The Burden of Proof

Preparing a Case from Intake through Verdict and on Appeal

PHILIP M. HALPERN

AMERICAN**BAR**ASSOCIATION

Solo, Small Firm and
General Practice Division

Printed in the United States of America.

24 23 22 21 20   5 4 3 2 1

Library of Congress Cataloging-in-Publication Data

Names: Halpern, Philip M., 1956– author. | American Bar Association. Solo, Small Firm and General Practice Division, sponsoring body.
Title: The burden of proof / Philip M. Halpern.
Description: Chicago : American Bar Association, 2020. | Includes bibliographical references and index. | Summary: "This book's mission is to demystify the theory and workings of the burden of proof in civil trials."—Provided by publisher.
Identifiers: LCCN 2020008678 (print) | LCCN 2020008679 (ebook) | ISBN 9781641056694 (paperback) | ISBN 9781641056700 (epub)
Subjects: LCSH: Burden of proof—New York (State)
Classification: LCC KFN6031 .H35 2020 (print) | LCC KFN6031 (ebook) | DDC 347.747/06—dc23
LC record available at https://lccn.loc.gov/2020008678
LC ebook record available at https://lccn.loc.gov/2020008679

Discounts are available for books ordered in bulk. Special consideration is given to state bars, CLE programs, and other bar-related organizations. Inquire at Book Publishing, ABA Publishing, American Bar Association, 321 N. Clark Street, Chicago, Illinois 60654-7598.

www.shopABA.org

Contents

Dedication

I want to acknowledge the love and support of my wife, Carolyn and my children, Alexander, Tommy and Emily. They are the center of my universe.

I wrote this book for my son, Thomas P. Halpern, Esq., a well-educated, young, and determined lawyer whom I love and of whom I am most proud. It represents a compilation of thoughts I have gathered over the past forty years of an active trial and appellate practice. I believe that the burden of proof for trial and appellate work is the *sine qua non* to litigation success. I also believe that success is grounded in the principles and approach set forth in this book. I hope this book is a helpful guide for my son's future as a litigator, if that is his desire, and for any lawyer who believes that the burden of proof is worth considering.

Acknowledgments

I would like to express my gratitude to a former associate of mine, Shari B. Hochberg, Esq., a graduate of the Elisabeth Haub School of Law at Pace University, for her devotion to this project. The book was researched almost exclusively by law students from the Elisabeth Haub School of Law at Pace University over a three-year period, during which Shari kindly hired the students and shepherded them, organizing, reviewing, and editing their work.

I would like to thank another former associate of mine, Lorenzo Venditti, Esq., for all of his hard work and devotion to this project. His contribution was immeasurable.

I would finally like to thank the interns who helped make this project possible: Sheila Arjomandi, Emily Rawdon Bandovic, Kayla Delpo, Carlianna Dengel, Courtney Dunn, Marisa Finkelberg, Daniel James Gillis, Emily Golban-Moghaddam, Jake Goldstein, Chelsea Hebert, Rosemarie Hebner, Timothy J. Henesy, James P. Kearns, Emma Lagle, Angeliki Ellie Laloudakis, Vito Marzano, Christopher J. Matcovich, Christina Oddo, Bianca Olliver, Andrea Osgood, Christian Radoi, Melissa Ryan Reitberg, Atasia Richardson, Joseph Russo, Matthew Shock, Arianna T. Sotos, and Katerina Sperl. The thoroughness and ability displayed by these students, most of whom are now attorneys, reflect favorably on the quality of the education each received at the Elisabeth Haub School of Law at Pace University.

About the Author

The Honorable Philip M. Halpern is a United States District Judge of the District Court for the Southern District of New York. Prior to receiving his judicial commission, Judge Halpern was the managing partner of Collier Halpern & Newberg, LLP, a practice focusing on commercial litigation, estates, employment litigation, real estate litigation, and securities litigation, and had more than ninety reported decisions and more than three decades of experience in representing individuals, corporations, and Fortune 500 companies. While in private practice, Judge Halpern was certified by the National Board of Trial Advocacy as a civil trial advocate and a civil pretrial advocate, and was selected as a Super Lawyer every year since 2008. He has also served as a mediator in U.S. Federal Court for the Southern District of New York and in New York State Supreme Court in the Civil Branch for New York County and in the Ninth Judicial District, Commercial Division, for Westchester County.

Judge Halpern also teaches a course entitled The Anatomy of a Trial: The Burden of Proof as an Adjunct Professor at The Elisabeth Haub School of Law at Pace University, dealing exclusively with trial skills.

Judge Halpern is a magna cum laude graduate of Fordham University, where he majored in economics and is a graduate of the Elisabeth Haub School of Law at Pace University School where he obtained his juris doctor. He began his legal career in 1980 as a law clerk to Federal Judge Irving Ben Cooper in the Southern District of New York.

In 2002, Mr. Halpern authored a two-volume book for Thompson Publishing Company on civil procedure entitled *Civil Pretrial Proceedings in New York*. He has also authored several articles for the Westchester Bar Association, New York State Bar Association, American Bar Association, and the Pace Law Review, and in addition to his adjunct professorship, he has lectured for the Office of Court Administration, New York State Bar Association, New York City Bar Association and a number of Bar Associations on a variety of litigation topics. Judge Halpern received the Pace Law School Alumni Leadership Award in 2006, Westchester County Business Journal Pace Setter Award in 2007, the American Diabetes Association Father of the Year Award in 2009, and was the Honoree for the Legal Services of the Hudson Valley Equal Access to Justice Award in 2017.

1 | The Historical Origins

INTRODUCTION

To hear this history rehearsed, for that there be inserted in it no fables, shall be perhaps not delightful. But he that desires to look into the truth of things done and which (according to the condition of humanity) may be done again, or at least their like, he shall find enough herein to make him think it profitable. And it is compiled rather for an everlasting possession than to be rehearsed for a prize.

—Thucydides (Hist. I, 20, 23)

Thucydides, a renowned Athenian historian, is widely recognized as the father of the "scientific history" method. The scientific history method entails impartially gathering evidence and then applying an objective cause-effect analysis to understand the underlying causes of historical events. In his book on the Peloponnesian War, Thucydides explained this approach, observing that history is inherently cyclical: that which occurred in the past will certainly recur in the future, in one form or another. Thus, Thucydides argued, using the scientific method to study history helps us understand the present, including by using history as a guide when past causes of historical events occur again in the present. Our study of the law draws from this approach.

In this book we consider the burden of proof and all that it entails. We know that in present-day civil actions, whoever lodges a claim shoulders the burden of establishing her contentions and the initial burden of going forward with the evidence. To fully understand civil procedural law, one must embrace these burdens and all attendant implications. This book demystifies the theory and workings of the burden of proof in civil trials, with New York State as its primary example. To this end, and in keeping with the teachings of Thucydides regarding the "scientific history" method, our first step must be to investigate the historical roots of the concept of the burden of proof. In doing so, we must not allow the opaque prism of hindsight to cloud our efforts to understand this topic. Rather, we must first consider the historical rules of procedure without regard to our present understanding of the burden of proof as applied in today's practice. Stated simply, our journey must start from the very beginning.

The oldest court system in the Western world was established by the Greeks, so our quest for the origin of the burden of proof starts with ancient Athenian procedural law.[1] Traditionally, Athens' history has been roughly divided into two different periods: first, the archaic era, which spans from 776 BC to 479 BC, and, second, the so-called classical period, which spans from 479 BC to 323 BC. According to modern scholars, the siege of Sestos marked the transition between the archaic era and the classical period.[2]

The archaic era adds little to our quest for understanding of the historical underpinnings of the burden of proof. Indeed, what little evidence we have describing procedures for settling disputes in the archaic era comes not from any legal documents, but from poetry, most notably Hesiod's works such as *The Theogony* and *The Works and Days*, and Homer's *Iliad* and *Odyssey*.[3] From these sources, we learn that in ancient Athens, the victim of a wrong had numerous avenues for obtaining redress. First, the injured party could resort to self-help; second, the king could intervene and settle the controversy; and, third, a group of elders (aided by people assembled in the public marketplace) could render a verdict settling the matter.[4] Eventually, a number of officers (known as *Arkhons*) were appointed and, during the archaic era, these officers were endowed with the authority to adjudicate disputes.

---

1. Modern literature debates whether the use of the term "ancient Greek law" is accurate or misleading, because in ancient Greece there were numerous city-states with different laws. *See* Michael Gagarin, *The Unity of Greek Law, in* THE CAMBRIDGE COMPANION TO ANCIENT GREEK LAW 30 (Michael Gagarin & David Cohen eds., Cambridge University Press 2005); S. C. TODD, THE SHAPE OF ATHENIAN LAW 15 (Clarendon Press Oxford 1993). Because this chapter is going to delve into the history of Athens only, we need not weigh in on that debate.
2. DAVID D. PHILLIPS, THE LAW OF ANCIENT ATHENS 10 (The University of Michigan Press 2013).
3. RUSS VERSTEEG, THE ESSENTIALS OF GREEK AND ROMAN LAW 4 (Carolina Academic Press 2010).
4. DOUGLAS M. MACDOWELL, THE LAW IN CLASSICAL ATHENS 14 (Cornell University Press 1978); VERSTEEG, *supra* note 3, at 5.

This rudimentary structure leaves little room for an in-depth and meaningful analysis of the origin of the burden of proof. We turn, then, to the trial procedural law of the classical period.

In the archaic period, in the middle of the sixth century BC, the *Arkhon* Solon,[5] an Athenian ruler, introduced several reforms repealing the laws previously in force in Athens.[6] Before Solon's reforms, Athenian institutions were substantially controlled by the aristocracy because (1) lawmakers, (2) magistrates, and (3) state officers were selected exclusively from the privileged upper class.[7] In the early classical period, as Athenian democracy was gradually being established, the upper class slowly agreed to cede its previously exclusive control over the city's institutions. Probably, this was so because the aristocracy feared that resisting the pressure to establish a fairer system would have caused a revolution in Athens.

The transfer of power in the administration of justice from the aristocracy to the body of Athenian citizens occurred gradually. Initially, Solon's law afforded litigants a *de novo* appeal of magistrates' rulings to the assembly of the entire body of Athenian citizens. Although that was a well-intentioned reform, by the end of the fifth century BC, proceedings before the judicial officers began to be viewed as a vain ceremonial step. This is not surprising, given that under Solon's law, the losing party at the first stage of the litigation was vested with the absolute right to appeal the magistrate's verdict to the assembly. Put differently, the result of the constant *de novo* appeals was that magistrates stopped rendering verdicts. That left the assembly as the only institution empowered to adjudicate controversies.[8] When convened to adjudicate a specific controversy, the assembly of the Athenian citizens was known as *Eliaia*. Notably, the same assembly was also bestowed with the power to legislate; when meeting for that purpose, the assembly was called *Ekklesia*.[9]

As the Athenian population grew, it became increasingly inconvenient to have cases heard and decided before the general assembly. That prompted the Athenians to allow a relatively small number of people sitting as jurors to represent the whole body of citizens (i.e., the *Eliaia*) and so render judgments more expeditiously.[10] Jury courts known as *dikastai* were thus established.[11]

---

5. Solon was an Athenian statesman, lawmaker, and poet.
6. Before Solon's reform, a special officer named Drakon had codified the then-existing Athenian laws. The term "Draconian" comes from Drakon's codification of existing laws, which imposed the death penalty for almost all offenses, however minor.
7. MacDowell, *supra* note 4, at 29.
8. *Id.* at 32.
9. *Id.* at 30.
10. *Id.* at 34.
11. *Id.*

Understanding how the administration of justice worked in the classical period might prompt the reader to conclude that today's jury system traces its origins to classical Athens. That isn't the case; in reality, Athenian jury-courts were dramatically different from today's courts. Indeed, Athenian jury-courts were more akin to a parliament in that: (1) the panel comprised no less than 500 jurors,[12] (2) the verdict was rendered without deliberations and the jurors simply voted individually by secret ballot,[13] (3) a simple majority was enough to approve a verdict, (4) the panel's verdict was always final and not subject to appeal,[14] (5) there was no direction or instructions on points of law given to the panel,[15] (6) issues of fact and matters of law were equally considered to be in the exclusive purview of the jury,[16] (7) the presiding magistrate, who was appointed by lot, had a merely ministerial role in administering justice,[17] and (8) it was customary to tender irrelevant evidence of the parties' character so as to paint for the jury a very broad picture of the events leading to the litigation.[18] This exemplifies why we ought not to study history looking backward through the fractured prism of hindsight.

Given all the differences between the historical courts and present-day courts, this chapter will argue that the link between ancient Greek law and today's practice is a very tenuous one when compared to the influence that Roman law exerted over virtually all modern Western legal systems.

Modern literature seems to agree that ancient Greek law did not significantly influence modern practice. By way of example, S. C. Todd put the point thus:

> Law is one of the very few areas of social practice in which the ancient Greeks have had no significant influence on subsequent societies. To grasp the significance of this statement, it is worth examining for a moment the contrast with politics, that other area of life in which relationships between human beings are publicly regulated. The Greeks invented not merely the terminology of politics, but many of its fundamental concepts. [. . .] Politics, it must be admitted, is an extreme example of the Greek legacy. But it is by no means unique. [. . .] Law, however, is a different matter because ancient Greek law has had a negligible influence on posterity. Even when there are superficial similarities

---

12. *Id.* at 37.
13. Gagarin & Cohen, *supra* note 1, at 115; Todd, *supra* note 1, at 31.
14. Todd, *supra* note 1, at 89.
15. Phillips, *supra* note 2, at 40.
16. *Id.*
17. Todd, *supra* note 1, at 83.
18. *Id.* at 90.

between Athenian practice and that of modern jurisdiction, there may be no direct descent. [. . .] [I]t is to Rome [. . .] that we must look for the origins of modern European legal systems.[19]

Greek law's tenuous influence on posterity notwithstanding, we shall nonetheless (briefly) analyze Athenian procedural law of the classical period because it provides us with a general understanding of the backdrop against which Roman jurists devised the system that so profoundly influenced modern law. After all, there is evidence showing that in the year 454 BC Roman jurists tasked with the duty to draft the statute called "the XII tables" were sent to Athens to observe and learn from their legal system.[20]

Offering a similar argument, Russ VerSteeg wrote: "[T]he Romans [. . .] who are world-famous for their influence on subsequent legal development, read and studied Greek Philosophers who wrote about law. Thus the ancient Greeks had a profound effect òn legal progress and evolution, albeit in an indirect manner."[21]

Therefore, this chapter delves into ancient Roman civil procedure, which will be the focus of our research. The reader might be tempted to pay little attention to the historical origins of the burden of proof under Roman law, thinking that (1) Roman law bears little relation to the English common law and (2) the burden of proof is a creation of modern jurisprudence. As this chapter explains, however, the evolution of the English common law and the burden of proof in today's practice are rooted in this history.

Traditionally, Roman law is said to have had two lives.[22] The first "life" was the Roman law regulating ancient Rome's rural society, which itself evolved into a vast multicultural empire wherein domestic and international trade were an essential part of its political and economic structure. The second "life" was the reemergence of Roman law like a phoenix from the ashes of the demise of the Roman Empire that occurred when, in the twelfth century AD, jurists started studying the so-called Justinian compilation of Roman law, which was originally put together at the behest of a Byzantine Emperor (i.e. Justinian) of the sixth century AD. Roman law was studied at universities, reinterpreted by jurists, and utilized by courts as a common transnational law (i.e., a *ius commune*) in continental Europe

---

19. TODD, *supra* note 1, at 3 *et seq.*
20. KATHLEEN FREEMAN, THE MURDER OF HERODES AND OTHER TRIALS FROM THE ATHENIAN LAW COURTS 15 (Macdonald & Co. 1946).
21. VERSTEEG, *supra* note 3, at 3.
22. *See* J. A. C. THOMAS, TEXTBOOK OF ROMAN LAW 3 (North Holland Publishing Company 1976).

and it ultimately became the basis of the major civil law codifications of the nine-teenth and twentieth centuries.[23]

The so-called second life of Roman law has had little or no influence over the evolution of the English common law.[24] However, that cannot be said as to the first life of Roman law. The first life of Roman law significantly influenced the formation and basic structure of the common law. Examples of similarities between Roman law and the basic features of the English common law include (1) the dichotomy between the *ius civile*—that is, the statutory law—and the *ius honorarium*—that is, judge-made law; (2) the existence of a magistrate-made body of equitable rules devised to supplement and correct the statutory law; and (3) the principle according to which rules of law existed well before their formal declaration.[25] These similarities support the proposition that Roman law did influ-ence the formation of the basic structure of the common law.

The modern notion imposing a burden of proof on litigants in civil trials along with the related rules employed to allocate such burden among the parties orig-inated at Rome when the system of the *legis actiones* gave way to the formulary civil procedure.

In the early days of the oligarchic domination of the patricians, the newly formed state gradually forbade self-help for redressing private wrongs such that the need for a civil action for vindicating citizens' rights arose. Therefore, the pro-cedure *per legis actiones* was created. This procedure was "prehistoric in origin"[26] and largely consisted of a highly formalistic recital of ritual declarations which closely resembled a symbolic combat among the parties.[27]

---

23. *Id.* at 9.

24. *Id.* at 10. In England, for political reasons, the Court of Chancery, on the one hand, and courts of law, on the other hand, remained separated for centuries. Conversely, at Rome, the original dichotomy between *ius civile* and *ius honorarium*, the former representing strict law and the latter equity, gradually blended together as a consequence of the flexibility of the formulary procedure. During the so-called second life of Roman law, in laying the foundations of the eigh-teenth- and nineteenth-century codifications, jurists looked mostly to the final stage of the evo-lution of Roman law such that the law-equity dichotomy did not make its way into the modern civil law systems.

25. *See, e.g.* W. W. Buckland, Equity in Roman Law 1 (University of London Press 1911); Peter G. Stein, *Roman Law, Common Law, and Civil Law*, 66 Tul. L. Rev. 1591, 1604 (1991–1992); Thomas, *supra* note 22, at 6 (stating that "[i]f one substitute[s] judge for jurist and writ for *formula*, there is a parallel between the first life of Roman Law and that of English law . . . .").

26. Thomas, *supra* note 22, at 71.

27. W. W. Buckland, The Main Institutions of Roman Private Law 346 (Cambridge at The University Press 1931); Henry R. Danner, Roman Law Pleading 12 (Fred B. Rothman 1983) ("When both the disputants appeared before the magistrate a mimic combat (*manuum consertio*)

The most representative form of action was the *legis actio per sacramentum in rem* through which a party could claim title to a *res* (i.e., a thing). From a procedural standpoint, in an action *sacramentum in rem*, both parties had to claim legal title to the thing in dispute.[28] As a consequence, the roles of plaintiff and defendant were not well defined.[29] Stated differently, if the defendant did not actively claim legal title to the thing in dispute after the plaintiff had put forth her claim of ownership, she would immediately lose the case. Pursuant to this form of action, after reciting the ritual declarations, the parties challenged each other to a wager of a sum of money which was forfeited to the state if the party's claim turned out to be unjust.[30]

Subsequently, after the recitals and the wagers were carried out, the case was assigned to a lay arbiter (called *iudex*) and the party whose claim of ownership appeared more plausible in the eyes of the arbiter won the case. Indeed, in the *legis actio sacramentum in rem* the burden of proof, as this concept is understood in modern parlance, was shouldered by both parties.[31]

The procedure *per legis actiones* was meant to be used for redressing violations of the ancient statutory law called *ius civile*: literally, the private law of the citizens of Rome. In fact, the word *Cives*, from which *ius civile* derives, means "citizens." In other words, under the *ius civile*, noncitizens (called *peregrinui*) did not have any private law rights or obligations. Consequently, they did not have access to the *legis actiones* procedure.[32]

Rome rapidly evolved from being a small rural community located in central Italy to being a vast empire where international trade with noncitizens was extremely common. The inadequacy of the *legis actiones* procedure in dealing with increasingly complex disputes—including with foreigners—became apparent.[33] This caused the Romans to add a magistrate competent to administer justice as to foreigners, and the new formulary procedure was eventually introduced.

---

ensued over the property in dispute [. . .]"); A. H. J. GREENIDGE, THE LEGAL PROCEDURE OF CICERO'S TIME 57 (Oxford at The Clarendon Press 1901); THOMAS, *supra* note 22, at 75; LEOPOLD WENGER, INSTITUTES OF THE ROMAN LAW OF CIVIL PROCEDURE, 127 (Otis Harrison Fisk trans., Fred B. Rothman & Co. 1986).

28. GREENIDGE, *supra* note 27, at 59.

29. DANNER, *supra* note 27, at 13.

30. SHELDON AMOS, THE HISTORY AND PRINCIPLES OF THE CIVIL LAW OF ROME 41 (Wm. W. Gaunt & Sons, Inc. 1989); DANNER, *supra* note 27, at 12; GREENIDGE, *supra* note 27, at 53.

31. BUCKLAND, *supra* note 27, at 346.

32. WILLIAM L. BURBICK, THE PRINCIPLES OF ROMAN LAW 635 (Wm. W. Gaunt & Sons, Inc. 1989); DANNER, *supra* note 27, at 16.

33. THOMAS, *supra* note 22, at 83.

Pursuant to a statute (*lex Licinia*), the magistrate who was competent for matters involving citizens (i.e., the *Praetor Urbanus*), and the magistrate who was competent for matters involving noncitizens (i.e., the *Praetor Peregrinus*), were endowed with discretionary authority, or *imperium*, to administer justice. The magistrate having authority over noncitizens—taking advantage of the discretionary nature of the power accorded to him—began granting the so-called *formulae* to foreigners who sought to have their grievances redressed in court.[34] To put it differently, since the old procedure *per legis actiones* was not applicable to foreigners, a new and more flexible procedure was devised by the magistrate to resolve their claims.

The *formula* has been defined as a "synopsis of the case"[35] summarizing claims and defenses and ultimately directing a lay arbiter (i.e., a *iudex*) to find for the plaintiff or for the defendant depending on what facts among those indicated in the *formula* itself were proved by the litigants.[36] Under this new procedure, the defendant was allowed to simply object to the plaintiff's contentions; thus, actively lodging a counterclaim seeking ownership of the thing in dispute was not required. Given the flexibility of this procedure, a statute, the *lex Aebutia*, eventually extended it to controversies among citizens.[37]

Pursuant to this new system, therefore, "the broad principle was that the burden of proof of an assertion rested upon the party who made it."[38] From a practical standpoint, given the syllogistic structure of the *formula*, the litigant bearing the burden of establishing her assertions was the party who would prevail if a certain contention was deemed to be true by the lay arbiter.

I. ATHENIAN LAW

In the classical period (i.e., from 479 BC to 323 BC), Athenian trial procedure was strongly influenced by the establishment and further development of democracy such that the structure of the court system closely resembled that of the newly

---

34. Burbick, *supra* note 32, at 636; Thomas, *supra* note 22, at 84.
35. Thomas, *supra* note 22, at 84.
36. Danner, *supra* note 27, at 16 (stating that a *formula* is "a grant to the plaintiff of the right to prosecute his suit before a judex therein named [. . .]"); Greenidge, *supra* note 27, at 130 ("The *formula* was a written statement of a case meant to be presented to a *iudex*; it was supposed to be an expression of the law applicable to this particular case and contained in a conditional form a judgment which the finding of the *iudex* was to make absolute [. . .]"); Wenger, *supra* note 27, at 191 (arguing that the rendering of judgment was prescribed to the *iudex* in the formula itself which contained a "command to adjudicate according to the result of the investigation of the state of facts").
37. Thomas, *supra* note 22, at 84.
38. *Id.* at 87.

created democratic institutions.[39] Accordingly, to fully understand Athenian procedural law, it is necessary to recount (in passing) how democratic institutions were established in Athens.

By the end of the seventh century BC, the hereditary monarchy had been discontinued. Eventually, most of the powers the king previously held were transferred to a number of state officials. These officers were the *Basileus*, literally meaning the "king" (a term confusingly used in an idiosyncratic way), who handled religious matters and homicide cases; the *Arkhon*, that is, literally the "leader," who was intended to be the top official in the state's hierarchy; the *Polemarch*, meaning "war commander," who dealt with military and immigration matters; and the (six) *Thesmothetai*, meaning "rule makers," who had authority to pass regulations in a number of fields. Collectively, these officers were known as *The Nine Arkhons*.[40] Probably, in the seventh century BC, the Nine *Arkhons* directly adjudicated controversies.[41] Until the establishment of democracy in the classical period, all these state officials were selected from among the privileged upper class.

The onset of democratic ideas gradually brought about significant change. Specifically, Athenians felt the need to impose checks and limitations on the absolute power of state's authorities. At first, the limiting of state officials' power was simply achieved by putting Athenian laws in writing so as to significantly curb the *Arkhons'* unbridled discretionary power.[42] To this end, in the year 621 BC, an independent official—named *Drakon*—tasked with the duty to record existing customs in writing was appointed. Under the Draconian codification,[43] the penalty for almost all offenses was death.[44]

Subsequently, regular citizens' resentment against the aristocracy—whose members held virtually all available public posts—grew significantly. Fear of a revolution spurred a re-codification of Athenian law.[45] In fact, in the year 594/3 BC, the *Arkhon* Solon repealed and replaced most of Drakon's laws. In so doing Solon laid the foundations upon which Athenian democracy was built.[46]

---

39. Harvey Yunis, *The Rhetoric of Law in Fourth-Century Athens, in* GAGARIN & COHEN, *supra* note 1, at 191–195.
40. MACDOWELL, *supra* note 4, at 25.
41. *Id.*
42. *Id.* at 27.
43. Drakon's (infamous) reputation for devising such a harsh body of laws might be misplaced as Drakon was tasked with the duty to record existing customs in writing. *See generally* VERSTEEG, *supra* note 3, at 8.
44. MACDOWELL, *supra* note 4, at 42.
45. *Id.* at 29.
46. VERSTEEG, *supra* note 3, at 9.

Solon's Code included several significant innovations that are important to our discussion. First, the new code introduced the right to appeal magistrates' rulings to the assembly of the whole body of Athenian citizens that reviewed cases *de novo*; and, second, since in Athens there was neither a police force nor a public prosecutor,[47] Solon allowed, under certain circumstances, volunteer citizens to vindicate others' rights by bringing a lawsuit on behalf of the aggrieved party.[48]

When the assembly of the entire body of Athenian citizens was convened for legislative sessions it was known as the *Ekklesia*; however, when the assembly was convened for adjudicating cases it was called *Eliaia*. Despite the name difference, the composition and internal practice of the *Ekklesia* and of the *Eliaia* were essentially the same.[49]

By the end of the fifth century BC, *Arkhons*' judgments were being appealed to the assembly in virtually every instance. That rendered the first phase of the proceedings redundant and irrelevant, which caused magistrates to completely cease adjudicating controversies. Putting it differently, the initial hearing before the magistrate became a purely procedural step that allowed the official to make arrangements for convening the assembly.[50] Eventually, Athenians began to appoint magistrates exclusively by lot. It follows that in the classical period magistrates were amateurs tasked with merely ministerial duties.

Convening the general assembly for adjudicating every single lawsuit was incredibly impractical. Therefore, Athenians came up with the idea that a relatively small panel of citizens could represent the general assembly in administering justice such that the verdict of the smaller panel was considered to be equivalent to the verdict of the people of Athens as a whole.[51]

Every year, six thousand lay jurors were chosen by lot from the pool of volunteer citizens who wished to be selected for service.[52] A jury trial never lasted for more than one day. For every single day in which a court of law was in session, at least five hundred jurors for each trial were selected by lot from the general pool of eligible jurors.[53] When chosen to sit on a particular jury, each juror was paid a small stipend. The standard trial court was called *dikastai*.

---

47. TODD, *supra* note 1, at 79.
48. MACDOWELL, *supra* note 4, at 29; TODD, *supra* note 1, at 113.
49. *Id.* at 31.
50. *Id.* at 32.
51. *Id.* at 34.
52. TODD, *supra* note 1, at 83.
53. MACDOWELL, *supra* note 4, at 34; TODD, *supra* note 1, at 83.

One of the most conspicuous idiosyncrasies of Athenian trial procedure vis-à-vis modern procedure is certainly evidence law. Broadly speaking, there were two kinds of evidence: *nonartistic evidence*, including laws, witnesses, contracts, slaves' testimony under torture, and oaths,[54] and *artistic evidence*, including parties' speeches written (and delivered) according to the principles of rhetoric—that is, the art of persuasion.[55] Under this system, the parties' speeches were considered to be evidence in and of themselves, upon which a verdict could be based.[56]

Athenian courts were structured as direct-democracy institutions wherein lay jurors voted without prior deliberations by secret ballot. Jurors were not given any instructions on principles of law.[57] Juries' findings were always in the nature of a general verdict;[58] only a simple majority quorum was required to approve a verdict, and juries' findings were not subject to review.[59] Clearly, truth finding and consistency of judgment were not the primary goals of the Athenian justice system.[60] Quite to the contrary, the primary goal of litigation was merely to settle disputes "democratically" rather than revealing the truth of the matter brought before the court.[61] In this system, the concept of ensuring that justice was served meant nothing more than guaranteeing a fair and democratic adversarial process wherein litigants had an equal opportunity to be heard and judged by their fellow citizens.[62]

This system of administering justice had some interesting features that bear discussion before we consider the question of how the burden of proof worked (if at all) under Athenian law.

---

54. *Id.* at 242; Gerhard Thür, *The Role of the Witness in Athenian Law, in* GAGARIN & COHEN, *supra* note 1, at 146; TODD, *supra* note 1, at 59.

55. FREEMAN, supra note 20, at 31 ("The art of persuasion is as old as human speech itself; but the systematic study of this art, and its application to public life, which the Greeks called Rhetoric, first emerges into the light of history [. . .] when [. . .] a citizen of the Greek colony of Syracuse, first wrote a handbook on Rhetoric . . . ."); Hervey Yunis, *The Rhetoric of Law in Fourth-Century Athens, in* GAGARIN & COHEN, *supra* note 1, at 191, 193.

56. Gerhard Thür, *The Role of the Witness in Athenian Law, in* GAGARIN & COHEN, *supra* note 1, at 146, 148; TODD, *supra* note 1, at 130.

57. Adriaan Lanni, *Relevance in Athenian Courts, in* GAGARIN & COHEN, *supra* note 1, at 112, 115; PHILLIPS, *supra* note 2, at 40; TODD, *supra* note 1, at 31.

58. TODD, *supra* note 1, at 89.

59. Yunis, *supra* note 55, at 191, 194.

60. Thür, *supra* note 54, at 146, 147.

61. *Id.* at 146.

62. Yunis, *supra* note 55, at 191, 194; TODD, *supra* note 1, at 68.

To start, Athenians did not think about jurisprudence as a scientific discipline.[63] In Athens, all actors who were involved in the administration of justice were amateurs: the jurors were lay citizens, the magistrates were nonprofessional officers tasked with purely ministerial duties,[64] and the litigants were not allowed to hire lawyers. Given all this, the contents of statutes had to be proved by the parties, since the court was not expected to know the law. Indeed, litigants often disputed before the jury what the law of the land actually was.[65] Parenthetically, it should be noted that the parties did hire speechwriters to ghostwrite their summations but these professionals were neither jurists nor advisers.

Second, the parliamentary-like procedure adopted by Athenian courts allowed litigants to paint for the jury a very broad picture of the events leading to the litigation; in other words, tendering irrelevant character evidence or highlighting the parties' past good (or bad) unrelated deeds was common practice.[66]

Third, an Athenian trial was a debating contest of sorts, so to speak.[67] Indeed, the parties' speeches, delivered pursuant to the principles of rhetoric, were deemed to be standalone (artistic) evidence and were considered as such by the jury. In fact, in the classical period, it is likely that artistic evidence was given the most weight when reaching a verdict.[68] This is evident in the trial procedural rules that did not allow live testimony from witnesses, disqualified the parties, women, and children from testifying,[69] and allowed testimony from eligible witnesses exclusively by reading witnesses' out-of-court statements to the jury.[70]

The parties to a lawsuit were not permitted to hire lawyers to represent them in court.[71] That was quite by design; the justice system was intended to be navigated by amateurs only.[72] There was no room (or need) for professional jurists. However, since few people were well versed in the art of rhetoric[73] and considering the weight given to artistic evidence by juries, litigants commonly hired professional

---

63. Yunis, *supra* note 55, at 191; TODD, *supra* note 1, at 53.

64. S. C. Todd, *Law and Oratory at Athens, in* GAGARIN & COHEN, *supra* note 1, at 97, 100; TODD, *supra* note 1, at 83.

65. Yunis, *supra* note 55, at 191, 201.

66. Lanni, *supra* note 57, at 112, 113; TODD, *supra* note 1, at 90.

67. Yunis, *supra* note 55, at 191, 193.

68. TODD, *supra* note 1, at 130 ("In an Athenian trial witnesses are relatively insignificant and everything hangs on the speech . . . .").

69. MACDOWELL, *supra* note 4, at 243.

70. *Id.* at 242; Michael Gagarin, *Early Greek Law, in* GAGARIN & COHEN, *supra* note 1, at 82, 91.

71. TODD, *supra* note 1, at 77.

72. *Id.*

73. FREEMAN, *supra* note 20, at 31.

speechwriters (known as *logographers*) to ghostwrite their summations.[74] As a practical matter, the ghostwriters prepared the speeches that were then memorized and personally delivered by litigants.[75] Collectively, these professional speechwriters are known as the *Sophists* and their work was preserved throughout history because of its literary and artistic significance.[76]

To get a better picture of how an Athenian trial by jury worked, let us consider for a moment an actual case tried in the classical period. The case, *In re assault and Battery of Ariston*, was decided in the year 340 BC by an ordinary jury-court.[77] Athenian law did not distinguish between criminal offenses and civil wrongs. The only relevant distinction in Athens was between lawsuits that could be brought only by the interested party, which were called private suits, and lawsuits that could be prosecuted by anyone, which were called public suits.[78] Oddly, murder was considered a private lawsuit that could be prosecuted only by the victim's family.[79]

The case in question was a private lawsuit, prosecuted by our plaintiff, a man named Ariston. Since Athens had no public prosecution service,[80] it follows that Ariston as the prosecutor of this private lawsuit, was also the victim of the alleged assault and battery. Ariston employed Demosthenes, a renowned Attic orator, as *logographer* to ghostwrite his summation to the jury. Ariston then memorized the speech and orally delivered it in open court.

In *In re assault and Battery of Ariston*, the plaintiff and the defendant's two sons were stationed together at a military base on garrison duty in a town, called Panactum, located at the frontier of Attica. Plaintiff and defendant's two sons were lodged in neighboring tents. Apparently, while at camp, the defendant's sons were often intoxicated and caused numerous disturbances. As a result, plaintiff reported defendant's sons to the commanding officer. A feud between the two families resulted. However, the main events underlying this lawsuit took place after plaintiff and defendant's sons returned to Athens.

One day, after sunset, Ariston was walking in the marketplace when he came across the defendant and his two sons who happened to be intoxicated and belligerent. Unsurprisingly, an altercation resulted, and Ariston was beaten nearly

74. S. C. Todd, *Law and Oratory at Athens, in* GAGARIN & COHEN, *supra* note 1, at 97, 99.
75. FREEMAN, *supra* note 20, at 11.
76. *Id.* at 33.
77. *Id.* at 114.
78. MacDOWELL, *supra* note 4, at 57; TODD, *supra* note 1, at 99, 113.
79. *Id.* at 59.
80. TODD, *supra* note 1, at 79.

to death by his comrade-in-arms' father. After miraculously recovering from the beating, Ariston filed this lawsuit.

Forensic speeches written according to the principles of rhetoric were divided into several parts, namely (1) the proem, which provided an opening statement; (2) the narrative, which set out the facts of the case; (3) the arguments, which contained the main legal reasoning; (4) the epilogue, wherein the speaker drew his conclusions; and (5) a section dealing with the parties' character.

For our purposes, the most relevant parts of Ariston's speech delivered in open court ran thus:

> [Proem . . .] I have experienced an outrage of such violence at the hands of the defendant Conon that for a long time my family and all the doctors despaired of my life. [. . .] I now call upon you and beg you all alike, first to hear me sympathetically while I describe my injuries, and then, if you agree that I have been wronged and criminally treated, to aid me with the just redress [. . .].
>
> [Narrative] Two years ago, I was ordered away on garrison duty [. . .] [t]he sons of the defendant Conon pitched tent near us [. . .] this was the origin of all our feud [. . .] Conon and his son and Theogenes attacked me [. . .] I will tell you—a thing that is a sign of the defendant's brutality and a proof that he was the ring-leader: he crowed, in imitation of a fighting-cock that has won a battle, and the others made him clap with his elbows against his sides like wings! [. . .] [During the narrative part of the speech the plaintiff asked the clerk to read to the jury witnesses' statements.]
>
> [Arguments] It has now, I think, been sufficiently demonstrated to you that the blows I received were of the utmost force and severity [. . .] I gather [the defendant] will try to divert attention from the assault and what actually happened by turning the matter to ridicule and making fun of it, saying that there are plenty of lads in Athens [. . .] who in sport, as young men will apply opprobrious epithets to one another [. . . and] that his son is one of their number, and has many a time taken and given beatings [. . .]. I shall be surprised if there is any excuse or plea acceptable to your Court by which a man, if convicted of violence and of inflicting blows, can escape punishment. The law takes a quite opposite view: it has anticipated the inevitable excuses, and tried to prevent them from growing more serious. for instance [. . .] take the process for verbal abuse: this, it is asserted, exists to prevent men from being led on from angry words to blows. Then there is the process for assault, to prevent a man when he is getting the worst of it from defending himself with a stone [. . .] and induce him to seek legal redress. Then there is the indictment for inflicting wounds, to prevent murder following on wounding. [. . .] [B]y making legal provision for these various kinds of law-suits [the law takes care] that differences shall not be settled by the fury or caprice of any individual [. . .].

[Allegations regarding character] The most scandalous device, however, which I hear he is going to try, I think it best to warn you of in advance. I am told he is going to bring his children into court, and swear an oath on their heads [. . .]. I learn gentlemen that a certain Bacchius, who was executed by order of your court [. . .] and other men of the same sort, including Conon here, were comrades in their boyhood and called themselves the Huns. They used to collect the food offered to the dead whenever they were dining together [. . .].

[Epilogue] [. . .] Conon will importune you and shed tears. But consider which of us is the more deserving of pity: the man who suffers injuries like mine at his hands, if I am to be sent away with added insult and without redress; or Conon if he pays the penalty? Which is to the advantage of each one of you: that there shall be license to beat and assault people, or not? [. . .] I could tell at great length, members of the jury, of our good record, both mine and brother's, and our father's when he was alive: how we contributed to the equipment of a war-ship, and did our military service, and performed every duty laid upon us [. . .].[81]

Unfortunately, we do not know how the court ultimately ruled but what emerges from reading the above excerpted passage is that Athenian litigants did seek to convince the jury both that their version of the events underlying the lawsuit, and their interpretation of the law, were more probable than not—albeit this was done using peculiar means of persuasion vis-à-vis what is acceptable under modern evidence law. In fact, in Athens: (1) persuasive speeches were considered in and of themselves evidence,[82] (2) character traits of the parties were always mentioned even when not related to the events underlying the lawsuit,[83] and (3) the standing of a litigants' family in the community was an important consideration when adjudicating the merits of a case.[84]

As it has been aptly noted, the development of the law has always been "akin to a meandering journey." It follows that burden-of-proof law did not begin with a (comprehensive) legal theory.[85] Tellingly, in Athens, it began as a practical consideration. Indeed, as a matter of practicality, in order to win their case, litigants routinely sought to convince juries—by offering artistic and nonartistic evidence—that their arguments were more probable than not so. But the burden of proof was

---

81. Freeman, *supra* note 20, at 114 *et seq.*
82. Todd, *supra* note 1, at 130.
83. Lanni, *supra* note 57, at 112, 113, 121; Todd, *supra* note 1, at 90.
84. Todd, *supra* note 1, at 90, 154.
85. *See generally* Nicholas Broadbent, Probable Flaws: Toward a Revised Tort of Malicious Prosecution 8 (Apr. 2017) (unpublished LL.M. thesis, Harvard University) (on file with the Harvard University Library system) (making the same argument with reference to tort law, citing Oliver Wendell Holmes Jr., The Common Law 1 [1881]).

not formalized as such. Instead, convincing juries in this manner was most likely perceived as a simple practical necessity rather than a legal requirement.

We can see that in Athens, rhetoric—that is, the art of persuasion, which mainly employs the concept of probability when making a point—played a very important role in the administration of justice. However, in our opinion, the widespread use of such rhetorical arguments in court cannot be considered as evidence of the existence of a legal theory of the burden of proof.

II. ROMAN LAW: THE *LEGIS ACTIO SACRAMENTUM IN REM*

It has been said[86] that the procedure *per legis actiones* (which can be translated into "through legal actions") was so named either because it was introduced by statute (i.e., by a *lex*), or because the procedural words that had to be uttered by the parties during trial closely reflected the wording of a statute.[87] According to Gaius, there were five legal actions: *sacramentum, iudicis arbitrive postulatio, condictio, manus iniecto,* and *pignoris capio.*

The *sacramentum* was the general-purpose civil action as it was applicable to all cases except when a statute mandated otherwise.[88] We will therefore focus on the *sacramentum* proceeding. Such procedure included both *in rem* and *in personam* actions. Specifically, we take up the *in rem* procedure because it was regarded as the paradigmatic civil action until the introduction of the formulary trial.

The Roman civil trial was split in two distinct phases: first, the so-called *in iure* phase, and, second, the *apud iudicem* part. During the *in iure* stage, the parties appeared before the magistrate and carried out the various rituals that characterized the *legis actiones* system. Subsequently, with the magistrate's permission, the litigants entered into an agreement called *litis ontestation* wherein the parties jointly appointed a lay arbiter, the *iudex*, to adjudicate the case. The intervention of the state-appointed magistrate rendered the arbiter's judgment legally enforceable. Conversely, if the litigants were to enter into an agreement appointing an arbiter without the formal sanction of the magistrate, the judgment entered by the arbiter so appointed would constitute a mere private resolution of the controversy.

---

86. Gaius, G.IV.10-20.
87. BUCKLAND, *supra* note 27, at 345.
88. THOMAS, *supra* note 22, at 74.

From a procedural standpoint, after the plaintiff had summoned the defendant (through the *in ius ontesta*) and both parties had appeared before the magistrate, a mimic combat ensued over the thing in dispute.[89] Specifically, the procedure unfolded as follows:[90] First, the thing in dispute (or a symbolic part thereof) had to be physically brought to court.[91] Second, the plaintiff put forth his or her formal claim by laying her hand on the object proclaiming: "I say that this [object] is mine by Quiritary title, [. . .] as I have declared, behold I lay my rod on [it] . . .".[92] Having so stated, the plaintiff then actually laid a rod on the object. This procedure was probably intended to mimic the act of drawing a sword in anticipation of combat. Third, the defendant followed the same ritual actively claiming legal title to the thing in dispute.[93] Failure to properly assert a counterclaim in this manner resulted in a default judgment for the plaintiff.[94] Fourth, the magistrate ordered both parties to let go of the object. In this way, the magistrate exercised his authority, simultaneously forbidding self-help in redressing legal rights and intervening in settling the controversy.[95]

Having both parties let go of the object, the plaintiff asked the defendant: "I ask you to say on what ground you claim [the object]." Immediately thereafter, the defendant replied: "I did what was right as I laid on my rod." Finally, the plaintiff challenged the defendant to enter into a wager by saying: "[s]ince you have wrongly claimed, I challenge you with [. . .] a wager of 50 [. . .]" and the defendant replied: "and I challenge you." Both litigants were then required to deposit the amount indicated with a public official or alternatively, to provide a guarantor. The losing party's deposit was forfeited to the state.[96]

As soon as all of the above formalities were carried out, the parties—with the magistrate's approval[97]—entered into a contract, called *litis ontestation*, through

---

89. DANNER, *supra* note 27, at 12; WENGER, *supra* note 27, at 127 (stating that this procedure is a "symbolic reminder of the manual struggle for the thing, of self-help, before the state established the order of the peace").
90. THOMAS, *supra* note 22, at 75.
91. BUCKLAND, *supra* note 27, at 346.
92. THOMAS, *supra* note 22, at 74.
93. W. W. BUCKLAND, A TEXT-BOOK OF ROMAN LAW FROM AUGUSTUS TO JUSTINIAN 606 (Cambridge at The University Press 1921); THOMAS, *supra* note 22, at 75.
94. GREENIDGE, *supra* note 27, at 56; WENGER, *supra* note 27, at 127 n.12 ("If the opponent were to keep silent, the allegation of right would be without contradiction, and the Praetor would adjudge the thing to the Plaintiff in accordance therewith.").
95. GREENIDGE, *supra* note 27, at 56; WENGER, *supra* note 27, at 128.
96. BUCKLAND, *supra* note 27, at 346.
97. WENGER, *supra* note 27, at 129 (stating that the *Praetor* authorized and obligated the appointed arbiter to render a state-recognized judgment).

which they (1) established the issues that were to be decided, and (2) appointed a lay arbiter empowered to render judgment.[98] Theoretically, each party could refuse to enter into the contract. However, the magistrate had several means of indirect coercion at his disposal, including the power to order the seizure of the disobedient party's assets.[99]

The stipulation of the *litis ontestation* marked the end of the *in iure* part and the beginning of the *apud iudicem* phase of the proceedings.[100] The *apud iudicem* phase took place before the lay arbiter in a different location than where the magistrate held the hearings. Both parties submitted evidence supporting their contentions and after hearing all evidence the lay arbiter returned a judgment determining which wager was unjust (i.e., *iniustum*). In other words, based on the evidence tendered by the parties, the arbiter's judgment simply indicated which one of the formal assertions of ownership was unlawfully made.[101] If neither party was able to prove title to the object in dispute, then "things stood as they were."[102] Indeed, it can safely be said that the burden of proof was borne by both parties in that neither litigant "could get judgment, without proving his title; there was no question of burden of proof, on one rather than on the other."[103]

For the sake of completeness, let us briefly consider the *Sacramentum in personam* action. The *in personam* action did not differ substantially from the *in rem* action. However, since this procedure was applicable to torts and contractual obligations only, there was no object over which the parties claimed title. Thus, after summoning the defendant to appear before the magistrate, the plaintiff had to formally state: "I say that you ought to give me [x amount] for [xyz reason . . .]" and the defendant had to reply: "I deny that I ought to give you [xyz . . .]." Subsequently, both parties entered into the wager called *sacramentum*. Finally, the lay arbiter in the *apud iudicem* phase determined which wager—that is, the plaintiff's or the defendant's—was lawfully made.

The *legis actiones* procedure was "ill-suited to an advance[d] state of society"[104] in that: (1) this procedure was only available to Roman citizens; (2) under

---

98. BUCKLAND, *supra* note 93, at 76.

99. *See, for example,* BUCKLAND, *supra* note 93, at 608.

100. WENGER, *supra* note 27, at 106 (highlighting the "fundamental principle of the contractual character of the Roman *litis contestatio*" but also noting that the magistrate could impose indirect sanctions on the uncooperative defendant).

101. BUCKLAND, *supra* note 27, at 348; THOMAS, *supra* note 22, at 76.

102. *Id.* at 348. *Contra* GREENIDGE, *supra* note 27, at 58 (stating that in the *legis actiones* procedure the burden of proof in substance lay on the original claimant as the "injustice of [the defendant's claim] established the relative justice of his rival's [. . .].").

103. BUCKLAND, *supra* note 93, at 611.

104. DANNER, *supra* note 27, at 16.

this system, suing through an agent was not possible; (3) form and ritualism had a paramount importance in court, whereas substantial justice had none; (4) substantive law rights merged into the action such that failure to obtain judgment for whatever reason extinguished plaintiff's rights; (5) the fact that both parties shouldered the burden of proof was impractical; and (6) the rigidity of the system meant that courts could not give protection to new interests not provided for under the *legis actiones* system, however meritorious they might have been.[105]

In the third century BC, as Rome was rapidly changing from being a rural community in central Italy to becoming a vast empire wherein international trade occupied a prominent role in the state's economy, the need to get rid of the treacherous clutches of *legis actiones* procedure became apparent.[106]

III. ROMAN LAW: THE FORMULARY PROCEDURE

A statute, the *lex Licinia*, conferred Roman magistrates—that is, the *Praetor Urbanus* and the *Praetor Peregrinus*—a sweeping discretionary power in administering justice. As stated above, the *Praetor Urbanus* was competent for matters involving Roman citizens and the *Praetor Peregrinus* was competent for matters involving noncitizens.

Taking advantage of the authority conferred by the aforesaid power, the *Praetor Peregrinus* began granting the so-called *formulae* to noncitizens who sought to have their rights protected in court.[107] A *formula* was a writ-like command[108] couched as an outline of the case containing a conditional judgment ordering the defendant to pay the plaintiff a certain amount of money,[109] provided that the arbiter appointed therein ascertained the existence of certain facts listed in the *formula* itself.[110]

The discretionary nature of the magisterial power afforded the *Praetor Peregrinus* great latitude in molding the new procedure according to the needs of the evolving, advanced, and diverse Roman society.[111] Magistrates took advantage of

---

105. GREENIDGE, *supra* note 27, at 155 (noting how the magistrate gave protection to new interests beyond the bounds of the *ius civile* employing the formulary procedure).

106. *See* THOMAS, *supra* note 22, at 83.

107. *Id.* at 83.

108. *See* BURBICK, *supra* note 32, at 649.

109. The judgment was always rendered in the form of an order to pay a sum of money even when the parties put forth a claim to title of a thing. *See* GREENIDGE, *supra* note 27, at 158; THOMAS, *supra* note 22, at 97.

110. *See* DANNER, *supra* note 27, at 24 (defining formula as "the right granted by the magistrate to a plaintiff to prosecute his cause before a *judex*").

111. THOMAS, *supra* note 22, at 95.

their discretionary power[112] in devising the new system such that the superiority of the new procedure as compared to the old *legis actiones* was soon appreciated by Roman authorities.[113] Sometime between the years 149 and 126 BC, the statute *l. Aebutia* and around the year 17 BC, the statutes *ll. Juliae*, extended the formulary procedure to all controversies. Specifically, the former is said to have merely allowed the plaintiff to choose which action to pursue, whereas the latter are regarded as having overruled the old procedure.[114]

The introduction of the formulary procedure represented a great innovation brought about within the basic framework of the old *legis actiones* procedure. Nonetheless, the formulary system preserved the basic two-phased structure of the old proceedings.[115] Indeed, as under the old system, the plaintiff summoned the defendant to appear before the magistrate for the first part of the trial. That phase ended when the parties entered into the agreement called *litis contestatio*. Through the *litis contestatio*, with magisterial approval, the parties appointed a lay arbiter who was vested with the authority to adjudicate the merits of the case and return a final judgment.[116]

Despite maintaining the two-phase structure, the new system was substantively different from the old *legis actiones* procedure. Significantly, the revised *in iure* phase did not consist of a mere recitation of invariable words. It is here that we find most of the innovations of the formulary procedure. Formerly, in the old *in iure* stage of the *legis actiones* procedure, the parties had to utter fixed ritual words determined by statute (i.e., *certa verba*), and anything short of strict compliance with the ritual forms caused either the plaintiff or the defendant to lose the case. The formulary system broke with this tradition and allowed the parties to appear before the magistrate and utter *concepta verba*: essentially, the litigants stated in their own words[117] (1) what the issue was, and (2) what *formula* they requested.[118]

---

112. *See* BUCKLAND, *supra* note 93, at 625.
113. The change in procedure was also brought about for political reasons. In fact, the exact contents of the *legis actiones* procedure remained secret for a long time. This secrecy favored the patrician rulers who were privy to these secrets. However, the publications of the rules contained in the so-called *arcana* in the third century BC certainly facilitated the widespread adoption of the new procedure because the value of the *legis actiones* procedure to the patricians decreased after said publication. *See* BUCKLAND, *supra* note 27, at 353.
114. BUCKLAND, *supra* note 93, at 624.
115. *Id.* at 622; BUCKLAND, *supra* note 27, at 352.
116. THOMAS, *supra* note 22, at 84.
117. It was not uncommon, however, to engage legal advisers even though the parties might have acted for themselves only as a formality. *See* BUCKLAND, *supra* note 27, at 354.
118. BUCKLAND, *supra* note 93, at 623; DANNER, *supra* note 27, at 23.

Having heard the parties in court, the magistrate then summarized (1) claims, (2) possible counterclaims, and (3) affirmative defenses in a written charge (i.e., the *formula*) addressed to the lay arbiter. Through the *formula*, the magistrate directed the arbiter to find in favor of the defendant or in favor of the plaintiff depending on what facts, among the relevant ones indicated therein, were proved at the second phase of the trial (i.e., *apud iudicem*). Under this procedure, the lay arbiter was a mere fact finder, as the law of the case had been fixed in the *formula*.[119]

The magistrate served for a one-year term and, immediately after taking office, each newly appointed magistrate issued a decree, that is, the *edict*, listing the *formulae* that were made available to potential litigants.[120] Indeed, at the outset of each term, the magistrate could devise new *formulae* and modify those that were listed in his predecessor's decree. Furthermore, while in office, the magistrate retained sweeping discretionary powers in administering justice; in fact, at any time, magistrates could (1) refuse to grant a *formula* even if it were listed in the decree, (2) devise new *formulae*, (3) reshape old actions, and (4) grant new equitable defenses.[121]

Now, let us delve into the procedural technicalities of the formulary trial. Once the parties appeared before the magistrate, the plaintiff stated the nature of her claim (*editio actionis*) and requested the issuance of a specific *formula* (*impetratio actionis*).[122] Subsequently, the defendant could (1) simply object,[123] (2) counterclaim following the same procedure employed by the plaintiff, and/or (3) raise an affirmative defense (*exceptio*), which was usually an equitable one.[124] Thereafter, the plaintiff had a chance to reply (*replicatio*) to the defendant's contentions raising defenses or counterclaims thereto. This back-and-forth procedure continued until the magistrate deemed the case ripe for decision.[125]

---

119. *But see* GREENIDGE, *supra* note 27, at 150 (arguing that the *iudex*'s role was not limited to a finder of points of fact because the formula "does not state the law requisite for the very condition of the formula").

120. *Id.* at 86 ("The *edictum* was the proclamation through which the Roman magistrate communicated with the public and expressed his commands, prohibitions and offers of assistance").

121. THOMAS, *supra* note 22, at 84.

122. BUCKLAND, *supra* note 27, at 354 ("The magistrate and the parties no longer recite ritual words *in iure*, but have a discussion, often long, as to the proper *formula*").

123. GREENIDGE, *supra* note 27, at 229.

124. DANNER, *supra* note 27, at 19; *See also* GREENIDGE, *supra* note 27, at 231 (stating that the exception was largely unknown at the time of the *legis actiones* procedure).

125. THOMAS, *supra* note 22, at 85.

Stated another way, during the first phase of the trial pending before the magistrate, the parties alleged a set of facts upon which their claims were based. At this stage, the magistrate viewed the facts put forth by the litigants in the light most favorable to the party making the allegation, including because the magistrate was determining whether a prima facie case warranting the kind of relief sought was properly made out.[126] Failure to set forth a prima facie case resulted in a dismissal. Conversely, for the reasons below, during the second phase of the proceedings before the lay arbiter, the abovementioned favorable inference was dropped and each party had to prove the allegations made during the first part of the trial.

The *formula* included several parts, namely (1) a clause appointing an arbiter, (2) a *demonstratio*, (3) an *intentio*, (4) a *condemnatio*, (5) an *adjudicatio*, (6) one or more possible *exceptiones*, (7) one or more *replicationes*, and (8) a *praescriptio*.[127] Not all elements had to be present in every issued formula as the magistrate adapted *formulae* to the specific circumstances of each case.[128]

For example, a simple formula ran thus:

To Titus who is appointed [arbiter]: Whereas [plaintiff] sold [x] to [defendant] [*demonstratio*], if it be proved that [defendant] owes [plaintiff] ten thousand Sesterces [*intentio*], do thou condemn [defendant] to pay [plaintiff] ten thousand Sesterces; but if it is not proved absolve him [*condemnatio*].[129]

At the outset of the *formula* an arbiter was appointed. Next, the *demonstratio* consisted of a brief statement of the subject matter of the dispute. The *intentio* specified in detail the elements of the claim; to put it differently, in modern parlance we would say that the *intentio* in combination with the *demonstratio* set forth the prima facie case. Then, the *condemnatio* vested the arbiter with the power to acquit or condemn the defendant.[130]

If the defendant chose not to simply deny plaintiff's allegations but pleaded additional facts intended to bar plaintiff's recovery, the magistrate could grant an *exceptio*. In the *formula*, the *exceptio* followed the clause setting out the elements

126. WENGER, *supra* note 27, at 192 ("we shall not fail to recognize the fundamental difference between apparently parallel courses of proceedings: *in iure* is involved the legal evaluation for the time being of not yet proven but alleged (by the parties) facts of legal importance; *apud iudicem* is involved the proving of those facts, whereupon judgment is rendered in accordance with the program set up *in iure*").
127. BURBICK, *supra* note 32, at 642; DANNER, *supra* note 27, at 20; GREENIDGE, *supra* note 27, at 151.
128. GREENIDGE, *supra* note 27, at 154.
129. BURBICK, *supra* note 32, at 641 (internal citation omitted).
130. DANNER, *supra* note 27, at 20; THOMAS, *supra* note 22, at 97.

of the prima facie case[131] and was couched as a negative condition qualifying the *intentio*.[132] For example, a *formula* comprising an *exceptio* ran thus: if it be proved that xyz happened and "if in that matter there was and is no fraud of [plaintiff . . .]."[133]

Subsequently, as stated above, the plaintiff could either (1) simply deny the defendant's allegations, or (2) raise an affirmative defense in the form of an *exceptio* to the *exception,* which was called *replicatio.*

By way of example, a *formula* comprising a *replicatio* ran thus:

> Titius is appointed [arbiter]. Whereas [plaintiff] stipulated for 10,000 sesterces from [defendant] [*demonstratio*], if it be proved that [defendant] ought to pay [plaintiff] 10,000 sesterces [*intentio*], provided that [plaintiff] and [defendant] did not agree that the money should not be demanded [*exceptio*], and if there was no subsequent agreement that [plaintiff] might sue [*replicatio*], do thou condemn [defendant] to pay [plaintiff] ten thousand Sesterces; but if it is not proved absolve him [*condmenatio*].[134]

A *praescriptio* was a clause placed before anything else in the formula so as to narrow the scope of the judicial inquiry and limit the preclusive effect of the judgment. This clause was normally introduced by the words "let only this question be considered."[135]

It is worth highlighting that the words "if it be proved" or "if it seems" always appeared in the *formula* right before both (1) the clause setting forth the elements of the prima facie case, and (2) any possible affirmative defense. Considering the features of the formulary trial we have been discussing, two important conclusions need be drawn here.

First, plaintiff's claim had to fit into one of the claim types listed in the magistrate's decree; thus, it was the claimant's *de facto* duty to allege all the elements of the prima facie case at the hearing.[136] If the claimant did not do so, the magistrate—either *sua sponte* or on an appropriate demurrer lodged by the other party—could deny the issuance of the *formula* (i.e., *denegatio actionis*), thus prematurely ending the trial.[137]

---

131. Thomas, *supra* note 22, at 99.
132. *Id.* at 100.
133. Burbick, *supra* note 32, at 643.
134. *Id.* at 644.
135. *Id.* at 645.
136. Buckland, *supra* note 27, at 354.
137. Danner, *supra* note 27, at 19.

Second, the inclusion of the if-it-be-proved clause stands for the proposition that the defendant's general denial of plaintiff's assertions was potentially sufficient to defeat plaintiff's claim, provided that the underlying factual contentions set forth by the claimant turned out to be *un*supported by the evidence.[138]

Under this system, only one of the parties shouldered the burden of establishing her allegations. This is so, because given the syllogistic structure of the *formula,* only one of the parties suffered the adverse consequences of failure to tender sufficient evidence, that is, losing the case. Indeed, per the explicit language of the *condemnatio* clause, failure to submit sufficient evidence caused the other party to win the case. In fact, as stated above, the *condemnatio* was expressed as an alternative command to condemn or to acquit depending on the sufficiency of the evidence submitted by a certain party. The reason for the need of an explicit condemn-if/acquit-if clause seems to be historical: as stated above, in the *legis actiones* procedure both parties shouldered the burden of proving title to the thing in dispute. Therefore, the magistrate probably couched the *formula* so as to make clear to the arbiter that—differently than what was done before—if one party's contentions were not proved, then judgment should go for the other party.[139] This conclusion is supported by the fact that the *formula* was worded as a conditional judgment[140] ordering the defendant to pay the plaintiff a sum of money *provided that* plaintiff's contentions proved to be supported by the evidence.[141] Obviously, the same argument can be made in reverse as to defendant's counterclaims and affirmative defenses.[142]

Turning again to the course of proceedings, let us consider the contract called *litis contestatio,* which marked the transition of the proceedings from the *in iure* stage to the *apud iudicium* part.[143] Having heard the parties at the hearing, the

---

138. *See, for example,* BURBICK, *supra* note 32, at 643; DANNER, *supra* note 27, at 20.

139. GREENIDGE, *supra* note 27, at 154 (stating that the reason for the dual structure of the *condemnatio* was "intimately connected with the history of the formula. [In fact,] if the latter was originally a mode of extra-legal assistance not recognized by the *ius civile* it is probable that the mere fulfilment of the action based on it did not (as in the case of the *legis actio*) *ipso iure* extinguish the claim and prevent a renewal of the case").

140. *Id.* at 150 (stating that the formula "contained in a conditional form a judgment which the finding of the iudex was to make absolute"); WENGER, *supra* note 27, at 191 (stating that the rendering of judgment was a "logical activity [. . .] indeed prescribed [. . .] in the formula and the command to adjudicate . . .").

141. This concept being quite similar to the modern order to show cause.

142. *Id.* at 232 ("The *exceptio* is always a sentence that conditions the condemnation. . . ."); *See also* THOMAS, *supra* note 22, at 99 (stating that the *exceptio* "raised a counter-question for the judge").

143. GREENIDGE, *supra* note 27, at 244.

magistrate could either dismiss the case (*denegatio actionis*), or issue the *formula* submitting the case to a lay arbiter for judgment. However, for the *formula* to issue, both parties had to enter into an agreement jointly appointing an arbiter tasked to return a final judgment.[144] Hypothetically, each party could refuse to enter into such agreement[145] but, should a party frivolously refuse to stipulate the *litis contestatio*, the magistrate had several indirect means of coercion at his disposal. For example, the magistrate could issue an order dispossessing the disobedient party of all her assets.[146]

The stipulation of the *litis contestatio* and the concurrent issuance of the *formula* had several important effects. Once the *formula* issued (1) the subject matter of the dispute was definitively established, (2) the law of the case became fixed such that the arbiter had no choice but to apply the law as spelled out in the *formula* no matter how unjust it might appear to him,[147] and (3) the preclusive effect of the judgment attached to every issue mentioned in the *formula*.[148]

After the *formula* issued, the lay arbiter set the hearing date.[149] Typically, the parties appeared accompanied by advisers and orators.[150] Then, the *formula* was presented to the arbiter and he was sworn in.[151] Should one of the parties fail to appear, a default judgment could be entered forthwith.[152] Next, upon the advice

---

144. BUCKLAND, *supra* note 93, at 627.

145. GREENIDGE, *supra* note 27, at 265.

146. *Id.* at 257.

147. WENGER, *supra* note 27, at 191 (stating that it was not part of the *iudex*'s job to "answer the question whether or not it is also reasonable to draw from the premises of the *intentio* the inference of the *condemnatio* . . .").

148. GREENIDGE, *supra* note 27, at 244; The preclusive effect of judgment was obtained by granting an exception, that is, the *exceptio rei iudicatae vel in iudicium deductae*, to a defendant who was sued on a claim that shared the same subject matter as that which was previously decided; *See* THOMAS, *supra* note 22, at 100; Alternatively, if the action originated from the *ius civile*, a second attempt to sue on the same transaction or occurrence would be met with an *in limine* dismissal of the action; *See Id.* at 104.

149. BUCKLAND, *supra* note 27, at 359.

150. The attorneys' role in litigation was split in two. In fact, two different professionals assisted the parties: the adviser who can be equated to a solicitor trained in the law but not allowed to address the court, and an orator trained in the oratory art who delivered the speech addressed to the court.

151. GREENIDGE, *supra* note 27, at 270 ("The *iudex* was on an appointed day approached by the parties in the forum. His first act was, perhaps, to take the oath, and then he was made aware of the outlines of the case, chiefly by the *formula* being presented to him, perhaps also by a short discourse with the parties or their counsel.") (Internal citation omitted); WENGER, *supra* note 27, at 193.

152. BUCKLAND, *supra* note 27, at 359.

of counsel, the orators delivered their speeches on behalf of the parties and seam-lessly tendered written and oral evidence supporting their clients' case.[153]

Rules of evidence were quite lax in that the litigants were permitted to submit any sort of written or testimonial evidence.[154] Hearsay testimony as well as opinion testimony was permissible.[155] However, the parties themselves and their close relations were not allowed to testify. Furthermore, giving testimony was a voluntary act in that the parties could not *subpoena* witnesses' attendance. The parties were allowed to cross-examine the other party's witnesses.[156]

After both parties presented their case, the arbiter entered a judgment in the form of an opinion[157]—rendered without stating the arbiter's reasoning—in accordance with the *formula's* acquit-if/condemn-if clause.[158] The wording of the *condemnatio* and, specifically, the if-it-be-proved or if-it-seems clause empowered the arbiter to freely weigh the credibility of the parties' evidence and thus determine whether claims or affirmative defenses were to be considered established.[159] In turn, the *formula* directed the arbiter to find in favor of the plaintiff on the condition that her evidence appeared convincing enough such that the "if it seems" question posed by the *formula* could be answered in the affirmative. Obviously, for a fact to "seem" true in the eyes of the arbiter it had to appear more plausible than not so.

Notably, the formula did not require the finder of fact to positively believe beyond a reasonable doubt that the plaintiff's allegations of fact definitely reflected reality. Perhaps in an attempt to acknowledge the subjectivity of this kind of adjudication method, the *formula* literally spoke of what "seemed" to be true or not true in the eyes of the finder of fact.[160] The lay arbiter was thus endowed with the authority to assess credibility.

---

153. BUCKLAND, *supra* note 27, at 359.

154. GREENIDGE, *supra* note 27, at 275.

155. BUCKLAND, *supra* note 27, at 359; BUCKLAND, *supra* note 93, at 632.

156. BURBICK, *supra* note 32, at 650; GREENIDGE, *supra* note 27, at 272.

157. GREENIDGE, *supra* note 27, at 276 ("There were no fixed terms in which the sentence was delivered; the cautiousness of the Roman character was betrayed in the fact that the *iudex* gave his binding judgment as an opinion (*videri*), generally with the hesitating addition *si quid mei iudcii est*.") (Internal citation omitted).

158. BURBICK, *supra* note 32, at 653.

159. BUCKLAND, *supra* note 93, at 633; *see also* WENGER, *supra* note 27, at 201 ("the classical law of procedure has the theory of *free weighing of proof* [. . .] Fundamentally—not without restrictions—the *iudex* can and must form his opinion concerning the weight of evidence according to his own free will.") (Internal citation omitted).

160. *See* GREENIDGE, *supra* note 27, at 276 ("According to the principle laid down by Cicero, which was the principle of Roman criminal as well as civil process, the general subjective impression

IV. ROMAN LAW AND THE COMMON LAW

An in-depth analysis of how the common law originated in England is beyond the scope of this book. We will, nevertheless, quickly outline certain features of the early common law so as to highlight a number of similarities between the common law and Roman law.

From a cultural and economic standpoint, ancient Romans had exerted great influence over Great Britain since Julius Caesar's expeditions in the years 55 and 54 BC. It was, however, in the year 43 AD, when Emperor Claudius militarily conquered the island, that Roman influence over Great Britain reached its climax.

After the Roman Empire's demise as a result of the so-called barbaric invasions, western European institutions (including Britain's) regressed considerably, falling back to what can be described as a primitive system of government. Put differently, in the middle ages, the sophisticated and highly centralized type of government that had been established by the Romans (temporarily) vanished.

In early feudal Great Britain, justice was administered locally by lords. A number of political subdivisions operated a court system. By way of example, civil justice was administered in the County Court, Hundred Court, Manorial Court, and other similar community-based courts.[161]

Numerous shortcomings characterized the feudal justice system: first, every court had its own rules of procedure and enforced local customary law; second, compulsory execution of judgments was not possible; and third, outlandish mechanisms such as trial by ordeal, trial by battle, and trial by compurgation were employed as fact-finding methods.

The ordeal or "judgment of God" was very popular among the Saxons. Different kinds of ordeals were employed, namely (1) the fire ordeal under which the defendant had to walk barefoot over a wooden plank that had been previously set aflame—if she successfully carried out the task, she was deemed innocent; (2) the hot water ordeal wherein the defendant had to plunge her arm into boiling water—if she managed to do so without suffering fatal consequences, she was acquitted; and (3) the cold water ordeal under which the defendant, whose arms and legs had been previously bound together, was thrown into a pool filled with

---

derived by the judge from the proceedings must decide his verdict, the only modifying rule being the obvious one that, with certain exceptions, the burden of proof lies on the plaintiff . . .").

161. JOHN H. LANGBEIN ET AL., HISTORY OF THE COMMON LAW 7 (Wolters Kluwer 2009); THEODORE PLUCKNETT, A CONCISE HISTORY OF THE COMMON LAW 15 (Liberty Fund 2012) (stating that "in the reign of Henry I the law was substantially anglo-Saxon and administered by the Sheriffs locally according to ancient custom . . .").

cold water—if the defendant sank, she prevailed. The assumption underlying these procedures was that God would have helped the respondent overcome these torments, should she deserve to be found innocent.[162]

Trial by compurgation or by "wager of law" required the defendant to give a sworn statement setting forth her rights. Subsequently, the defendant had to bring forward a certain number of neighbors who confirmed her credibility under oath. If the prescribed number of oaths were sworn, judgment was issued for the respondent. The idea underlying this procedure was that people involved in the litigation, for fear of God, would not swear a false oath.[163]

Trial by battle entailed actual fighting among the parties. Under certain circumstances, litigants were allowed to hire so-called "champions" for carrying out the duel.[164]

In 1066 AD, England was conquered by the Normans. Among other things, Norman kings brought to England their customs, which were derived from Germanic traditions. England's new rulers established a more centralized state, a period of relative political stability, and the idea that the king himself was the ultimate "fountain of justice" of the kingdom.

After the conquest, the new Norman rulers administered the kingdom wisely. When making important decisions, Norman kings regularly consulted with the most influential aristocrats and landowners of the country. This group of advisers became to be known as the *Curia Regis* (or King's Council).[165]

Because of the numerous shortcomings of the feudal justice system, aggrieved parties who failed to obtain redress in regular local courts started petitioning the king directly pleading for special redress.[166] Typically, the king delegated the investigation and resolution of these grievances to his advisers, that is, the members of the *Curia Regis*.

This unusual avenue for obtaining justice became exponentially more popular as Britain's economy started to flourish. Eventually, landowners and other litigants increasingly refused to prosecute cases before feudal courts, as they came to be perceived as unreliable. Probably to strengthen the power of the central government, the king started to accept a large number of these special petitions

---

162. GEORGE CRABB, A HISTORY OF ENGLISH LAW; OR AN ATTEMPT TO TRACE THE RISE, PROGRESS, AND SUCCESSIVE CHANGES, OF THE COMMON LAW; FROM THE EARLIEST PERIOD TO THE PRESENT TIME 27 (Baldwin and Cradock 1829); Plucknett, *supra* note 161, at 114 *et seq.*

163. CRABB, *supra* note 162, at 29.

164. *Id.* at 47.

165. *Id.* at 53.

166. 77 R. C. VAN CAENEGEM, ROYAL WRITS IN ENGLAND FROM THE CONQUEST TO GLANVILL 25 (Professional Books Ltd 1972).

for review. By the middle of the twelfth century AD, the king and his council, the *Curia Regis*, administered justice concurrently with local courts on a regular basis.[167] As it turns out, the *Curia Regis* was the very first common-law court—that is, a court enforcing rules *common* to the whole kingdom as opposed to feudal courts, which enforced local customs.

Initially, the *Curia Regis* literally followed the king as he traveled around Great Britain. Thus, the King's Council dispensed justice operating as an itinerant court of special jurisdiction. Subsequently, by the end of the twelfth century AD, the Court of Common Pleas and the King's Bench were established as offshoots of the *Curia Regis*.[168] In contrast to the *Curia Regis*, the Common Pleas and the King's Bench permanently sat at Westminster in London.

Central courts sitting in London ultimately supplanted the King's Council in administering justice because, *inter alia*, the itinerant nature of the latter rendered carrying out the day-to-day judicial business impractical.

Both the Common Pleas and the King's Bench were trial courts. Thus, theoretically, litigants had to travel to London to prosecute their case at common law. Because of the inconvenience of primitive traveling, the King frequently commissioned special judges, called justices *in eyre*, to travel the realm holding hearings in every county.[169] Eventually, this practice was codified and the kingdom was subdivided into circuits.[170] Justices of the central courts regularly rode the circuits holding hearings.

Common-law courts ultimately overshadowed local feudal courts. Probably, as we will argue below, it was the greater impartiality of royal courts resulting from the empanelment of lay juries that ultimately determined their success.[171]

The legal instrument through which central courts removed cases from local courts was the writ. Specifically, a plaintiff who intended to file a civil action before common-law courts had to obtain a writ from the chancellor. The writ was an order of the king directing the sheriff or another officer to allow the action to proceed at common law before royal courts. Simultaneously, the writ barred local courts from hearing the case. At trial, pursuant to the writ's language, the presiding judge instructed the finder of fact to condemn the defendant provided that the

167. Matthew Hale, The History of the Common Law of England, and an Analysis of the Civil Part of the Law 22 (London, H. Butterworth, 1820) (defining the common law as that law "by which proceedings and determinations, in the king's ordinary courts of justice, are directed and guided . . .").
168. Plucknett, *supra* note 161, at 146 *et seq.*
169. Crabb, *supra* note 162, at 99.
170. Van Caenegem, *supra* note 166, at 19.
171. Plucknett, *supra* note 161, at 81.

facts of the case—as alleged and subsequently proved—fit into one of the typical fact patterns indicated in the issued writ itself.

The oldest writ, the Writ of Right, was originally worded thus:

> William, king of England, to [. . .] the chamberlain and his justices and all his lieges, greeting. Inquire by the county court who had more justly a forfeiture of this kind in the time of my father, whether the abbot of [. . .] or the predecessor of [. . .] and if the county court agrees that it is rather the abbot who ought rightly to have the said forfeiture, then I order that the 100 shillings which [. . .] impleaded about be restored to the abbot without delay [. . .].[172]

Essentially, this writ ordered local courts to do justice and subtly signaled to local authorities that should they fail to do so the king would intervene in the matter. Thereafter, the writ employed to prosecute cases at common law gradually evolved into an order to show cause—that is, a so-called writ *Praecipe*. By way of example, a writ *Praecipe* ran thus:

> William, king of England, to Robert, earl of Northumberland, greeting. I will that the bishop of Durham be seised of the land of Ross, as he was seised on that day on which he departed from me from Windsor for wrath. And whatsoever your men have received thence since I restored his land to the bishop of Durham, cause to be returned to him without delay. And if you claim anything in the said land, show me your claim and I will reply to you what is fitting [. . .].[173]

Soon thereafter the order to show cause was phased out and the writs made available to litigants were couched as a simple injunction whereby the king ordered the defendant to do something. One such writ was worded thus:

> Henry, king of England and duke of Normandy [. . .], to the sheriff of Essex, greeting. I order that Gilbert [. . .] shall hold well and in peace, freely and justly all his lands and tenures, as abbot Hugh, his predecessor, held them on the day when he was alive and dead. And I forbid that he be impleaded because of any peasant who claims [. . . a tenure] as his hereditary tenure. And unless you do it my justices shall do it.[174]

The language of this writ implied that if the defendant wished to disobey the king's order, she had to appear before royal justices seeking to quash the injunction. Eventually, the king's injunction to do or refrain from specific acts

---

172. VAN CAENEGEM, *supra* note 166, at 413.
173. *Id.* at 427.
174. *Id.* at 504.

came to be considered a mere formality and this writ morphed into a pure writ of summons directing the sheriff to compel a certain person to appear before one of the king's courts.

Under this system, the available causes of action were undoubtedly limited. Moreover, the causes of action upon which relief could be granted at common law were determined by the chancellor, who was endowed with the authority to devise and issue writs. To this end, the chancellor maintained a register of the various kinds of writs made available to litigants. The claimant who intended to bring suit was required to purchase one of the writs the chancellor listed in his registry. It goes without saying, if the legally operative facts of plaintiff's case did not match any of the causes of action listed in the chancellor's registry, a writ could not issue and royal courts could not afford relief.[175]

To sum up, around the year 1066 AD, the crown established a system of central courts. Simultaneously, the chancellor devised a set of writs that allowed prospective litigants to prosecute their cases before the newly created royal courts. In consequence, central courts gradually overshadowed local courts.

The establishment of central royal courts had several consequences significant to our discussion. First, there was a formal shift of power from the feudal court system to the royal court system. Second, the royal court system strengthened the central government. Most importantly, new rules were promulgated by the crown and, eventually, common-law judges completely set aside the medieval and irrational methods of proof (i.e. trial by battle, ordeal, and compurgation), and replaced them with jury trials. The institution of the lay jury marked the creation of modern evidence law.[176]

Now, let us delve into the technicalities of jury trials in the twelfth century.

After the Conquest of 1066, Norman kings brought several new traditions to England. One such new tradition was the inquest. Under the inquest procedure, a panel of lay citizens for each village was appointed by royal authorities. Members of the panel were routinely interrogated under oath by royal officers so as to gather all sorts of information concerning the community in which they resided.[177]

At this early stage, the inquest was mainly employed as a simple administrative (i.e., nonjudicial) method of fact finding through which "foreign" rulers

---

175. Stein, *supra* note 25, at 1592.
176. PLUCKNETT, *supra* note 161, at 111.
177. *Id.*

(i.e., Norman kings) obtained relevant information from potentially uncooperative local (Anglo-Saxon) communities.[178]

By way of example, King William the Conqueror issued the following order directing his officers to carry out an inquest:

> Enquire by the oath of the sheriff and of all the barons and of their Frenchmen, and of all the hundred, of the priest, of the reeve, and of six villeins of every vill, what is the name of the manor, who held it in the time of King Edward, who now, how many hides, how many ploughs,—how many men, how many villeins [. . .] how much it was worth and how much now; and all these at three times, the time of King Edward, the time when King William gave it, and now.[179]

Subsequently, once the new central courts were established, King Henry II issued an ordinance that effectively adopted the inquest procedure as a fact-finding mechanism for judicial proceedings.[180] This ordinance, called the Grand assize (assize generally means "enactment"), mandated that the defendant in a judicial proceeding initiated by writ of right could elect to put himself on trial by inquest, instead of trial by battle.[181] Under the Grand assize procedure, four "lawful knights" of the neighborhood where the case originated were summoned to choose twelve other lawful knights of the neighborhood to be sworn in and serve as jurors. Ultimately, the panel of twelve knights was required to "recognize" under oath who among the litigants was vested with the greater right.[182]

The inquest procedure was made applicable to several forms of action. The king enacted a number of so-called Petty assizes; namely: the assize *Utrum*, the *Novel Disseisin*, *Mort d'ancestor*, and *Darrein Presentment*.[183] By way of contrast with the Grand assize wherein only knights could be summoned for jury service, under the Petty assizes, simple "lawful men" of the neighborhood could serve as jurors.[184] The assumption underlying the adoption of the inquest procedure as a method of fact finding was that the jurors could shed light upon the facts

---

178. *Id.*
179. *Id.*
180. Crabb, *supra* note 162, at 48.
181. *See* Plucknett, *supra* note 161, at 111 *et seq.*
182. Van Caenegem, *supra* note 166, at 82.
183. Plucknett, *supra* note 161, at 112.
184. Van Caenegem, *supra* note 166, at 82.

of the case at bar because they had direct knowledge of major events relating to their communities.

This assumption was certainly true so far as the so-called "open-fields agriculture" was the prevalent method of farming in England. In fact, the principal tenet of open-field agriculture was that the whole community participated in cultivating communal fields. Thus, widespread knowledge of the main events concerning one's neighborhood was certainly to be expected.[185]

This new procedure was significant in several respects. First, the jury was a self-informing panel. As such, the jurors were expected (and, in fact, required) to have direct knowledge of the facts of the case at bar. It followed that, if a juror did not have such knowledge, another "lawful man" having prior firsthand knowledge had to be summoned.[186] In other words, at the outset, the so-called "instructional trial" in which litigants tendered evidence to inform an impartial and neutral finder of fact as to the merits of their claims did not exist.

Second, since no evidence was tendered at (or before) trial, one can easily argue that none of the parties shouldered a burden of proof. However, having considered the structure of the inquest procedure, it seems that the *standard of proof* applicable to common-law actions was the absolute-certainty standard. In fact, jurors were simultaneously fact finders and witnesses. Under this system, the jurors/witnesses swore an oath confirming that judgment should go to the plaintiff or to the defendant precisely because the jury had actual knowledge of the facts of the case.[187]

Third, given the exacting standard of proof required, appeals or motions to set aside verdicts were not allowed, save and except that verdicts could be vacated for bribery, fraud, or other misconduct.

We must also consider the historical socioeconomic context in which the judicial inquest procedure was established. The system of self-informing juries developed between the year 1066 and the year 1300. During this time, Britain's population doubled in number. Indeed, labor-intensive farming spurred this sharp natality rate increase. Against this backdrop, as it has been said above, the so-called open-fields agriculture was prevalent and nearly all available communal fields were intensively cultivated to meet the need of a growing population. Conversely, noncommunal cultivation of enclosed fields was of marginal importance.[188]

---

185. *Id.* at 91.
186. LANGBEIN ET AL., supra note 161, at 209.
187. *Id.*
188. *Id.* at 224.

This situation suddenly changed in the summer of 1348 when the Black Death, that is, a plague epidemic, reached England, wiping out forty percent of the population in just one year. This steep population decline caused a shortage of labor and in turn a dramatic wage hike. As a result, relatively richer agrarian workers who survived the plague started acquiring fee simple tenements. Thus, the open-fields communal agriculture quickly disappeared.[189]

After the year 1349, on average, the pool of eligible jurors having firsthand knowledge of local events shrank sharply. This was so because of (1) the great number of deaths caused by the plague, (2) the establishment of a new noncommunal agriculture brought about the loosening of social ties in agrarian communities, and (3) the wage hike that caused an increased level of mobility of the workforce and ultimately massive urbanization.[190]

All of the sudden, employing self-informing juries for judicial proceedings no longer seemed a sensible policy choice. However, change did not happen overnight. The transition from the self-informing jury to the modern (uninformed) jury occurred incrementally. Initially, litigants dealt with the difficulty of finding previously informed jurors by informally offering evidence to the prospective members of the panel before trial. In other words, the parties and their lawyers regularly approached jurors out of court attempting to convince them of their alleged entitlement to judgment by giving speeches or offering evidence.[191]

In the year 1563, the informal practice of offering evidence to jurors in order to persuade them about the merits of the parties' claims or defenses was finally regulated by a statute. Among other things, litigants were afforded the right to compel witness's attendance at trial where they could be subjected to direct and cross-examination under the supervision of the judge.

Initially, this modernization of trial procedure was brought about by Queen Elizabeth, who enacted the statute of perjury. The statute provided that:

> [I]f any person or persons, upon whom any process out of any of the courts of record [. . .] shall be served to testify or depose concerning any cause or matter depending in any of the same courts, and having tendered unto him or them, according to his or their countenance of calling, such reasonable sums of money

---

189. *Id.* at 225.
190. *Id.* at 227.
191. David J. Seipp, *Jurors, Evidences and the Tempest of 1499, in* THE DEAREST BIRTH RIGHT OF THE PEOPLE OF ENGLAND: THE JURY IN THE HISTORY OF THE COMMON LAW 75, 82 (John Cairns & Grant McLeod eds., Hart Publishing 2002).

for his or their costs and charges, as having regard to the distance of the places is necessary to be allowed in that behalf, do not appear according to the tenor of the said process, having not a lawful and reasonable let or impediment to the contrary, that them the party making default, to lose and forfeit for every such offense ten pounds, and to yield such further recompense to the party grieved, as by the direction of the judge of the court [. . .].[192]

Subsequently, offering evidence to the finder of fact became possible only at trial under the direction of the royal judge,[193] and that judge was given a concurrent opportunity to evaluate and weigh that evidence independent of the jury's view of it. In *Wood v. Gunston*,[194] we have the first reported case in which the court set aside a jury verdict for being against the weight of the evidence. In *Wood*, the plaintiff brought a libel action against Gunston for allegedly uttering "scandalous words." The jury returned a verdict of £1,500, but the court set aside the verdict and granted a new trial because in the view of the court, the damages award was excessive in light of the evidence tendered to establish the triviality of the alleged insult.

Obviously, if the court could grant a new trial when the verdict was against the weight of the evidence, it follows that approaching jurors out of court was no longer possible. In fact, the evidence offered out of court would not be taken into account when judging a motion to set aside a verdict.[195]

To sum up, by the year 1655, to obtain redress at common law, the plaintiff had to (1) purchase an appropriate writ from the chancery, (2) serve the writ on the defendant, and (3) tender sufficient evidence *at trial* so as to persuade the (uninformed) jury that she was entitled to judgment. For each cause of action, the chancery issued a different writ that listed the elements of the *prima facie* case. The writ ordered the court to do justice on the condition that each legally operative factual element of the cause of action listed in the writ was found to be proven.

As it has been said above, after the year 1655, presiding judges were empowered to set aside jury verdicts for being against the weight of the evidence. Therefore, pursuant to their new authority conferred by the *Wood* case and its progeny, judges began instructing the jury *in limine* about principles of law

---

192. Langbein et al., supra note 161, at 246.
193. *Id.* at 441.
194. (1655) 82 Eng. Rep 867.
195. Langbein et al., *supra* note 161, at 440.

relating to the case at bar and specifically about the sufficiency of the evidence tendered at trial.[196]

Under the old inquest procedure, none of the parties shouldered the burden of proof because no evidence was offered at trial. Under the new system, in which litigants tendered evidence at trial, it can safely be said that the burden of proof rested on the party seeking the relief indicated in the writ. In fact, failing to convince the jurors of the existence of any of the elements of the *prima facie* case listed in the writ resulted in judgment for the other party. Indeed, the royal writ granted relief on the condition that a number of factual circumstances listed therewith were proven to be true.

As to the standard of proof, per *Wood*, after 1655, members of the jury were not allowed to have direct knowledge of the facts of the case. Therefore, to win the lawsuit, litigants had to tender enough evidence to persuade the (uninformed) jury of their entitlement to relief. Thus, the new standard fell short of the absolute certainty required under the inquest procedure. However, at this time, courts did not articulate the exact standard of proof required. In other words, courts did not distinguish among persuading the jury beyond a reasonable doubt, by a preponderance of the evidence, or by clear and convincing evidence.

In the year 1285, in an attempt to curb royal courts' powers, the Statute of Westminster II forbade the chancellor from devising new writs, thus effectively restricting the evolution of the common law.[197]

The writ system, no doubt, brought about a certain level of rigidity in the administration of justice.[198] Against this backdrop, the need for broadening the kinds of relief the royal justice system could afford became apparent.[199] Thus, litigants began petitioning the king, though the chancellor, pleading to issue injunctions or to afford protection for interests not provided for at common law. The chancellor began granting these prayers whenever he deemed appropriate given the specific circumstances of each case. Gradually, the Chancery Court was established to ensure that the remedial gaps caused by the rigidity of the common law were filled.[200] As a result, the Chancery Court became a court of equity wherein the chancellor, by contrast with the rigidity of the common law, administered

---

196. See Chapter 7 for a discussion of modern motions *in limine*.
197. Plucknett, *supra* note 161, at 28 ("its primary object was to authorize the extension of remedies which already existed between parties [. . .]. Chancery clerks did not regard this statute as giving them wide powers of creating new forms of action . . ."); Van Caenegem, *supra* note 166, at 27.
198. Stein, *supra* note 25, at 1594.
199. *Id.* at 1593.
200. *Id.* at 1594.

justice (without empaneling a jury) according to the principles of fairness and elasticity.[201]

In conclusion, it should be noted that the basic structure of early common law seems to resemble the framework of the third-century BC ancient Roman civil procedure. Specifically, the following similarities should be noted.

First, common-law courts could hear cases only after the claimant obtained a document, the writ, directing the finder of fact to return a verdict for the plaintiff provided that certain facts were deemed established; under the Roman formulary procedure, the claimant could obtain relief only after the magistrate issued a document, the *formula*, directing a lay arbiter to condemn the defendant on the condition that certain facts indicated therein seemed to be proven in the eyes of the lay arbiter.[202] Moreover, both the chancellor in England and the Roman magistrate published a list of possible actions that were made available to litigants: the former published the writ registry while the latter issued the decree, that is, the *edict*, listing the *formulae*.[203]

Second, at common law and under the Roman formulary procedure, civil trials were divided into two phases, namely (1) the first stage wherein the parties and the magistrate framed the issues to be submitted for adjudication, and (2) the second part in which laymen (the jury and the arbiter, respectively) rendered a verdict based on the directions received from the magistrate.

Third, since at common law and under Roman law the finder of fact was not a professional judge, money damages was the only possible relief that could be granted.[204] As a result, under both systems, a parallel jurisdiction was established to fill the remedial gaps created by the traditional civil procedure, namely, the Court of Equity in England and the system of *interdicta* administered by the Roman magistrate wherein fairness, substantial justice, and elasticity were of paramount importance.[205]

Furthermore, in both systems, legal discussion revolved around remedies rather than around rules of law. Put differently, English and (early) Roman jurists were more concerned with the legally operative facts of the case and with framing issues for submitting the case to the lay finder of fact, rather than with discussing the legal implications of abstract rules of law.[206]

---

201. *Id.*
202. THOMAS, *supra* note 22, at 6.
203. Stein, *supra* note 25, at 1592.
204. *Id.* at 1593.
205. *Id.* at 1594.
206. *Id.* at 1592.

V. CONCLUSION: THE RECEPTION OF THE ENGLISH COMMON LAW IN AMERICA

The legal status of the thirteen British colonies on the east coast of North America founded in the seventeenth and eighteenth centuries was set by various charters granted by the King of England. These charters laid out both the rights and duties of the settlers, and the relationship between the colonies and the Mother Country. Generally, these charters provided that the laws of the colonies could never be contrary to the laws of England.

After the Declaration of Independence and the Revolutionary War, the newly established U.S. Court of Appeals for the Pennsylvania Circuit acknowledged that:

> When the American colonies were first settled by our ancestors, it was held, as well by the settlers, as by the Judges and lawyers of England, that they brought hither, as a birth-right and inheritance, so much of the common law, as was applicable to their local situation, and change of circumstances.[207]

Subsequently, in *Van Ness v. Pacard*,[208] the United States Supreme Court clarified that: "The common law of England is not to be taken in all respects to be that of America. Our ancestors brought with them its general principles, and claimed it as their birthright. But they brought with them, and adopted only that portion which was applicable to their situation." In other words, in *Van Ness*, the Supreme Court acknowledged that, although American law was largely based on the English common law, it later diverged in a number of fields.

In New York, before the year 1798, state court judges delivered their opinions orally in open court and no record of their reasoning was made. Thus, lawyers and judges simply crafted their legal arguments and opinions on the basis of English precedents found in law reports and treatises imported from England.[209]

This situation suddenly changed when the New York governor appointed James Kent to the highest court of the state at the time: the New York Supreme Court. Justice Kent insisted that Supreme Court opinions had to be delivered in writing and that the state should subsidize a system of New York law reports.[210]

---

207. United States v. Worrall, 2 U.S. 384, 394 (C.C.Pa. 1798).
208. Van Ness v. Pacard, 27 U.S. 137, 141 (1829).
209. John H. Langbein, *Chancellor Kent and the History of Legal Literature*, 93 COLUM. L. REV. 547 et seq. (1993) *in* HISTORY OF THE COMMON LAW 824 (Wolters Kluwer 2009).
210. Langbein, *supra* note 209, at 825.

Soon thereafter, a number of states followed suit, paving the way for the creation of regional law reports. Eventually, American law reports overshadowed English reports and American common law started to drift apart from that of England.

Current trial procedure in New York has been certainly influenced by the English common law which, in turn, had been influenced by Roman law of the classical period.[211] Therefore, the brief historical analysis of the developments of trial procedure throughout the last 2,800 years provided in this chapter should help the reader in understanding how the theory of the burden of proof profoundly shapes litigation practice in New York and, more generally, in the United States.

---

211. Occasionally, the U.S. Supreme Court explicitly referenced Roman law to support its arguments. *See, e.g.* United States v. Chavez, 175 U.S. 509 (1899) (discussing Roman law when analyzing adverse possession); Hovey v. Elliott, 167 U.S. 409 (1897) (discussing the right to be heard under Roman law); Hurtado v. California, 110 U.S. 516, 530-31 (1884) ("The Constitution of the United States was ordained, it is true, by descendants of Englishmen, who inherited the traditions of English law and history; but it was made for an undefined and expanding future, and for a people gathered and to be gathered from many nations and of many tongues. and while we take just pride in the principles and institutions of the common law, we are not to forget that in lands where other systems of jurisprudence prevail, the ideas and processes of civil justice are also not unknown. Due process of law, in spite of the absolutism of continental governments, is not alien to that code which survived the Roman Empire as the foundation of modern civilization in Europe, and which has given us that fundamental maxim of distributive justice—suum cuique tribuere. There is nothing in Magna Charta, rightly construed as a broad charter of public right and law, which ought to exclude the best ideas of all systems and of every age; and as it was the characteristic principle of the common law to draw its inspiration from every fountain of justice, we are not to assume that the sources of its supply have been exhausted. On the contrary, we should expect that the new and various experiences of our own situation and system will mould and shape it into new and not less useful forms."); Columbian Ins. Co. v. Ashby, 38 U.S. 331, 338 (1839) ("That the case of jettison was here understood to be put as a mere illustration of a more-general principle, is abundantly clear from the context of the Roman law, where a ransom paid to pirates to redeem the ship is declared to be governed by the same rule. Si navis a piratis redempta sit—omnes conferre debere. Dig. lib. 14, tit. 2, c. 2, s. 3. The same rule was applied to the case of cutting away or throwing overboard of the masts or other tackle of the ship to avert the impending calamity; Dig. lib. 14, tit. 2, c. 3, c. 5, s. 2; and the incidental damage occasioned thereby to other things. Without citing the various passages from the Digest which authorize this statement, it may be remarked that the Roman law fully recognized and enforced the leading limitations and conditions to justify a general contribution, which have been ever since steadily adhered to by all maritime nations.").

2 | What Is the Burden of Proof?

INTRODUCTION

The term burden of proof is often used to mean different concepts. On the one hand, it refers to the requirement that a litigant has to convince the court of the existence of certain propositions of fact to obtain a favorable ruling. On the other hand, the term burden of proof has been used to refer to the necessity of producing (or going forward with) evidence that is initially assigned to one of the litigants, which burden may subsequently shift.[1] At times, too, the term burden of proof has been considered analogous to the burden of persuasion.[2]

As it turns out, in this field, terminology appears to be misleading.[3] In fact, in the year 2005, the U.S. Supreme Court, citing McCormick's treatise, stated that, "[t]he term 'burden of proof' is one of the slipperiest members of the family of legal terms."[4] In this chapter, therefore, we shall attempt to shed light upon the meaning of each of the abovementioned terms delving into the technicalities of trial practice.

We shall take up each one of these concepts in turn. The first section shall explain what the burden of proof is. To be sure, the burden of proof has been

---

1. James Flaming, Jr., *Burdens of Proof*, 47 Va. L. Rev. 51 (1961).
2. Dir. v. Greenwich Collieries, 512 U.S. 267, 272 (1994).
3. James B. Thayer, *The Burden of Proof*, 4 Harv. L. Rev. 46 (1890).
4. Schaffer v. Weast, 546 U.S. 49, 56 (2005) (citing 2 J. Strong, McCormick on Evidence § 342, p 433 (5th ed. 1999)).

defined as being the burden of convincing the decider of fact that a proposition of fact is more likely true than not so.[5] Furthermore, it could be briefly summarized as describing "which party loses if the evidence is closely balanced."[6]

In the second section, we shall take up the burden of production, also called the burden of going forward with the evidence. The burden of production can be described as "the obligation to come forward with evidence of a litigant's necessary proposition of fact."[7] The burden of production requires a party to put forth evidence to support their argument, or in some cases, to rebut evidence put forth by the other party.

Finally, we shall explain how these concepts relate to the burden of persuasion and to each other. Understanding the interplay and importance of these distinct concepts is essential to the prosecution and defense of any action or proceeding. It is, thus, imperative to be ever mindful of them from the inception of a case, throughout trial, and on appeal.

To be sure, recognizing and identifying the correct burden of proof is merely the first step. It is equally necessary to be cognizant of the varying quantum or standards of proof that apply to determine whether the burden of proof is met. The standards range from a preponderance of the evidence, the least demanding, to beyond a reasonable doubt, representing the highest standard applied by the courts. In civil matters, courts will apply a preponderance of the evidence, substantial evidence, or a clear and convincing standard of proof, according to the type of action at issue.

I. THE BURDEN OF PROOF

The burden of proof can be described as a tiebreaker mechanism employed by courts for deciding cases when the evidence is closely balanced.[8] The logic behind the theory and workings of this device are critical to understand today's trial practice.

Obviously, forbidding self-help and ultimately keeping the peace are fundamental goals of our system of government. To this end, the government has to intervene to settle private disputes so as to deliver justice for the aggrieved party. Indeed, people may, and very often do, find themselves involved in controversies

---

5. People v. Tzitzikalakis, 864 N.E.2d 44, 46 (N.Y. 2007).

6. *Schaffer*, 546 U.S. at 56.

7. Skoczen v. Shinseki, 564 F.3d 1319, 1324 (Fed. Cir. 2009).

8. *Dir*, 512 U.S. at 272 (1994); *see also Schaffer*, 546 U.S. at 56.

with one another. Failing to intervene in settling disputes would likely be unacceptable in modern society. This is not to say that, should the government fail to deliver justice in every single case, litigants would automatically be harmed. More generally, however, laws forbidding self-help and the establishment of a state-sanctioned impartial system of dispute resolution are essential features of our modern democracy.

The basic structure of a legal norm is typically shaped thus: *if A, B, and C occurred, then xyz effect results*; where A, B, and C represent distinct propositions of fact and *xyz* represents a legal effect. Or, to put it in a mathematical format, A + B + C = xyz. To be sure, the syllogism is the basic paradigm on which legal norms are ordinarily based.

Needless to say, if each party to the transaction or occurrence at issue is in good faith and agrees on the legal consequences of the facts in question, then the legal effect set forth by the law will occur without friction and the state-sanctioned system of dispute resolution will not come into play. By way of contrast, should a dispute ensue among the parties concerning the transaction or occurrence in which they are involved, the appropriate court of law will (probably) be asked to intervene causing the *legal* effect set forth by the law to be brought about compulsorily—that is, against the wishes of the non-moving litigant. Stated differently, when people disagree over either (1) the existence or (2) the effect of propositions of fact upon which a cause of action is based, the government has to intervene and authoritatively settle the matter, if the *rule of law* has to be preserved.

As it has been explained in the previous chapter, under our modern system of state-sanctioned dispute resolution, the court of law is a neutral and impartial institution that adjudges controversies based on an evaluation of evidence submitted by the parties.[9] Thus, judge and jury ought not to have prior direct knowledge of events underlying the pending lawsuit.[10]

To be sure, the justice system is ultimately tasked with the responsibility of ascertaining the truth of the matter submitted for consideration (i.e., the transaction or occurrence at issue) so as to grant (or decline) the relief afforded by law to

---

9. Ronald J. Allen, *Burdens of Proof, Uncertainty, and Ambiguity in Modern Legal Discourse*, 17 Harv. J.L. & Pub. Pol'y 627 (1994) ("In virtually all cases, decision is reached by uninvolved third parties (judge or jurors) evaluating reports of events rather than by viewing the events themselves. In all such cases, the reports might be in error, and in many cases the reports offered at trial conflict. Indeed, that is usually why there is a trial. Even when primary data exist, such as exhibits or videos, typically those data must be interpreted, so again there is often a considerable distance between the actual event and the decision about that event. Consequently, decision must be taken under uncertainty, and the burden of persuasion merely provides the decision rule under uncertainty.")
10. Flaming, *supra* note 1, at 55.

the aggrieved party. to this end, courts are equipped with fact-finding mechanisms (such as jury or bench trials) for authenticating the actual existence of the events underlying the lawsuit.

Parenthetically, we should keep in mind that a court of law does not usually act *sua sponte*. This is because, generally, civil courts stand in a state of inertia, so to speak.[11] In other words, a civil court will take steps to actively modify the present real-world state of affairs (e.g., issuing orders, money judgments, and so on) only upon the application of one party and for good reason. To borrow terminology from Newton's first law of motion, civil courts tend to stand still until a sufficient "external force" is applied such that it causes them to actively take action.

Therefore, the proponent has to overcome the court's natural state of inaction if he or she wants to obtain a favorable ruling. A prospective litigant who is interested in causing the court to take steps so as to obtain relief must: (1) formally request (i.e., plead for) such intervention, and (2) show the court why what is being sought is warranted under the law. Conversely, the opponent, who would be adversely affected by a judicial order in favor of the proponent, will logically attempt to prevent such order, usually by seeking to negate the proponent's assertions of fact.

For the sake of illustration, going back to our terminology, the previous point can be put thus: the party who wishes that the (*xyz*) legal effect set forth by a legal norm be brought about has to convince the court of the existence of the A, B, and C propositions of fact. Conversely, the party who disfavors such legal effect will be incentivized to either show non-A, non-B, and/or non-C, or to impeach the credibility of the other party's proof.

As stated above, judge and jury ought not to have direct knowledge of the events underlying the lawsuit. Therefore, ascertaining the truth of the matter submitted to the court is achieved through evaluating the evidence tendered by litigants.

Generally speaking, an item of proof can be described as an event that is caused to come about in the courtroom so as to represent for the benefit of the decider of fact the occurrence of a different (historical) event disputed among the parties. The evidence *par excellence* is testimony. Essentially, a witness says on the stand that he or she saw, heard, or otherwise perceived a past event taking place. The questioning of the witness in court is a fact occurring in the courtroom on the record, which tends to represent a past event happening outside the courtroom sometime in the past.

---

11. Thayer, *supra* note 3, at 58.

Needless to say, when a number of human beings are to evaluate evidence tending to show the existence (or nonexistence) of a fact in question, different assessments of the credibility to assign the evidence may result.[12] Tellingly, reasonable people could weigh the same evidence differently and, vice versa, different evidence similarly. Indeed, at trial, it is possible that the decider of fact will assign the same weight (i.e., the same convincing force) to *inconsistent* evidence tending to show, on the one hand, that a fact did actually occur, and tending to negative, on the other hand, that same proposition of fact.[13] In other words, as to matters submitted for trial, the finder of fact is said to be in equipoise when, following an evaluation of the evidence and arguments, it is determined that the existence of a fact in question is *as likely as* its nonexistence.[14]

Therefore, at trial, when the decider of fact believes that a proposition of fact is as likely true as not so, or when none of the parties submits any admissible evidence, there is potential for a stalemate situation wherein the decider of fact is unable to make a decision.[15] Hypothetically, under these circumstances, the court could simply issue a refusal to adjudge the merits of the case—a mistrial of sorts. However, as a matter of policy, this is not an acceptable outcome.[16] In fact, as it has been said at the outset, since the government forbids self-help, it follows that courts must decide the merits of every single case submitted for consideration.

From all of the above, it appears that a tiebreaker mechanism is needed to adjudicate cases wherein the evidence is closely balanced or where parties for whatever reason fail to tender any admissible evidence.[17]

The burden of proof does precisely that.[18] In general, the law creating a cause of action casts upon the party prosecuting the case an obligation to plead and establish those facts which are essential to the cause of action or else it will be defeated.[19]

---

12. Flaming, *supra* note 1, at 52.

13. *Id.* at 51.

14. Matter of Santer v. Board of Educ. of E. Meadow Union Free Sch. Dist., 23 N.Y. 3d 251, 275 (2015).

15. Flaming, *supra* note 1, at 51–52.

16. *Id.* at 51.

17. *Schaffer*, 546 U.S. at 56, 57 (speaking of the burden in terms of a default rule); *Dir*, 512 U.S. at 273.

18. Flaming, *supra* note 1, at 52. In our party-oriented justice system, an obvious need exists for a mechanism to structure the orderly presentation of information so that a decision can be reached. *See* Allen, *supra* note 9.

19. The burden of proof, or *onus probandi*, is often associated with the Latin maxim derived from Roman law *semper necessitas probandi incumbit et qui agit* or "the necessity of proof always lies with the person who lays charges." http://legaldictionary.net/burden-of-proof/

The party to whom this burden is assigned by the substantive law[20] retains it throughout trial—the burden of proof does not shift.[21] Indeed, the party shouldering the burden of proof bears the risk that a judgment on the merits will be entered against him or her if that party is unable, for any reason whatever, to carry his or her case beyond the point of equilibrium of proof *in the eyes of the finder of fact*—that is, to convince the jury (or the judge in a bench trial) that the propositions of fact constituting a disputed case are at least fifty-one percent likely true.[22]

Such is the import of *Farmers' Loan & Trust Co. v. Siefke,*[23] a case involving an action brought upon a sealed promissory note. The defendant alleged that the seal had been appended on the instrument without his consent. The trial unfolded as follows: the plaintiff tendered the note and rested; thereafter, the defendant put in evidence tending to establish that the seal was affixed illegally; and, finally, the plaintiff rebutted defendant's contentions giving evidence to the effect that the seal was appended with the debtor's consent. At the close of the evidence, the trial court instructed the jury that, on that record, the plaintiff bore the ultimate burden of proof. Being so instructed, the jury found for the defendant. On appeal, the Court of Appeals of New York ruled that the charge was not erroneous.

Chief Judge Andrews, writing for the court, stated:

> The burden is upon a plaintiff to establish his cause of action when it is in proper form denied by the other party. In actions upon a promissory note this burden is in the first instance discharged by giving evidence tending to show that the note was signed by the defendant. Proof of signing also identifies and proves the seal when the action is upon a sealed instrument. This prima facie establishes the cause of action. But a defendant is not concluded. He may give evidence, under a general denial, to show that the signature is a forgery, or that the note had been materially altered by the plaintiff without his consent, or many other things which might be mentioned, showing that the plaintiff never had a cause of action. It is very common to say in such cases that the burden is upon the defendant to

---

20. Am. Dredging Co. v. Miller, 510 U.S. 443, 454 (1994).

21. Fleming, *supra* note 1, at 62; Thayer, *supra* note 3, at 51. However, in some cases the substantive law may cause the burden of proof to shift once a party makes a showing of a certain fact. *See* Plough, Inc. v. Mason & Dixon Lines, 630 F.2d 468, 470 (6th Cir. 1980) ("the carrier's delivery of damaged goods which were in good condition when it received them created a presumption of negligence, not a mere inference. The burden which shifts to the carrier once a shipper makes out a prima facie case is not the burden of going forward with the evidence. It is the burden of proof which "shifts to the carrier and remains there.")

22. John T. McNaughton, Burden of Production of Evidence: A Function of a Burden of Persuasion, 68 Harv. L. Rev. 1382 (1955).

23. Farmers' Loan & Trust Co. v. Siefke, 39 N.E 358, 359 (N.Y. 1895).

establish the fact relied upon. All that this can properly mean is that when the plaintiff has established a prima facie case the defendant is bound to controvert it by evidence, otherwise he will be cast in judgment. When such evidence is given, and the case upon the whole evidence, that for and that against the fact asserted by the plaintiff, is submitted to court or jury, then the question of the burden of proof as to any fact, in its proper sense, arises, and rests upon the party upon whom it was at the outset, and is not shifted by the course of the trial, and the jury may be properly instructed that all material issues tendered by the plaintiff must be established by him by a preponderance of evidence. The general rule of pleading, which also accords with reason, is, that defenses which assume or admit the original cause of action alleged, but are based upon subsequent facts or transactions which go to qualify or defeat it, must be pleaded and proved by the defendant; and on the other hand the cause of action alleged by the plaintiff, and all its material incidents, must be asserted and proved by him, and in both cases the final event must be supported by a preponderance of evidence in favor of the party tendering the issue.[24]

Thus, ultimately, if the evidence is closely balanced or if the parties fail to tender any admissible evidence, the burden-of-proof rule will determine who wins the lawsuit. Ascertaining who shoulders the risk of not being able to convince the decider of fact is a matter of interpretation of the substantive law which creates the cause of action being prosecuted.[25] In this respect, the U.S. Supreme Court has stated, "There are no hard-and-fast standards governing the allocation of the burden of proof in every situation. The issue, rather, 'is merely a question of policy and fairness based on experience in the different situations.'"[26]

Usually, whoever prosecutes an affirmative case bears the burden of proof.[27] This is so because, as it has been said above, civil courts are ordinarily disinclined to intervene and modify the present real-world state of affairs unless the party

---

24. *Farmers' Loan & Tr. Co.*, 39 N.E. at 359 (internal citation omitted).

25. At times the law from which a party's cause of action derives will directly impact a party's burden of proof. The above stated description of the burden of proof can be properly classified as "the ordinary rule," which is applicable to common law claims and statutory claims where the statute in question does not give explicit direction concerning the burden of proof. Further, in very few situations, a statute may place the entire burden of proof on the defendant; Alaska Dept. of Environmental Conservation v. EPA, 540 U.S. 461, 493–94 (2004) (finding that the Clear Air Act places the burden of persuasion entirely on the defendant when a stop-construction order is challenged).

26. Keyes v. Sch. Dist., 413 U.S. 189, 209 (1973) (internal citation omitted).

27. *Farmers' Loan & Tr. Co.*, 39 N.E. at 359. *See also* Grossman v. Rankin, 373 N.E.2d 267, 271 (N.Y. 1977) ("The general rule is that the burden is on the party asserting the affirmative of an issue"); Heinemann v. Heard, 62 N.Y. 448, 455 (N.Y. 1875) ("The question of which party has the affirmative of an issue is in many cases very material, as the case might be one in which the jury

seeking such intervention overcomes the court's reluctance to act by carrying his or her case to the required height.[28]

To sum up, the proponent of an affirmative case $(A + B + C)$[29] will want to overcome the court's reluctance to intervene by: (1) petitioning the court for obtaining relief (the *xyz* legal effect, in our example), and (2) demonstrating the existence of each proposition of fact upon which the cause of action rests (i.e., A, B, and C, employing our terminology). Under the above stated rule, since the proponent normally shoulders the burden of proof, should the latter fail to carry his or her evidence beyond the point of equilibrium, he or she will lose.

The opponent, who disfavors the legal effect sought by the proponent (i.e., *xyz*), will logically want to ward off the adversary's "attack"—so to speak. To this end, a number of courses of action are available to the opponent.

First, the opponent could simply deny the propositions of fact upon which the proponent based his or her case, impeach the credibility of the adversary's evidence, and hope that the proponent will fail to carry the evidence to the required height *in the eyes of the finder of fact*. Thus, in this scenario, the opponent will win the lawsuit if the proponent fails to meet the burden of proof.

Second, the opponent could attempt to proactively undermine the proponent's assertions of fact (attempting to show non-A, non-B, or non-C, in our example), hoping that, as a result, the decider of fact will find the matter to be at least in equipoise (i.e., the assertions of fact are found to be no more than fifty percent likely true). Thus, if so, the court will find for opponent—that is, the party who does not bear the burden of proof. This is so because, to use Judge O'Brien's words, the party who does not bear the ultimate burden of proof

> need not overcome [proponent's] evidence. If he neutralizes it, he proceed as far as the law requires. If he acts with equal force, if he supplies an equivalent weight, he compensates the evidence against him and leaves the scales in equipoise. For him counterweight is enough. For [proponent of an affirmative proposition] over-weight is required.[30]

Third, the opponent could raise an affirmative defense. In this scenario, opponent will argue that even though the propositions of fact on which the

---

might hesitate in finding that the plaintiff had established the charge, and yet when they would not find that it had been satisfactorily answered."); Root v. Conkling, 199 A.D. 90 (App. Div. 1921).
28. Flaming, *supra* note 1, at 58.
29. For ease of exposition, let us recall our sketch of the basic paradigm of legal norms: if A, B, and C facts occurred, xyz legal effect results.
30. *In re* Schillinger's Will, 179 N.E. 380, 383 (N.Y. 1932).

adversary based her claim (A, B, and C) may be true, the requested relief (i.e., the *xyz* legal effect) is not warranted under the applicable law. The opponent will argue that another fact ("D") occurred and that the additional fact, considered alone, neutralizes the opponent's case-in-chief.[31] In a mathematical format, we would represent this concept thus: A + B + C + D = non-xyz. Therefore, the truthfulness of the proponent's propositions of fact notwithstanding, when a new fact is submitted such that, considered alone, it could defeat the proponent's claim, judgment should go for the opponent, provided that the latter proves that additional fact. In other words, generally speaking, whoever raises an affirmative defense bears the burden of proof as to that defense, because that party is putting forth an affirmative case within the already pending case.[32] As to affirmative defenses, the U.S. Supreme Court stated, "The ordinary default rule, of course, admits of exceptions. . . . for example, the burden of [proof] as to certain elements of a plaintiff's claim may be shifted [i.e., assigned] to defendants, when such elements can fairly be characterized as affirmative defenses or exemptions."[33]

At this point, the original proponent could attempt to defeat the affirmative defense through the same avenues available to the original opponent, namely, (1) by denying the additional fact and impeaching the adversary's evidence, (2) by submitting evidence intended to negative that fact,[34] or (3) by introducing additional propositions of facts that could neutralize the affirmative defense.

Of course, there is some overlap between the burden of proof and the burden of production as they are two sides of the same coin.[35] This brings us to the burden of production, which we shall take up in the next section.

---

31. *See, for example*, Dean v. Pitts, 10 Johns. 35, 35 (N.Y. Sup. Ct. 1813) (holding that burden of proof was borne by defendant when he admitted to a debt but claimed his partner had paid it); Huntingon v. Conkey, 33 Barb. 218, 220–221 (N.Y. Sup. Ct. 1860).
32. Manion v. Pan Am. World Airways, Inc., 434 N.E.2d 1060, 1062 (N.Y. 1982) ("The party asserting an affirmative defense generally bears the burden of proof on that issue . . . "); *In re* Schillinger's Will, 179 N.E. at 382.
33. Schaffer v. Weast, 546 U.S. 57 (2005) (internal citation omitted).
34. *In re* Schillinger's Will, 179 N.E. at 382.
35. In 1871, the New York Court of Appeals, without identifying the two distinct burdens, stated that the party who puts forth the fact in question bears the burden for the duration of the trial, to persuade the jury. Lamb v. Camden & A. R. & T. Co., 46 N.Y. 271, 279–280 (1871) ("It has, in such cases, frequently been said, that the burden of proof was changed to the other side, but it was never intended thereby that the party bound to prove the fact was relieved from [persuading the jury]; and that the other party, to entitle him to a verdict, was required to satisfy the jury that the fact was not as alleged by his adversary. In such cases, the party holding the affirmative is still bound to satisfy the jury, affirmatively, of the truth of the fact alleged by him, or he is not entitled to a verdict.")

II. THE BURDEN OF PRODUCTION

The burden of production can be described as "the obligation to come forward with evidence of a litigant's necessary proposition of fact."[36]

When it comes to fully understanding the burden of production, the above quoted (seemingly) exhaustive definition represents just the tip of the iceberg. There are, in fact, a number of layers that need be unearthed, so to speak. Preliminarily, two considerations need to be made.

First, the law or, in some cases, procedural rules cast the burden of production (initially) on one of the litigants. Subsequently, this burden may shift back and forth among the parties.[37] At the outset of the trial, the party shouldering the burden of production is usually the same litigant who bears the burden of proof. In fact, policy reasons for allocating both the burden of proof and the burden of production are similar.[38] However, occasionally, the burden of production is assigned to a party other than the one who bears the burden of proof. Typically, this is so because, at times, for special policy reasons, the law assigns the burden of producing evidence to the party on whom it rests the lightest.[39] Put differently, the

---

36. Skoczen v. Shinseki, 564 F.3d 1324 (Fed. Cir. 2009).

37. Flaming, *supra* note 1, at 58.

38. Cabrera v. Jakabovitz, 24 F.3d 372, 381 (2d Cir. 1994); Flaming, *supra* note 1, at 58. As to presumptions, *see also* USCS Fed Rules Evid R 301 ("The same considerations of fairness, policy, and probability which dictate the allocation of the burden of the various elements of a case as between the prima facie case of a plaintiff and affirmative defenses also underlie the creation of presumptions. . . .")

39. Flaming, *supra* note 1, at 58, 66; Thayer, *supra* note 3, at 51; Commercial Molasses Corp. v. New York Tank Barge Corp., 314 U.S. 104 (1941). *See also* Haft v. Lone Palm Hotel, 478 P.2d 465 (Cal. 1970). In *Haft*, plaintiff sued Lone Palm Motel for the wrongful death of her husband and five-year-old son who drowned in the motel's swimming pool. At trial, a witness testified seeing the victims playing in the water; half an hour later they were found dead. It was shown that defendant did not provide the safety measures mandated by statute. The trial judge refused to instruct the jury that failure to post the sign required by law was *prima facie* negligence. The jury returned a verdict for defendant. Thereafter, plaintiff appealed. The court reversed saying that the requested instruction was proper. In fact, failing to comply with the safety statute which was designed to protect persons such as plaintiff makes the motel *per se* negligent. Consequently, the burden to show the lack of proximate causation is cast upon defendant; in *Kingston v. Chi. & N. W. R. Co.*, 211 N.W. 913 (Wis. 1927), plaintiff sued defendant to recover damages sustained to his lumber yard. A forest fire had been burning the northwest corner of plaintiff's yard. At the same time another fire was burning the northeast corner. The two fires united and destroyed the lumber. It was shown that the northeast fire was ignited by sparks coming from defendant's trains, while the origin of the other one was not known. Either fire would have destroyed the lumber on its own. The jury found for plaintiff. Defendant appealed. The court affirmed the judgment for plaintiff saying that the burden is on the defendant to prove that the fire ignited by its trains united with another fire which was either of

burden of production is sometimes cast on the party who has easier access to the evidence regardless of other policy considerations.[40] Determining who shoulders the burden of production is a matter of interpretation of the applicable law. Frequently, the law allocates the burden of production through so-called presumptions which we shall take up in the next section.

By way of example, in *Martin v. Herzog*,[41] Judge Cardozo writing for the court identified one such case where the law initially assigns the burden of production to the opponent. In *Martin*, plaintiff and her husband suffered injuries when the defendant's car struck plaintiff's wagon. Plaintiff's husband died as a result of the collision. Allegedly, the defendant's lack of reasonable care consisted in not driving on the right-end side of the highway. In addition, plaintiff's deceased husband, the driver of the buggy, was charged with contributory negligence in that he was ostensibly travelling without night lights in violation of a statute. The jury found for plaintiff and the appellate division reversed. According to the appellate division, the trial court had erroneously instructed the jury that the absence of lights on the buggy was merely *some* evidence of contributory negligence.

The Court of Appeals affirmed the Appellate Division's reversal. The court ruled that the omission of the statutorily required night lights was more than *mere* evidence of contributory negligence. Indeed, here, it was negligence *per se* such that the duty and breach elements of the *prima facie* case were made out by simply showing noncompliance with the statute. As to the issue of the existence of the causation element of the *prima facie* case for which the proponent of the affirmative defense, the defendant in this case, bore the burden of proof, the court said:

> "Proof of negligence in the air, so to speak, will not do". . . . We think, however, that evidence of a collision occurring more than an hour after sundown between a car and an unseen buggy, proceeding without lights, is evidence from which a causal connection may be inferred between the collision and the lack of signals. *If nothing else is shown to break the connection, we have a case, prima facie sufficient, of negligence contributing to the result.* There may indeed be times when the lights on a highway are so many and so bright that lights on a wagon are superfluous. If that is so, it is for the offender to go forward with the evidence, and prove the illumination as a kind of substituted performance.[42]

---

much greater proportions or of a natural origin such that the defendant's fire was not the proximate cause of the damage.

40. Flaming, *supra* note 1, at 58.
41. Martin v. Herzog, 126 N.E. 814, 816 (N.Y. 1920).
42. *Martin*, 126 N.E. at 816 (internal citation omitted) (emphasis supplied).

Parenthetically, recall that a *prima facie case* "is evidence required to satisfy every element of a cause of action or every element of an affirmative defense."[43] If a *prima facie* case is properly made out, the adversary will lose unless he or she: (1) denies the proponent's assertions while impeaching the credibility of the evidence put forth by the other party; (2) proactively submits rebuttal evidence; and/or (3) proves an affirmative defense.

Ordinarily, a *prima facie* case for negligence is made out when proponent asserts and proves the following elements: (1) the wrongdoer had a duty of reasonable care toward the plaintiff (2) that he or she breached; (3) the breach was a factual and proximate cause of the injury; and (4) plaintiff suffered damages. Here, as to the causation element, Judge Cardozo assigned the burden of production to the opponent in that a *prima facie* case was deemed to be made out by simply showing noncompliance with the statute. Thus, to avoid a ruling as a matter of law, the opponent had to go first and come forward with evidence tending to negate the existence of causation in fact and/or proximate causation.

Second, recall that the judge typically has the authority of resolving questions of law and the jury (or, the judge in bench trials) has the responsibility to decide questions of fact. Indeed, weighing the convincing force of the evidence is in the purview of the finder of fact—typically, the jury.[44] However, when it is determined that reasonable minds cannot differ in assessing the convincing force of the evidence as its weight allows only one credible conclusion, the judge may, as a matter of law, take away the issue from the jury, either issuing summary judgment or directing a verdict for one of the parties.[45]

The burden of production can be simultaneously described as (1) a procedural device meant to police how, as a matter of practicality, parties submit evidence at trial; (2) the risk borne by one of the litigants of losing the case *as a matter of law* for not being able to produce (more) evidence when required to do so;[46] and (3) a standard.[47]

Now, let us take up each in turn.

First, the burden of production can be explained as a device for determining in what order each party has to submit evidence at trial.[48] This appears to be the

---

43. The Wolters Kluwer Bouvier Law Dictionary Desk Edition; *See also* United States v. Stephens, 445 F.2d 192, 198 (3d Cir. 1971).

44. McNaughton, *supra* note 22, at 388.

45. Fane v. Zimmer, Inc., 927 F.2d 124, 128 (2d Cir. 1991) ("In reviewing a grant of a directed verdict, we must resolve all issues of credibility in favor of the appellant. . . .")

46. Thayer, *supra* note 3, at 50.

47. Flaming, *supra* note 1, at 51; McNaughton, *supra* note 22, at 383.

48. FLEMING, *supra* note 1, at 55, 58.

oldest meaning of the burden of production. In fact, already in 1886, Lord Justice Bowen stated:

> In every lawsuit somebody must go on with [the evidence]; the plaintiff is the first to begin, and if he does nothing he fails. If he makes a prima facie case, and nothing is done by the other side to answer it, the defendant fails. The test, therefore, as to burden of [production] is simply to consider which party would be successful if no evidence at all was given, or if no more evidence was given than is given at this particular point of the case, because it is obvious that during the controversy in the litigation there are points at which the onus . . . shifts, and at which the tribunal must say, if the case stopped there, that it must be decided in a particular way. Such being the test, it is not a burden which rests forever on the person on whom it is first cast, but as soon as he, in his turn, finds evidence which, prima facie, rebuts the evidence against which he is contending, the burden shifts until again there is evidence which satisfies the demand. Now, that being so, the question as to onus of proof is only a rule for deciding on whom the obligation rests of going further, if he wishes to win.[49]

For the sake of exposition, let us (temporarily) assume that both parties are able to produce relevant evidence tending to (1) sustain each proposition of fact comprising a claim, and (2) rebut the adversary's evidence.

Against this backdrop, the burden of production merely determines which party goes first tendering evidence. Usually, the burden of production is initially assigned to the litigant shouldering the burden of proof. Thus, the proponent of an affirmative case will typically bear the burden of production.[50] It follows that, at the outset, the proponent has to come forward with evidence supporting the propositions of fact upon which his or her cause of action is based. Subsequently, it is the opponent's turn to tender evidence. Then, the original proponent will have a chance to rebut the opponent's evidence,[51] and on and on this back-and-forth procedure will go until either (1) the judge deems the case ripe for decision, or (2) one of the parties merely impeaches the other party's evidence without submitting new proof.

Second, when one or both parties are unable to submit evidence tending to authenticate the elements of the *prima facie* case, the burden of production represents the risk assigned to a litigant of losing the case *as a matter of law* for not submitting (more) evidence when required to do so.[52]

---

49. *See* Abrath v. No. East. Ry. Co., 32 W. R. 50, 53.
50. Flaming, *supra* note 1, at 58.
51. *Id.* at 55.
52. *Id.* at 55; McNaughton, *supra* note 22, at 383.

To meet the burden of production, the party who shoulders it has to tender enough evidence making out a *prima facie* showing so as to allow a reasonable finder of fact to return a verdict for the propounder. If the party (initially) shouldering this burden fails to lift it, the judge[53] will either issue summary judgment or direct a verdict against that litigant.[54] In other words, the case will not go to the jury.[55]

Such is the import of the case of *Pacific Mail S. S. Co. v. Panama R. Co.*[56], wherein judge Learned Hand clearly stated how the burden of production operates vis-à-vis the burden of proof. In *Pacific Mail S. S. Co.*, defendant's dock collapsed causing great damages to a steamer that was moored there. Plaintiff sued on a negligence theory. The trial judge found for the defendant because plaintiff failed to show an element of the *prima facie* case. On appeal, appellant, plaintiff at the trial court level, argued that the dock's collapse speaks for itself such that an inference of negligence should have been drawn. Judge Hand, writing for the court, affirmed the District Court's ruling. Judge Hand explained how the burden of proof interacts with the burden of production thus:

> We think that the collapse of the wharf created a presumption of negligence. . . . That presumption does not change the burden of proof, strictly speaking, since the libelant, though it makes a case by showing the collapse, does not put upon the respondent the duty of satisfying us that it was not negligent. When the respondent once put in proof that the wharf and embankment were well made and well maintained, it had done all that was required of it under the presumption. The libelant must convince the court of the truth of all its allegations in this as in every other case.

Furthermore, in *Celotex Corp. v. Catrett*,[57] the United States Supreme Court clarified how the burden of production interacts with the burden of proof in the context of a motion for summary judgment and/or judgment as a matter of law.[58] In this case, plaintiff sued Celotex on strict liability and negligence theories

---

53. McNaughton, *supra* note 22, at 383.
54. Flaming, *supra* note 1, at 55.
55. Thayer, *supra* note 3, at 52.
56. Pacific Mail S. S. Co. v. Panama R. Co., 251 F. 449 (2d Cir. 1918).
57. Celotex Corp. v. Catrett, 477 U.S. 317 (1986).
58. Recall that in the context of a motion for summary judgment, the movant bears the initial burden of demonstrating that there exists no material issue of fact and that judgment as a matter of law is warranted. CPLR Rule 3212(b); Suffolk County Dep't Social Services v. James M., 630 N.E.2d 636 (1994). If and when the movant's initial burden is met, the burden of production shifts to the non-moving party to establish that a genuine issue of fact does exist. Zolin v. Roslyn Synagogue, 545

because plaintiff's husband allegedly died as a result of exposure to defendant's asbestos products. However, in response to interrogatories, plaintiff failed to identify witnesses or other evidence tending to show such contact. The District Court granted the defendant's motion for summary judgment; however, a divided panel of the Court of Appeals reversed because the defendant/movant had failed to come forward with affidavits of decedent's nonexposure to its products. The Supreme Court reversed and remanded. The Court clarified that, in the context of a motion for summary judgment or, generally, of judgment as a matter of law, the moving party will prevail so long as the latter points to specific parts of the record showing lack of a genuine issue of material fact for failure to tender proof of one or more elements of the *prima facie* case. In other words, when the nonmoving party bears the burden of proof at trial as to the elements of a cause of action (or affirmative defense), the party moving for summary judgment (and/or a directed verdict) does not have to come forward with affidavits (or other evidence) tending to negate the non-movant's assertions of fact in order to prevail. Justice Rehnquist, writing for the Court, put the point thus:

> In our view, the plain language of Rule 56(c) mandates the entry of summary judgment, after adequate time for discovery and upon motion, against a party who fails to make a showing sufficient to establish the existence of an element essential to that party's case, and on which that party will bear the burden of proof at trial. In such a situation, there can be "no genuine issue as to any material fact," since a complete failure of proof concerning an essential element of the nonmoving party's case necessarily renders all other facts immaterial. The moving party is "entitled to a judgment as a matter of law" because the nonmoving party has failed to make a sufficient showing on an essential element of her case with respect to which she has the burden of proof. [. . .] [U]nlike the Court of Appeals, we find no express or implied requirement in Rule 56 that the moving party support its motion with affidavits or other similar materials negating the opponent's claim.[59]

The Court of Appeals of New York, in *Tyler v. Gardiner*,[60] explained the logic underpinning the interplay between the burden of proof and the burden of production thus:

N.Y.S.2d 846 (N.Y. App. Div. 1989). If the non-movant fails to point to evidence to demonstrate the existence of a genuine issue of material fact, then the movant is entitled to the relief sought. However, if the non-movant does produce such evidence, then the burden shifts to the movant to produce rebuttal evidence. Importantly, throughout the summary judgment process, the movant always maintains the burden of proof, while the burden of production shifts between parties.

59. *Celotex Corp.*, 477 U.S. at 323.
60. Tyler v. Gardiner, 35 N.Y. 559, 574 (N.Y. 1866).

When we find the party, whose right and interest it was to countervail the force of the facts by evidence, content to leave them unrebutted and unexplained, and to abide by the conclusions to which they so clearly tend, we have nothing to do but to draw the inevitable inference, and, applying the settled rules of law, to sustain the rejection of the will. It may be that the whole truth of the case is not before us; that facts exist, which, if proved, would relieve it from some of its unfavorable aspects; but we are bound to take the evidence as we find it, and to give it effect in accordance with our clear convictions.

Third, the production burden also represents a standard for evaluating the convincing force of a litigant's evidence.[61] When deciding if a party met their burden of production, the judge has to determine if the evidence tendered would allow a (hypothetical) reasonable jury to return a verdict against the other party.[62] At this stage, to preserve the right to a jury trial, the judge must view the evidence in the light most favorable to the propounding party. In other words, the judge (temporarily) draws all inferences and resolves all questions of credibility in favor of the propounding party.[63]

In *Scocozza v. Erie Railroad. Co.*,[64] a case involving a railroad employee injured by a locomotive's loose bolt, the Second Circuit, in affirming a directed verdict in favor of defendant for failure of making out a *prima facie* showing, explained that:

The railroad is liable in this suit only if it was guilty of negligence which caused the accident. But the plaintiffs were entitled to have that issue submitted to the jury if the evidence, viewed in its light most favorable to them, was sufficient to make out a prima facie case. This does not mean, however, that the assertion of an interested party is alone sufficient to carry the issue of the railroad's negligence to the jury when it is so opposed to known facts and reasonable inferences drawn from them that members of a jury could not fairly reconcile it with those established facts. The requirement that conflicts in the evidence be resolved as favorably to the plaintiff as is possible always means that the judge must decide whether impartial members of the jury could, with reason, decide that the plaintiff's alleged cause of action was proved by evidence which outweighed at least a little all that was to the contrary. Applied to this case that means that before the jury could lawfully return a verdict for the plaintiffs, it had to be able to find not only that the boy's version of the cause of his injuries was the correct one, but

---

61. McNaughton, *supra* note 22, at 383.
62. *Id.* at 386.
63. *Id.*
64. Scocozza v. Erie R. Co., 171 F.2d 745 (2d Cir. 1949).

also that prudence required the defendant to foresee some likelihood that such an explosion as that described by him might occur and to take steps to protect the boy from such a danger. The defendant railroad was not an insurer, and there is nothing whatever in this record to show that it did, or should, have had even the slightest intimation that hitting the nuts on this engine would cause anything to explode. There was, therefore, insufficient evidence of negligence of the defendant on which to go to the jury.[65]

Furthermore, as to the standard for granting summary judgment, the Court of Appeals of New York, in *Forrest v. Jewish Guild for the Blind*,[66] stated:

[T]he facts must be viewed in the light most favorable to the nonmoving party. For the purposes of appealing a summary judgment motion, appellant's allegations of fact must be taken as true. Of course, the standard for determining the outcome of the motion is whether or not there are any genuine issues of material fact in dispute. Moreover, for the purposes of review, the facts as stated by the nonmovant must be taken as true.[67]

If the proponent does make out such a *prima facie* case, then the production burden shifts to the other litigant: generally, the opponent.[68] Afterwards, if the opponent, who now bears the burden of production, wishes to avoid an unfavorable ruling as a matter of law, he or she has to ward off the adversary's "attack."[69] Opponent has to meet the burden by either: (1) impeaching proponent's proof so as to create a question of credibility of the evidence upon which reasonable minds may differ, (2) adduce proof tending to negate proponent's evidence, or (3) make a *prima facie* showing of an affirmative defense by proving an additional fact which, considered alone, would neutralize proponent's claim.[70]

---

65. *Scocozza*, 171 F.2d at 745 (internal citation omitted).
66. Forrest v. Jewish Guild for the Blind, 819 N.E.2d 998 (N.Y. 2004).
67. *Forrest*, 819 N.E.2d at 1014 (internal citation omitted). As to a motion to set aside a verdict, in *Haskell v. Kaman Corp.*, Judge Mansfield explained that:

    [a] district court may enter a judgment notwithstanding the verdict when, viewing the evidence in the light most favorable to the non-moving party, '(1) there is such a complete absence of evidence supporting the verdict that the jury's findings could only have been the result of sheer surmise and conjecture, or (2) there is such an overwhelming amount of evidence in favor of the movant that reasonable and fair minded men could not arrive at a verdict against him.'
68. Thayer, *supra* note 3, at 52–53; *Farmers' Loan & Tr. Co.*, 39 N.E. 359 (N.Y. 1895); Baum v. New York & Q.C. Ry. Co., 124 A.D. 12 (App. Div. 1908).
69. Flaming, *supra* note 1, at 56.
70. *Id.*

Logically, if the judge determines that the convincing force of the evidence is such that reasonable minds cannot differ on its interpretation, then opponent's only options for repelling proponent's "attack" will be either to undermine the *prima facie* showing with new evidence, or to prove an affirmative defense.

At this point, the burden of production may shift again to the proponent, provided that the opponent met the burden of production. Thus, the proponent will have to go forward with the evidence if he or she wishes to avoid an adverse ruling. The burden will keep shifting until one of the parties either fails to meet the burden (causing summary judgment or a directed verdict to issue), or simply rests having impeached the adversary's evidence without tendering new proof (prompting the judge to submit the case to the jury for deliberations).

To be sure, when one party avoids a directed verdict or summary judgment by *merely* impeaching adversary's evidence, the production burden does *not* shift back to the other party. In this scenario, litigants will rest and the case will be submitted to the jury. Therefore, the jury will only be concerned with the burden of proof because the burden of production was effectively met and did not shift.[71]

A clear example of how the burden of production works comes from the area of employment discrimination. The United States Supreme Court established a three-step inquiry to test enforcement of Title VII claims.[72] New York State has adopted the federal standards for recovery in a discrimination action under the New York State Human Rights Law, and thus, New York courts mirror the inquiry set forth for Title VII.[73] The first question a court must consider is whether the plaintiff has met the initial burden of establishing a *prima facie* case of discrimination. This burden is met by the plaintiff demonstrating that he or she: (1) is a member of a protected class, (2) is qualified to hold the position, (3) was terminated from the position or suffered other adverse employment action, and (4) the discharge or adverse employment action occurred under circumstances that give rise to an inference of discrimination.[74] If the plaintiff successfully establishes these four elements, "[t]he burden [of production] then shifts to the employer to rebut the presumption of discrimination by clearly setting forth, through the introduction of admissible evidence, legitimate, independent, and nondiscriminatory reasons to support its employment decision."[75]

---

71. *Id.* at 57.
72. McDonnell Douglas Corp v. Green, 411 U.S. 792 (1973).
73. *Forrest*, 819 N.E.2d at n.3.
74. *Id.* at 305, 390.
75. *Id.*

The inquiry, however, does not end there. Recognizing that employers may use the plaintiff's conduct as a pretext for prohibited discriminatory action, the United States Supreme Court in *McDonnell Douglas* added a second shifting of the burden of production. To rebut the nondiscriminatory reasons proffered by the employer, a plaintiff is afforded the opportunity to prove that the legitimate reasons were in fact a pretext for discrimination and that the discrimination was the true reason for termination.[76] In meeting this pretext burden, a plaintiff need not present direct evidence. Circumstantial evidence is sufficient to establish that a legitimate reason was in fact discriminatory.[77] Thus, where a plaintiff has responded with some evidence to demonstrate that the reason for the adverse employment action provided by the employer was false, misleading, or incomplete there exists "a host of determinations properly made only by a jury" or other fact finder. In those scenarios where credible pretext evidence is offered by the plaintiff, summary judgment in nearly every such case must be denied and the case tried.[78]

III. PRESUMPTIONS

As a matter of semantics, the word "presumption" carries several meanings.[79] Generally speaking, a presumption involves a relationship between a fact that is proven or admitted and another fact whose existence has not been, as yet, authenticated.[80] Specifically, from a legal standpoint, a presumption is a device through which the existence of an unproven fact in question can be *deduced* from the existence of a different proven (or admitted) fact.[81]

In *Wisniewski v. New York Central Railroad Co.*,[82] a case involving a train running over a pedestrian at a grade crossing, the Appellate Division reversed the trial court for having incorrectly charged the jury that there existed a presumption of the victim's reasonableness in crossing the tracks. The Court explained:

---

76. *McDonnell Douglas Corp.*, 411 U.S at 804; *see also Forrest*, 819 N.E.2d at 305, 391.

77. *Forrest,* 819 N.E.2d at 325, 405 (Smith concurring).

78. Sandiford v. City of New York Dept. of Educ., 943 N.Y.S.2d 48 (N.Y. App. Div. 2012).

79. *See* Cambridge English Dictionary ("a belief that something is true because it is likely, although not certain").

80. Flaming, *supra* note 1, at 63.

81. *See* The Wolters Kluwer Bouvier Law Dictionary Desk Edition ("A conclusion inferred from sufficient but inconclusive evidence. A presumption is a finding of fact derived from evidence that would not otherwise be sufficient to demonstrate the finding conclusively, but which reaches a threshold of sufficiency to be accepted as a fact.)

82. Wisniewski v. New York C. R. Co., 238 N.Y.S. 429, 436 (App. Div. 1930).

There is a marked distinction between burden of proof and a presumption. Ordinarily, a presumption rests upon a logical inference which may properly be drawn from other facts which have been proven, or which are admitted, because of the experienced course of human conduct and affairs, and the connection which is usually found to exist between the fact which is assumed and those from which it is drawn. While we may assume that a person is desirous of preserving his life and limb, it is common knowledge that multitudes are daily taking all kinds of chances at railroad crossings. Common experience does not warrant the conclusion that one who is struck and killed by a locomotive at a railroad crossing was conducting himself as a reasonably prudent person would under like circumstances.

Deducing the existence of an unproven fact in question from a known linked fact can be achieved through two different avenues: first, by employing logic or lay reasoning as stated in the above quoted case; or, second, by complying with a legal norm that directs courts to do so. Generally, the former type is called *inference* or *presumption of fact*,[83] whereas the latter is called *presumption of law*. Presumptions of law may be further subcategorized into *conclusive presumptions* (also called *iuris et de iure*), and *true presumptions* (also called *iuris tantum*).[84]

The Court of Appeals of New York defined *presumptions of fact* as: "inferences drawn from other facts and circumstances in the case [which inferences] should be made upon the common principles of induction,"[85] whereas the Court defined *presumptions of law* as: "a rule which requires that a particular inference must be drawn from an ascertained state of facts."[86]

Usually, the finder of fact is permitted, but not required, to draw reasonable inferences from circumstantial evidence. Circumstantial evidence is proof of a fact that is not directly part of, but is connected to, the transaction or occurrence

---

83. Judge Learned Hand in *United States v. Sherman*, 171 F.2d 619, 624 (2d Cir. 1948), said: "In discussions among lawyers and judges of the difference between a permissible inference and a presumption, the terminology may be unimportant. But the jury may be misled by the word 'presumption'; and here it may have interpreted that word as far stronger than a permissible inference."
84. 2 Bender's New York Evidence § 127.01 (2018) ("In dealing with presumptions, the practitioner must first recognize the distinctions between a "conclusive presumption" and a "true presumption"—which is rebuttable—and between a true "presumption of law"—which is mandatory in the absence of rebuttal evidence—and a "presumption of fact"—which is merely an inference.") Parenthetically, one should keep in mind that terminology in this field is often used loosely as the Court of Appeals of New York "has not specifically set forth comprehensive definitions of the various types of presumptions and inferences. . . ." 2 Bender's New York Evidence § 127.01 (2018).
85. O'Gara v. Eisenlohr, 38 N.Y. 296, 303 (N.Y. 1868).
86. Platt v. Elias, 79 N.E. 1, 2 (N.Y. 1906).

under consideration at trial.[87] Indeed, such evidence is offered to prove *indirectly* the truth of the matter at issue.

Frequently, as a matter of logic and lay reasoning, numerous inferences can be drawn from a proven fact. When this happens, selecting from the spectrum of possible reasonable inferences the most plausible one is in the exclusive purview of the decider of fact. However, ascertaining whether the inference drawn is a reasonable one is the judge's responsibility.

To be sure, the following three scenarios are conceivable.

First, if—as a matter of experience and lay reasoning—there are no possible avenues through which reasonable minds may infer the existence of a fact in question from a showing of a different (but connected) fact, then judgment as a matter of law *against* the party bearing the burden of production may be warranted.

Second, exceptionally, when there is *only one* possible logical inference that can be drawn from a piece of circumstantial evidence tending to establish the existence of a fact in question, then judgment as a matter of law may be warranted *for* the party shouldering the burden of production.[88]

Third, if multiple *reasonable* inferences can be drawn from a showing of a fact, then judgment as a matter of law is not warranted and the case has to be submitted to the decider of fact for deliberations.

In *Platt v. Elias*,[89] a case involving an inference of undue influence arising out of disbursements made by a man to a woman while engaged in (at the time) illegal cohabitation, the Court of Appeals said:

> If . . . the presumption of undue influence in the case of a gift by a man to a woman with whom he has a meretricious connection is only a presumption of fact, it merely warrants the trial court in deducing the exercise of undue influence from the fact that the sexual relations between the parties were improper, but does not absolutely demand that such an inference shall be drawn from that fact. In other words, a presumption of fact leaves the trial court at liberty to infer certain conclusions from a certain set of circumstances, but does not compel it to do so. . . .

Furthermore, it should be highlighted that a permissible inference may be used as a shield from an adverse judgment as a matter of law or summary judgment.

---

87. *See* The Law Dictionary, Anderson Publishing Co. ("evidence from which a fact is reasonably inferred, although not directly proven. It is often introduced when direct evidence is not available.")
88. Flaming, *supra* note 1, at 69.
89. *Platt*, 79 N.E. 1, 2 (N.Y. 1906).

In fact, the existence of a reasonable inference tending to establish an element of the *prima facie* case creates a question of material fact for the jury to decide.[90]

By way of example, one such case occurs when plaintiffs rely on the doctrine of *res ipsa loquitur* to make out a *prima facie* case of negligence absent direct proof of how defendant breached a duty of care.

In *George Foltis, Inc. v. New York*,[91] plaintiff, a restaurateur, sued the City of New York to recover damages caused to his restaurant by a leak in the underground water main installed and maintained by defendant. At trial, plaintiff produced no evidence pointing to a specific breach of duty by defendant. At the close of the evidence, the specific cause of the pipes' break remained unexplained. In order to make out a *prima facie* case for negligence, plaintiff relied on the doctrine of *res ipsa loquitur* according to which:

> where the instrumentality which produced an injury is within the exclusive possession and control of the person charged with negligence, and such person has exclusive knowledge of the care exercised in the control and management of that instrumentality, evidence of circumstances which show that the accident would not ordinarily have occurred without neglect of some duty owed to the plaintiff is sufficient to justify an inference of negligence and to shift the burden of explanation to the defendant.[92]

Against this backdrop, defendant offered evidence to the effect that the pipes were new when laid and that City's employees had properly inspected said pipes before laying them. However, defendant did not submit evidence explaining the specific cause of the pipes' break. On this record, the Court of Appeals of New York ruled that a genuine issue of material fact existed and thus the defendant was not entitled to the direction of a verdict in its favor. Furthermore, the Court clarified that the doctrine of *res ipsa loquitur* does not generally entitle the plaintiff to a directed verdict on the issue of breach of duty. In other words, in the context of a summary judgment motion, simple inferences, such as those allowed by the *res ipsa loquitur* doctrine, can usually be used as a shield but not a sword.[93]

A *conclusive presumption of law* is an inference that is commanded by a legal norm. This kind of presumption is not necessarily grounded on principles of lay reasoning or laws of nature but rather on policy considerations.

---

90. Flaming, *supra* note 1, at 65.
91. George Foltis, Inc. v. New York, 38 N.E.2d 455 (N.Y. 1941).
92. *Id.* at 459.
93. Flaming, *supra* note 1, at 65.

Indeed, when a legal norm sets forth a presumption of law, courts are directed to find as established an unproven fact in question from a showing of a different, but related, proposition of fact. This kind of presumption is *irrebuttable*. Thus, courts will neither entertain arguments nor admit evidence tending to negate the presumed fact.

From the above, it follows that a conclusive presumption of law has nothing to do with the burden of production in that said presumption is not a procedural device.[94] Rather, it is a technique employed by rule makers for formulating legal norms. Essentially, when the law sets forth an irrebuttable presumption, the existence (or nonexistence) of the fact being presumed is deemed to be irrelevant for the purpose of making out a *prima facie* case. However, the law falls short of saying so openly.[95] Tellingly, the presumed fact remains an element of the *prima facie* case and as such it has to be pleaded, albeit as a mere formality.[96]

Similarly, a *true presumption of law* is an inference that is mandated by a legal norm.[97] However, by way of contrast with a *conclusive* presumption, a *true* presumption is a procedural device employed for allocating (i.e., shifting)[98] the burden of production.[99] This is so because a *true* presumption of law allows the party against whom it is cast to dispel it through rebuttal evidence tending to negate the presumed fact.[100] For policy reasons, the law directs courts to draw inferences from known facts until proof to the contrary is tendered. In other words, through

---

94. *Id.* at 63.
95. *Id.*
96. By way of example, prior to being repealed by L 1993, ch. 602, § 4, effective Jan 1, 1995, NY CLS RPTL § 1020 provided that after two years from the recordation of a tax deed by a City or County, the presumption of regularity of the deed became irrebuttable. *See* Peak Realty & Mgmt. v. Lajon Enters., Inc., 500 N.Y.S.2d 38, 39 (App. Div. 1986) ("Since more than two years had passed between the recordation of the respective city and county tax deeds and the commencement of the action, the presumption of regularity afforded to each had become conclusive when the action was commence.")
97. *See, for example,* ITC Ltd. v. Punchgini, Inc., 482 F.3d 135, 148 (2d Cir. 2007) ("Although the term 'presumption' is not specifically defined in the Rules of Evidence, it is generally understood to mean 'an assumption of fact resulting from a rule of law which requires such fact to be assumed from another fact or group of facts found or otherwise established in the action.'") (internal citations omitted). *See also* 2 Chamberlayne, Modern Law of Evidence §§ 1087, 1160 (1911).
98. *See, for example,* Golden v. Kentile Floors, Inc., 512 F.2d 838, 849 (5th Cir. 1975) ("[a presumption] does not shift the burden of proof unless a shift is dictated by an independent rule of law").
99. On the other hand, the burden of proof remains unaffected.
100. "In a civil case, unless a federal statute or these rules provide otherwise, the party against whom a presumption is directed has the burden of producing evidence to rebut the presumption. But this rule does not shift the burden of persuasion, which remains on the party who had it originally." Fed. R. Evid. 301 (2010).

this type of presumption, because of convenience, expedience, or fairness considerations, legal norms assign the burden of production to a litigant other than the one putting forth an affirmative case.[101]

By way of example, let us consider CPLR § 2103(b)[102] which provides: "service upon an attorney shall be made: . . . by mailing the paper to the attorney at the address designated by that attorney for that purpose . . .; service by mail shall be complete upon mailing. . . ." Indeed, should a dispute ensue between the sender and the addressee concerning the parcel's delivery, an inference of receipt ought to be drawn from the act of depositing papers into the carrier's postbox with proper postage. Consequently, the addressee will have to produce evidence of nonreceipt if he or she wants to avoid an unfavorable ruling as a matter of law.

In *Vita v. Heller*,[103] defendant's attorney moved to dismiss plaintiff's ostensibly untimely complaint arguing that fourteen weeks had passed since he served a *notice of appearance and demand for complaint*. Plaintiff's attorney claimed he never received such a *notice of appearance* and offered his secretary's affidavit to support that contention. The Second Department said:

> Service of papers by mail is deemed complete upon deposit of such papers in the mail and such manner of service creates a presumption of proper mailing to the addressee. The burden then falls upon the addressee to present evidence sufficient to overcome the presumption and establish non-receipt. In the case at bar, the affidavit of plaintiff's counsel's secretary was sufficient to overcome the presumption and create a question of fact, the resolution of which requires a hearing.[104]

---

101. *See, for example,* Usery v. Turner Elkhorn Mining Co., 428 U.S. 1, 27 (1976) ("Each presumption is explicitly rebuttable, and the effect of each is simply to shift the burden of going forward with evidence from the claimant to the operator.")

102. *See also* NY CLS Lien § 75 ("Failure of the trustee to keep the books or records required by this section shall be presumptive evidence that the trustee has applied or consented to the application of trust funds actually received by him as money or an instrument for the payment of money for purposes other than a purpose of the trust as specified in section seventy-one of this chapter.") In *Medco Plumbing, Inc. v. Sparrow Constr. Corp.,* 802 N.Y.S.2d 730, 731–32 (N.Y. App. Div. 2005), plaintiff sued the defendant construction company seeking to enforce a trust under NY CLS Lien § 75. Plaintiff argued that the construction company was liable for divesting trust funds and relied on said statutory presumption in order to make out a *prima facie* case. The Court held that evidence put forth by defendant to the effect that Manhattan DA's office had seized company's books was not enough to dispel the presumption arising from the missing books and records.

103. Vita v. Heller, 467 N.Y.S.2d 652, 653 (N.Y. App. Div. 1983).

104. *Vita,* 467 N.Y.S.2d at 653 (internal citations omitted). *See also* Nassau Ins. Co. v. Murray, 386 N.E.2d 1085, 1086 (N.Y. 1978) ("Where, as here, the proof exhibits an office practice and procedure followed by the insurers in the regular course of their business, which shows that the notices

In *Engel v. Lichterman*,[105] defendant filed a motion for summary judgment claiming that plaintiff had failed to comply with a *conditional order of preclusion* allegedly served on plaintiff's attorney with notice of entry. To this end, defendant's attorney filed an affidavit of service. Plaintiff's attorney filed an affidavit merely denying receipt. The Second Department reversed the trial court's conditional summary judgment, granted unconditional summary judgment, and explained:

> Evidence of proper mailing of the conditional order of preclusion was submitted by defendant in the form of a correct and accurate affidavit of service by mail. Under these circumstances, a presumption arose that the conditional order of preclusion was received by plaintiff's attorney. Plaintiff's attorney's mere denial of receipt was insufficient to rebut that presumption. [. . .] Finally, the mere denial of receipt of the conditional order of preclusion, did not, under the circumstances of this case, raise an issue of fact as to the initial mailing of the conditional order of preclusion.[106]

A true presumption of law may be used both as a shield, to avoid judgment as a matter of law (or summary judgment), and as a sword,[107] to obtain such a ruling against the other litigant.[108] Now, suppose for a moment that the substantive law identifies three facts comprising a *prima facie* case necessary for obtaining a certain legal effect. Suppose further that a legal norm provides that on a showing of

---

of cancellation have been duly addressed and mailed, a presumption arises that those notices have been received by the insureds. . . .")

105. Engel v. Lichterman, 467 N.Y.S.2d 642, 647 (N.Y. App. Div. 1983).

106. *Engel*, 467 N.Y.S.2d, at 647. *See also* News Syndicate Co. v. Gatti Paper Stock Corp., 176 N.E. 169, 170 (N.Y. 1931) (stating that the mailing of a check established a presumption of receipt on the next business day when the originating postbox and the addressee are both located in the City of New York such that plaintiff had to go forward with evidence to the effect he received the check on a different day); Dulberg v. Equitable Life Assurance Soc'y, 12 N.E.2d 554, 555 (N.Y. 1938) (stated that proper mailing of a check created a presumption of receipt on the next business day such that the addressee had to go forward with proof of a late receipt).

107. On the other hand, as stated above, a permissible inference can usually be used only as a shield to prevent said rulings.

108. *See, for example,* United States v. Ahrens, 530 F.2d 781, 787 n.9 (8th Cir. 1976) ("our disposition makes unnecessary consideration of the government's argument that the initial burden of proof rested with the taxpayer to prove the validity of the notice of deficiency. Even assuming, without deciding, that the initial burden of proof rested with the government, the presumption shifted the burden of going forward with the evidence to the taxpayer. Since the taxpayer produced no evidence rebutting the presumption, the only permissible inference from the circumstances is that the notice of deficiency was valid. We hold that the district judge was required to draw that inference as a matter of law.") (internal citations omitted).

the first two propositions of fact the third one has to be presumed until evidence to the contrary is introduced.

From the above, it follows that the proponent makes out a *prima facie* case by simply tendering evidence showing the existence of the first two propositions of fact—the third one being presumed. As such, proponent is shielded from judgment as a matter of law. At this point, since the *prima facie* showing has been made out, the burden of production is automatically assigned to the opponent.[109] Proponent may, therefore, move for summary judgment. Consequently, at the outset of the trial, opponent must go forward with evidence tending to negate the proposition of fact, which is presumed, or else be defeated as a matter of law.

To dispel the presumption, the party shouldering the burden of production has to produce enough evidence to convince a hypothetical reasonable jury of the nonexistence of the presumed fact.[110] Or, according to some courts, enough evidence that would have been sufficient to avoid a directed verdict on the issue.[111]

Under the general burden-of-production rule, once opponent tenders evidence sufficient to dispel the presumption, proponent will have to either: (1) introduce evidence showing the existence of the formerly presumed fact, and/or (2) impeach the credibility of opponent's evidence, or else be defeated as a matter of law.

Generally speaking, a rebuttable presumption of law disappears from the case once it is dispelled with evidence negating the presumed fact.[112] Consequently, the jury need not be instructed about said presumption. In contrast, in weighing the convincing force of each party's evidence, the finder of fact is always permitted (but not required) to draw all reasonable inferences from proven or admitted propositions of fact. Thus, the decider of fact may still draw the conclusion that the previously presumed fact exists *as a matter of lay deductive reasoning.* Conversely,

---

109. *See, for example,* Klein v. Trustees of Indiana Univ., 766 F.2d 275, 280–281 (7th Cir. 1985).
110. *See, for example,* United States v. Bailey, 707 F.2d 19, 22 (1st Cir. 1983) ("The burden imposed on the defendants by the presumption, however, is not to prove that the stock was valueless or that it had a particular value lower than that urged by the government, but only to come forward with enough evidence to support a finding that the stock exchange quotations are not a reliable indicator of the actual value of the stock on the day in question.")
111. *See, for example,* Howing Co. v. Nationwide Corp., 927 F.2d 263, 265 (6th Cir. 1991) ("If the adverse party presents evidence suggesting the insignificance of the omitted information, the right of the plaintiffs to have the jury consider the significance of the information persists, and the jury may infer that the information would be significant, unless and until evidence has been received which would require a directed verdict for the defendants on the significance of the information.")
112. Also called *bursting the bubble* theory. *See, for example, In re* Tomeo, 1 B.R. 673, 679 (Bankr. E.D. Pa. 1979).

if such inference cannot be reasonably drawn, then the dispelled presumption will not have any residual effect.[113]

Such is the import of the case of *People ex rel. Wallington Apartments, Inc. v. Miller*,[114] where the Court of Appeals of New York clarified that a dispelled presumption has no residual effect in the case. In *Wallington Apartments*, a case involving a presumption of correctness of an apartment's value assessment made by a State assessor, the Court said that:

> There is a presumption of sorts that the assessors' valuations are not excessive. The assessors "are sworn officers, and as such, in absence of evidence to the contrary, are presumed to have done their duty." This rule so stated is an application, almost a translation, of the ancient maxim "*omnia praesumuntur rite et solemniter esse acta donec probetur in contrarium.*" The important qualifying phrase "in absence of evidence to the contrary" must not be overlooked. If the opponent does offer evidence to the contrary the presumption disappears. Thereupon "the case ceases to be one for presumptions, and becomes a case for proof."[115]

Nevertheless, in *Wellisch v. John Hancock Mutual Life Insurance Co.*,[116] plaintiff sued defendant insurance company to recover benefits under her deceased husband's life insurance. Defendant countered by submitting evidence to the effect that plaintiff's husband committed suicide and argued that said evidence overcame the presumption against suicide. The Court of Appeals of New York affirmed a jury verdict for plaintiff. As to the residual effect of a presumption that has been countered with evidence capable, if believed, to negate the presumed fact, the Court stated:

> [this] presumption is not one of those that takes the place of evidence so as to create a question of fact even when all the real proof is the other way. Nor is it the sort of "presumption" that serves only to shift the burden of proof and

---

113. *In re* Tomeo, 1 B.R. 673, 679 n.9 (Bankr. E.D. Pa. 1979) ("However, the "bursting of the bubble" does not necessarily dilute the strength of the logical inferences which have arisen as a result of the plaintiff-creditor's evidence. Hence, it is quite possible that, even if the debtor has come forward with evidence that he did not intend to deceive the creditor, thereby effectively rebutting the presumption, ("bursting the bubble") the court may still choose to disbelieve the debtor's evidence. Therefore, the plaintiff-creditor could carry its burden of persuasion if the logical inferences created by the evidence showed clearly and convincingly that the debtor performed the acts alleged with intent to deceive the creditor.")

114. People *ex rel.* Wallington Apartments, Inc. v. Miller, 41 N.E.2d 445, 446 (N.Y. 1942).

115. *Wallington Apartments, Inc.*, 41 N.E.2d at 446 (internal citation omitted).

116. Wellisch v. John Hancock Mutual Life Insurance Co., 56 N.E.2d 540 (N.Y. 1944).

disappears from the case as soon as evidence to the contrary is offered. It is really a rule or guide for the jury in coming to a conclusion on the evidence. Suicide "is contrary to the general conduct of mankind" and the presumption against it is one of the "judicial recognitions of what is probable." Juries are authorized to take heed of the truth drawn from general human experience, that death by suicide is an improbability, that most men cling to life. The "presumption against suicide" means that when death by violence is shown and an inference must be drawn by the jury as to suicide or not, then the jury should in justice and good conscience draw the inference of accident, not suicide. This presumption is one aspect of the broader rule that where evidence is susceptible of two constructions, the construction which does not imply criminality or moral turpitude is to be favored. Of course, that does not mean that there should be a finding against suicide when the circumstances are wholly inconsistent with a finding of accident and there is no reasonable hypothesis available except that of suicide. It means only that a fair question of fact as to accident or suicide should be answered: "accident". When in such a case the jury gives that answer, then no question of law is left for us.[117]

In other words, the presumption in *Wellisch*, unlike the presumption in *Wallington Apartments*, was grounded on principles of lay reasoning such that the jury could draw reasonable inferences from all the facts shown at trial finding the existence of the presumed fact even after the presumption was dispelled. Indeed, common experience leads us to believe that usually people do not commit suicide. Conversely, in *Wallington Apartments*, the presumption of non-excessiveness of the assessor's evaluation was merely grounded on policy considerations. Tellingly, the fact that the assessor was an employee of the state, as a matter of common experience, in and of itself, does not command the conclusion that the assessment made by such employee was not excessive.

IV. THE BURDEN OF PERSUASION

The burden of proof, the burden of production, and the burden of persuasion are distinct concepts, yet they constantly interact with one another so as to profoundly shape the anatomy of any given civil trial. Perhaps, at this point, to understand the burden of persuasion, a brief summary of what has already been explained is needed.

---

117. *Wellisch*, 56 N.E.2d at 543 (internal citations omitted).

To sum up, a litigant who wishes to obtain relief must (1) plead the elements of a cause of action, and (2) carry his or her evidence beyond the point of equilibrium of proof on each one of the pleaded elements of the *prima facie* case, or else be defeated.[118] It goes without saying that, to prevail, each party is incentivized to produce proof so as to show—depending on the party's role—either the existence or the nonexistence of the elements of the cause of action being prosecuted. To that end, the burden of production dictates the order in which litigants actually submit evidence to the court.

Once the parties' evidence is introduced, if the judge finds there is a genuine issue of material fact, then the case will be submitted to the jury for deliberations—or, alternatively, the judge will take it under advisement in bench trials. At this stage of the trial, should the finder of fact believe the evidence to be closely balanced, the burden of proof will break the tie and determine who wins the lawsuit.[119] As such, the burden of proof may be described as a fallback rule.

Thus, from a court's perspective, the burden of proof simply represents a tie-breaker mechanism. Conversely, from the litigant's viewpoint, the burden of proof also operates so as to "stack the deck" against one of the parties, so to speak. Indeed, to win the case, the party shouldering the burden of proof has to carry his or her evidence to a certain height, while the other party may still prevail by *merely* matching (or impeaching) the adversary's evidence and/or by undermining the adversary's arguments.

Consequently, it appears that—in addition to the burden of proof and the burden of production—litigants bear a supplemental obligation *of actually persuading the court* that the elements of the cause of action have (or have not) been established under the applicable standard, if they wish to prevail.[120] Specifically, considering the

---

118. *See, for example, In re* Capoccia, 453 N.E.2d 497 (N.Y. 1983).

119. *See, for example,* Rinaldi & Sons, Inc. v. Wells Fargo Alarm Serv., Inc., 347 N.E.2d 618 (N.Y. 1976).

120. The Supreme Court of the United States efficiently spells out this reality in its recent decision of a patent infringement suit. In *Medtronic, Inc. v. Mirowski Family Ventures, LLC,* 571 U.S. 191, 197 (2014), the Supreme Court was tasked with deciding whether the burden of persuasion shifts to the licensee from the patentee when the relief sought is not damages but for a declaratory judgment. When analyzing the question presented, the Supreme Court asked "who bears the burden of proof, or, to be more precise, the burden of persuasion? Must the patentee prove infringement or must the licensee prove noninfringement?" In framing the question with this language the Supreme Court impliedly realizes that the burden of proof is a function of the burden of persuasion, but nevertheless elects to distinguish the two, focusing on the latter. Further highlighting this versatile relationship between the burden of production and burden of persuasion is the Supreme Court's decision in *St. Mary's Honor Center v. Hicks,* 509 U.S. 502, 507 (1993), an action for employment discrimination under Title VII. While reanalyzing the *McDonnell Douglas* burden-shifting criteria,

automatic operation of the fallback mechanism, the party who shoulders the burden of proof has to *actually persuade* the jury (or the judge) that, given the evidence submitted, the averments put forth are more likely true than not, whereas the party who does not bear the burden of proof is incentivized to persuade the jury (or the judge) that, having considered the evidence, the averments at issue are *as* likely true *as* not so—or, alternatively, more likely untrue than true.

For the sake of exposition, let us recall once again our terminology describing the basic structure of a legal norm: if *A, B, and C* facts occurred, then *xyz* legal effect ensues. Now, let us assume that, under the applicable law, the proponent in a lawsuit shoulders the burden of proof and the burden of production. Thus, the trial will likely run somewhat like this: First, proponent will pray the court for obtaining (the xyz) relief and, to that end, plead the (A, B, and C) elements of the *prima facie* case. Second, opponent will file an answer (probably) denying the adversary's allegations. Third, proponent will presumably tender evidence showing A, B, and C. Finally, opponent will either rebut (trying to show non-A, non-B, and/or non-C) or impeach the adversary's evidence. Let us recall that if the evidence is deemed to be in equipoise, proponent will lose. Therefore, at the close of the evidence, proponent has the burden of *actually convincing* the court that A, B, and C occurred and, ultimately, that his or her averments are correct. Conversely, opponent is incentivized to convince the court that the adversary's averments are not true—or at least as likely true as not so. If proponent fails to actually persuade the court, *then by operation of the burden of proof mechanism*, he or she will lose the case.

Generally speaking, to *actually persuade the court* means that a litigant who wishes to succeed must *bring the judge and/or the jury to believe* that his or her argument is correct under the law and supported by the facts. Indeed, at one point or another during the lifespan of a case, the determination of some, if not all, issues will inevitably be influenced by at least some degree of personal or subjective reasoning. In short, satisfaction of the burden of persuasion will always be at least somewhat dependent upon who needs to be convinced.

Specifically, a party to a lawsuit ought to employ the art of rhetoric[121] and use appropriate communication strategies such as choosing the right courtroom

---

the Court notably emphasized one critical aspect, stating, "[i]t is important to note, however, that although the McDonnell Douglas presumption shifts the burden of production to the defendant, the ultimate burden of persuading the trier of fact that the defendant intentionally discriminated against the plaintiff remains at all times with the plaintiff."

121. KATHLEEN FREEMAN, THE MURDER OF HERODES AND OTHER TRIALS FROM THE ATHENIAN LAW COURTS 31 (Macdonald & Co. 1946) ("The art of persuasion is as old as human speech itself;

attire, the appropriate voice tone, and the proper vocabulary, if he or she wishes to sway the court. By way of example, a litigant will want to marshal his or her evidence for the finder of fact and point to the appropriate reasoning to connect the dots. In so doing, the litigant will want to use language that closely matches that which is generally employed by jury instructions normally given by the judge so as to facilitate the whole process.

In *Roberge v. Bonner*,[122] a case involving an alleged breach of an oral contract to pay a sum of money either in cash or through a testamentary disposition, the Court of Appeals of New York approved the following jury's instruction as an accurate statement of the law of the burden of persuasion:

> The law in this case, and indeed in every case, is that a party coming into a court of justice must satisfy the jury by what is called a fair preponderance of evidence as to the justice of his claim. What we mean by the fair preponderance of evidence is this: Preponderance refers to something that may be weighed. Of course, we cannot get a pair of scales, and by some arbitrary method put on one side the testimony of the plaintiff and on the other side the testimony of the defendant and say which one outweighs the other, or whether it is evenly balanced, but you are to try to do that mentally as far as possible. The law says that unless the plaintiff satisfies you throughout the entire case of the correctness of his story to such an extent that it outweighs the proof of the defendants, he cannot recover. In other words, if the testimony is evenly balanced, it shows that there is some doubt in your mind; that is not sufficient; that is, if the testimony of the plaintiff weighs just the same as that of the defendant you must find for the defendant; that is the law. The plaintiff can only recover where his testimony outweighs that of the defendant.[123]

Perhaps, the importance of the burden of persuasion vis-à-vis the employment of theatrics, rhetoric, and communication skills is best brought to light by an outlandish and somewhat extreme case. In *Zabin v. Picciotto*,[124] plaintiffs, attorneys at law, sued their former clients for outstanding fees. At trial, which took place at the end of October, the jurors asked the judge if they could wear costumes for Halloween. The judge, having consulted counsels, allowed the request without

but the systematic study of this art, and its application to public life, which the Greeks called Rhetoric, first emerges into the light of history [. . .] when [. . .] a citizen of the Greek colony of Syracuse, first wrote a handbook on Rhetoric . . .").
122. Roberge v. Bonner, 77 N.E. 1023 (N.Y. 1906).
123. *Roberge*, 77 N.E. at 1024.
124. Zabin v. Picciotto, 896 N.E.2d 937 (Mass. App. Ct. 2008).

objections. Furthermore, "one of the plaintiffs' counsel handed out candy to the jurors."[125] Among other things, on appeal defendants argued that those shenanigans turned the "trial into a circus and denied their rights to due process."[126] on that issue, the Court of Appeals observed:

> with or without the consent of counsel to the parties, it is regrettable that the trial judge agreed to the jurors' request. The introduction of Halloween costumes cannot but have detracted from the seriousness and gravity of formal court proceedings. However, as to the defendants' claim of a due process violation, the judge did not merely accommodate the jurors' request; he consulted with counsel for all parties before doing so, and all counsel agreed. The issue is waived.[127]

In *Zobin*, the court characterized court proceedings as *serious* and *grave*. In a way, a trial is a staged representation of real life, thus to some extent drama plays a role in determining the outcome of a case. The successful litigant ought to present the evidence and the arguments so as to be the most appealing to the audience, be it the jury or the judge. In *Zabin*, perhaps in a misguided attempt to be completely amenable to the jury's requests, plaintiffs and defendants went along with the Halloween theme. This is certainly an unusual and outlandish case but it does show how details like dress code and communication skills play an important role in litigation.

Therefore, from the above, it appears that in presenting their arguments, litigants ought to heed the teachings of rhetoric, that is, literally the art of persuasion, so as to meet their burden of persuasion.

---

125. *Id.* at 961 n.42.
126. *Id.* at 961.
127. *Id.*

3 | What Is the Standard of Proof?

INTRODUCTION

The first step in preparing a civil litigation is identifying the proper burdens of proof associated with the action. Once you have answered "what is the burden of proof," the next question a civil litigator must ask is: how *much* proof do I need to establish that I have met the burden of proof? Thus, the next step will be identifying what burden of persuasion you have in order to effectively demonstrate that you have met the burden of proof. That question is answered by determining the *standard of proof* associated with the burden of proof. Standards of proof tell the finder of fact "the degree of confidence our society thinks he should have in the correctness of factual conclusions for a particular type of adjudication."[1] Generally, the standards of proof are (1) by a preponderance of the evidence, (2) by clear and convincing evidence, (3) by substantial evidence, and (4) beyond a reasonable doubt. Unfortunately, there is no clear-cut formula to determine the standard of proof, but one can assess which standard is applicable by reviewing statutes and case law.

Typically, most causes of action in civil actions require that the facts prove the proponent's position by a preponderance of the evidence.[2] This standard is

---

1. *In re* Carter, 424 N.Y.S.2d 833, 835 (Sup. Ct. 1980).
2. *See* Ferrante v. Am. Lung Ass'n, 687 N.E.2d 1308, 1312 (N.Y. 1997) (noting New York law in cases of discrimination is preponderance of the evidence, in accord with federal standards of discrimination under Title VII).

similarly applied to affirmative defenses.[3] Therefore, it is up to the finder of fact to determine from the properly submitted evidence presented whether it is more probable than not that a particular factual position is true.[4]

An alternate, slightly higher standard applied in some civil cases, particularly those with allegations of fraud or similar quasi-criminal behavior, is that facts be proved by clear and convincing evidence.[5] Unlike the ease with which the preponderance of the evidence is summarized, clear and convincing is less easily described. Sometimes the "clear and convincing" standard is described as "whether there is 'concrete' or 'affirmative evidence' in the record that would allow a jury to conclude with 'convincing clarity'" the truth of the fact asserted.[6]

The standard of proof known as "substantial evidence" is applicable in administrative proceedings and is less than the "preponderance of the evidence" standard. It is the lowest standard by which a litigant must meet its burden of proof. Article 78 proceedings in New York, to appeal a decision by a state or local agency, require substantial evidence.[7] From the quality and quantity of the entire record, the litigant must establish that a conclusion or ultimate fact may be reasonably extractive.[8] In this context, the fact finder will pay deference to the

---

3. *See, for example*, Pogo Holding Corp. v. N.Y. Prop. Ins. Underwriters, 468 N.E.2d 291 (N.Y. 1984).

4. Metro. Stevedore Co. v. Rambo, 521 U.S. 121, 137 n.9 (1997) ("The burden of showing something by a preponderance of evidence . . . simply requires the trier of fact to believe that the existence of a fact is more probable than its nonexistence before [he] may find in favor of the party who has the burden to persuade the [judge] of the fact's existence." [quoting Concrete Pipe & Prods. of Cal., Inc. v. Constr. Laborers Pension Trust for S. Cal., 508 U.S. 602, 622 (1993)]) (quotations omitted); *see, for example*, Sandiford v. City of N.Y. Dep't of Educ., 943 N.Y.S.2d 48, 51 (App. Div. 2012) (noting a question of fact regarding discriminatory practices).

5. Gaidon v. Guardian Life Ins. Co. of Am., 725 N.E.2d 598, 607 (N.Y. 1999).

6. Kipper v. NYP Holdings Co., 912 N.E.2d 26, 30 (N.Y. 2009) (citations omitted).

7. CPLR § 7804 sets forth the procedure for an Article 78 proceeding; *see id.* § 7804(g) ("Hearing and determination; transfer to appellate division. Where the *substantial evidence* issue specified in question four of section 7803 is not raised, the court in which the proceeding is commenced shall itself dispose of the issues in the proceeding. Where such an issue is raised, the court shall first dispose of such other objections as could terminate the proceeding, including but not limited to lack of jurisdiction, statute of limitations and res judicata, without reaching the substantial evidence issue. If the determination of the other objections does not terminate the proceeding, the court shall make an order directing that it be transferred for disposition to a term of the appellate division held within the judicial department embracing the county in which the proceeding was commenced. When the proceeding comes before it, whether by appeal or transfer, the appellate division shall dispose of all issues in the proceeding, or, if the papers are insufficient, it may remit the proceeding.") (emphasis added).

8. *For example*, 300 Gamatan Ave. Assocs. v. State Div. of Human Rights, 379 N.E.2d 1183, 1188 (N.Y. 1978) (holding substantial evidence in the record to support commissioner's finding of a violation of the Human Rights Law, N.Y. Exec. Law § 296(5)(a)(1)).

decision of the previous fact finder but will ultimately determine if another conclusion is more reasonable.[9]

Some cases will require a party to prove its claim beyond a reasonable doubt. Used primarily in criminal cases, this requires that the fact finder determine that the evidence points to no other logical explanation.[10] Courts have interpreted this standard to require the prosecution to have put forth evidence that allows all reasonable inferences to lead to a conclusion in its favor.[11]

I. STANDARD OF PROOF—PREPONDERANCE OF THE EVIDENCE

The majority of civil litigations are adjudicated by a preponderance of the evidence standard with the exception of specific civil actions or quasi-criminal actions.[12] Thus, in civil cases, the plaintiff has the burden of proving facts sufficient to support the causes of action asserted in their complaint.[13] The plaintiff is not required to exclude every other possible cause, but only needs to prove the elements of his

---

9. *See* FMC Corp. v. Unmack, 699 N.E.2d 893, 898 (N.Y. 1998).

10. People v. Bonifacio, 82 N.E. 1098, 1100 (N.Y. 1907) (using the phrase "no other reasonable conclusion [is] possible").

11. *See* People v. Robinson, 411 N.Y.S.2d 793, 802–03 (Sup. Ct. 1978).

12. *For example*, Killon v. Parrotta, 28 N.Y.3d 101, 65 N.E.3d 41 (N.Y. 2016) (battery claim); People v. Tzitzikalakis, 864 N.E.2d 44 (N.Y. 2007) (restitution hearing); Kurz v. Doerr, 83 N.Y.S. 736 (App. Div. 1903) (assault claim); *In re* Crystal A. (Chigorizim C.A.), 18 N.Y.S.3d 393 (Sup. Ct. 2015) (child neglect claim); Fernandez v. State of N.Y., 14 N.Y.S.3d 49 (Sup. Ct. 2015) (negligence claim); In *re* Falk, 845 N.Y.S.2d 287 (Sup. Ct. 2007) (breach of contract claim); Maracallo v. Bd. of Educ., 769 N.Y.S.2d 717 (Sup. Ct. 2003) (negligent infliction of emotional distress claim); McCormack v. Cty. of Westchester, 731 N.Y.S.2d 58 (Sup. Ct. 2001); (defamation claim); Hanna v. Hanna, 700 N.Y.S.2d 532 (Sup. Ct. 1999) (custody claim); N.Y. Life Ins. Co. v. V.K., 711 N.Y.S.2d 90 (Civ. Ct. 1999) (appointment of a guardian ad litem); Sandra S. v. Larry W., 667 N.Y.S.2d 632 (Fam. Ct. 1997) (paternity showing); Farrell v. Stram, 644 N.Y.S.2d 395 (Sup. Ct. 1996) (nuisance claim); State of N.Y. v. Fermenta ASC Corp., 630 N.Y.S.2d 884 (Sup. Ct. 1995) (trespass to land claim); Murphy v. Murphy, 486 N.Y.S.2d 457 (Sup. Ct. 1985) (intentional infliction of emotional distress claim); Wiltse v. State, 380 N.Y.S.2d 175 (Sup. Ct. 1976) (false imprisonment claim); Nat Koslow, Inc. v. Bletterman, 197 N.Y.S.2d 583 (Sup. Ct. 1960) (conversion claim).

13. *See Fernandez*, 14 N.Y.S.3d at 50 ("[T]o prevail at trial in a negligence case, a [claimant] must establish by a preponderance of the evidence that the defendant's negligence was a proximate cause of [claimant's] injuries. A [claimant] is not required to exclude every other possible cause, but need only offer evidence from which proximate cause may be reasonably inferred." (quoting Burgos v. Aqueduct Realty Corp., 706 N.E.2d 1163, 1165 (N.Y. 1998)); *see also* Canonico v. Beechmont Bus Serv., Inc., 790 N.Y.S.2d 36, 37 (Sup. Ct. 2007) (noting in a negligence case proximate cause is to be established by a preponderance of the evidence).

or her own cause of action.[14] Likewise, if the defendant asserts a counterclaim or an affirmative defense, the defendant only needs to prove the elements of his counterclaim or defense by a preponderance of the evidence.

The weight of evidence required to meet the preponderance standard should not be reduced to a simple formula. However, for simplification purposes, it has been described as a fifty-one percent chance that each element of the cause of action more likely than not occurred because of the person or entity at fault.[15] A preponderance of evidence has been explained as the existence of an alleged fact "being more probable than its non-existence."[16] If at the end of the trial, the evidence "as a matter of logical necessity is equally balanced, plaintiff has failed to meet his burden and the cause of action is not made out."[17]

The court will decide which party has the burden of proving the preponderance of the evidence in a hearing or proceeding.[18] Generally, the proponent or plaintiff has to prove his argument by a preponderance of the evidence. This holds true in restitution hearings, appointment of a guardian ad litem hearings, custody and paternity hearings, will contests, holdover proceedings, and many other types of proceedings.[19]

Unlike the higher standard, beyond a reasonable doubt, a preponderance of evidence does not require that the fact finder exclude all reasonable doubt but, rather, that the presumption in favor overcome and outweigh the opposing party's presumptions and evidence.[20] Preponderance of the evidence only requires that the convincing force of the evidence appeal to the jury's mind by tilting the scale

---

14. *Fernandez*, N.Y.S.3d at 51.

15. *See* Rinaldi & Sons, Inc. v. Wells Fargo Alarm Serv., Inc., 347 N.E.2d 618, 619 (N.Y. 1976) (exemplifying that when the evidence is evenly balanced, the plaintiff has not met its burden as a matter of logic or of law).

16. Universal Open MRI of the Bronx, P.C. v. State Farm Mut. Auto Ins., 819 N.Y.S.2d 852, 852 (Civ. Ct. 2006).

17. *Rinaldi*, 347 N.E.2d at 620.

18. *See, for example*, Morejon v. Rais Constr. Co., 851 N.E.2d 1143, 1148 n.12 (N.Y. 2006) (discussing how negligence on a *res ipsa loquitor* theory shifts the burden to the defendant).

19. *For example*, 3657 Realty Co. LLC v. Jones, 859 N.Y.S.2d 434 (App. Div. 2008) (summary holdover proceeding); People v. Tzitzikalakis, 864 N.E.2d 44 (App. Div. 2007) (restitution hearing); Hanna v. Hanna, 700 N.Y.S.2d 532 (Sup. Ct. 1999) (custody claim); N.Y. Life Ins. Co. v. V.K., 711 N.Y.S.2d 90 (Civ. Ct. 1999) (appointment of a guardian ad litem); Sandra S. v. Larry W., 667 N.Y.S.2d 632 (Fam. Ct. 1997) (paternity showing); *In re* Huber's Will, 170 N.Y.S. 901 (Surr. Ct. 1918).

20. Kurz v. Doerr, 83 N.Y.S. 736 (App. Div. 1903) (explaining the question to be asked is, "which [side] has presented to you a preponderance of the evidence; that is, does the evidence in favor of the story told by the plaintiff *outweigh* the testimony which makes against that claim?") (emphasis in original).

more favorably one way than the other.[21] The more probable argument will win, even if both arguments seem to be doubtful. Indeed, courts have recognized that a decision based on the preponderance of the evidence, "does not require much proof to tip the scales in favor of one party."[22]

For example, in *Meyers v. Hines*, the plaintiff accused the defendant train company of being responsible for his personal injuries when he allegedly was pushed and fell off the train platform.[23] Several witnesses testified that the plaintiff attempted to board the moving train and fell of his own negligence.[24] The court ruled that this testimony established, by a preponderance of the evidence, that the defendant could not be held liable for the injuries.[25] In contrast, the court in *Fernandez v. State of New York* ruled that the plaintiff failed to prove his cause of action by a preponderance of the evidence when he blamed a pipe's proximity to a wall for his injuries, but photographs of the accident site submitted by the plaintiff showed that the pipe was at least one foot from the wall.[26]

Finally, it should be noted that although this standard does not hold difficult to prove, it claims authority in the justice system as unable to be set aside unless it plainly appears that the preponderance could not weigh in favor of the side the jury chose by any fair interpretation.[27] The strength in the jury's verdict upon a preponderance of the evidence reiterates that the questions of fact are to be decided by the jury and their answer in jury trials is conclusive.[28] In either a bench or jury trial, proving one's case by a preponderance of the evidence can be effectuated in a variety of manners, depending on the cause of action at issue.[29]

---

21. *Id.* (describing the weight of the evidence as the "convincing force of the evidence" appeals more to a jury's mind).

22. *Hanna*, 700 N.Y.S.2d at 533.

23. 191 N.Y.S. 773, 774 (App. Div. 1922).

24. *Id.*

25. *Id.*

26. 14 N.Y.S.3d 49, 51 (App. Div. 2015).

27. *Hines*, 191 N.Y.S. at 773.

28. *Id.*

29. *For example*, People v. Tzitzikalakis, 864 N.E.2d 44 (App. Div. 2007) (showing that at a restitution hearing for unjust enrichment, the People bear the burden of proving the victim's out of pocket loss the amount necessary to make the victim whole by a preponderance of the evidence. To prove the burden, the People must show both components of the restitution equation, the amount taken minus the benefit conferred. The People may satisfy their burden by simply proving the amount taken); *see also* Welsh v. Cornell, 61 N.E. 891 (N.Y. 1901) (showing that to entitle the

II. STANDARD OF PROOF—CLEAR AND CONVINCING EVIDENCE

More stringent than the preponderance of the evidence standard common to the majority of civil litigation, but less than the criminal standard of "beyond a reasonable doubt" discussed in section V of this chapter is proof by a "clear and convincing" standard.[30] The clear and convincing standard has been interpreted in a variety of ways, including "evidence of a very high order," "clear, positive and convincing evidence," "evidence of the clearest and most satisfactory character," and "proof of 'the most substantial and convincing character.'"[31] The trend, however, is to subsume all of these intermediate levels under the rubric of "clear and convincing evidence."[32] To succeed on a clear and convincing standard, the party with the burden of proof must show that its side is "highly probable."[33] Under this heightened standard of proof, the evidence presented must be found to be more highly probable to be true than not, must provide the finder of fact with a firm belief or conviction of the evidence, and must show that the facts more likely than not prove the issue that they are asserted in support of. This heightened standard is meant to stress the importance of the issues in the case and to avoid relief whenever the evidence may be loose or "in its texture open to doubt or to opposing presumptions."[34]

---

plaintiff to recover in a negligence action, that it was necessary for him to establish by a fair preponderance of the evidence that the accident which caused his injury was occasioned by the omission of the defendant to discharge some duty which rested upon him); *Fernandez*, 14 N.Y.S.3d 49 (App. Div. 2015) (showing that to prevail at trial in a negligence case, a claimant must prove by a preponderance of the evidence that the defendant's negligence was proximate cause of the claimant's injuries; a claimant is not required to exclude every other possible cause, but need only offer evidence from which proximate cause may be reasonably inferred); Canonico v. Beechmont Bus Serv., 790 N.Y.S.2d 36 (App. Div. 2005) (noting in a negligence case, in which plaintiff bears the burden of proof by a preponderance of the evidence, he must prove that the defendant's negligence was a proximate cause of his injuries); McCormack v. Cty. of Westchester, 731 N.Y.S.2d 58 (App. Div. 2001) (noting for a defamation cause, in order to recover damages where the content of the article is arguably within the sphere of public concern, the defamed party must demonstrate by a preponderance of the evidence that publisher acted in a grossly irresponsible manner without due consideration for standards of information gather and dissemination ordinarily followed by responsible parties).

30. *In re* Carter, 424 N.Y.S.2d 833, 835 (Sup. Ct. 1980).
31. George Backer Mgmt. Corp. v. Acme Quilting Co., 385 N.E.2d 1062, 1066 (N.Y. 1978).
32. Ausch v. St. Paul Fire & Marine Ins. Co., 511 N.Y.S.2d 919, 921 (App. Div. 1987).
33. Firmes v. Chase Manhattan Auto. Fin. Corp., 852 N.Y.S.2d 148, 160 (App. Div. 2008).
34. Southard v. Curley, 31 N.E. 330, 331 (N.Y. 1892).

This standard has been found by courts to be "appropriate where the 'interests at stake' are deemed more substantial than mere loss of money."[35] Courts have applied this heightened standard, inter alia, when confronting questions of whether to allow the refusal of treatment to terminally ill patients unable to confer their desires,[36] involving allegations of fraud upon the court,[37] determining the element of malice for claims of libel against public figures,[38] deciding whether to terminate a father's parental rights,[39] or considering a party's entitlement to a collateral source setoff.[40] In these circumstances, courts have been guided by the belief that the decision requires a finding of high probability and that the necessary evidentiary requirement be a "weighty caution upon the minds of all judges, and it forbids relief whenever the evidence is loose, equivocal or contradictory."[41]

At times, the clear and convincing standard of proof is described as that of "reasonable certainty."[42] Interpreting this standard, which is more than a preponderance of the evidence but less than proof beyond a reasonable doubt, courts have held that the evidence is clear and convincing where the result drawn from it is "highly probable."[43]

"Mere speculation" of experts is not clear and convincing evidence.[44] However, in *CDR Créances S.A.S. v. Cohen,* fraud upon the court was proven by clear and convincing evidence when there was a record of ignoring discovery requests, forging documents, and submitting scripts to witnesses for their depositions and trial testimony.[45] It is this level of detail that is required for the clear and convincing evidence standard to be successfully met.

---

35. *In re* Eichner *ex rel.* Fox, 426 N.Y.S.2d 517, 545 (App. Div. 1980) (discussing and quoting the *Addington* court).

36. *For example, In re* Eichner *ex rel.* Fox, 426 N.Y.S.2d 517.

37. *For example,* CDR Créances S.A.S. v. Cohen, 15 N.E.3d 274, 284 (N.Y. 2014) (discussing and determining whether a party's action in discovery amounts to fraud against the court); Gaidon v. Guardian Life Ins. Co of Am., 725 N.E.2d 598, 606 (N.Y. 1999) (holding that plaintiff had not met the heightened evidentiary threshold to support its common-law fraud cause of action but had with respect to the lesser standard necessary under GEN. BUS. LAW § 349.

38. *For example,* Kipper v. NYP Holding Co., 912 N.E.2d 26 (N.Y. 2009).

39. *For example, In re* Annette B., 829 N.E.2d 661 (N.Y. 2005).

40. Firmes v. Chase Manhattan Auto. Fin. Corp., 852 N.Y.S.2d 148 (App. Div. 2008).

41. *Southard,* 31 N.E. at 331; *see also In re* Westchester Cty. Med. Ctr. *ex rel.* O'Connor, 531 N.E.2d 607, 612 (N.Y. 1988).

42. *Firmes,* 852 N.Y.S.2d at 160.

43. *Id.*

44. Welsh v. Cornell, 61 N.E. 891, 891 (N.Y. 1901).

45. 15 N.E.3d 274, 280–81 (N.Y. 2014).

III. STANDARD OF PROOF—SUBSTANTIAL EVIDENCE IN ARTICLE 78 PROCEEDINGS

Article 78 allows parties to appeal decisions of New York state and local agencies.[46] There are many types of decisions made by agencies.[47] In a proceeding brought pursuant to Article 78, the reviewing court is charged with applying a substantial evidence standard of review.[48] The reviewing court must ask whether the determination made as a result of a hearing is supported by substantial evidence.[49] Where substantial evidence is not raised, the court disposes *sua sponte* of the issues in the proceeding.[50] A determination by an administrative agency will be affirmed where the evidence presented is "so substantial that from it an inference of the existence of the fact found may be drawn reasonably."[51]

When seeking reversal of an administrative determination, deference is given to the administrative agency.[52] Therefore, the petitioner bears the burden of demonstrating that the decision was arbitrary and capricious, rather than supported by substantial evidence.[53] Substantial evidence has been defined "as such relevant proof as a reasonable mind may accept as adequate to support a conclusion or ultimate fact, and 'is less than the preponderance of the evidence, overwhelming evidence or evidence beyond a reasonable doubt.'"[54] Said differently, substantial evidence is met where the quality and quantity of the entire record presented is such to "generate conviction in and persuade a fair and detached fact finder that, from the proof as a premise, a conclusion or ultimate fact may be extracted

---

46. CPLR § 7801.

47. *For example, In re* Ridge Rd. Fire Dist. v. Schiano, 947 N.E.2d 140 (N.Y. 2011) (challenging award of benefits to respondent firefighter); 300 Gramatan Ave. Assocs. v. State Div. of Human Rights, 379 N.E.2d 1183 (N.Y. 1978) (challenging Division of Human Rights); FMC Corp. v. Unmack, 699 N.E.2d 893 (N.Y. 1998) (challenging property value by tax assessor); Stork Rest. v. Boland, 26 N.E.2d 247 (N.Y. 1940) (challenging ruling that labor practice is unfair); *In re* Macri v. Kelly, 935 N.Y.S.2d 295 (App. Div. 2011) (challenging pension benefits); *In re* 25-24 Cafe Concerto Ltd. v. N.Y. State Liq. Auth., 881 N.Y.S.2d 427 (App. Div. 2009) (challenging State Liquor Authority determination); *In re* Soho All. v. N.Y.C. Bd. of Standards & Appeals, 703 N.Y.S.2d 150 (App. Div. 2000) (challenging local zoning laws).

48. CPLR § 7803(4).

49. *Id.*

50. *Id.* § 7804(g).

51. *300 Gramatan Ave. Assocs.*, 379 N.E.2d at 1185 (quoting *Stork Rest.*, 26 N.E.2d at 255).

52. *In re* Ridge Rd. Fire Dist., 947 N.E.2d at 142.

53. *Id.* at 141.

54. *Id.* at 143 (quoting *300 Gramatan Ave. Assocs.*, 379 N.E.2d at 1187); *see also FMC Corp.*, 699 N.E.2d 893.

reasonably—probatively and logically."[55] "The concept of substantial evidence, a term of art as related to administrative decision making, is rather easily verbalized but, when put to use in respect to a particular determination, frequently causes difficulty and disagreement."[56]

The decision of the administrative agency or department is normally afforded a presumption of validity in an Article 78 proceeding.[57] By statutory authority, however, this initial presumption of validity can be removed from respondent and placed with the petitioner, thus shifting the burden of proof to the petitioner. For example, Administrative Code § 13-252.1(1)(a) states that first responders who develop health conditions as a result of their assistance with the September 11 relief effort do not have the burden of proving their entitlement to benefits; instead, the administrative agencies must prove with substantial evidence that the petitioners are not entitled to the benefits.[58] In such a case, it is consequently petitioner's burden to demonstrate that the respondent is not entitled to the statutorily defined presumption.[59] This presumption can be overcome by substantial evidence, as opposed to a heightened standard.[60] This standard need not find that an inference is the most probable; rather, only that it is reasonable and plausible.[61] Substantial evidence only requires proof that a reasonable mind "may accept as adequate."[62] Because under this standard of analysis petitioners and respondents may produce substantial evidence on both sides, including expert reports, that production is not controlling. Either side may reasonably

55. *300 Gramatan Ave. Assocs.*, 379 N.E.2d at 1187; *see In re* Haug, 112 N.E.3d 323, 325 (N.Y. 2018) ("Where substantial evidence exists to support a decision being reviewed by the courts, the determination must be sustained, 'irrespective of whether a similar quantum of evidence is available to support other varying conclusions.'") (quoting *In re* Collins, 342 N.E.2d 524, 524 (N.Y. 1976).

56. *300 Gramatan Ave. Assocs.*, 379 N.E.2d at 1185–86.

57. *See FMC Corp.*, 699 N.E.2d at 896 (N.Y. 1998) (noting the Court's analysis "begins with the recognition that a property valuation by the tax assessor is presumptively valid and thus obviates any necessity, on the part of the assessors, of going forward with proof of the correctness of their valuation") (citations omitted).

58. *In re* Macri, 935 N.Y.S.2d 295, 299 (App. Div. 2011).

59. *Id.* (discussing while the burden of proof concerning entitlements normally rests with the petitioner to establish a right to benefits, by action of the Legislature in enacting N.Y.C. ADMIN. CODE § 13-252.1, et seq., a presumption in favor of accidental line-of-duty causation is afforded to first responders that performed recovery duties in connection with the World Trade Center attacks.).

60. Carriage House Motor Inn, Inc. v. Watertown, 524 N.Y.S.2d 930, 931 (App. Div. 1988).

61. *In re* Ridge Rd. Fire Dist. v. Schiano, 947 N.E.2d 140, 143 (N.Y. 2011).

62. *In re* 25-24 Cafe Concerto Ltd. v. N.Y. State Liq. Auth., 881 N.Y.S.2d 427, 432 (App. Div. 2009) (quotations omitted).

prevail based upon the amount of evidence a court is obligated to accept to support the agency's determination.[63] Equally so, although an administrative determination must be assessed based on the credibility of witnesses and reasonable inferences drawn, the reviewing court "may not weigh the evidence or reject the conclusions of the administrative agency where the evidence is conflicting and room for choice exists."[64] Courts may not substitute their own judgments for that of the administrative agency where the findings are supported by substantial evidence.[65]

Where the petitioner fails to present substantial evidence (and in excess of the respondent agency), the agency decision should be upheld as presumptively *valid*.[66] However, where substantial evidence is presented and the presumption of validity has been rebutted, the reviewing court must then weigh the entire record to determine whether the petitioner has established by a preponderance of the evidence that its contention is the correct one.[67]

The court in *300 Gramatan Avenue Associates. v. State Division of Human Rights*, ruled that there was substantial evidence to support race discrimination where a landlord lied to a black man about the room's availability, failed to mention other available rooms, had actually been trying quite hard to rent the room for a lower rate than the one agreed upon, and had no black tenants out of all ninety tenants.[68] In contrast, the court in *Matter of 25-24 Cafe Concerto Limited v. New York State Liquor Authority*, ruled that there was not substantial evidence.[69] In this case, police imposed a penalty on "possession and consumption of alcohol by a minor."[70] However, six of the individuals in question did not present identification, and the officer at the scene only thought he smelled alcohol but did no further testing and could not remember what kind of alcohol he smelled.[71]

---

63. *Compare id.* at 431–35, *with* Retail Prop. Trust v. Bd. of Zoning Appeals, 774 N.E.2d 727, 731 (N.Y. 2002).

64. *In re 25-24 Cafe Concerto Ltd.*, 881 N.Y.S.2d at 436 (quoting *In re* Cafe, La China Corp., N.Y.S.2d 30, 32 (App. Div. 2007)).

65. *Retail Prop. Trust*, 774 N.E.2d at 731.

66. FMC Corp. v. Unmack, 699 N.E.2d 893, 896–97 (N.Y. 1998).

67. *Id.* (holding that the preponderance of the evidence after the petitioner challenging tax assessment met his burden of producing substantial evidence challenging the agency's determination established that the valuation was accurate).

68. *300 Gramatan Ave. Assocs.*, 379 N.E.2d at 1187 (N.Y. 1978).

69. *In re 25-24 Cafe Concerto Ltd.*, 881 N.Y.S.2d at 431.

70. *Id.* at 433.

71. *Id.* at 430.

IV. STANDARD OF PROOF—BEYOND REASONABLE DOUBT

Reserved almost exclusively for criminal prosecutions and overruling the statutes of the legislature,[72] the "beyond a reasonable doubt" standard requires that the evidence presented amounts to a determination that no other logical explanation can be derived from the facts except that the accused committed the charged crime. "[T]he defense bears no burden and . . . it is the prosecution that must introduce evidence sufficient to persuade the fact finder, beyond a reasonable doubt, of the defendant's guilt."[73] It is a long held and firmly established rule that in criminal cases a defendant's guilt must be proven beyond a reasonable doubt. In so doing, the presumption that a person is innocent until proven guilty is overcome. "Proof 'beyond a reasonable doubt' has been well defined to be that which amounts to a moral certainty, as distinguished from an absolute certainty."[74]

Doubt itself must be defined before one can establish what proof beyond a reasonable doubt is. In a trial setting, doubt arises in the finder of fact from the absence of a material fact or from a fact that has not sufficiently been established by the evidence.[75] The doubt referenced to in "proof beyond a reasonable doubt" has also been defined as "a doubt for which you can conscientiously express a reason, based on logic and the credible evidence or lack of credible evidence."[76] If the plaintiff's attorney successfully proved the elements of his case through the evidence, the finder of fact should not have any doubt.

Reasonable doubt, as with other standards of proof, is not easy to define precisely.[77] Courts have consistently viewed beyond a reasonable doubt as being

---

72. People v. Jones, 26 N.E.3d 754 (N.Y. 2014) (rape); People v. Antommarchi, 604 N.E.2d 95 (N.Y. 1992) (possession of controlled substance); People v. Quinones, 507 N.Y.S.2d 417 (App. Div. 1986) (burglary, criminal mischief, possession of burglary tools); People v. Malloy, 434 N.E.2d 237 (N.Y. 1982) (robbery, criminal possession of stolen property, unlawful imprisonment); People v. Barnes, 406 N.E.2d 1071 (N.Y. 1980) (assault, criminal possession of stolen property, unauthorized use of a vehicle); People v. Patterson, 347 N.E.2d 898 (N.Y. 1976) (defense of extreme emotional distress in relation to manslaughter charge); People v. Bonifacio, 82 N.E. 1098 (N.Y. 1907) (murder); United States v. Eury, 286 F.2d 517 (2d Cir. 1959) (destroying and concealing mail); *see for example*, N.Y. Cty. Lawyer's Ass'n v. State, 745 N.Y.S.2d 376, 386 (Sup. Ct. 2002) ("In order to declare a statute or a provision thereof unconstitutional, the invalidity of the law must be demonstrated beyond a reasonable doubt.")
73. *Antommarchi*, 604 N.E.2d at 98.
74. *Bonifacio*, 82 N.E. at 1099.
75. *Id.*
76. *Malloy*, 434 N.E.2d at 239.
77. *See Antommarchi*, 604 N.E.2d at 98.

satisfied when considering the facts proved and the inferences that could reasonably be drawn from them leads to the conclusion that there is no reasonable doubt that the defendant committed the charged criminal act.[78] It is also a necessary aspect to a criminal proceeding and indication of the proper working of the judicial system that decisions not be based on the "whim" of jurors.[79] Proper jury instructions may state that if a reasonable person would hesitate in their decision to rule for the plaintiff, then proof beyond a reasonable doubt has not been established.[80] However, if the evidence excludes every hypothesis except for guilt, then the proof beyond a reasonable doubt standard has been met.[81] Indeed, the finder of fact is expected to "engage in reasoned discussion of the evidence" to arrive at its decision.[82]

Importantly, in a criminal case, the burden of proof never shifts from the People to the defendant.[83] If the People, through their presentment of evidence, fail to satisfy their burden the defendant must be found not guilty.[84] Of course, when dealing with human nature and affairs, there are very few things that can be known with absolute certainty. Therefore, the standard of proof is not that a defendant is proved guilty beyond any *possible* doubt. Nor is it sufficient to prove guilt by a degree of probability.[85] Rather, proof *beyond* a reasonable doubt is what is required.

For example, the defendant in *United States v. Upchurch* was found guilty of mail fraud beyond a reasonable doubt when there was evidence that: he was in the vicinity of the post office during its operating hours on the day of the incident;

---

78. People v. Barnes, 406 N.E.2d at 1074.

79. *Antommarchi*, 604 N.E.2d at 98.

80. *Quinones*, 507 N.Y.S.2d at 418 (noting "[i]t was not error for the court to instruct the jury that if they had a doubt upon which they believed "a reasonable person [would] hesitate to act," that was a reasonable doubt").

81. United States v. Upchurch, 286 F.2d 516, 518–519 (4th Cir. 1961) (noting the evidence and possible inferences).

82. *Antommarchi*, 604 N.E.2d at 98.

83. *Compare* People v. Getch, 407 N.E.2d 425, 429 (N.Y. 1980) ("In the Getch case the defendant claims that the use of the 'natural consequences' charge and the phrase 'unless the act was done under circumstances to preclude existence of such intent' effectively shifted the burden of proof to him on the element of intent. The court, however, did not err in informing the jury that they "may infer that a person intends that which is the natural and necessary and probable consequences of the act done by him."), *with* People v. Patterson, 374 N.E.2d 898, 903 (N.Y. 1976) ("If the burden of proof was improperly placed upon the defendants, defendant was deprived of a properly conducted trial.").

84. *See* Taylor v. Kentucky, 436 U.S. 478 (1978).

85. People v. Malloy, 434 N.E.2d 237, 239 (N.Y. 1982) (noting beyond reasonable doubt does not mean "proof beyond all doubt or proof to a mathematical certainty, or scientific certainty").

that he owned and operated the same make and model of the vehicle seen at the crime scene; that he left witnesses in the car and returned with letters; that the witnesses opened the letters in front of the defendant and disposed of them in the ravine where they were found; and that the witness had possession of the adding machine also stolen from the scene of the crime.[86]

In contrast, the court in *People v. Jones* doubted whether the standard of beyond a reasonable doubt was met and reversed the lower court's ruling.[87] In the lower court, the defendant was convicted of rape when DNA evidence showed another man's DNA and the only evidence was the victim's testimony that she was certain the defendant had raped her.[88]

---

86. *Upchurch,* 286 F.2d at 518–519.
87. People v. Jones, 26 N.E.3d 754, 762 (N.Y. 2014).
88. *Id.* 758–59.

4 | Common-Law and Statutory Burdens of Proof

OUTLINE

INTRODUCTION

The essential legal questions should always be: who has the burden of proof and has it been met? The burden of proof in civil litigation usually rests initially with the plaintiff. The plaintiff wins if, by the appropriate standard of proof, the plaintiff's evidence meets the burden of proof. Sure, it is not always that simple, but now that you have a better understanding of the basics of the burden of proof, its origins, and the standards by which it is met, let us explore how those burdens are associated with some key common law and statutory causes of action. What follows in this chapter should demystify the complexities surrounding the burden of proof with respect to choosing and establishing a litigant's causes of action.

There are but two worlds in the arena to consider when first deciding what causes of action to bring: the common law and statutes. The civil common law of New York can be broken down to two basic theories: contracts and torts. These "theories" govern the day-to-day of interpersonal affairs. In court, a *prima facie* case marks the completion of a party's initial burden of proof. In this chapter, we examine how a litigant makes out a *prima facie* case under some important common law and statutory theories of recovery, and highlight when and where the burdens of proof and/or production shift.

I. COMMON LAW

A. Contracts

How many contracts did you enter into today? Almost everything a person does is structured by the rules of contract law, such as buying a cup of coffee and a bagel in the morning, signing up for a television provider, or executing a car or apartment lease.

A contract is an agreement between two or more parties creating obligations that are enforceable or otherwise recognizable at law.[1] In short, a contract is a negotiation between two or more parties where terms are offered and accepted.

Forming an enforceable contract requires mutual assent, an offer, acceptance, and consideration.[2] A contract may be express or implied.[3] An express contract is a written or oral agreement between two parties. An implied contract, on the other hand, is formed by the conduct of the parties. If it is shown that two parties intend to enter into an agreement, the formation of a contract may be implied. This is true even in the absence of a written or oral agreement, and implied contracts are no less legally binding than an express contract.[4] Under New York law, an implied-in-fact contract requires all of the elements of any valid contract.[5]

---

1. *Contract*, BLACK'S LAW DICTIONARY (10th ed. 2014).
2. Civil Serv. Employees Ass'n, Inc. v. Baldwin Union Free Sch. Dist., 924 N.Y.S.2d 126, 128 (App. Div. 2011).
3. Pache v. Aviation Volunteer Fire Co., 800 N.Y.S.2d 228, 229 (App. Div. 2005); RESTATEMENT (SECOND) OF CONTRACTS § 4 cmt. a. (AM. LAW. INST. 1981).
4. European Am. Bank v. Cain, 436 N.Y.S.2d 318, 321 (App. Div. 1981).
5. Murray v. Northrop Grumman Info. Tech., Inc., 444 F.3d 169, 178 (2d Cir. 2006) (applying New York Law).

The existence of a contract requires one party to make an offer which, when accepted by the other party,[6] creates mutual assent to the essential terms of the agreement.[7] Further, all contracts must be supported by consideration, consisting of a benefit to the promisor or a detriment to the promisee.[8]

Conversely, if a valid contract does not exist, we must look to the legal concept of quasi-contract, also known as implied or constructive contracts. In New York, there are two kinds of implied contracts: (1) those implied in fact and (2) those created in law—known as "quasi" or "constructive contracts"—which are unrelated to the intentions of the parties.[9] An implied-in-law contract is thus not a contract at all, but rather an obligation created by law from the circumstances present based upon equitable principles that operate whenever justice requires that compensation be paid.[10] In short, the equitable theory of quasi-contract is used to compensate the injured party even in the absence of a valid contract so as to prevent injustice.[11]

1. Breach of Contract

When the inevitable occurs—inevitable here only because you are reading a book about litigation and if things went the way they were originally intended, we would not have anything to write about—and one or both parties to the contract has not obtained the benefit of the bargain, one of the first theories of recovery crossing a litigator's mind is a cause of action for breach of contract. Under New York law, it is axiomatic that, in order to prevail on a breach of contract cause of action, a plaintiff must establish all of the following four elements: (1) the existence of a valid contract, (2) plaintiff's performance of the contract, (3) defendant's material breach of the contract, and (4) resulting damages.[12] In a breach of contract action, the plaintiff has the burden of establishing each of the essential elements of the cause of action by a preponderance of the evidence.[13]

---

6. Resorb Networks, Inc. v. YouNow.com, 30 N.Y.S.3d 506, 510 (N.Y. Sup. Ct. 2016).
7. RESTATEMENT (SECOND) OF CONTRACTS, *supra* note 3, at § 22(1) ("The manifestation of mutual assent to an exchange ordinarily takes the form of an offer or proposal followed by acceptance by the other party or parties").
8. Beitner v. Becker, 824 N.Y.S.2d 155, 156 (App. Div. 2006).
9. Judge Rotenberg Educ. Ctr. Inc. v. Blass, 882 F. Supp. 2d 371, 377 (E.D.N.Y. 2012) (applying New York Law); *see, for example,* Goldman v. Metro. Life Ins. Co., 841 N.E.2d 742 (N.Y. 2005).
10. *Judge Rotenberg Educ. Ctr. Inc.,* 882 F. Supp. 2d at 377.
11. *See* Paramount Film Distrib. Corp. v. State, 285 N.E.2d 695 (N.Y. 1972).
12. JP Morgan Chase v. J.H. Elec. of New York, Inc., 893 N.Y.S.2d 237 (App. Div. 2010); Hermandad Y Asociados, Inc. v. Movimiento Misionero Mundial, Inc., 880 N.Y.S.2d 873 (N.Y. Sup. Ct. 2009).
13. Enercomp, Inc. v. McCorhill Pub., Inc., 873 F.2d 536, 542 (2d Cir. 1989) (applying New York law).

In the sections that follow, we will highlight the burden of proof required on each element of the cause of action.

a. Existence of a Contract

To establish an express contract under New York law, a plaintiff must establish an offer, acceptance of the offer, consideration, mutual assent, and an intent to be bound.[14] In essence, there must be an objective meeting of the minds that results in a binding, enforceable contract.[15] An express contract may be written or oral.

With respect to a written contract, meeting the burden of establishing its existence could be achieved as early as the filing and service of your complaint by attaching the contract as an exhibit. This strategy can save time and money in discovery, at summary judgment, and at trial if properly used. The contract annexed to the pleading is deemed a part of the pleading.[16] The defendant then has to admit (usually admits) or deny its existence—whereupon the plaintiff has proven that element of the cause of action: the existence of a contract.[17] However, if that is not the right strategy at the time, or if the contract is an oral one, a litigant can still meet its burden to prove the existence of a contract.

The plaintiff's initial burden of establishing the existence of a contract is satisfied by proving there was a sufficiently definite offer such that its unequivocal acceptance will give rise to an enforceable contract.[18] Acceptance requires that the terms of the offer to contract be clear, unambiguous, and unequivocal.[19] The plaintiff's burden is to provide documents, testimony, or other relevant evidence of the existence of the offer and acceptance.[20]

---

14. Kolchins v. Evolution Markets, Inc., 8 N.Y.S.3d 1 (App. Div. 2015) (*quoting* 22 N.Y. JUR. CONTRACTS § 9 (AM. LAW REP. 2008)).

15. "Generally, courts look to the basic elements of the offer and the acceptance to determine whether there is an objective meeting of the minds sufficient to give rise to a binding and enforceable contract." Express Indus. & Terminal Corp. v. New York State Dep't of Transp., 715 N.E.2d 1050, 1053 (N.Y. 1999).

16. CPLR § 3014 ("A copy of any writing which is attached to a pleading is a part thereof for all purposes").

17. *See* Certain Underwriters at Lloyd's, London v. William M. Mercer, Inc., 801 N.Y.S.2d 231 (N.Y. Sup. Ct. 2005) (document not annexed to complaint); Wilmington Trust Co. v. Metropolitan Life Ins. Co., 2008 WL 3819698 (N.Y. Sup. Ct. 2008).

18. Express Indus. & Terminal Corp. v. New York State DOT, 715 N.E.2d 1050, 1053 (N.Y. 1999).

19. *Kolchins*, 8 N.Y.S.3d at 9.

20. New York courts apply the "best evidence rule" for breach of contract actions and require the production of an original writing where its contents are in dispute and sought to be proven. Secondary evidence, however, of the contents of an unproduced original may be admitted upon threshold factual findings by the trial court that the proponent of the substitute has sufficiently explained the

Once the litigant has established proof of the offer and acceptance, it must demonstrate that the purported contract is supported by consideration, which consists of a benefit to the promisor or a detriment to the promisee.[21] The plaintiff's burden is to establish that there has been an exchange for something of value (monetary, property, etc.) between the parties.[22] Conversely, the party defending a breach of contract cause of action may successfully attack the existence of the contract element of the claim by alleging a lack of consideration. Lack of consideration occurs when there is a promise made but only one party gets something in exchange for that promise. If only one side is bound to perform, making the obligation illusory, consideration does not exist.[23]

After the basic elements leading to the formation of a contract are met (offer, acceptance, and consideration), there must be mutual assent, which is essential to the formation of an enforceable contract. Mutual assent is when two or more parties are in agreement and there is a meeting of the minds on all fundamental terms of the contract to assure that the parties are truly in agreement with respect to all material terms.[24] Without a "meeting of the minds" the contract is voidable.[25] Demonstrating that an offer was made and that it was accepted can prove this element.[26] Also note that mutual assent can be oral or in writing.

b. Performance by Plaintiff

The plaintiff has the burden to prove that he or she has satisfied or performed all conditions of the contract. In a case that involves bilateral contracts, the plaintiff has the burden of proving that he or she performed the duties and obligations contemplated by the contract. However, once the plaintiff has met this burden, the burden of production and/or the burden of proof associated with an affirmative defense then shifts to the defendant.[27] The defendant might allege that he or she did not breach the contract, must show that the obligations were met, and the plaintiff did not perform in accordance with the agreed upon contract.

---

unavailability of the primary evidence and has not procured its loss or destruction in bad faith. Additionally, under New York law, writings creating a contract may be signed by only one party, and in fact, need not be signed by either party.

21. *Beitner,* 824 N.Y.S.2d at 156.

22. *See, generally,* Apfel v. Prudential-Bache Sec. Inc., 616 N.E.2d 1095 (N.Y. 1993).

23. *See* Curtis Properties Corp. v. Greif Companies, 628 N.Y.S.2d 628, 632 (App. Div. 1995).

24. *Express Indus. & Terminal Corp.,* 715 N.E.2d at 1053.

25. Schultz v. Hourihan, 656 N.Y.S.2d 526, 528 (App. Div. 1997).

26. *See, generally, Express Indus. & Terminal Corp.,* 715 N.E.2d at 1050.

27. Special Prod. Mfg., Inc. v. Douglass, 564 N.Y.S.2d 615, 617 (App. Div. 1991) ("[P]laintiff sustained its burden of showing that defendant's breach contributed in a substantial measure to its loss, and the burden shifted to defendant to prove that some intervening cause contributed to the loss").

c. Breach by Defendant

Plaintiff's next step in demonstrating his or her breach of contract claim is to prove that the defendant breached the contract. Breaches come in one of two forms: material or nonmaterial.[28] A "material" breach is a failure to do something required under the contract that is so fundamental to the contract that the failure to perform that obligation defeats the essential purpose of the contract or makes it impossible for the other party to perform under the contract.[29] This type of breach allows the injured party to stop its performance and sue for damages. An example of a material breach with respect to a real property matter would be where plaintiff agreed to purchase residential real property, both parties signed a contract of sale and the plaintiff returned it with a personal check for the down payment, which was then dishonored for irregular signature.[30] The plaintiff then provided a cashier's check for the payment but the defendant refused to accept the cashier's check and rescinded the contract; the plaintiff then sued for specific performance.[31] In this example, the Appellate Division held that the dishonor of the down payment check constituted a material breach of the agreement and the defendant was not obligated to accept a replacement check.[32]

Where the plaintiff alleges a nonmaterial breach of the contract by the defendant, the plaintiff carries the burden of establishing his continuing performance under the contract in order to sue for damages.[33] An example of a nonmaterial breach would be if a homeowner and an electrician agreed to use a yellow wire to connect a television from the bedroom to the living room and the electrician instead used a black wire. This breach is nonmaterial because even though it deviates from the original agreement, it does not affect the functionality of the agreement; in other words, it does not affect the heart of the contract.

d. Resulting Damage

Generally, the party asserting the breach of contract cause of action has the burden of proving the harm suffered as a result of that breach[34] with reasonable certainty.[35] When the existence of damage is certain, and the only uncertainty is

---

28. *See, generally,* 23 Williston on Contracts § 63:3 (4th ed. 2018).
29. *Id.*
30. Daimon v. Fridman, 773 N.Y.S.2d 441, 442 (App. Div. 2004).
31. *Id.*
32. *Id.*
33. Williston, *supra* note 28, at § 63:4.
34. J.R. Loftus, Inc. v. White, 649 N.E.2d 1196, 1198 (N.Y. 1995).
35. City of New York v. State, 801 N.Y.S.2d 8, 11 (App. Div. 2005).

as to its amount, the plaintiff will not be denied recovery of substantial damages, but even then the plaintiff must show "a stable foundation for a reasonable estimate" of damages.[36] "It is always the breaching party . . . who must shoulder the burden of the uncertainty regarding the amount of damages."[37] Equitable remedies are available to a party who has been injured when a contract has been breached and monetary damages are inadequate; these include specific performance, recession, restitution, or reformation of the contract.

2. Quasi-Contract Causes of Action

Where there is not an express contract governing the relationship between the parties, a litigant may consider an action founded on a "quasi-contract" theory of recovery. In this section, we discuss two of those causes of action; namely, unjust enrichment and *quantum meruit*. Although these two theories of recovery are similar in nature, they are not interchangeable. A successful litigant must carefully choose which theory is representative of its cause.

a.   Unjust Enrichment

The term "unjust enrichment" applies when there is no contract between the parties, but one party is unfairly benefiting from the efforts of the other without providing compensation. The general principle of contract law is that one must not unreasonably fail to perform one's promise to another.[38] The quasi-contract theory of unjust enrichment applies to implied or constructive contracts. It is said that "a party may not recover in . . . unjust enrichment where the parties have entered into a contract that governs the subject matter."[39] It is well settled that the fundamental inquiry in an action for unjust enrichment is "whether it is against equity and good conscience to permit the defendant to retain what is sought to be recovered."[40] Thus, the first burden of proof to keep in mind when considering a claim of unjust enrichment is the burden to establish that there is not an express contract between the parties governing the same subject matter at issue.

A plaintiff therefore cannot simultaneously have valid claims for both unjust enrichment and breach of contract; a claim for unjust enrichment is foundationally

---

36. ESPN, Inc. v. Office of the Comm'r of Baseball, 76 F. Supp. 2d 416, 418 (S.D.N.Y. 1999) (applying New York law).
37. Wathne Imports, Ltd. v. PRL USA, Inc., 953 N.Y.S.2d 7, 11 (App. Div. 2012).
38. Restatement (Second) of Contracts, *supra* note 3, at § 90.
39. Pappas v. Tzolis, 982 N.E.2d 576, 580 (N.Y. 2012).
40. Mandarin Trading Ltd. v. Wildenstein, 944 N.E.2d 1104, 1110 (N.Y. 2011).

based on the fact that there is no enforceable contract. The New York Court of Appeals has held that the existence of a valid and enforceable written contract governing a particular subject matter ordinarily precludes recovery in quasi-contract (i.e., unjust enrichment) for events arising out of the same subject matter.[41]

To state a cause of action for unjust enrichment, the plaintiff's burden is to establish that it conferred a benefit upon the defendant, that the defendant will obtain such benefit without adequately compensating plaintiff therefor,[42] and there is an absence of an express agreement made between the parties. The New York Court of Appeals recently articulated the plaintiff's burden of proof on a cause of action for unjust enrichment[43] as follows: "[T]he plaintiff must allege that (1) the other party was enriched, (2) at that party's expense, and (3) that it is against equity and good conscience to permit the other party to retain what is sought to be recovered."[44] The plaintiff must also establish a relationship between the parties, or at least an awareness by the defendant of the plaintiff's existence.[45] The burden of proof rests with the plaintiff, who must establish the truth and validity of each of the three elements by a fair preponderance of the credible evidence.[46]

Unjust enrichment occurs whether the defendant has obtained the money by wrongdoing, illegality, mere mistake,[47] or without the intention to injure the plaintiff by such acts.[48] The plaintiff does not have the burden to prove the defendant's motivations; the plaintiff need only establish the three elements of the cause of action—keeping in mind, however, that such a claim will not be supported unless there is a connection or relationship between the parties that could have caused reliance or inducement on the plaintiff's part.[49] Recently, *UETA Latinamerica, Inc. v. Zafir* provided a clear example of a litigant successfully meeting its burden of proof on a cause of action for unjust enrichment.[50] In *UETA*, the defendant received luxury watches worth millions of dollars from UETA's predecessor in interest, with the understanding and reasonable expectation that the defendant would pay for those goods. The trial court dismissed plaintiff's breach of contract

---

41. MacDraw, Inc. v. CIT Grp. Equip. Fin., Inc., 157 F.3d 956, 964 (2d Cir. 1998) (applying New York law).
42. Nakamura v. Fuji, 253 A.D.2d 387, 390, 677 N.Y.S.2d 113, 116 (App. Div. 1998).
43. Georgia Malone & Co., Inc. v Rieder, 973 N.E.2d 743, 746 (N.Y. 2012).
44. *Id.*
45. *Id.*
46. *See, generally,* Goli Realty Corp. v. Halperin, 5 N.Y.S.3d 328 (N.Y. Sup. Ct. 2014).
47. *See, for example,* Parsa v. State of New York, 474 N.E.2d 235, 237-38 (N.Y. 1984).
48. *See, for example,* Corsello v. Verizon N.Y. Inc., 967 N.E.2d 1177 (N.Y. 2012).
49. *Mandarin Trading Ltd.* 944 N.E.2d at 1111 (N.Y. 2011).
50. UETA Latinamerica, Inc. v. Zafir, 10 N.Y.S.3d 566, 568 (App. Div. 2015).

and unjust enrichment claims. However, the Second Department reversed the dismissal of the unjust enrichment claim and held that such a quasi-contract only applies in the absence of an express agreement and is not really a contract at all; rather, it is an equitable obligation imposed by law to prevent a party's unjust enrichment. The court held the defendant was personally enriched by taking the luxury watches worth millions of dollars—while failing and refusing to pay for said merchandise—and concluded that these allegations are sufficient to state a cause of action for unjust enrichment.[51]

Additionally, in *Alan B. Greenfield, M.D., P.C. v. Beach Imaging Holdings, LLC*, Dr. Greenfield filed an assumed name certificate and started to practice under the name of "Islandwide Medical Imaging" and entered into a lease and services agreement with the defendant, Long Beach Imaging Holdings, LLC.[52] He then subleased a medical office to the plaintiff for a term of ten years. Under the lease, Islandwide was to provide MRI and mammography machines, an ultrasound system, diagnostic imaging technologists to operate the machines, as well as nonmedical personnel for administration, bookkeeping, scheduling, maintaining patient files, and complying with managed care contracts.[53] The defendant was to be paid "usage fees" and to have a "continuing security interest" in the plaintiff's bank accounts in which revenues from his business were to be deposited, as well as accounts receivable generated from medical services performed at the office.[54] The defendant eventually terminated the lease and services agreement claiming several breaches of the agreement. Because the defendant took over the plaintiff's practice and used his name—Islandwide Medical Imaging—without regard to the contractual relationship, the plaintiff made a claim for unjust enrichment.[55]

The Second Department reversed the trial court's judgment, finding in favor of the plaintiff and allowing recovery of damages for unjust enrichment.[56] The court found that the cause of action was properly pled and that "unjust enrichment . . . does not require the performance of any wrongful act by the one enriched. Innocent parties may frequently be unjustly enriched. What is required, generally, is that a party hold property under such circumstances that in equity and good conscience he ought not to retain it."[57] Further, the defendant

---

51. *UETA*, 10 N.Y.S.3d at 568.
52. Alan B. Greenfield, M.D., P.C. v. Long Beach Imaging Holdings, LLC, 2012 N.Y. Slip Op. 33807[U] (N.Y. Sup. Ct. 2012) *rev'd*, 981 N.Y.S.2d 135 (App. Div. 2014).
53. *Id.*
54. *Id.*
55. *Id.*
56. *Id.* at 137.
57. *Id.*

wrongfully held and barred access to the plaintiff's files and records to enrich itself at the plaintiff's expense.[58]

b. *Quantum Meruit*

A cause of action for *quantum meruit* may allow a party to recover for the value of labor, services, or work performed based upon a finding of an implied promise by the defendant to pay the plaintiff the reasonable value for said services.[59] This legal concept parallels that of unjust enrichment,[60] which, as discussed above, is used to prevent one party from benefiting at the expense of the other in the absence of a valid contract. The elements of a cause of action sounding in *quantum meruit* are: (1) the performance of services in good faith, (2) the acceptance of services by the person to whom they are rendered, (3) the expectation of compensation therefor, and (4) the reasonable value of the services rendered.[61,62] The burden of proof for each element—especially with respect to the acceptance of services and expectation of compensation—rests with the plaintiff. The idea that the burden lies with the plaintiff is based on the fact that it is generally assumed that an individual does not work without cost or payment for services rendered presumably without the defendant's acceptance or knowledge. In addition, the plaintiff has the burden of proving damages incurred.

There are limited circumstances in which it is appropriate to seek the recovery of *quantum meruit* damages when a written contract exists. Typically, courts do not allow quasi-contract claims like *quantum meruit* where a valid agreement exists between the parties.[63] However, when a contract has been terminated prior to completion (a material breach), *quantum meruit* is the appropriate measure of damages.[64] In *American Underground Engineering, Inc. v. City of Syracuse*,[65] the plaintiff contracted to construct a parking garage in Syracuse and, prior to completion, the city materially breached the contract and failed to pay the plaintiff for the work performed in accordance with the contract terms. The

---

58. *Id.*
59. Sogeti, U.S.A., L.L.C. v. Whirlwind Bldg. Systems, Inc., 496 F. Supp. 2d 380 (S.D.N.Y. 2007) (applying New York law).
60. *See, generally,* Super v. Abdelazim, 527 N.Y.S.2d 591, 592 (App. Div. 1988).
61. DiSario v. Rynston, 30 N.Y.S.3d 129, 133 (App. Div. 2016).
62. Paramount Film Distrib. Corp. v. State, 285 N.E.2d 695, 698 (N.Y.1972).
63. Clark–Fitzpatrick, Inc. v. Long Island R.R. Co., 516 N.E.2d 190, 193 (N.Y. 1987).
64. MCK Bldg. associates, Inc. v. St. Lawrence Univ., 754 N.Y.S.2d 397, 399 (App. Div. 2003).
65. Am. Underground Eng'g, Inc. v. City of Syracuse, No. 5:00-CV-278 FJS/DEP, 2011 WL 4809882 (N.D.N.Y. Oct. 11, 2011), *aff'd,* 526 F. App'x 37 (2d Cir. 2013) (applying New York law).

District Court, applying New York law, held that "once an agreement has been wrongfully terminated, the non-breaching party may elect to pursue *quantum meruit* damages."[66]

3. Account Stated

A party to an express or implied contract may also seek to recover on a cause of action for an account stated if they can meet the burden of proof associated therewith. "An account stated is an agreement between parties to an account based upon prior transactions between them with respect to the correctness of the account items and balance due."[67] Further, "[t]he agreement may be express or . . . implied from the retention of an account rendered for an unreasonable period of time without objection and from the surrounding circumstances."[68] At common law, the elements of a cause of action for account stated require only that: (1) the parties stand in a debtor-creditor relationship, (2) there has been mutual examination of the claims of the respective parties, (3) a balance has been struck, and (4) there has been an agreement either express or implied that the balance is correct and that the party against whom it is found will pay it.[69] The plaintiff generally need not prove the details of the original debt; instead, a plaintiff may merely show the defendant received the account and kept it for a reasonable time without objection. It is said that the burden is then on the party receiving the account to show fraud, mistake, or that it was never accepted by him as an account stated.[70]

To recover on a cause of action for an account stated under New York law, a plaintiff must show that: "(1) an account was presented; (2) it was accepted as correct; and (3) the debtor promised to pay the amount stated."[71] For example, in *Haselton Lumber Co., Inc. v. Bette & Cring, LLC*, the plaintiff-seller was a family-owned business in Wilmington, New York, that sold, distributed, and manufactured building supplies for use in the construction industry.[72] The plaintiff was contacted by the defendant-debtor to arrange for the purchase

---

66. *Id.* at *2.
67. Jim-Mar Corp. v. Aquatic Const., Ltd., 600 N.Y.S.2d 790, 791 (App. Div. 1993).
68. *Id.*
69. Bank of New York-Delaware v. Santarelli, 491 N.Y.S.2d 980, 981 (Cnty. Ct. 1985); *See* 1 N.Y. Jur. 2d § 10 Accounts and Accounting.
70. *Santarelli*, 491 N.Y.S.2d at 981.
71. Prof'l Merch. Advance Capital, LLC v. C Care Servs., LLC, No. 13-CV-6562 RJS, 2015 WL 4392081, at *6 (S.D.N.Y. July 15, 2015).
72. 998 N.Y.S.2d 491, 492 (App. Div. 2014).

of building materials.[73] Plaintiff provided the defendant with a business credit application and a personal guarantee requesting an extension of credit in order to purchase materials and supplies—both of which were executed by the defendant.[74] During the next several months, the plaintiff furnished the contractor with various building materials, sent out invoices and monthly billing statements that itemized the charges to the contractor's account, and recorded any payments submitted to the account.[75] After the defendant failed to pay certain invoices, the plaintiff commenced an action for account stated to recover the outstanding balance due, accumulated finance charges, and the personal guarantee.[76] The Appellate Division found the plaintiff provided evidence sufficient to establish an account stated claim. The plaintiff submitted copies of the invoices and itemized billing statements to demonstrate the unpaid balance due, as well as an affidavit from the plaintiff's president to establish that the defendant never objected to the imposition of the accrued finance charges.[77] The court found that the plaintiff met its initial burden of demonstrating an account stated claim, further finding that neither partial payment nor a subsequent offer to settle—unaccompanied by a specific complaint regarding the propriety of the sum due—was sufficient to constitute an objection to the payment of the account rendered.[78]

B. Torts

1. *Tortious Interference with Contract*

Torts also arise in the contract setting. Tortious interference is a cause of action that arises when an individual or business that is not a party to the contract engages in behavior that intentionally disrupts a business relationship formalized by a contract.[79] A third party may intentionally interfere with the contract. Where the contract has not yet been entered into and the third party—one who is not an employee or agent of one of the parties to the contract—prevents a deal from

---

73. *Id.*
74. *Id.*
75. *Id.*
76. *Id.*
77. *Id.* at 493.
78. *Id.* at 491, 493–494.
79. *Tortious Interference with Contractual Relations*, BLACK'S LAW DICTIONARY (10th ed. 2014) ("A third party's intentional inducement of a contracting party to break a contract, causing damage to the relationship between the contracting parties.").

being made, a claim arises under tort law.[80] New York law recognizes the tort of interference with both *prospective* and *existing* contracts, but

> greater protection is accorded an interest in an existing contract (as to which respect for individual contract rights outweighs the public benefit to be derived from unfettered competition) than to the less substantive, more speculative interest in a prospective relationship (as to which liability will be imposed only on proof of more culpable conduct on the part of the interferer).[81]

In New York, a plaintiff seeking to recover on a cause of action for tortious interference with a contract has the burden to establish, by clear and convincing evidence, the following: (1) a valid contract between the plaintiff and a third party, (2) the defendant's knowledge of that contract, (3) the defendant's intentional procurement of the third party's breach of that contract, and (4) damages.[82] A plaintiff must specifically allege that the contract would not have been breached but for the defendant's conduct.[83] To prevail on a claim for tortious interference with contractual or prospective contractual relations, a party must demonstrate that the alleged tortfeasor wrongfully interfered with the contract for the sole purpose of harming the plaintiff, or that he committed independent torts or predatory acts toward the third party.[84] Furthermore, courts require that this conduct be knowing or intentional—mere negligence is not enough.[85] A tort cause of action for interference with contractual relations of a plaintiff is not established when the only interference asserted is not intentional, but only incidental to another legitimate business purpose of the defendant.[86]

Additionally, to establish a defendant's liability for damages, the plaintiff must establish that the defendant engaged in wrongful conduct that interfered with a prospective contractual relationship between the plaintiff and a third party.[87] Where procurement of the breach by defendant is established, the burden shifts to the defendant to plead and prove justification for inducing the breach.[88] Furthermore, New York courts have recognized tortious interference

80. *See, for example*, State Enterprises, Inc. v. Southridge Co-op. Section 1, Inc., 238 N.Y.S.2d 724 (App. Div. 1963).
81. White Plains Coat & Apron Co. v. Cintas Corp., 867 N.E.2d 381, 383 (N.Y. 2007).
82. Iacono v. Pilavas, 4 N.Y.S.3d 250 (App. Div. 2015).
83. Burrowes v. Combs, 808 N.Y.S.2d 50, 53 (App. Div. 2006).
84. Lerman v. Med. Associates of Woodhull, P.C., 554 N.Y.S.2d 272, 273 (App. Div. 1990).
85. *White Plains Coat & Apron Co.*, 867 N.E.2d at 384-85.
86. Alvord & Swift v. Stewart M. Muller Const. Co., 385 N.E.2d 1238 (N.Y. 1978).
87. Smith v. Meridian Techs., Inc., 927 N.Y.S.2d 141, 144 (App. Div. 2011).
88. Bogoni v. Friedlander, 610 N.Y.S.2d 511, 514-15 (App. Div. 1994).

with contractual relations as an independent tort under which punitive damages may be awarded.[89]

Tortious interference with a contract can occur, for example, in landlord/tenant matters when a holdover tenant of a property intentionally prevents a new lessee from taking possession of the property.[90] New York law states that a tenant must surrender possession of the entire leased premises at the end of the lease term and must vacate any sublease occupying said space.[91] In *Havana Central NY2, LLC*, the Appellate Division found that a holdover tenant or sublessee might be liable to the new tenant for tortious interference with a contract with respect to the new tenant's lease.[92] The Appellate Division held that the tenant became a trespasser once it held over and did not surrender the premises, resulting in the landlord materially breaching the contract because the landlord could not timely deliver the premises to the incoming tenant due to the existing tenant's holdover.[93]

2. Negligence

To prevail in a negligence claim, the plaintiff must prove: (1) the defendant owed the plaintiff a cognizable duty of care,[94] (2) the defendant failed to exercise that duty of care, (3) the plaintiff suffered injury,[95] and (4) the defendant's failure to exercise his or her duty of care caused the plaintiff's injury.[96] Thus, for a negligence claim to survive the pleading stage, a plaintiff must provide sufficient facts in his or her complaint to support each of the four necessary elements required for a *prima facie* case.[97]

Conversely, to defend against a negligence claim, a defendant can present evidence to overcome each element that the plaintiff is required to prove. For

---

89. Anesthesia Assoc. of Mount Kisco, LLP v. N. Westchester Hosp. Ctr., 873 N.Y.S. 2d 679, 682 (App. Div. 2009).

90. Kronish Lieb Weiner & Hellman LLP v. Tahari, Ltd., 829 N.Y.S.2d 7 (App. Div. 2006).

91. Stahl Associates Co. v. Mapes, 490 N.Y.S.2d 12 (App. Div. 1985).

92. Havana Cent. NY2 LLC v. Lunney's Pub, Inc., 852 N.Y.S.2d 32 (App. Div. 2007).

93. *Id.* at 37.

94. 2 NY EVID. PROOF OF CASES § 26:1 Generally (addressing duty to person injured).

95. *Id.* (addressing proximate cause).

96. *Id.*; Buckley v. State, 938 N.Y.S.2d 734 (N.Y. Ct. Cl. 2011) (reiterating that a *prima facie* negligence claim requires proof of (1) defendant's duty, (2) defendant breaching said duty, (3) injury suffered by the plaintiff, and (4) plaintiff's injury being the proximate result of defendant's breach of duty. *See also* Atkins v. Glens Falls City Sch. Dist., 424 N.E.2d 531, 534 (N.Y. 1981).

97. Schweitzer v. Mindlin, 162 N.E. 524 (N.Y. 1928) (opining that a mere accusation of negligence, without more, will not support a cause of action in a negligence case).

example, the defendant may prove that he owed no duty of care, or, in the alternative, that he did not have sufficient notice of that duty of care.[98] A defendant may also overcome the two elements of duty and breach by proving that the injury was foreseeable, and that the plaintiff assumed the risk of obtaining that injury.[99] Still, it is worth noting that assumption of risk is not an absolute defense in a negligence action; rather, it is simply a way to measure the scope of the defendant's duty of care, along with the liability that may follow.[100]

a.   The Defendant's Duty of Care and Breach of Duty of Care

To succeed in a negligence case, a specific duty of care to the plaintiff is required; without a specific duty of care, defendants would be subjected "to limitless liability. . . ."[101] Accordingly, the injured party bears the burden of proving not only that the defendant owed a general duty to society, but also a specific duty to the injured party. "Without a duty running directly to the injured person there can be no liability in damages, however careless the conduct or foreseeable harm."[102] Still, a specific duty of care is not easily proved in all factual circumstances. Therefore, courts will often measure a defendant's duty of care against whether the harm or injury was foreseeable.

Foreseeability is a tool that courts use to measure almost every element in a negligence claim. Thus, foreseeability in itself is never dispositive in evaluating a negligence suit. However, courts have differed in using foreseeability to evaluate a duty of care. In New York, the Court of Appeals has explicitly and repeatedly held that "[f]oreseeability should not be confused with duty."[103] Instead, it should be used to measure the scope of duty once that duty has been determined to have existed.[104] "The duty owed by one member of society to another is a legal issue

---

98. 2 NY Evid. Proof of Cases § 26:5 foreseeability. Danielenko v. Kinney Rent A Car, Inc., 441 N.E.2d 1073, 1075 (N.Y. 1982) (holding that determining whether a breach of duty has occurred will ultimately depend upon whether the resulting injury was a reasonably foreseeable result of the defendant's conduct.)

99. Danielenko v. Kinney Rent A Car, Inc., 441 N.E.2d at 1075. Buckley v. State, 938 N.Y.S.2d 734, 741 (N.Y. Ct. Cl. 2011).

100. Morgan v. State, 685 N.E.2d 202, 207 (N.Y. 1997).

101. In re New York City Asbestos Litig., 840 N.E. 2d 115, 119 (N.Y. 2005) (internal citations omitted).

102. Hamilton v. Beretta U.S.A. Corp., 750 N.E.2d 1055, 1060 (N.Y. 2001) *opinion after certified question answered*, 264 F.3d 21 (2d Cir.) (internal citations omitted).

103. Pulka v. Edelman, 358 N.E.2d 1019, 1022 (N.Y. 1976).

104. *Id.*

for the courts."[105] Thus, foreseeability—in the context of measuring a defendant's duty—is a question of law for the courts to determine. Nonetheless, foreseeability is also surrounded by factual questions that must be used to measure the other elements of a negligence suit.[106]

b.   The Causation of a Plaintiff's Injury

Proving the element of causation is possibly the most difficult burden to meet, because causation contains two subelements. The first is *cause in fact*—otherwise known as *but for causation*. Ultimately, a plaintiff must prove that there is a relationship between the act (or omission) and the injury suffered. The second subelement—the *proximate cause* to the injury—is met by showing that the injuries were a foreseeable result of the defendant's actions or omissions. In assessing foreseeability, courts will consider whether an objective, reasonable person would have foreseen the injury. In evaluating proximate cause, courts consider (1) the extent of injury, (2) the type of injury, (3) the person injured, and (4) the linear distance between the *but for causation* and the injury suffered.

(1)   Cause in Fact

Although *cause in fact* (also known as *but for causation*) is the easier sub-element of causation to meet, the Court of Appeals has nonetheless reiterated its importance. Recently, in *Burlington Ins. Co. v. NYC Transit Authority*, the Court of Appeals engaged in an analysis echoing the appropriate standard for causation in fact, renewing its well-known definition.[107] "It is well established in [New York] law that 'but for' causation, or causation in fact, is '[t]he cause without which the event could not have occurred.'"[108] To break it down further, let us consider an example:

> *John Smith is driving while texting and does not see Suzie Q. crossing the street; he subsequently hits Suzie Q. with his car.*

---

105. Miglino v. Bally Total Fitness of Greater New York, Inc., 937 N.Y.S.2d 63, 71 (App. Div. 2011), *aff'd but criticized*, 985 N.E.2d 128 (N.Y. 2013).

106. *See Id.* ("However, '[u]nlike foreseeability and causation, both generally factual issues to be resolved on a case-by-case basis by the fact finder, the duty owed by one member of society to another is a legal issue for the courts" (quoting Eiseman v. State of New York, 511 N.E.2d 1128, 1134 (N.Y. 2004)).

107. Burlington Ins. Co. v. NYC Transit Auth., 79 N.E.3d 477, 481 (N.Y. 2017).

108. *Id.* (quoting *But-for Cause*, BLACK'S LAW DICTIONARY (10th ed. 2014); DAN B. DOBBS ET AL., TORTS § 186 (2d ed. 2011 & June 2017 Update); *see also* Koehler v. Schwartz, 399 N.E.2d 1140 (N.Y. 1979)).

In the example above, John Smith's act of texting was the cause in fact to Suzie Q.'s injury. In other words, *but for* John Smith's texting while driving, he would have seen Suzie Q. crossing the street, and would not have injured her. However, as stressed in *Burlington Ins. Co.*, "not all 'but for' causes result in liability and '[m]ost causes can be ignored in tort litigation.'"[109] In other words, *but for causation* does not per se assign liability in a negligence suit—there must be more.

Let us return to our John Smith texting example. John Smith is texting while driving, and therefore does not see Suzie Q. walking across the street. For purposes of discussion, let us assume:

> *John Smith was only driving three miles per hour. Thus, when John Smith hits Suzie Q., she walks away with a minor hip injury. To ease her pain, the next day, Suzie Q. sits in a hot tub for twelve hours. Shortly thereafter, Suzie Q. suffers from chemical poisoning from sitting in the hot tub for such a long time.*

If Suzie Q. were to commence a negligence suit against John Smith for the burns suffered from her chemical poisoning, and *not* for the minor hip injury, who would prevail? John Smith. It is true that *but for* John Smith's texting, Suzie Q. would not have injured her hip and sat in the hot tub for twelve hours, which resulted in her suffering from chemical poisoning. However, permitting such a lenient standard of causation would lead to endless liability. *But for causation* refers to a link in the chain leading to an outcome, and in the abstract does no more than state the obvious, that "[a]ny given event, including an injury, is always the result of many causes."[110] Courts have long reasoned that the chain of causation must have an endpoint in order "to place manageable limits upon the liability that flows from negligent conduct."[111] Accordingly, to assign liability in a negligence suit, courts must determine the *legal causation* of a plaintiff's injury.[112] The "legal cause" of an injury is referred to as the "proximate cause."[113]

(2)   Proximate Causation

A plaintiff will not prevail in a negligence claim without a showing that an act of commission or omission by the defendant was the proximate cause of the

---

109. *Burlington Ins. Co.*, 79 N.E.3d at 481 (internal citations omitted).
110. *Id.*
111. Hain v. Jamison, 68 N.E.3d 1233, 1237 (N.Y. 2016).
112. *Burlington Ins. Co.*, 79 N.E.3d at 481 (emphasis added) (internal citations omitted).
113. *Id.*

plaintiff's injury.[114] *Palsgraff v. Long Island Railroad*[115] is perhaps the most well-known case to address issues surrounding causation. A man had been running to catch a train; as he stumbled onto the train, the package he had been carrying, which contained fireworks, exploded when it hit the train tracks.[116] The plaintiff had been waiting on the platform and was injured as a result of the explosion.[117] In the famous majority opinion by Justice Cardozzo, the court held that the defendant Railroad Company owed no duty to the plaintiff, and thereby could not have been the proximate cause to the injury.[118] The dissent, however, opined that issues surrounding proximate causation is a question for the jury. The dissenting opinion is the law that we follow today.[119]

Authored by Justice Andrews, the *Palsgraff* dissent most clearly articulates the meaning of proximate causation.[120] His dissent stresses that "damages must be so connected with the negligence that the latter may be said to be the proximate cause of the former."[121] The explosion was *a* cause of plaintiff's injuries, but not the *proximate cause*. What we mean by the word "proximate" is that, because of convenience, public policy, and a rough sense of justice, the law arbitrarily declines to trace a series of events beyond a certain point. That is not logic. It is practical politics.[122]

What does this mean? It means that, as previously discussed, without boundaries, we can essentially trace an accident or injury all the way back to whomever we wish to point the blame.[123] "The proximate cause, involved as it may be with many other causes, must be, at the least, something without which the event would not happen. The court must ask itself whether there was a natural

---

114. 2 NY EVID. PROOF OF CASES § 26:3 Act of Commission or Omission; Camillery v. Halfman, 584 N.Y.S.2d 605 (App. Div. 1992) (holding that the plaintiff failed to prove, by preponderance of the evidence, that the defendants had caused his injury); *see* Ruback v. McCleary, Wallin & Crouse, 115 N.E. 449, 450 (N.Y. 1917) (holding that where there are several possible causes of injury, for one or more of which the defendant is not liable, the plaintiff must prove that the injury was sustained wholly or in part by cause for which defendant was responsible, and mere possibility that the defendant's negligence may have been the proximate cause of damage is not sufficient).

115. 162 N.E. 99 (N.Y. 1928).

116. *Id.* at 340-41.

117. *Id.*

118. *Id.*

119. *Id.* at 351 (Andrews, J., dissenting).

120. *Id.*

121. *Palsgraff*, 248 N.Y. at 351 (Andrews, J., dissenting).

122. *Id.*

123. *See* Hain v. Jamison, 68 N.E.3d 1233, 1237 (N.Y. 2016).

and continuous sequence between the cause and effect."[124] Thus, Justice Andrews offered a consistent opinion that articulates the *but for* and *proximate causation* subelements. The plaintiff bears a burden of proving these two subelements by preponderance of the evidence.

As proximate causation is perhaps the most complex factor to a negligence suit, let us consider more examples. In *Ottenstein v. City of New York*, a plaintiff who slipped and fell on an icy crosswalk commenced a personal injury suit against a construction company, alleging that the company had applied the asphalt patch that caused his injury.[125] The Appellate Division held that the construction company had not applied the asphalt patch that the pedestrian alleged contributed to his slip and fall.[126] In other words, the plaintiff had failed to meet his burden of proving, by preponderance of the evidence, that the construction company's commission had caused his injury. Similarly, in *Mercer v. City of New York*, the Appellate Division held that the sponsor of a youth baseball league was not liable for injuries that a child sustained when he was struck in the eye by a baseball during practice because he had not been the proximate cause of the injury.[127] The Appellate Division reasoned that, because the sponsor had no control over the coaching, training, supervision, or organization of the league participants, the sponsor had no role in enforcing a rule regarding age limitations for joining the league, and could not have proximately caused the injury.[128]

The two subelements of causation strike a balance between blame and fairness. Where a plaintiff is injured, the law seeks to remedy that injury by placing blame where warranted. Thus, the *cause in fact* subelement is ultimately a question of who to blame out of fairness to the plaintiff. Who is the plaintiff seeking to blame for his injury and why? The *proximate causation* subelement is more of a legal question of fairness to the defendant. Under the law, is it fair to hold the defendant legally responsible for the harm suffered by the plaintiff? These questions are imperative to avoid endless liability.

(3) Attenuation and Superseding Cause as a Defense

As previously discussed, to prove a *prima facie* case, the plaintiff bears the burden of proving that the defendant's negligence was a "substantial cause of the

---

124. *Palsgraff*, 248 N.Y. at 354 (Andrews, J., dissenting).
125. Ottenstein v. City of New York, 922 N.Y.S.2d 153, 155 (App. Div. 2011).
126. *Id.*
127. 679 N.Y.S.2d 694 (App. Div. 1998).
128. *Id.*

events which produced the injury."[129] However, where a defendant raises an argument of a superseding or intervening cause as a defense, the burden shifts to the defendant to prove that the alleged intervening cause broke the causal connection between the defendant's negligence and the plaintiff's injury.[130] The New York Court of Appeals has explained: "If the intervening act is extraordinary under the circumstances, not foreseeable in the normal course of events, or independent of or far removed from the defendant's conduct, it may well be a superseding act which breaks the causal nexus."[131] It is worth noting that questions surrounding the foreseeability of an intervening act are questions of fact that the jury must resolve.[132]

An "act of God"[133]—or *vis major*[134]—is also recognized as an affirmative defense. The New York Court of Appeals has continuously held that, for an intervening cause to constitute an "act of God," "human activities cannot have contributed to it in any degree."[135] Other acts of God, however, can be harder to prove. Let us consider fallen trees as an example: Is a fallen tree an act of God, or an act of negligence? In cases of fallen trees, New York courts have held that a property owner will only be held liable if he knew or should have known about the defective condition of the tree.[136] Where the property owner *had previous knowledge* of a defective tree condition but failed to take any protective measures, the property owner's omission to act will be found to have contributed to the tree's fall, whereas if the property owner *had no previous knowledge* of its defective condition, the tree's fall will be deemed an act of God.

In *Piore v. New York City Dep't of Parks & Rec.*, a plaintiff brought a personal injury action after his vehicle was struck by a falling tree located on the defendant church's property.[137] The defendant church argued that a tornado had touched down in the area where the accident had occurred within that same timeframe, and argued that it could not be held liable for damages caused by an act of God.[138] However, the court denied the church's motion for summary judgment,

---

129. Derdiarian v. Felix Contracting Corp., 414 N.E.2d 666, 670 (N.Y. 1980).
130. *Id.*
131. *Id.*
132. *Id.*
133. *See* Cangialosi v. Hallen Const. Corp., 723 N.Y.S.2d 387 (App. Div. 2001).
134. An unforeseeable act of God may include acts of nature, such as hurricanes, tornadoes, earthquakes, and floods.
135. Sawicki v. GameStop Corp., 966 N.Y.S.2 447, 449 (App. Div. 2013).
136. 2 N.Y.3d 170, 171 (App. Div. 2015).
137. *Id.*
138. *Id.*

holding that the church had failed to establish its *prima facie* defense.[139] The court reasoned that the church did not put forward any facts to support a finding that the tree had fallen solely due to the tornado.[140] Accordingly, to assert an act of God as a defense, the defendant bears the burden of proving that the harm was caused solely by the act of God.

(4) Injury

Injury is closely related to the subelement of proximate causation. To succeed in a negligence claim, the plaintiff bears the burden of proving that he or she suffered injury to his or her person or property as the proximate result of the defendant's alleged negligence.[141] This means that even if a defendant's actions were the but for causation of the plaintiff's injury, unless the defendant's actions *proximately caused* the injuries, the plaintiff will be unable to meet its burden required to prevail under a negligence claim.[142] However, it is important to note that a plaintiff will not prevail in a negligence suit where he or she only seeks economic damage. Rather, the plaintiff must suffer a physical damage to his or her person or property resulting from a negligent cause.[143]

Emotional injury may be compensable, but only where the plaintiff proves that the emotional injury was a direct result of the defendant's breach of duty, rather than a consequential result.[144] For example, in *Kennedy v. McKesson*, the New York Court of Appeals held that the parents to a newborn infant could not recover damages for their emotional distress resulting from their newborn infant being abducted from the hospital's nursery.[145] The parents had alleged negligence on behalf of the hospital for its poor management of the nursery and lack of care

---

139. *Id.*

140. *Id.* (the court noted that the church did not prove (1) that it conducted a reasonable inspection of the subject tree; (2) that the tree had not manifested any indicia of decay; and (3) that the incident was solely caused by an act of God).

141. 2 NY Evid. Proof of Cases § 26:4 Injury to Person or Property; *see* Becker v. Schwartz, 386 N.E.2d 807 (N.Y. 1978).

142. 2 NY Evid. Proof of Cases, *supra* note 141; *see* Brazos v. Brumidge, 179 N.Y.S.2d 730 (App. Div. 1958).

143. 2 NY Evid. Proof of Cases, *supra* note 141; *see* Goldberg Weprin & Ustin, LLP v. Tishman Const. Corp., 713 N.Y.S.2d 57 (App. Div. 2000); *see also* Antel Oldsmobile-Cadillac, Inc. v. Sirus Leasing Co., 475 N.Y.S.2d 944 (App. Div. 1984) (holding that the plaintiff could not recover on the grounds that a computer system broke down, causing stored bookkeeping, inventory, and financial data to be erased).

144. 2 NY Evid. Proof of Cases, *supra* note 141; *see* Kennedy v. McKesson Co., 448 N.E.2d 1332 (N.Y. 1983).

145. *Kennedy*, 448 N.E.2d at 1332.

for the child. However, the parents were not within the zone of danger and did not suffer injuries resulting from contemporaneous observation of serious physical injury or death caused by the hospital's negligence. Thus, the Court of Appeals held that the necessary element of injury could not be satisfied for the parents to prevail under a negligence claim.[146]

c. Assumption of Risk as a Defense

A plaintiff makes a successful *prima facie* case after proving (1) the defendant owed the plaintiff a cognizable duty of care,[147] (2) the defendant failed to exercise its duty of care, (3) the plaintiff suffered an injury,[148] and (4) the defendant's failure to exercise his or her duty of care was the proximate cause of the plaintiff's injury.[149] However, where the defendant relies on *assumption of risk as a defense*, liability may be mitigated if properly proven. By raising assumption of risk as a defense, the defendant is essentially arguing that the plaintiff could have, should have, or did, in fact, foresee the injury, but assumed the risk nonetheless. Again, courts may analyze assumption of risk under the objective reasonable standard.

New York follows a comparative fault system. Therefore, where a defendant asserts assumption of risk as a defense, that defendant has the burden of proving the plaintiff's comparative liability resulting from the assumption of risk.[150] Implied assumption of risk is a defense that may mitigate damages where properly proven by the defendant. It is not the plaintiff's burden to prove implied assumption of risk as an element in the plaintiff's cause of action.[151] Still, the defendant bears a similar burden to establish, as a matter of law, that the plaintiff's action is barred by the doctrine of *primary* assumption of risk.[152]

---

146. *Id.*
147. 2 NY EVIDENCE PROOF OF CASES, *supra* note 94 (addressing duty to person injured).
148. *Id.* (addressing proximate cause).
149. *Id.*; Buckley v. State, 938 N.Y.S.2d 734 (N.Y. Ct. Cl. 2011) (reiterating that a *prima facie* negligence claim requires proof of (1) defendant's duty; (2) defendant breaching said duty; (3) injury suffered by the plaintiff; and (4) plaintiff's injury being the proximate result of defendant's breach of duty); *see also Atkins*, 424 N.E.2d at 534.
150. CPLR § 1412.
151. Abergast v. Bd. of Educ., 480 N.E.2d 365 (N.Y. 1985); *see also* Maddox v. City of New York, 487 N.E.2d 553 (N.Y. 1985); Mesick v. State, 504 N.Y.S.2d 279 (App. Div. 1986) (distinguishing between express assumption of risk and implied assumption of risk).
152. *See* Turcotte v. Fell, 502 N.E.2d 964 (N.Y. 1986) (acknowledging the doctrine of primary assumption of risk, which precludes a plaintiff's recovery based on the rationale of no duty and therefore no cause of action); Weller v. Colleges of Senecas, 635 N.Y.S.2d 990 (App. Div. 1995).

In a comparative fault jurisdiction, such as New York, an assumption of risk defense may reduce the percentage of damages that a plaintiff may recover.[153] Thus, in incidents where a plaintiff voluntarily assumes a known risk of injury, that express assumption of risk will pardon the defendant's duty owed to the plaintiff. [154] The minority approach, however, follows a contributory negligence approach, where assumption of risk may be used as a complete defense.[155] In New York, prior to the enactment of the comparative negligence statutes, the plaintiff had the burden of proving his or her freedom from contributory negligence.[156] Thus, as New York shifted from contributory negligence to comparative fault, the burden of proof shifted by statute[157] from the plaintiff to the defendant.[158] In *Sigue v. Chemical Bank*,[159] for example, the First Department addressed a slip-and-fall case. The court ultimately held that the plaintiff did not bear the burden of proving that she was not negligent in moving her cleaning cart down the ramp on which she fell; instead, it was the defendant's burden to show that there was an alternative, safer route that the plaintiff elected not to take.[160] However, to fully understand comparative negligence, we should further explore the concept of assumption of risk.

To understand the concept of assumption of risk, let us once again return to our John Smith texting example, but with slightly modified facts. John Smith is texting while driving. For purposes of discussion, let us assume that John Smith had the right of way with a green light, but Suzie Q. elected to jaywalk. Although John Smith had the right of way, because he was texting, he did not see Suzie Q. jaywalking, and subsequently hit her with his car. Was John Smith negligent for

---

153. Morgan v. State, 685 N.E.2d 202, 207 (N.Y. 1997) (quoting "assumption of risk is not an absolute defense but a measure of the defendant's duty of care and thus survives the enactment of the comparative fault statute." (internal citations omitted)); *see* CPLR § 1411.

154. *Abergast*, 480 N.E.2d 365.

155. *See* McQuiggan v. Boy Scouts of Am., 536 A.2d 137, 139 (Md. Ct. Spec. App.1988) (Maryland court following a contributory negligence approach, quoting that "[a] plaintiff is said to have assumed the risk of injury when, with full knowledge and understanding of an obvious danger, [he] exposes [himself] to that particular danger, thus voluntarily abandoning [his] right to complain." (internal citations omitted)).

156. *See* Fitzpatrick v. International Ry. Co., 169 N.E. 112 (N.Y. 1929); Lyman v. Village of Potsdam, 127 N.E. 312 (N.Y. 1920).

157. *See* CPLR § 1412.

158. *See* Gonzalez v. Medina, 417 N.Y.S.2d 953 (App. Div. 1979); *see also* Woods v. J.R. Liquors, Inc., 446 N.Y.S2d 64 (App. Div. 1982) (holding that failure to assign burden of proof to the defendant as to plaintiff's contributory negligence required a reversal and a new trial).

159. 727 N.Y.S.2d 86 (App. Div. 2001).

160. *Id.*

texting while driving? Yes, because all four elements are satisfied. First, John Smith had a duty not to text and drive. Second, he breached that duty by nonetheless texting while driving. Third, John Smith's breach caused him to hit Suzie Q. with the car. Finally, Suzie Q.'s injury resulted from John Smith's conduct. However, here, John Smith can mitigate his liability by invoking the assumption of risk doctrine. By jaywalking, Suzie Q. assumed the risk of being hit by a car. Although this does not diminish John Smith's liability for texting and driving, it can reduce the percentage of damages that Suzie Q. may recover.

It is important to note that mere negligence on behalf of the defendant is insufficient for the plaintiff to invoke the assumption of risk doctrine as a defense. Another causation element must be considered. The defendant's assumption of risk must also be connected to the accident, thereby contributing to the injury. In our John Smith example, we already understand that *but for* John Smith's texting, Suzie Q. would not have been injured. However, *but for* Suzie Q.'s jaywalking, John Smith would not have hit her with the car. Accordingly, the fact finder would determine how much should be deducted from John Smith's total damages due to Suzie Q.'s jaywalking. Next, the apportionment of fault in causing the collision would be applied to reduce the damages figure.[161] For example, the court may find John Smith sixty percent at fault for texting and driving, while finding Suzie Q. forty percent at fault for jaywalking. As a result, a jury would reduce Suzie Q.'s damages by forty percent.

(1) Assumption of Risk in Sports and Recreational Activities

The assumption of risk doctrine is applied differently throughout jurisdictions. The New York Court of Appeals, for example, has articulated that "[a]s a general rule, application of assumption of the risk should be limited to cases appropriate for absolution of duty, such as personal injury claims arising from sporting events, sponsored athletic and recreative activities, or athletic and recreational pursuits that take place at designated venues."[162] New York has long recognized that "by engaging in a sport or recreational activity, a participant consents to those commonly appreciated risks which are inherent in and arise out of the nature of the sport generally and flow from such participation."[163] Nevertheless, a participant will not be deemed to have assumed the risk of injury by activities

---

161. *See* Stein v. Penatello, 587 N.Y.S.2d 37 (App. Div. 1992); DiMauro v. Metropolitan Suburban Bus Auth., 483 N.Y.S.2d 383, 390 (App. Div. 1984).
162. Custodi v. Town of Amherst, 980 N.E.2d 933, 936 (N.Y. 2012).
163. *Morgan*, 685 N.E.2d at 207.

that are not within the proper character of the sport.[164] For example, a participant does not assume the risk of another participant's negligent play, which
in turn, enhances the risk.[165] Such standard applies to sports and recreational
activities, including "games as well as frolic."[166] Similarly, a participant is not
presumed to have assumed the risk where faced with unique dangers that are
abnormal to the sport.[167]

In *Custodi v. Town of Amherst*, a plaintiff brought a common-law negligence
claim against a landowner defendant for injuries sustained by the plaintiff while
rollerblading. The New York Court of Appeals held that the plaintiff was not
precluded under the doctrine of assumption of risk. The court reasoned that the
plaintiff was not rollerblading at a rink, a skating park, or in a competition; moreover, the defendants did not actively sponsor or promote the activity in question.
As New York applies the assumption of risk doctrine to limited personal injury
cases, the court found that these facts did not fit within the parameters of the
doctrine. The Court of Appeals, however, acknowledged certain exceptions might
apply to this general rule, but declined to engage in any such analysis under the
facts of *Custodi*.[168]

Still, it is important to note that a highly experienced participant that is fluent
in the particular sport will be held to a higher degree of awareness.[169] Just as a
spectator at a sporting event is deemed to assume the risk of injury resulting from
obvious dangers incidental to the game, a referee, umpire, or similar individual
officiating at a sporting event will also be deemed to have assumed the risk.[170]
However, exceptions may exist when such officials are presented with dangers
unique to the sport.

---

164. *See* Alpert v. Finkelstein, 344 N.Y.S.2d 649 (App. Div. 1973).

165. Convey v. City of Rye Sch. Dist., 710 N.Y.S.2d 641, 645 (App. Div. 2000).

166. *Id.*

167. Sauray v. City of New York, 690 N.Y.S.2d 716 (App. Div. 1999) (holding a bicyclist's collision
with a chain suspended over a path in a city park was not within the scope of dangers in mountain
biking; thus, the bicyclist had not assumed the risk of injury).

168. *Custodi*, 20 N.Y.3d at 89 ("Resolution of this appeal requires us only to conclude that no
exception is warranted under the facts presented").

169. *See* Surace v. Lostrappo, 673 N.Y.S.2d 543 (N.Y. Sup. Ct. 1998) (Where an experienced skater
assumed the risk that he might collide with another inexperienced skater; absent proof that the
inexperienced skater acted recklessly in slowly skating across the parking lot, the experienced skater
was deemed to have assumed the risk of collision).

170. *See* Honohan v. Turrone, 747 N.Y.S. 2d 543 (App. Div. 2002) (where a spectator at a children's
soccer game was deemed to have assumed the risk of being struck by a soccer ball).

(2) Applying Assumption of Risk to Rescuers

Wagner v. International Ry. Co. provides another well-known Justice Cardozo opinion for purposes of negligence suits under New York law.[171] Noting that "[d]anger invites rescue[,]"[172] the New York Court of Appeals held that a defendant may be liable to both a plaintiff and the plaintiff's rescuer. "The cry of distress is the summons to relief. The law does not ignore these reactions of the mind in tracing conduct to its consequences. . . . The wrong that imperils life is a wrong to the imperiled victim; it is a wrong also to his rescuer."[173]

A remedy exists for police officers, firefighters, or their survivors. Such rescuers may sue for injuries sustained in their line of duty caused by another person's negligence, resulting from the failure of complying with an applicable law or regulation. The burden of proof under this type of action requires a plaintiff to (1) identify the statute or ordinance in which the defendant failed to follow, (2) describe the manner in which the police officer or professional rescuer was injured, and (3) assert those facts from which an inference can be drawn that the defendant's negligence directly or indirectly caused the harm.[174] This is also referred to as the *firefighter's rule* or *firefighter's doctrine*. Some jurisdictions impose this doctrine through case law,[175] while others, such as New York, impose liability through statute.[176]

d. Negligence Per Se

The New York Court of Appeals has held that "[a] violation of a statute may constitute negligence per se or it may give rise to absolute liability."[177] Although negligence per se is a close relative to negligence, it is important to distinguish the two. As we have already discussed, negligence requires four distinct elements: duty, breach, causation, and injury. Negligence per se, however, requires a plaintiff to prove different elements from those of traditional negligence. First, the plaintiff must prove that the defendant violated a state statute. Next, the plaintiff must

---

171. *See* Wagner v. International Ry. Co., 133 N.E. 437 (N.Y. 1921).

172. *Id.*

173. *Id.*

174. Gammons v. City of New York, 25 N.E.3d 958 (N.Y. 2014) (internal citations omitted); *See* N.Y. GEN. MUN. LAW § 205-e (Consol. 2018).

175. *See* Ruiz v. Mero, 917 A.2d 239, 240 (N.J. 2007).

176. *Gammons*, 25 N.E.3d 958 (internal citations omitted); *See* N.Y. GEN. MUN. LAW § 205-e (Consol. 2018).

177. Van Gaasbeck v. Webatuck Cent. Sch. Dist., 234 N.E. 2d 243, 245 (N.Y. 1967) (internal citations omitted).

prove that the defendant's violation of that statute caused the defendant's injury. Last, the plaintiff must prove that the plaintiff's injury was of the nature that the statue intended to prevent. Accordingly, the elements of negligence per se look something like: (1) statutory duty, (2) breach of statutory duty, (3) causation, (4) injury, and (5) statutory purpose.

It is important to note that, to constitute negligence per se under New York law, a New York statute must be violated. The New York Court of Appeals has held that violating a local regulation or ordinance does not give rise to a level of negligence per se; rather, it only rises to the level of traditional negligence.[178] "As a rule, violation of a State statute that imposes a specific duty constitutes negligence per se, or may even create absolute liability. . . . By contrast, violation of a municipal ordinance constitutes only evidence of negligence."[179] Where a defendant is charged with violating a statute, the New York Court of Appeals has broken liability into three categories: "(1) a statutory violation resulting in absolute liability without regard to negligence; (2) a statutory violation amounting to negligence per se and (3) a violation of a local ordinance or an administrative rule which is evidence of negligence."[180] To understand the distinction between these three categories, we should once again return to our hypothetical between Suzie Q. and John Smith.

For purposes of discussion, let us assume that there is a local city ordinance that prohibits drivers from texting while operating a vehicle. Nonetheless, John Smith elected to send a text message while driving. Because he was texting, John Smith did not see that he was approaching a red light. Suzie Q. was crossing the street as a pedestrian and John Smith subsequently hit her with his car. Does John Smith's conduct of texting and driving give rise to statutory liability? No! Even if Suzie Q. was able to prove that the purpose behind enacting such an ordinance was to prevent injuries such as her own, this is not a statutory regulation; rather, it is an administrative regulation.[181] Accordingly, for Suzie Q. to prevail in New York, she would have to resort to the four traditional elements of negligence: duty, breach, causation, injury. However, because there is a local ordinance imposing a duty upon individuals not to text and drive, that will be an easier element for her to prove.

---

178. Elliot v. City of New York, 747 N.E.2d 760, 762 (N.Y. 2001) (holding that "[t]his Court has long recognized a distinction between State statutes on the one hand, and local ordinances or administrative rules and regulations on the other, for purposes of establishing negligence").

179. *Id.*; *see* Major v. Waverly & Ogden, Inc., 165 N.E.2d 181, 183 (N.Y. 1960).

180. Utica Mut. Ins. Co. v. Paul Mancini & Sons, 192 N.Y.S.2d 87, 91 (App. Div. 1959).

181. *See Major*, 165 N.E.2d 181 ("The rules of an administrative body or even the ordinances of a municipality lack the force and effect of a substantive legislative enactment. This principle is a salutary one.")

Now, let us assume the exact same facts as those referenced above, except instead of a local ordinance, there is a New York State statute that prohibits texting and driving. Is John Smith statutorily liable for Suzie Q.'s injuries under the doctrine of negligence per se? Probably! Suzie Q. would have a very easy burden. First, she would need to prove that John Smith violated the statute.[182] Next, Suzie Q. would have to prove that John Smith's violation of that statute caused her subsequent injuries.[183] Last, Suzie Q. would have to prove that her injury was of the nature that the New York statute intended to prevent.[184] Do we have all elements for negligence per se? Absolutely. We have: (1) statutory duty, (2) breach of that statutory duty, (3) causation, (4) injury, and (5) statutory purpose.

That leaves us with one missing category of statutory violations: "a statutory violation resulting in absolute liability without regard to negligence. . . ."[185] Because absolute liability is a cousin of negligence, rather than a distant relative, we will only touch on it briefly. If there was a state statute that imposed absolute liability[186] upon individuals that violated the statute prohibiting texting while driving, then John Smith would be absolutely liable for any subsequent harm. Let us return to Suzie Q. and John Smith, once again, but with slightly different facts. For purposes of discussion, let us assume that John Smith had a green light while he was texting and driving, but Suzie Q. elected to jaywalk when he hit her with his car. He would be strictly liable for any and all subsequent harm suffered by Suzie Q., regardless of the fact that he had a green light. To make things more interesting, let us assume the same facts, but that Suzie Q. was not injured. Rather, she jumped backwards to avoid injury, which resulted in her phone falling out of her pocket, shattering on the sidewalk, and breaking into pieces. Would John Smith be strictly liable for the harm to Suzie Q.'s cell phone? Yes. This would ultimately diminish Suzie Q.'s burden of proof. All she would need to do is prove that there was a state statute that prohibited texting while driving, and that John Smith violated it.

---

182. Because John Smith was texting and driving, Suzie Q. would likely meet her burden of proving this element.

183. Suzie Q. would likely meet her burden of proving this element, as John Smith hit Suzie Q. with his car because he had been texting while driving.

184. Suzie Q. would likely meet her burden of proving this element, so long as she has a sufficient argument to prove that the legislature intended to enact a statute prohibiting texting while driving for the purposes of protecting pedestrians from distracted drivers, such as John Smith.

185. *Utica Mut. Ins. Co.*, 192 N.Y.S.2d at 91.

186. Absolute liability is also referred to as "strict liability."

e. Res Ipsa Loquitur

The doctrine of res ipsa loquitur is a relative to the negligence doctrine. Under the doctrine of res ipsa loquitur, the plaintiff must establish that the event: (1) is of the nature that would not ordinarily exist in the absence of someone's negligence,[187] and (2) was caused by an agency or instrumentality within the *exclusive control* of the defendant.[188] Prior to becoming a comparative fault jurisdiction, New York previously mandated that a plaintiff must also prove that his or her injury was not caused by any voluntary action or contribution on the part of the plaintiff.[189] However, this no longer applies in comparative fault jurisdictions.[190]

In *Ramirez v. New York City Housing Authority*, for example, the First Department held that the jury instruction on res ipsa loquitur was proper.[191] There, the plaintiff tenant brought an action against a city housing authority after suffering injury from an incinerator chute hopper slamming shut on her hand.[192] As the incident was of a nature that ordinarily does not occur in the absence of negligence, and the housing authority was in exclusive control of the internal mechanism of the apparatus, the plaintiff established her *prima facie* case under the doctrine of res ipsa loquitur.[193] In sum, res ipsa loquitur is warranted "only where a plaintiff establishes that (1) the type of accident at issue ordinarily does not occur in the absence of negligence, [and] (2) the instrumentality causing the accident was in the defendant's exclusive control."[194]

3. Fraud

Fraud is a knowing misrepresentation or knowing concealment of a material fact made to induce another to act to their detriment;[195] any kind of artifice by

---

187. 2 NY EVID. PROOF OF CASES § 26:129 Elements of doctrine. *See generally* § 26:132.

188. *Id.* See generally §§ 26:133-35.

189. 2 NY EVID. PROOF OF CASES, *supra* note 187; *see* Kambat v. St Francis Hosp., 678 N.E.2d 456 (1997).

190. 2 NY EVID. PROOF OF CASES, *supra* note 187; *see* Davis v. Vantage Homes, Inc., 536 N.Y.S.2d 864 (App. Div. 1989).

191. 671 N.Y.S.2d 456 (App. Div. 1998).

192. *Id.*

193. *Id.*

194. Abrams v. Excellent Bus Service, Inc., 937 N.Y.S.2d 117 (App. Div. 2012) (holding that a plaintiff's "fall on a moving bus is not the kind of event that ordinarily does not occur in the absence of negligence"). *See generally* 2 NY EVID. PROOF OF CASES § 26:129.

195. *Fraud*, BLACK'S LAW DICTIONARY (10th ed. 2014).

which another is deceived.[196] Hence, surprising, tricking, cunning, dissembling, and engaging in other unfair ways to cheat anyone, is considered fraud.[197] Fraud is usually a tort and, within the context of contract cases, this creates a problem because a plaintiff may not pursue a simultaneous case for breach of contract and fraud when it is premised on the same facts, as it is considered duplicative.[198]

New York courts have struggled when deciding whether to dismiss a tort claim that arises out of the same contractual relationship as the breach of contract claim.[199] The Court of Appeals has identified several different ways to separate tort and contract claims. A contracting party may be charged with a separate tort liability arising from a breach of a duty distinct from, or in addition to, the breach of contract.[200] A tort may arise from the breach of a legal duty independent of the contract, but merely alleging that the breach of contract duty arose from a lack of due care will not transform a simple breach of contract into a tort.[201] Justice Fried held that a fraud claim must be based on some additional representation, omission, or conduct, other than the contract itself, which was fraudulent when performed.[202] In other words, tort claims that add something extra or in addition to the contract claim should not be dismissed merely because they related to the contractual relationship.

In New York, a party pleading fraud must establish the following elements of a cause of action: that there was a material misrepresentation of an existing fact, made with knowledge of the falsity, with an intent to induce reliance thereon, justifiable reliance upon the misrepresentation, and the party suffered damages.[203] It is well settled that a misrepresentation of material fact, which is collateral to the contract and serves as an inducement for the contract, is sufficient to sustain a cause of action alleging fraud.[204] A fraud claim may be based on an allegation that the defendant fraudulently induced the plaintiff to enter into a contract. A party who has fraudulently been induced to enter into a contract may then have a cause of action for both breach of contract and fraud, where those misrepresentations

---

196. *Id.*

197. John Willard, *A Treatise on Equity Jurisprudence* 147 (Platt Potter ed., 1879).

198. Clark-Fitzpatrick, Inc. v. Long Island R. Co., 516 N.E.2d 190, 193-94 (N.Y. 1987).

199. Sommer v. Fed. Signal Corp., 593 N.E.2d 1365, 1368 (N.Y. 1992).

200. N. Shore Bottling Co. v. C. Schmidt & Sons, Inc., 239 N.E.2d 189, 193 (N.Y. 1968).

201. *Sommer,* 593 N.E.2d at 1369.

202. Gotham Boxing Inc. v. Finkel, 856 N.Y.S.2d 498 (N.Y. Sup. Ct. 2008).

203. Stortini v. Pollis, 31 N.Y.S.3d 90, 92 (App. Div. 2016).

204. Deerfield Communications Corp. v. Chesebrough-Ponds, Inc., 502 N.E.2d 1003, 1004 (N.Y. 1986); First Bank of Americas v. Motor Car Funding, 690 N.Y.S.2d 17 (App. Div. 1999).

add something extra, more than just a promise to do something in the future.[205] The circumstances giving rise to the cause of action for fraud must be pled in sufficient detail.[206]

In addition, the fraud may arise in the form of fraudulent misrepresentation or negligent misrepresentation, both of which are discussed below. Negligence and fraud are not synonymous terms; nor, in legal effect, are they equivalent terms. Fraud is a deceitful practice or willful device, resorted to with the intent to deprive another of his or her right, or in some manner to do him or her an injury. It is positive in that the purpose concurs with the act, designedly and knowingly committed. Negligence does not include a purpose to do a wrongful act. It may be some evidence of fraud but is not fraud.[207] Fraud always has its origin in a purpose, but negligence is an omission of duty minus the purpose.[208]

a.   Fraudulent Misrepresentation

In order to prevail on a cause of action for fraudulent misrepresentation, whether for rescission of the contract or for damages, the plaintiff must establish a misrepresentation of a material fact, which was false and known to be false by the defendant, made for the purpose of inducing the other party to rely upon it, justifiable reliance of the other party, and injury.[209] A cause of action to recover damages for fraudulent concealment requires, inter alia, an allegation that the defendant had a duty to disclose material information.[210]

b.   Negligent Misrepresentation

Unlike fraud, negligent misrepresentation does not require a showing of malicious intent or recklessness by the defendant. In an action for negligent misrepresentation, the plaintiff has to prove by a preponderance of evidence: "(1) the existence of a special or privity-like relationship imposing a duty on the defendant to impart correct information to the plaintiff; (2) that the information was incorrect; and (3) reasonable reliance on the information."[211] In determining whether a special relationship exists in the commercial context, the New York Court of Appeals

---

205. *See generally* W.I.T. Holding Corp. v. Klein, 724 N.Y.S.2d 66 (App. Div. 2001).
206. CPLR § 3016.
207. Gardner v. Heartt, 1846 WL 4315 (N.Y. Sup. Ct. 1846).
208. Reno v. Bull, 124 N.E. 144, 145 (N.Y. 1919).
209. Sitar v. Sitar, 878 N.Y.S.2d 377, 379 (N.Y. 2009).
210. E.B. v. Liberation Publications, Inc., 777 N.Y.S.2d 133, 134 (App. Div. 2004).
211. Ginsburg Dev. Companies, LLC v. Carbone, 22 N.Y.S.3d 485, 490 (App. Div. 2015).

has held that a fact finder should consider whether the person making the representation held or appeared to hold unique or special expertise, whether a special relationship of trust or confidence existed between the parties, and whether the speaker was aware of the use to which the information would be put and supplied it for that purpose.[212] Under New York law, negligent words are not actionable unless they are uttered directly, with knowledge or notice that they will be acted upon. The words must be directed to one to whom the speaker is bound by some relation of duty, arising out of public calling, contract or otherwise, to act with care if he acts at all.[213]

4. Conversion

A cause of action sounding in conversion is a common-law tort in New York. A conversion takes place when someone, intentionally and without authority, assumes or exercises control over personal property belonging to someone else, interfering with that person's right of possession.[214]

To establish a *prima facie* cause of action for conversion, the plaintiff has the burden to prove: (1) plaintiff's possessory right or interest in the property, and (2) defendant's dominion over the property or interference with it, in derogation of plaintiff's rights.[215] The plaintiff must set forth sufficient facts to support each element of a conversion claim to survive a *prima facie* case, and each element must be established by a preponderance of the evidence.[216]

A wrongful intention to possess the property of another is not an element of a conversion.[217] The only "intent" required is the intent to exercise dominion or control over the property, not an intent to deprive one of such property permanently. "It is sufficient if the owner has been deprived of his property by the defendant's unauthorized act in assuming dominion and control."[218]

To defend against a cause of action for conversion, the defendant should present evidence that negates the elements of the cause of action. One alternative

---

212. Kimmell v. Schaefer, 675 N.E.2d 450 (N.Y. 1996).

213. Ultramares Corp. v. Touche, 174 N.E. 441, 447 (N.Y 1931).

214. Colavito v. New York Organ Donor Network, Inc., 860 N.E.2d 713 (N.Y. 2006).

215. *Id*. at 717; Castellotti v. Free, 27 N.Y.S.3d 507 (App. Div. 2016); Chen v. Dai, 2017 WL 252460 (N.Y. Co. January 18, 2017); Jackson K. v. Parisa G., 37 N.Y.S.3d 207 (N.Y. Sup. Ct. 2016).

216. Icy Splash Food & Beverage, Inc. v. Henckel, 789 N.Y.S.2d 505, 507 (App. Div. 2005); Tinsley v. State, 598 N.Y.S.2d 734 (App. Div. 1993); Sternberg v. Schein, 71 N.Y.S. 511, 512 (App. Div. 1901).

217. Gen. Elec. Co. v. Am. Exp. Isbrandtsen Lines, Inc., 327 N.Y.S.2d 93, 95 (App. Div. 1971).

218. *Id.*

is for the defendant to produce evidence that shows they did not substantially interfere with the plaintiff's property. An example would be if a person opened a car door that was already unlocked and moved that car from one parking spot to another while the owner of the car was at work. In this instance, the car owner was not substantially deprived of her property.

Alternatively, the defendant could establish that plaintiff did not have any interest in or possess the property. For example, say instead of moving the car, the defendant took a joyride in the car. In this hypothetical, title to the car in question was not actually held by the plaintiff, but rather it was his friend's car that he was borrowing for work that day. In such a case, the defendant should argue that the plaintiff did not have title or any interest in the car, therefore negating that element of conversion.

These facts do not always exist, of course, but a defendant cannot simply argue that he was unaware that he was committing conversion.[219] Being unaware or mistakenly committing the act of conversion may not be enough to escape liability. As discussed above, the intent to exercise dominion and control of the property is the only intent required—it does not matter whether the person committing the act believed he had possessory rights to the property or simply made a mistake.[220]

The exercise of dominion over the property in question is a factor determinative of whether conversion has taken place. Dominion, simply put, is defined as having control or ownership over something.[221] The term is derived from the Latin word *dominium directum*.[222] When someone exercises dominion over another's legally possessed property, a tort has been committed.

In the case of *Mendelson v. Boettger*,[223] the plaintiff claimed that a trust company, without authority, "executed an instrument which effectually changed the nature of [the plaintiff's property]."[224] The trust company was given authority to represent and collect interest on two mortgages owned by the plaintiff. As an agent, the company acted, without the owner's authority or consent, to execute certain documents that changed the nature of the plaintiff's property. "To

---

219. William L. Prosser, *Nature of Conversion,* 42 Cornell L. Rev. 168 (1957).

220. *See, for example,* 160 Realty Corp. v. 162 Realty Corp., 113 N.Y.S.2d 618 (N.Y. Sup. Ct. 1952), *aff'd,* 113 N.Y.S.2d 678 (App. Div.).

221. Prosser, *supra* note 219.

222. In civil law, *dominium directum* is "strict ownership; that which was founded on strict law, as distinguished from equity. Property without use; the right of a landlord [; and] right or proper ownership." Black's Law Dictionary (10th ed. 2014).

223. 12 N.Y.S.2d 671 (App. Div. 1939).

224. *Id.* at 673.

constitute conversion there need not be an outright misappropriation of the property of another. It is sufficient if there be interference with the owner's dominion over his property to the exclusion of his rights."[225] The court thus held that the defendant committed an act of conversion.

After determining that a person exercised dominion over another's property, the next question is at what point did the exercise of dominion become an act of conversion? In other words, how much dominion over another's property has to be exercised to constitute conversion?[226] For instance, imagine someone tied their dog's leash up to a tree to secure the dog before entering a store. While in the store, someone else removed the leash and moved the dog to the adjacent tree that had more shade. Here, it can be argued that the person who moved the dog exercised dominion over the dog while moving him to another tree. Was that exercise of dominion enough to establish conversion? Moving the dog under the shade may not be enough to establish an act of conversion, as the owner of the dog was not substantially deprived of his property. In conversion, the measure of damages is the chattel's full value at the time and place of the tort.[227] Conversion has therefore been limited to those serious, major, and important interferences with the right to control the property that justify requiring the defendant to pay its full value.[228] Thus, understanding what it means to be substantially deprived of one's property is integral to the analysis.

The basic definition of the term deprivation is "the state of being kept from possessing, enjoying, or using something: the state of being deprived."[229] In *Tudisco v. Duerr*,[230] the Appellate Division determined that unlawfully exercising dominion over another's personal property for more than one year and returning the property in a damaged condition constitutes an act of conversion. In that case, after performing work on the plaintiff's property, the defendant took a piece of equipment owned by the plaintiff to another location. After four years, the plaintiff got the piece of equipment back in a worsened condition then it was four years earlier. The court found that the period of time the defendant had dominion over the property was sufficient for it to constitute conversion

---

225. *Id.*

226. Prosser, *supra* note 219.

227. *See* RESTATEMENT (SECOND) OF TORTS § 222A cmt. C (Am. Law Inst. 1979).

228. *Id.*

229. *Deprivation*, MERRIAM-WEBSTER, https://www.merriam-webster.com/dictionary/deprivation (last visited Jul 25, 2018).

230. Tudisco v. Duerr, 933 N.Y.S.2d 140 (App. Div. 2011).

because the true owner was totally deprived of the use of his equipment over the course of four years.

There are a number of factors to be considered in determining the seriousness of the deprivation that would require the defendant to pay the full value of the converted property. The Restatement (Second) of torts, § 222A, provides, in relevant part, as follows:

> In determining the seriousness of the interference and the justice of requiring the actor to pay the full value, the following factors are important:
>
>   a. the extent and duration of the actor's exercise of dominion or control;
>
>   b. the actor's intent to assert a right in fact inconsistent with the other's right of control;
>
>   c. the actor's good faith;
>
>   d. the extent and duration of the resulting interference with the other's right of control;
>
>   e. the harm done to the chattel;
>
>   f. the inconvenience and expense caused to the other.[231]

a. Conversion of Money

Like personal property or chattel, money may be the subject of an action in conversion.[232] A cause of action for "conversion of money will only lie where the money constitutes a specific identifiable fund"[233] and is "subject to an obligation to be returned or to be otherwise treated in a particular manner."[234] In other words, the action must be one for recovery of a particular and definite sum of money. The specific bills, of course, need not be identified.[235]

The subject money "must be capable of being described or identified in the same manner as a specific chattel."[236] The right to be paid is usually not the basis of an action for conversion; the plaintiff had to first have possession or an immediate right to possession of the money in question, since the essence of a conversion cause of action is the unauthorized dominion over the thing in question.[237]

---

231. RESTATEMENT (SECOND) OF TORTS § 222A(2) (Am. Law. Inst. 1979).

232. Thys v. Fortis Sec. LLC, 903 N.Y.S.2d 368, 369 (App. Div. 2010).

233. Montalvo v. J.P. Morgan Chase & Co., 906 N.Y.S.2d 781 (N.Y. Sup. Ct. 2009).

234. In re Clark, 45 N.Y.S.3d 41, 43 (App. Div. 2017), *leave to appeal denied*, 80 N.E.3d 404 (N.Y.).

235. *Thys*, 903 N.Y.S.2d at 369.

236. Mumin v. Uber Techs., Inc., 239 F. Supp. 3d 507, 537 (E.D.N.Y. 2017) (applying New York law).

237. Barker v. Amorini, 995 N.Y.S.2d 89, 92 (App. Div. 2014).

Conversion of money is frequently pled (and dismissed) in cases where a person is not paid for his services on a contract.[238] The fundamental issue is that tort claims are not properly interposed in a breach of contract action, except in special circumstances.[239] When establishing what the burden of proof is in a conversion case, it is important to establish whether or not the problem arises from a contract or a tort.

In the Nassau County case *Fiorenti v. Cent. Emergency Physicians*,[240] the trial court was faced with a conversion case where the plaintiffs had contracts with the defendants. The plaintiffs pled that within the contract, employees were to receive bonuses that were agreed upon by both parties. Instead of giving the bonuses to the plaintiffs, the defendants allegedly converted that money to themselves.[241] The trial court had held that payments for additional "administrative hours" were not contemplated in the contract such that the refusal to return same could satisfy the elements necessary for conversion.[242]

This holding was reversed by the Second Department. Returning to the elements of conversion, it is arguable that the defendant committed conversion; the fund was segregated from the contract. However, the Second Department held that to the extent the Supreme Court found that the bonuses due to the plaintiffs were improperly calculated pursuant to the employment agreements, such a finding establishes a breach of contract, upon which a conversion claim cannot be predicated.[243]

---

238. Res. Fin. Co. v. Cynergy Data LLC, 966 N.Y.S.2d 24, 25–26 (App. Div. 2013); Welch Foods, Inc. v. Wilson, 716 N.Y.S.2d 243, 248 (App. Div. 2000); Matzan v. Eastman Kodak Co., 521 N.Y.S.2d 917 (App. Div. 1987); Peters Griffin Woodward, Inc. v. WCSC, Inc., 452 N.Y.S.2d 599, 600 (App. Div. 1982).

239. *See* 431 Conklin Corp. v. Rice, 580 N.Y.S.2d 475, 476 (App. Div. 1992) ("A simple breach of contract is not to be considered a tort unless a legal duty independent of the contract itself has been violated. This legal duty must spring from circumstances extraneous to, and not constituting elements of, the contract . . ."); Retty Fin., Inc. v. Morgan Stanley Dean Witter & Co., 740 N.Y.S.2d 198 (App. Div. 2002) ("Plaintiff's conversion and breach of fiduciary duty claims were also properly dismissed, since they are duplicative of the breach of contract cause of action . . ."); Sutton Park Dev. Corp. Trading Co. Inc. v. Guerin & Guerin Agency Inc., 745 N.Y.S.2d 622, 625 (App. Div. 2002) ("All that plaintiffs allege in the 'conversion' cause of action is that [defendant] failed to use the quarterly payments paid by plaintiffs to purchase insurance from the insurers and its subsidiaries which, if true, would clearly be a breach of their contract, and conversion may not be predicated merely on a breach of contract . . ."); Wolf v. Nat'l Council of Young Israel, 694 N.Y.S.2d 424, 425 (App. Div. 1999) ("a claim to recover damages for conversion cannot be predicated on a mere breach of contract . . .").

240. 723 N.Y.S.2d 851 (N.Y. Sup. Ct. 2001).

241. *Id.*

242. *Id.*

243. Fiorenti v. Cent. Emergency Physicians, 762 N.Y.S.2d 402, 404 (App. Div. 2003).

Similarly, in *Meese v. Miller*,[244] the plaintiff claimed that the defendants committed conversion by depositing a check that was meant to satisfy payment for the purchase of computers, but that they neither received nor ordered any of the items for which the check was meant. The Appellate Division held that the facts presented did not establish a conversion cause of action, but rather a breach of a contract. Likewise, in *Citipostal, Inc. v. Unistar Leasing*,[245] the Appellate Division held that "[a]lthough 'specific money' can be the subject of a cause of action for conversion, 'a mere claim of monies paid out by mistake based upon contract will not support' such a cause of action."[246]

5. Defamation

Traditionally, defamation was a strict liability tort.[247] The law assumed that all persons are of good character such that any statement tending to belittle a person's reputation was presumed to be false and maliciously made.[248] At common law, in order to prevail on a defamation cause of action, the plaintiff had to plead and prove by a preponderance of the evidence that the defendant: (1) made a defamatory statement, (2) concerning the plaintiff, and (3) which statement was published (or broadcast) by the defendant to a third party.[249] Indeed, falsity of the alleged defamatory statement was not an element of the *prima facie* case.[250] Accordingly, truth was only an affirmative defense that had to be pled and proven by the defendant.[251]

In 1964, the Supreme Court clarified that the First Amendment to the U.S. Constitution places several restrictions on the states' ability to impose strict

---

244. 436 N.Y.S.2d 496 (App. Div. 1981).

245. 724 N.Y.S.2d 555 (App. Div. 2001).

246. *Id.* at 559 (citing Marine Midland Bank v. John E. Russo Produce Co., 410 N.Y.S.2d 730 (App. Div. 1978), *modified sub nom.*, 405 N.E.2d 205 (N.Y. 1980).

247. *See, for example*, Corrigan v. Bobbs-Merrill Co., 126 N.E. 260, 262 (N.Y. 1920) ("The appellant is chargeable with the publication of the libelous matter if it was spoken 'of and concerning' him, even though it was unaware of his existence or that it was written 'of and concerning' any existing person. Apart from the question of express malice, proof that the chapter actually referred to plaintiff would sustain his cause of action.")

248. *See, for example*, Bingham v. Gaynor, 96 N.E. 84, 85 (N.Y. 1911).

249. Dun & Bradstreet, Inc. v. Greenmoss Builders, Inc., 472 U.S. 749 (1985).

250. Rinaldi v. Holt, Rinehart & Winston, Inc., 366 N.E.2d 1299, 1301 (N.Y. 1977) ("[A]t common law the defendant had the burden of proving the truth of the libelous statement, the burden is now on plaintiff to show the falsity thereof, since he is a public official who must show actual malice and therefore must show knowledge of falsity or reckless disregard for the truth.")

251. *See, for example*, White v. Barry, 41 N.E.2d 448, 449 (N.Y. 1942).

liability for purportedly defamatory speech.[252] Subsequently, the New York Court of Appeals explained that the protection afforded to free speech by Article I, § 8 of the New York State Constitution is even broader than the protection required under the U.S. Constitution. Therefore, New York courts ought to be particularly vigilant in safeguarding the freedom of the press.[253]

As a result of the process of *constitutionalization* undergone by the tort of defamation—subject to certain qualifications contingent upon the status of the parties involved—the following are the elements necessary to establish a *prima facie* case: (1) a defamatory statement of fact, (2) regarding the plaintiff, (3) published (or broadcast) by the defendant to someone other than the plaintiff, (4) substantial falsity, (5) the statement was made with some degree of fault, and (6) some injury to the plaintiff resulted from the statement.[254]

Indeed, depending on the status of the parties and on the subject matter of the purportedly defamatory statement, the above listed ingredients of the cause of action have to be modified, supplemented, and/or, at times, replaced. Indeed, several qualifications reflecting the numerous *strati* of defamation law—which developed (somewhat) haphazardly[255]—ought to be made.

In the first place, defamation law varies depending upon: (1) the status of the plaintiff (i.e., whether the plaintiff is a *public official*, a *public figure*, or a *private figure*); (2) the subject matter of the statement (i.e., whether it regards a matter of public or private concern); and (3) the status of the defendant (i.e., whether the defendant is a media publisher or a nonmedia declarant).

Furthermore, defamation law varies depending upon the medium through which the defamatory statement is communicated (i.e., whether the statement is simply directed to the ear of a relatively limited number of people, communicated in writing, and/or broadcast through radio or television). The first kind is generally called *slander,* whereas the last two are called *libel.*

Now, for the sake of exposition, let us take up the first three elements of the cause of action (i.e., defamatory statement, regarding the plaintiff, and publication) as those elements are common throughout defamation law.

Subsequently, we shall discuss the balance of the cause of action's elements (i.e., falsity, fault, and harm) which vary depending upon the status of the parties and the medium of the communication.

---

252. New York Times Co. v. Sullivan, 376 U.S. 254 (1964).
253. Immuno AG v. Moor-Jankowski, 567 N.E.2d 1270, 1278 (N.Y. 1991).
254. *See, for example,* DiBella v. Hopkins, 403 F.3d 102, 110 (2d Cir. 2005) (applying New York law).
255. Prosser & Keeton on Torts 771, § 111 (5th ed. 1984).

Generally speaking, plaintiff bears the burden of pleading and proving *by a preponderance of the evidence* that the defendant made a defamatory statement of fact, concerning the plaintiff, and which statement has been communicated to a third party (i.e., published).

The New York Court of Appeals has defined the term defamation as "the making of a false statement which tends to expose the plaintiff to public contempt, ridicule, aversion or disgrace, or induce an evil opinion of him in the minds of right-thinking persons, and to deprive him of their friendly intercourse in society."[256]

Typically, determining whether words ascribed to the defendant have a defamatory import is a question of fact for the jury to decide. However, on a proper motion, the court may establish that the statement at issue is not capable of being given a defamatory meaning as a matter of law.[257]

In *Franklin v. Daily Holdings, Inc.*,[258] plaintiff, a DJ in a New York City nightclub, brought suit against an online newspaper for libel. According to plaintiff, the newspaper erroneously reported that he gave a certain statement to the press concerning a brawl that broke out in the club between two rappers. Essentially, the DJ alleged that he never uttered the statement imputed to him by the newspaper. Defendant erroneously reported that plaintiff said:

> So we're sitting in there. Me, a couple of others, Chris, Drake comes in and keeps eyeballing the table. Perhaps to show he didn't care that Drake had hooked up with his ex—or to flaunt the fact that he's rekindled his romance with her—Brown sent a bottle to Drake's table. Drake sent it back with a note, a witness told the New York Post. It read, "I'm f. . .ing the love of your life [Rihanna], deal with it," and then things erupted. As rappers Maino and Meek Mill looked on, Brown and Drake's entourages threw bottles and fists throughout the club. I was gonna start shooting in the air but I decided against it. . . .[259]

Plaintiff argued that in this field, club operators generally expect employees to refrain from giving any statement to the press concerning what happens at trendy events. Plaintiff further contended that, as a result of the defendant's article, his career suffered a major setback as after that publication he could no longer obtain the most coveted engagements as DJ. In fact, according to plaintiff, the operators

256. *See, for example*, Foster v. Churchill, 665 N.E.2d 153, 157 (N.Y. 1996).
257. *See* Arrington v. N.Y. Times Co., 434 N.E.2d 1319, 1323 (N.Y. 1982) ("The allegations of a complaint, supplemented by a plaintiff's additional submissions, if any, must be given their most favorable intendment. . . .")
258. 21 N.Y.S.3d 6 (App. Div. 2015).
259. *Id.* at 9.

of the best clubs in New York City ceased hiring him because they believed plaintiff did talk to the press about the aforesaid incident. Defendant countered that, as a matter of law, the statement at issue cannot have a defamatory import. Thus, defendant moved to dismiss.

The trial court denied the motion to dismiss. On appeal, the First Department held that in assessing whether words may be construed so as to carry a defamatory import, the court's inquiry "is guided by both the meaning of the words as they would commonly be understood and the context in which they appear."[260] In this case, the court stated that:

> ... [N]either the language, nor the implication that plaintiff was a witness to the incident, are libelous on their face, meaning that the complained of words are not commonly understood to subject a person to public contempt or ridicule. Stated another way, the import of this statement is innocent on its face since it merely conveys that plaintiff was sitting at a table observing his surroundings; even if false, this statement is not defamatory. The only way plaintiff alleges that these statements are susceptible to a defamatory meaning is by reference to extrinsic facts. No reasonable juror could interpret the alleged defamatory statements in the manner urged by plaintiff without knowing that employers expect DJs not to publicly discuss or give interviews about the happenings at trendy clubs and private parties where they work. . . .[261]

Generally, the defendant is liable only for defamatory statements of *fact*. Accordingly, statements conveying opinions are not actionable in tort. As a matter of semantics, a *statement of fact* is one that is susceptible of being verified (i.e., capable of being proven true or false). Conversely, a person expresses an opinion where he or she states what his or her feelings are about a certain set of facts or certain emotions. Needless to say, *pure* opinions are not capable of being objectively proven true or false.

The New York Court of Appeals has adopted a three-pronged test to determine whether an utterance is a *statement of fact* or a *protected opinion*. Specifically, courts should consider: (1) whether the words uttered have a "precise meaning" that is "readily understood," (2) if the statement is capable of being proven true or false through evidence, and (3) whether the full context of the utterance in which the statement at issue appears and surrounding circumstances are such that a reasonable person who perceives the statement is likely to infer that *only* an opinion is being expressed.[262]

---

260. *Id.* at 11.
261. *Id.*
262. Thomas H. v. Paul B., 965 N.E.2d 939, 942 (N.Y. 2012).

Furthermore, to determine whether a statement is actionable in tort, New York courts consider whether (1) an alleged opinion implies an underlying undisclosed basis in facts not revealed by the declarant, or (2) the statement of opinion is uttered in conjunction with a full disclosure of the facts upon which it is based. The New York Court of Appeals clarified that the former type is actionable in tort, whereas the latter is not.[263] Obviously, a pure statement of opinion that does not have an implied or express basis in certain propositions of fact is not actionable because it is not susceptible of being proven true or false.[264]

By way of example, calling a public official *incompetent* has been found to be a nonactionable protected opinion. Conversely, calling a public official *corrupt* has been found to be actionable because it implies that the declarant knows certain facts that are not disclosed—for example that the official committed certain crimes such as bribery or the like.[265]

To be actionable, the defamatory statement of fact complained of must be *of and concerning* the plaintiff. On a proper motion, the court should determine whether a reasonable person who was exposed to the statement at issue could infer that the plaintiff was the object of the purportedly defamatory communication. In other words, the court may grant a motion to dismiss where it appears that no reasonable juror may find the statement at issue to refer to plaintiff.[266]

In *Elias v. Rolling Stone LLC*, plaintiffs, three former members of the Phi Kappa Psi fraternity at the University of Virginia, brought suit against defendant online newspaper for libel. Plaintiffs contended that defendant published an article (erroneously) detailing a brutal gang rape that had allegedly occurred in 2012 at the fraternity house on campus.[267]

According to plaintiffs, even though the publication did not disclose the names of the purported perpetrators, the story's details as spelled out in the article made it clear that plaintiffs were responsible for such a heinous crime. As it turned out, shortly after the article's publication, it was discovered that the alleged victim's story was completely fabricated.

Defendants filed a motion to dismiss for failure to state a claim arguing that the article did not name plaintiffs as the alleged rapists such that the statements at issue were not "of and concerning" plaintiffs. The District Court for the Southern District of New York dismissed the complaint in its entirety.

---

263. Gross v. N.Y. Times Co., 623 N.E.2d 1163, 1168 (N.Y. 1993).
264. Howlett v. Bloom, 657 N.Y.S.2d 433, 433 (App. Div. 1997).
265. Rinaldi v. Holt, Rinehart & Winston, Inc., 366 N.E.2d 1299 (N.Y. 1977).
266. Lihong Dong v. Ming Hai, 969 N.Y.S.2d 144 (App. Div. 2013).
267. Elias v. Rolling Stone LLC, 872 F.3d 97 (2d Cir. 2017).

An appeal ensued. Plaintiffs argued that their collective claim should lie under a theory of small group defamation. Plaintiffs further contended that their individual claims should not have been dismissed because the article did contain a number of elements that would allow a reasonable reader who knew plaintiffs to identify them individually and collectively as members of the fraternity and as participants in the purported gang rape.

Specifically, plaintiffs alleged their distinguishing characteristics are as follows. Plaintiff Elias contended he lived in the first (large) room at the top of the fraternity house's main staircase—that room being the only one accessible without an electronic key and large enough to host about ten people. Plaintiff Fowler alleged that he was an avid swimmer and that he served as the fraternity's recruitment rush chair in the relevant timeframe. Plaintiff Hadford contended that after graduation he continued living on campus, where he frequently rode his bike.

Plaintiffs argued that the abovementioned distinguishing features are sufficient to allow a reader of the article to infer their identity because of the details of the alleged incident as described in the publication. Put it differently, the fraternity brothers contended that the relevant details of the published story matched their distinguishing features.

Indeed, the newspaper erroneously reported that (1) the alleged victim met with one of the fraternity brothers at the university's pool where they were working as lifeguards—probably, indirectly referring to Fowler who was an avid swimmer; (2) the aforesaid fraternity brother invited her to a frat-house party; (3) at the party, the alleged victim was supposedly brought to a large room upstairs where seven men raped her while two other men watched—thus, seemingly referring to Elias's room; (4) during the commission of the crime, someone encouraged another participant to rape the alleged victim by saying: "Don't you want to be a brother?"—so, obliquely, alluding to Fowler for being the recruiting rush chair; and (5) the victim supposedly saw one of the attackers riding his bike on campus after the attack—apparently, referring to Hadford, who often rode his bike on campus.

The Second Circuit Court of Appeals, applying New York law, clarified that a defamatory statement concerns the plaintiff where "those who know the plaintiff can make out that [he or she] is the person meant. . . ."[268] Here, the court reversed in part the District Court's dismissal and held that plaintiffs Elias and Fowler individually stated a claim upon which relief may be granted. The court, however, affirmed dismissal of Hadford's claim. Additionally, the court held that

---

268. *Id.* at 105.

the collective claim could proceed under a small-group defamation theory. Judge Forrest, writing for the court, explained:

> [As to Elias] the alleged rape took place on the second floor of the fraternity house; the complaint alleged that Elias's bedroom was one of only three in the Phi Kappa Psi house on the second floor that could fit ten people (the number involved in the alleged gang rape) and was the only bedroom on the second floor accessible by way of the staircase without having to pass through an electronic keypad lock. The complaint also alleged that upon release of the Article, family, friends, acquaintances, coworkers, and reporters easily identified Plaintiff Elias as one of the alleged attackers and, among other things, interrogated him, humiliated him, and scolded him. . . . At this stage of the proceedings, Elias has shown that it is plausible that a reader who knew Elias could identify him based on the allegedly defamatory statements in the Article.
>
> [Fowler alleged that] during the time of the purported rape, he was a Phi Kappa Psi brother in the class of 2013, he had a prominent role in initiating new fraternity members, and he regularly swam at the UVA aquatic center. As discussed above, Fowler was the rush chair for Phi Kappa Psi in the 2010–2011 academic year and was active in the rush process during the 2011–2012 academic year. . . . The Article described a kind of fraternity initiation ritual, with the alleged attackers egging on one unaroused participant by stating: "Don't you want to be a brother?". . . . The Article also stated that [a participant] worked as a lifeguard and Jackie ran into Drew at the UVA pool. We conclude that based on these facts, Fowler like Elias has plausibly alleged that the Article was "of and concerning" him.
>
> [As to Hadford] The District Court determined that Hadford failed to plausibly allege that the Article was "of and concerning" him. Hadford's defamation claim rests primarily on the fact that, in addition to being a Phi Kappa Psi member who graduated in 2013, he rode his bike through campus regularly for fifteen months after graduating. Like the District Court, we conclude that Hadford's allegations are too speculative to withstand Defendants' motion to dismiss.
>
> [As to small group defamation] Under the group libel doctrine, typically "a statement made about an organization is not understood to refer to any of its individual members unless that person is distinguished from other members of the group." But where a statement defames all members of a small group, the reference to the individual plaintiff reasonably follows from the statement. Accordingly, an individual belonging to a small group may maintain an action for individual injury resulting from a defamatory comment about the group, by showing that he is a member of the group.
>
> To evaluate a small group defamation claim, a court considers the size of the group, whether the statement impugns the character of all or only some of the group's members, and "the prominence of the group and its individual members"

in the community. Weighing these factors, we find that Plaintiffs have pled sufficient facts to establish a prima facie case that the Article contained defamatory
statements of and concerning all members of the UVA chapter of Phi Kappa Psi at
the time the Article was published.[269]

For liability to attach, a defamatory statement of fact that concerns the plaintiff must be *published* to a third party. In other words, the statement must be read,
heard, or otherwise perceived by someone other than the plaintiff. Generally, the
identity of the person or persons to whom the statement has been communicated
must be pled and proven with specificity by the plaintiff.[270] In this respect, Judge
Cardozo, speaking for the Court of Appeals of New York, said:

> In the law of defamation, publication is a term of art. A defamatory writing is not
> published if it is read by no one but the one defamed. Published it is, however, as
> soon as read by any one else. The reader may be a telegraph operator, or the com-
> positor in a printing house, or the copyist who reproduces a long hand draft. The
> legal consequence is not altered where the symbols reproduced or interpreted are the
> notes of a stenographer. Publication there still is as a result of the dictation, at least
> where the notes have been examined or transcribed. Enough that a writing defam-
> atory in content has been read and understood at the behest of the defamer. . . .[271]

Now, let us take up the balance of the cause of action's elements (i.e., falsity,
fault, and harm). As to those ingredients, different rules apply depending on the
status of the parties involved and on the medium through which the statement is
communicated.

If the plaintiff is either a *public official* or a *public figure*, then—in addition to
the elements listed above—he or she will have to prove by clear and convincing
evidence[272] that the published statement is (1) substantially false and (2) made (at
least) with constitutional malice.[273]

Public officials are "those among the hierarchy of government employees
who have, or appear . . . to have, substantial responsibility for or control over

---

269. *Id.* at 105–6 (internal citations and quotation marks omitted).
270. Raymond v. Marchand, 4 N.Y.S.3d 107, 108 (App. Div. 2015).
271. Ostrowe v. Lee, 175 N.E. 505 (N.Y. 1931) (internal citations omitted).
272. Bose Corp. v. Consumers Union of U.S., Inc., 466 U.S. 485, 486 (1984) (requiring clear and
convincing evidence of constitutional malice); DiBella v. Hopkins, 403 F.3d 102, 113 (2d Cir. 2005)
(predicting that the New York Court of Appeals will require a clear and convincing standard of
proof to show falsity).
273. New York Times Co. v. Sullivan, 376 U.S. 254 (1964) (requiring malice for public officials);
Curtis Pub. Co. v. Butts, 388 U.S. 130 (1967) (applying the same standard for public figures).

the conduct of governmental affairs. . . ."[274] Public figures are "those who [. . .] assumed roles of especial prominence in the affairs of society. Some occupy positions of such persuasive power and influence that they are deemed public figures for all purposes. More commonly, those classed as public figures have thrust themselves to the forefront of particular public controversies in order to influence the resolution of the issues involved. . . ."[275]

Recall that, at common law, malice requires a showing that a statement is uttered with spite or ill will toward the plaintiff.[276] Differently, per *New York Times Co. v. Sullivan*, for First Amendment purposes, a finding that a statement was made maliciously requires a showing that the declarant uttered the statement either with knowledge of its substantial falsity or with reckless disregard for its truth. Thus, for the purpose of the constitutional malice inquiry, the motive for which the declarant uttered the statement is not relevant.

Public officials or public figures must also plead and prove *substantial falsity*— that is, the statement at issue does not reflect reality. The Court of Appeals of New York explained that when "the truth is so near to the facts as published that fine and shaded distinctions must be drawn and words pressed out of their ordinary usage to sustain a charge of libel[,]" then the statement at issue may not be deemed substantially false.[277] Additionally, the U.S. Supreme Court held that the falsity must be material. The falsity is material where the pleaded truth would produce a different effect on the mind of the reader (or listener) from that which the false statement actually produced.[278]

In *Martin v. Daily News L.P.*,[279] plaintiff, a justice of the New York Supreme Court, brought suit against a newspaper and its columnist for libel. The newspaper published two columns accusing the judge of presiding over a real estate case between two Brooklyn businessmen despite having a conflict of interest.

---

274. Rosenblatt v. Baer, 383 U.S. 75, 85 (1966).

275. Gertz v. Robert Welch, Inc., 418 U.S. 323, 345 (1974). Alternatively, plaintiff may assume the status of limited-purpose public figure. In *Gertz*, the Court said: "In some instances an individual may achieve such pervasive fame or notoriety that he becomes a public figure for all purposes and in all contexts. More commonly, an individual voluntarily injects himself or is drawn into a particular public controversy and thereby becomes a public figure for a limited range of issues. In either case such persons assume special prominence in the resolution of public questions." *Id.* at 351.

276. Weir v. Equifax Servs., Inc., 620 N.Y.S.2d 675, 676 (App. Div. 1994) ("Common-law malice requires a showing that spite or ill will was the one and only cause for the publication. . . .").

277. Cafferty v. S. Tier Pub. Co., 123 N.E. 76, 78 (N.Y. 1919).

278. Air Wisconsin Airlines Corp. v. Hoeper, 571 U.S. 237 (2014) ("a materially false statement is generally one that would have a different effect on the mind of the reader [or listener] from that which the . . . truth would have produced") (internal quotation marks omitted).

279. 990 N.Y.S.2d 473 (App. Div. 2014).

Specifically, the column alleged that a lawyer for one of the parties also represented the judge in a separate matter.

As it turned out, the newspaper article was inaccurate in that (i) the judge presided over another lawsuit, a foreclosure action, which mainly involved only one of said parties; (ii) during the pendency of the foreclosure action, none of the parties was formally represented by the lawyer who represented the judge; and (iii) a letter in which one of the litigants authorized said lawyer (who also represented the judge) to handle the various pending real estate lawsuits was not disclosed during the pendency of the unrelated foreclosure case.

The trial court granted defendant's motion to dismiss because, among other reasons, the plaintiff failed to show constitutional malice on the part of the defendants. On appeal, the First Department affirmed and said that:

> Reckless conduct is not measured by whether a reasonably prudent man would have published, or would have investigated before publishing. There must be sufficient evidence to permit the conclusion that the defendant in fact entertained serious doubts as to the truth of his publication . . . In support of his argument that he satisfied the standard, [plaintiff] cites portions of [the author's] deposition testimony. [The author] explained that in his view, the claim of conflict of interest turned on whether or not [the lawyer who represented the judge] was involved in the case in any manner; he thought that the letter from February of 2005 authorizing [the lawyer] to resolve all of [the businessmen's] conflicts with [the other real estate businessman] was key. [Plaintiff] emphasizes [defendant's] admission that although he did not know what role [the lawyer] had played, he nevertheless accused [the judge] of a conflict of interest based on [the lawyer's] involvement. However, none of [the author's] testimony satisfies the actual malice standard. The only issue here is whether [plaintiff] presented evidence sufficient to create an issue of fact as to whether he could prove, by clear and convincing evidence, that [defendant] knew that [the judge's] conduct did not involve a conflict of interest. This he failed to do. The letter in which [the real estate businessman] authorized [the lawyer] to act as his agent to negotiate a settlement neither definitively established nor definitively disproved that [the appointed agent] was acting as [the businessman's] attorney before or at that time. [The author's] reliance on the authorization letter to justify his reasoning that [the lawyer] was actually representing [the businessman] was not entirely unreasonable; his testimony fails to rise to the level of establishing that he entertained serious doubts as to the truth of his publication, or acted with a high degree of awareness of [its] probable falsity. Rather, [defendant's] sometimes inaccurate reporting about the . . . lawsuit and [plaintiff's] conduct was simply sloppy and careless.[280]

---

280. *Id.* at 482–83 (internal citations and quotation marks omitted).

Where the plaintiff is a *private figure*, the purported defamatory statement is published by a *media defendant*, and said statement involves a *matter of public concern*, in addition to the elements listed above, plaintiff has to plead and prove *by a preponderance of the evidence*: (1) substantial falsity[281] and (2) some degree of fault to be determined by state law.[282]

As to the fault element, the New York Court of Appeals determined that such a private plaintiff must prove "by a preponderance of the evidence, that the publisher acted in a grossly irresponsible manner without due consideration for the standards of information gathering and dissemination ordinarily followed by responsible parties."[283]

In *Gertz v. Robert Welch, Inc.*,[284] the U.S. Supreme Court also held that a private plaintiff suing a media defendant who published a statement involving a matter of public concern may not obtain punitive or presumed damages unless constitutional malice is shown. From the above, it follows that such a plaintiff must show *actual damages* as part of his or her *prima facie* case.

In determining whether a piece of information is a matter of public or private concern, courts rarely second-guess an editorial decision of a media publisher. Deference is generally given to a media defendant's determination on whether the piece of information at issue is newsworthy and/or related to a matter of concern to the community.[285]

Where the plaintiff is a *private figure*, the statement at issue concerns a *private matter*, and the defendant is a *nonmedia declarant*, the common law applies. Thus, plaintiff must plead and prove only the following elements: (1) a defamatory statement of fact, (2) concerning the plaintiff, (3) publication, and—as explained below—in libel *per quod* and/or plain slander cases, (4) special damages.

Indeed, the U.S. Supreme Court held that the First Amendment does not bar recovery of presumed or punitive damages where a private plaintiff brings suit

---

281. Philadelphia Newspapers, Inc. v. Hepps, 475 U.S. 767, 777 (1986) ("because such a "chilling" effect would be antithetical to the First Amendment's protection of true speech on matters of public concern, we believe that a private-figure plaintiff must bear the burden of showing that the speech at issue is false before recovering damages for defamation from a media defendant.").

282. Gertz v. Robert Welch, Inc., 418 U.S. 323 (1974).

283. Chapadeau v. Utica Observer-Dispatch, 341 N.E.2d 569 (N.Y. 1975).

284. 418 U.S. 323 (1974).

285. Huggins v. Moore, 726 N.E.2d 456, 460 (N.Y. 1999) ("Yet we have stated repeatedly that the Chapadeau standard is deferential to professional journalistic judgments. Absent clear abuse, the courts will not second-guess editorial decisions as to what constitutes matters of genuine public concern. . . .")

against a nonmedia defendant where the statement at issue does not involve matters of public concern.[286] Thus, in this scenario, as explained below, actual damages need not be pled and proven.

If the plaintiff is a *private figure* and the defendant is a *media publisher*, in New York, a *negligence standard* is generally applied in defamation cases where the defamatory statement involves a purely *private matter*. Thus, in addition to the above listed elements set forth by the common law, private plaintiffs suing a media defendant for publishing a statement concerning a private matter ought to prove that the media publisher was negligent. By way of example, in *Krauss v. Globe Int'l, Inc.*,[287] plaintiff, the ex-husband of a celebrity, brought suit against a tabloid for libel. Plaintiff contended that the defendant published an article falsely accusing him of hiring a prostitute before divorcing his wife.

The trial court granted the defendant's motion to dismiss. On appeal, the First Department reversed and held that (i) plaintiff was not a public figure, (ii) the statement did not involve a matter of public concern, and (iii) a question of fact arose as to whether the media publisher was negligent in publishing the article.

Now, let us take up the last element of the cause of action—namely, *harm.* The tort of defamation may be cast in the form of *libel* or *slander*. Traditionally, libel is a defamatory statement that is perceived through the sense of sight because the publication is expressed in writing, printing, or by symbols, whereas slander is a defamatory statement that is perceived through the sense of hearing.[288] However, considering the wide reach of modern mass media, statements uttered on the radio or on television are now ascribed to the libel category.[289]

The libel/slander distinction is of consequence only with respect to whether harm has to be pled and proven as part of the *prima facie* case for defamation. Indeed, a written or broadcast statement that is defamatory on its face (i.e., libel *per se*) is always actionable as the common law presumes injury to reputation. In other words, the plaintiff does not have to plead and prove special damages flowing from the statement in order to make out a *prima facie* case.

A publication is libelous on its face where the statement itself "brings a party into hatred, ridicule or contempt by asserting some moral discredit upon his

---

286. Dun & Bradstreet, Inc. v. Greenmoss Builders, Inc., 472 U.S. 749, 760 (1985).
287. 674 N.Y.S.2d 662 (App. Div. 1998).
288. Ava v. NYP Holdings, Inc., 885 N.Y.S.2d 247, 251 (App. Div. 2009) ("generally speaking, slander is defamatory matter addressed to the ear while libel is defamatory matter addressed to the eye. . . ."); Privitera v. Town of Phelps, 435 N.Y.S.2d 402, 405 (App. Div. 1981).
289. Matherson v. Marchello, 473 N.Y.S.2d 998 (App. Div. 1984).

part" or "if [the statement] tends to make him be shunned or avoided, although it imputes no moral turpitude to him."[290]

By way of contrast, a written or broadcast statement that is innocent on its face but defamatory by way of reference to extrinsic facts (called libel *per quod*) is actionable only where the plaintiff pleads and proves special damages.[291]

Under the common law, slander can be broken down into two different types: plain slander and slander *per se*. In general, the former is actionable upon proof of special damages; conversely, the latter is actionable without such proof.

Plain slander consists of an oral statement "affecting a person's reputation or good name by malicious or scandalous words."[292] Reputation has been defined as the right "to enjoy the good opinion of others, and is as capable of growth, and has as real an existence, as an arm or leg."[293]

Slander *per se* consists of an oral defamatory statement that (1) imputes unchastity to a woman, (2) attributes a loathsome disease to a person, (3) imputes a character trait inconsistent with a person's trade, business, or occupation,[294] or (4) imputes the commission of a crime involving moral turpitude.[295] The *prima facie* case for slander *per se* does not comprise the special damages element. Thus, the plaintiff does not have to plead and prove said ingredient.[296]

As explained by the Fourth Department, the reason for distinguishing between plain slander and slander *per se* is that:

> certain classes of accusation [are] judged so noxious that pecuniary damage is the natural and probable consequence of the words spoken and those which require proof of resulting injury. It is not that the words are more or less offensive, but

---

290. Katapodis v. Brooklyn Spectator, 38 N.E.2d 112, 113 (N.Y. 1941). Glendora v. Kofalt, 616 N.Y.S.2d 138, 144 (N.Y. Sup. Ct. 1994) (holding that a statement is libelous where the "publication, expressed in printing or writing or by symbols or pictures, concerning a living person which is false and tends to injure his reputation and thereby expose him to public hatred, contempt, scorn, obloquy, or shame. . . .")

291. *Ava*, 885 N.Y.S.2d, at 251 ("Libel is broken down into two discrete forms—libel per se, where the defamatory statement appears on the face of the communication, and libel per quod, where no defamatory statement is present on the face of the communication but a defamatory import arises through reference to facts extrinsic to the communication. . . .")

292. *Glendora*, 616 N.Y.S.2d, at 144 (Internal quotation marks omitted).

293. Cohen v. N.Y. Times Co., 138 N.Y.S. 206, 208 (App. Div. 1912).

294. However, if the single instance rule applies plaintiff has to plead and prove special damages. *See* Armstrong v. Simon & Schuster, Inc., 649 N.E.2d 825, 828 (N.Y. 1995) ("The "single instance" rule applies where a publication charges a professional person with a single error in judgment, which the law presumes not to injure reputation. . . .")

295. Liberman v. Gelstein, 605 N.E.2d 344, 346 (N.Y. 1992).

296. Zetes v. Stephens, 969 N.Y.S.2d 298, 303-04 (App. Div. 2013).

rather that their injurious character is a matter of common knowledge in the first instance, permitting the court to take judicial notice of it, and not so in the latter.[297]

To sum up, at common law, to make out a *prima facie* showing of slander *per se* and libel *per se*, the plaintiff does not have to prove special damages flowing directly from the purported defamatory statement; conversely, in plain slander and libel *per quod* cases, the plaintiff must show special harm.[298]

Incidentally, the following should be highlighted. The First Department (in *dictum*) clarified that, under New York law, even in slander *per se* or libel *per se* cases, the complaint ought to allege *at least* that some harm to plaintiff's reputation resulted from the statement.[299]

Under the common law of defamation, proving special harm means showing that plaintiff suffered the loss of a pecuniary advantage that he or she would have received (or retained) but for the purported defamatory statement. Indeed, harm resulting from the *effects* of the alleged defamatory statement does not qualify as special damages. Generally speaking, neither loss of caste in the community nor standing-alone mental anguish may be considered special damages.[300]

Parenthetically, it should be emphasized that the common-law element of "special damages" necessary for making out a *prima facie* showing of plain slander or libel *per quod* is *not* equivalent to "actual damages," which is an element of the cause of action under *Gertz v. Robert Welch, Inc.*[301]

Generally speaking, the scope of the term *actual damages* is broader than the scope of *special damages*. In fact, the former comprises noneconomic harm, stand-alone personal humiliation, and/or reduced status in the community,[302] whereas the

---

297. Privitera v. Phelps, 435 N.Y.S.2d 402, 404 (App. Div. 1981).

298. Liberman v. Gelstein, 605 N.E.2d 344, 346 (N.Y. 1992).

299. Sandals Resorts Int'l Ltd. v. Google, Inc., 925 N.Y.S.2d 407, 412 (App. Div. 2011).

300. RESTATEMENT (SECOND) OF TORTS § 575 (AM LAW INST. 1977) ("Thus the fact that a slander has caused the person defamed to lose caste in the eyes of his friends and so has deprived him of many pleasant social contacts is not special harm. If, however, the loss of reputation results in material loss capable of being measured in money, the fact that the lowered social standing resulting from the slander itself causes the acts that produce the loss does not prevent the tangible loss from being special harm. . . .")

301. 418 U.S. 323 (1974).

302. Time, Inc. v. Firestone, 424 U.S. 448, 460 (1976) ("[In *Gertz*] we made it clear that States could base awards on elements other than injury to reputation, specifically listing "personal humiliation, and mental anguish and suffering" as examples of injuries which might be compensated consistently with the Constitution upon a showing of fault. Because respondent has decided to forgo recovery for injury to her reputation, she is not prevented from obtaining compensation for such other damages

latter comprises only pecuniary harm flowing *directly* from the statement which harm ought to be specifically itemized by the plaintiff in his or her complaint.[303]

The Fourth Department put the point thus:

> Although these constitutional rules are conceptually inconsistent with New York decisions, it is now established that even in cases of libel per se, damage may not be presumed in the absence of Times malice but must be proved. That is not the same, however, as saying that special damages, as the term is used by New York courts, i.e. as the loss of something having economic or pecuniary value must be pleaded or proved. While special damages as so defined are included in the term actual damages used in Gertz, supra, the Supreme Court did not limit actual damages to out-of-pocket or pecuniary damage as loss of reputation, humiliation and mental anguish. . . .[304]

Let us recall that in *Gertz* the U.S. Supreme Court held that because of First Amendment constraints—unless constitutional malice is shown—a *private plaintiff* suing a *media defendant* for publishing a defamatory statement regarding a matter of *public concern* may not recover presumed or punitive damages. Thus, under the First Amendment, such a plaintiff must show at least *actual damages* as part of his or her *prima facie* case irrespective of the type of defamation at issue.

Consequently, under *Gertz*, "actual damages" is an element of the slander *per se* and libel *per se* causes of action. Because the "special damages" threshold is more stringent than the "actual damages" threshold, in libel *per quod* and plain slander cases plaintiff must still plead and prove special damages and not simply actual damages.[305]

6. Breach of Fiduciary Duty

Breach of fiduciary duty is a cause of action sounding in tort whereby one party, the fiduciary, may be subject to liability for failing to act honestly, fairly,

---

that a defamatory falsehood may have caused her. The trial court charged, consistently with Gertz, that the jury should award respondent compensatory damages. . . .")

303. Elias v. Rolling Stone LLC, 872 F.3d, 97 (2d Cir. 2017).

304. Hogan v. Herald Co., 446 N.Y.S.2d 836, 843 (App. Div. 1982).

305. N.Y. PATTERN JURY INSTR. (Civil) 3:29 ("The pattern charge is only applicable in three categories: cases involving private plaintiffs and matters of purely private concern where the defamation takes the form of libel on its face or slander per se; cases involving public officials and public figures where the defamation takes the form of libel on its face or slander per se; and cases involving private plaintiffs and speech raising matters of public concern where the defamation takes the form of libel on its face or slander per se and where the plaintiff has proved constitutional malice.")

and in good faith toward the principal.[306] To make out a *prima facie* case for breach of fiduciary duty, a plaintiff must allege and prove by a preponderance of the evidence:[307] (1) the existence of a fiduciary relationship between the parties; (2) defendant's misconduct consisting, among other things, of self-dealing or acting under a conflict of interest; and (3) damages directly caused by the misconduct.[308]

Parenthetically, recall that under traditional common law, at the foundation of a tort lies a violation of a *legal* duty owed to another person. As explained below, a fiduciary owes a duty of undivided loyalty to the principal. Let us further recall that, generally speaking, breach of an obligation set forth by a contract is not *per se* actionable in tort because violation of a contractual obligation is something different than the violation of a legal duty. Put another way, conduct that constitutes breach of contract without more is not tortious. However, conduct constituting breach of contract may be also actionable in tort as a breach of fiduciary duty where additional circumstances are shown.[309] In fact, as a matter of policy, the law may impose a legal duty (of loyalty) springing out of the relation established by the contract.

The Court of Appeals of New York put the point thus:

Ordinarily, the essence of a tort consists in the violation of some duty due to an individual, which duty is a thing different from the mere contract obligation. When such duty grows out of relations of trust and confidence, as that of the agent to his principal or the lawyer to his client, the ground of the duty

---

306. Restatement (Second) of Torts § 874 (Am. Law Inst. 1979) ("one standing in a fiduciary relation with another is subject to liability to the other for harm resulting from a breach of duty imposed by the relation.") *See also* Birnbaum v. Birnbaum, 539 N.E.2d 574 (N.Y. 1989). *See also* N.Y. Bus. Corp. Law § 626(e) (Consol. 2019) ("If the action on behalf of the corporation was successful, in whole or in part, or if anything was received by the plaintiff or plaintiffs or a claimant or claimants as the result of a judgment, compromise or settlement of an action or claim, the court may award the plaintiff or plaintiffs, claimant or claimants, reasonable expenses, including reasonable attorney's fees, and shall direct him or them to account to the corporation for the remainder of the proceeds so received by him or them. This paragraph shall not apply to any judgment rendered for the benefit of injured shareholders only and limited to a recovery of the loss or damage sustained by them.")

307. *In re* Schulman, 568 N.Y.S.2d 660, 663 (App. Div. 1991).

308. *See, for example, Birnbaum*, 539 N.E.2d 574.

309. Charles v. Onondaga Cmty. Coll., 418 N.Y.S.2d 718, 720 (App. Div. 1979) ("A duty extraneous to the contract often exists where the contract results in or accompanies some relation between the parties out of which arises a duty of affirmative care as in cases involving bailor and bailee, public carrier and passenger, innkeeper and guest, lawyer and client, or principal and agent.") (internal citations omitted).

is apparent, and the tort is, in general, easily separable from the mere breach of contract.

. . .

It may be granted that an omission to perform a contract obligation is never a tort, unless that omission is also an omission of a legal duty. But such legal duty may arise, not merely out of certain relations of trust and confidence, inherent in the nature of the contract itself, as in the cases referred to in the respondent's argument, but may spring from extraneous circumstances, not constituting elements of the contract as such, although connected with and dependent upon it, and born of that wider range of legal duty which is due from every man to his fellow, to respect his rights of property and person, and refrain from invading them by force or fraud. It has been well said that the liability to make reparation for an injury rests not upon the consideration of any reciprocal obligation, but upon an original moral duty enjoined upon every person so to conduct himself, or exercise his own rights as not to injure another.[310]

In *Apple Records, Inc. v. Capitol Records, Inc.,*[311] plaintiffs, former members of the Beatles, brought suit alleging, inter alia, breach of fiduciary duty against a record company defendant. Plaintiffs claimed that an *informal* relationship of trust and confidence was established throughout the years as a result of the parties' business dealings. According to plaintiffs, the defendants breached their fiduciary duty by surreptitiously selling a number of records claimed as scrapped and by selling records branded as "promotional." In so doing, defendants allegedly diluted the Beatles' market.

As relevant here, defendants moved to dismiss for failure to state a claim for breach of fiduciary duty, arguing that plaintiff impermissibly attempted to plead a tort cause of action by simply restating the factual allegations upon which their breach of contract claim was based.

The motion court denied the motion. The Appellate Division affirmed on appeal, stating:

Courts have long grappled with the difficulty of formulating a precise test to determine under what circumstances a party to a contract may be held liable in tort to another party thereto as a result of some clash in the contractual relationship. While no precise test has ever evolved, it has at least been established that the focus is not, as the motion court misapprehended, on whether the tortious conduct is separate and distinct from the defendants' breach of contractual

---

310. Rich v. N.Y. C. & H. R. R. Co., 87 N.Y. 382, 390-98 (N.Y. 1882).
311. 529 N.Y.S.2d 279 (App. Div. 1988).

duties, for it has long been recognized that liability in tort may arise from and be inextricably intertwined with that conduct which also constitutes a breach of contractual obligations. Rather, the focus is on whether a noncontractual duty was violated; a duty imposed on individuals as a matter of social policy, as opposed to those imposed consensually as a matter of contractual agreement. Thus, unless the contract creates a relation, out of which relation springs a duty, independent of the mere contract obligation, though there may be a breach of the contract, there is no tort, since there is no duty to be violated.

An oft used example is when a special relationship of "trust and confidence" exists between the contracting parties (such as is typically found between bailor and bailee, lawyer and client, principal and agent, public carrier and passenger or innkeeper and guest), so that born of this relation is a special duty, which, when betrayed, is made actionable in tort.[312]

Thus, a fiduciary relationship may stem from the parties' agreement, from the parties' prior dealings, or from other formal or informal relations.[313] Typically, a relationship of trust and confidence is established where one party is under a duty to act (or to give advice) for the benefit of another, who thereby relies on the first party's superior knowledge, expertise, or abilities.[314] Accordingly, in a fiduciary relationship one party reposes trust and confidence on the integrity and fidelity of the other party who, as a result, acquires a position of superiority and/or influence over the former.[315]

Determining whether a fiduciary relationship exists is a fact-specific inquiry.[316] Normally, an arm's length business relationship without more does not give rise to fiduciary duty as a matter of course.[317] As said above, where special circumstances are shown, fiduciary liability may arise in connection with a business (or other formal or informal) relation. Among other things, *special circumstances* comprise situations in which (1) the defendant undertook to act mainly for the

312. *Apple Records, Inc.*, 529 N.Y.S.2d at 281–82 (internal citations and quotation marks omitted).

313. *See, for example*, Sergeants Benevolent Ass'n Annuity Fund v. Renck, 796 N.Y.S.2d 77, 79 (App. Div. 2005).

314. *See, for example*, AG Capital Funding Partners, L.P. v. State St. Bank & Tr. Co., 896 N.E.2d 61, 67 (N.Y. 2008).

315. *See, for example*, Ne. Gen. Corp. v. Wellington Advert., 624 N.E.2d 129, 138 (N.Y. 1993). *See also* RNK Capital LLC v. Natsource LLC, 907 N.Y.S.2d 476 (App. Div. 2010) (stating that reliance unilaterally reposed is not enough).

316. Eurycleia Partners, LP v. Seward & Kissel, LLP, 910 N.E.2d 976, 980 (N.Y. 2009).

317. HF Mgmt. Servs., LLC v. Pistone, 818 N.Y.S.2d 40, 42 (App. Div. 2006).

benefit of another,[318] (2) one party exercises control over the other for the good of the latter,[319] and (3) one party is appointed as agent for the other.[320]

In *EBC I, Inc. v. Goldman Sachs & Co.*,[321] an issuer of securities engaged Goldman Sachs to underwrite an initial public offering (IPO). Plaintiff, looking to raise new capital, hired defendant investment firm, who agreed to buy plaintiff's securities in bulk and resell them to the public for a set (augmented) price. After the securities issuer filed a petition for reorganization under Chapter 11 of the Bankruptcy Code, the company's Committee of Unsecured Creditors brought an action against the underwriter, Goldman Sachs. Plaintiff alleged that the defendant advised the issuer of the securities as to the IPO price without disclosing that the underwriter was to receive a share of its customers' profits made from subsequent resales of said securities. According to plaintiff, this undisclosed arrangement incentivized Goldman Sachs to advise the issuer to set a lower IPO price as compared to what the market would command. In fact, a lower initial price would result in a higher resale price and, in turn, in higher profits for the defendant.

Defendant moved to dismiss arguing that, as a matter of law, an arm's length business transaction between two sophisticated parties does not impose a fiduciary obligation upon the underwriter.

As relevant here, the trial court and the appellate division held that the pleading sufficiently raised the issue of the existence of an informal fiduciary relationship. On appeal, the Court of Appeals affirmed, stating:

> A fiduciary relationship exists between two persons when one of them is under a duty to act for or to give advice for the benefit of another upon matters within the scope of the relation. Such a relationship, necessarily fact-specific, is grounded in a higher level of trust than normally present in the marketplace between those involved in arm's length business transactions. Generally, where parties have entered into a contract, courts look to that agreement to discover . . . the nexus of [the parties'] relationship and the particular contractual expression establishing the parties' interdependency. [I]f the parties . . . do not create their own relationship of higher trust, courts should not ordinarily transport them to the higher realm of relationship and fashion the stricter duty for them. However, it

---

318. Restatement (Second) of Agency § 13 cmt. a (Am. Law Inst. 2010) ("The agreement to act on behalf of the principal causes the agent to be a fiduciary, that is, a person having a duty, created by his undertaking, to act primarily for the benefit of another in matters connected with his undertaking.")
319. In re *Entes*, 644 N.Y.S.2d 533, 535-36 (App. Div. 1996).
320. Cristallina S.A. v. Christie, Manson & Woods Int'l, 502 N.Y.S.2d 165, 171 (App. Div. 1986).
321. 832 N.E.2d 26 (N.Y. 2005).

is fundamental that fiduciary liability is not dependent solely upon an agreement or contractual relation between the fiduciary and the beneficiary but results from the relation.

Goldman Sachs argues that the relationship between an issuer and underwriter is an arm's length commercial relation from which fiduciary duties may not arise. It may well be true that the underwriting contract, in which Goldman Sachs agreed to buy shares and resell them, did not in itself create any fiduciary duty. However, a cause of action for breach of fiduciary duty may survive, for pleading purposes, where the complaining party sets forth allegations that, apart from the terms of the contract, the underwriter and issuer created a relationship of higher trust than would arise from the underwriting agreement alone.

Here, the complaint alleges an advisory relationship that was independent of the underwriting agreement. Specifically, plaintiff alleges eToys was induced to and did repose confidence in Goldman Sachs' knowledge and expertise to advise it as to a fair IPO price and engage in honest dealings with eToys' best interest in mind. Essentially, according to the complaint, eToys hired Goldman Sachs to give it advice for the benefit of the company, and Goldman Sachs thereby had a fiduciary obligation to disclose any conflict of interest concerning the pricing of the IPO. Goldman Sachs breached this duty by allegedly concealing from eToys its divided loyalty arising from its profit-sharing arrangements with clients.[322]

In *Roni LLC v. Arfa*,[323] a group of foreign investors brought suit against the promoters of a limited liability company (LLC) for, inter alia, breach of fiduciary duty. The complaint alleged that promoter defendants solicited the plaintiffs (foreign nationals) to invest in a New York LLC that was to purchase real estate for renovation and resale. According to plaintiffs, the promoters did not disclose that property sellers and brokers paid them commissions that inflated the purchase price. Defendant moved to dismiss, arguing that promoters of an LLC do not owe fiduciary obligations to investors. Plaintiffs countered that, in this case, a relationship of trust and confidence was established because the promoters solicited their involvement playing upon cultural identities and friendship of the parties and told investors they had special expertise in the field. As relevant here, the Supreme Court denied the motion. On appeal, the Appellate Division affirmed, stating:

Here, plaintiffs assert that the promoter defendants planned the business venture, organized the limited liability companies, solicited their involvement and

---

322. *Id.* (internal quotation marks and citations omitted).
323. 963 N.E.2d 123 (N.Y. 2011).

exercised control over the invested funds. We agree with plaintiffs that the promoters of a limited liability company are in the best position to disclose material facts to investors and can reveal those facts more efficiently than individual investors, who would otherwise incur expense investigating what the promoters already know. In addition, the complaint alleges that the promoter defendants represented to the foreign investors that they had "particular experience and expertise" in the New York real estate market. Although the promoter defendants describe plaintiffs as "sophisticated prospective investors," the complaint paints a different picture, stating that they were "overseas investors who had little or limited knowledge of New York real estate or United States laws, customs or business practices with respect to real estate or investments." Moreover, plaintiffs contend that the promoter defendants assumed a position of trust and confidence, in part, by "playing upon the cultural identities and friendship" of plaintiffs. Accepting the totality of these allegations to be true, as we must at this early stage of the litigation, the complaint adequately pleads a fiduciary relationship.[324]

In *Northeast Gen. Corp. v. Wellington Advertising*,[325] plaintiff-finder and defendant-seller entered into a finder/seller agreement whereby the finder would be entitled to a commission in the event it introduced a buyer to defendant where the parties so introduced entered into a purchase agreement for seller's company. Finder did introduce a buyer to seller and they entered into such an agreement. As it turned out, after closing, buyer gradually removed assets from the company rendering it almost insolvent.

Seller, as a minority shareholder, was injured by this conduct and refused to pay finder's commission. Thus, plaintiff finder brought suit against seller for payment of its commission. The jury found for the plaintiff. Defendant then moved to set aside the verdict, arguing finder was not entitled to the commission because it had breached a fiduciary duty. In fact, defendant contended that finder impermissibly failed to disclose adverse reputational information regarding the buyer, which information it had acquired before the purchase agreement closed.

The Supreme Court set aside the verdict, and the Appellate Division affirmed. On appeal, the Court of Appeals reversed, stating:

> If the parties find themselves or place themselves in the milieu of the "workaday" mundane marketplace, and if they do not create their own relationship of higher trust, courts should not ordinarily transport them to the higher realm of relationship and fashion the stricter duty for them.

---

324. *Id.*
325. 624 N.E.2d 129 (N.Y. 1993).

The Northeast-Wellington agreement contains no cognizable fiduciary terms or relationship. The dissent ascribes inordinate weight to the titles nonexclusive independent "investment banker and business consultant." These terms in the context of this agreement are not controlling, since [plaintiff] did not perform the services of an investment banker or consultant. Instead, [plaintiff's] sole function was "for the purposes of finding and presenting candidates" That drives the analysis of this case because he was a traditional finder functioning under a finder's agreement, and his role ceased when he found and presented someone. The finder was not described or given the function of an agent, partner or coventurer. . . . Probing our precedents and equitable principles unearths no supportable justification for such a judicial interposition, however highly motivated and idealistic. Indeed, responding to this fine instinct would inappropriately propel the courts into reformation of service agreements between commercially knowledgeable parties in this and perhaps countless other situations and transactions as well.

Also, a finder is not a broker, although they perform some related functions. Distinguishing between a broker and finder involves an evaluation of the quality and quantity of services rendered. The finder is required to introduce and bring the parties together, without any obligation or power to negotiate the transaction, in order to earn the finder's fee. While a broker performs that same introduction task, the broker must ordinarily also bring the parties to an agreement. A broker in New York, unlike a finder, thus carries a defined fiduciary duty to act in the best and more involved interests of the principal. . . .[326]

In *Marmelstein v. Kehillat*,[327] a congregant brought suit against a rabbi and a synagogue claiming, inter alia, damages for breach of fiduciary duty. The congregant contended that the rabbi convinced her to engage in a sexual relationship with him as part of counseling. According to plaintiff, the rabbi claimed that "sex therapy" was the only way to help the congregant find a husband. Plaintiff alleged that her standing in the community was impugned after she ended the sexual relationship with the rabbi. Defendant filed a motion to dismiss for failure to state a cause of action. As relevant here, the Supreme Court denied the motion. On appeal, the Appellate Division reversed, dismissing the cause of action. The Court of Appeals affirmed, explaining:

[W]e conclude that her breach of fiduciary duty cause of action fails . . .: the facts asserted insufficiently demonstrate that she developed a fiduciary relationship with [the rabbi]. A fiduciary relationship exists between two persons when one of

---

326. *Id.* (internal citations omitted).
327. 892 N.E.2d 375 (N.Y. 2008).

them is under a duty to act for or to give advice for the benefit of another upon matters within the scope of the relation. Whether a fiduciary relationship has been established is an inquiry that is "necessarily fact-specific." In undertaking that determination, we have noted that two essential elements of a fiduciary relation are . . . de facto control and dominance. [The congregant] claims that [the rabbi] held himself out as a counselor and advisor and that he provided those services to her.

But these general assertions alone are inadequate to cast [the rabbi] as a fiduciary beyond that of ordinary cleric-congregant affiliations. Nor can [the congregant] show that a duty existed by merely stating, in a conclusory fashion, that [the rabbi] acted as a fiduciary and that a relationship of trust existed. Rather, it is essential that a plaintiff articulate specific facts that will allow a court to distinguish a viable claim of breach of fiduciary duty from nonactionable seductive conduct, however reprehensible the offending conduct may be. Allegations that give rise to only a general clergy-congregant relationship that includes aspects of counseling do not generally impose a fiduciary obligation upon a cleric. To establish that a course of formal counseling resulted in a cleric assuming de facto control and dominance over the congregant, a congregant must set forth facts and circumstances in the complaint demonstrating that the congregant became uniquely vulnerable and incapable of self-protection regarding the matter at issue.

Judged by this standard, [plaintiff's] allegations fall short of a cause of action for breach of fiduciary duty. The facts alleged and the inferences derived therefrom demonstrate that [she] voluntarily consented to a 3 1/2-year intimate relationship with [the rabbi] because she subjectively believed that the "therapy" he suggested would help her find a husband.[328]

One who is shackled by fiduciary obligations may not act selfishly by putting his or her own interests before the interests of the beneficiary.[329] In other words, a fiduciary is bound to abide to the highest principles of morality.[330] The duty of undivided loyalty imposed on a fiduciary entails, inter alia, that such a person: (1) must disclose to the beneficiary all relevant information within the scope of the relationship,[331] (2) may not receive undisclosed compensation from anyone whose interests are adverse to the beneficiary's,[332] (3) may not engage in self-dealing,[333]

---

328. *Id.* at 378-79 (internal citations and quotation marks omitted).
329. Birnbaum v. Birnbaum, 539 N.E.2d 574 (N.Y. 1989).
330. Lamdin v. Broadway Surface Advert. Corp., 5 N.E.2d 66, 67 (N.Y. 1936).
331. Scher v. Stendhal Gallery, Inc., 983 N.Y.S.2d 219, 228–29 (App. Div. 2014).
332. People *ex rel.* Cuomo v. Wells Fargo Ins. Servs., Inc., 944 N.E.2d 1120, 1122 (N.Y. 2011).
333. Matter of Heller, 849 N.E.2d 262, 266 (N.Y. 2006).

(4) may not act under a conflict of interest,[334] and (5) must exercise the utmost good faith.[335]

Speaking for the Court of Appeals in *Meinhard v. Salmon*,[336] Judge Cardozo put the point thus:

> Many forms of conduct permissible in a workaday world for those acting at arm's length, are forbidden to those bound by fiduciary ties. A trustee is held to something stricter than the morals of the market place. Not honesty alone, but the punctilio of an honor the most sensitive, is then the standard of behavior. As to this there has developed a tradition that is unbending and inveterate. Uncompromising rigidity has been the attitude of courts of equity when petitioned to undermine the rule of undivided loyalty by the "disintegrating erosion" of particular exceptions. Only thus has the level of conduct for fiduciaries been kept at a level higher than that trodden by the crowd. It will not consciously be lowered by any judgment of this court.[337]

By way of example, the following relationships create fiduciary obligations: attorney-client, guardian-ward, trustee-beneficiary, and principal-agent.[338]

Now, let us briefly take up each in turn.

---

334. RESTATEMENT (SECOND) OF TRUSTS § 170 (AM. LAW INST. 2012).

335. Sokoloff v. Harriman Estates Dev. Corp., 754 N.E.2d 184, 189 (N.Y. 2001).

336. 164 N.E. 545, 545 (N.Y. 1928).

337. *Id.* at 546 (internal citations omitted).

338. *Apple Records, Inc.*, 529 N.Y.S.2d at 281-82. *See also In re* Will of Smith, 95 N.Y. 516, 522 (1884) ("[T]ransactions between guardian and ward, attorney and client, trustee and cestui que trust, or persons one of whom is dependent upon and subject to the control of the other, are illustrations of this doctrine.")

Special duties to act in good faith spring out of other contractual relations. Traditionally, common law courts have found that a passenger or a guest may seek damages in tort against a common carrier or innkeeper when the latter's bad faith causes damages. *See, for example*, Aaron v. Ward, 96 N.E. 736 (N.Y. 1911) ("It may be admitted that, as a general rule, mental suffering resulting from a breach of contract is not a subject of compensation, but the rule is not universal. It is the settled law of this state that a passenger may recover damages for insulting and slanderous words uttered by the conductor of a railway car as a breach of the company's contract of carriage. The same rule obtains where the servant of an innkeeper offers insult to his guest. It is insisted, however, that there is a distinction between common carriers and innkeepers, who are obliged to serve all persons who seek accommodation from them, and the keepers of public places of amusement or resort, such as the bathhouse of the defendant, theaters and the like. That the distinction exists is undeniable, and in the absence of legislation the keeper of such an establishment may discriminate and serve whom he pleases. Therefore, in such a case a refusal would give no cause of action. So, also, it is the general rule of law that a ticket for admission to a place of public amusement is but a license and revocable. . . . But granting both propositions, that the defendant might have refused the plaintiff a bath ticket and access to his premises, and that even after selling her a ticket he might

a. Attorney-Client

Generally speaking, an attorney has an obligation to represent his or her client diligently. Needless to say, the attorney may be subject to liability for failure to exercise due care in carrying out his or her duties. Additionally, considering the importance of the attorney-client relationship, the law directs lawyers to act honorably and in the best interests of their clients.

Put differently, in addition to a duty of reasonable care, the lawyer has a duty of conduct—that is, the attorney has an obligation to act loyally. The duty of undivided loyalty springs out of the relation of trust and confidence established *inter partes* by operation of law, and it exists regardless of the contractual obligations the lawyer may have towards the client. In sum, even where the attorney diligently carries out his or her services, he or she may be nonetheless subject to liability for (1) failing to act in the best interests of the client, (2) which failure causes damages, (3) provided that the damages and the misconduct are causally linked.

By way of example, the attorney may be liable for breach of fiduciary duty with respect to events that occur after the representation has ended. Moreover, the lawyer breaches his fiduciary duty when he or she advises a third party whose interests are in conflict with the former client's, or where the attorney discloses information relating to the representation to third parties.

In *TVGA Eng'g, Surveying, P.C. v. Gallick*,[339] plaintiff alleged that defendant attorney advised a third party whose interests where adverse to plaintiff's in matters substantially related to plaintiff's case. As relevant here, defendant moved to dismiss the breach of fiduciary duty cause of action as duplicative of the legal malpractice cause of action. The Supreme Court dismissed that branch of the complaint, and an appeal ensued.

Reversing in part, the Appellate Division explained:

> It is well settled that, where the breach of fiduciary duty cause of action arises from the same facts as the legal malpractice claim and allege[s] similar damages, the breach of fiduciary duty cause of action should be dismissed. A cause of

---

have revoked the license to use the premises for the purpose of bathing, which the ticket imported, neither proposition necessarily determines that the plaintiff was not entitled to recover damages for the indignity inflicted upon her by the revocation. We have seen that in the case of a common carrier or innkeeper, a person aggrieved may recover such damages as for a breach of contract, while on the other hand, on the breach of ordinary contracts, a party would not be so entitled, and the question is, to which class of cases the case before us most closely approximates.") (Internal citations and quotation marks omitted).

339. 846 N.Y.S.2d 506 (App. Div. 2007).

action for legal malpractice must be based on the existence of an attorney-client relationship at the time of the alleged malpractice, while a cause of action for breach of the fiduciary duty of an attorney extends both to current and former clients and thus is broader in scope than a cause of action for legal malpractice. As a result of an attorney's fiduciary duty, the attorney may not represent parties whose interests are adverse to the attorney's former clients in matters that are substantially related.

In the complaint and the exhibits attached to it, plaintiff alleges that Gallick continued to provide legal advice to Lehr after the attorney-client relationship between plaintiff and Gallick ended and that such advice was adverse to plaintiff's interests in matters that were substantially related. Thus, to the extent that Gallick's representation of Lehr continued after Gallick's representation of plaintiff ceased, the cause of action for breach of fiduciary duty arises from facts that are separate and distinct from those that form the basis of the legal malpractice cause of action, and the breach of fiduciary duty cause of action is not duplicative of the legal malpractice cause of action.[340]

b. Guardian-Ward

In a guardian-ward relationship, one party (the guardian) exerts influence and control over the other party (the ward) for the benefit of the latter. Typically, the ward is an incapacitated or otherwise impaired person who is not able to attend to his or her affairs. Accordingly, the law sets forth a mechanism through which the court may appoint an agent, that is, the guardian, who is tasked with the responsibility to take care of the ward's affairs.

For example, N.Y. MENTAL HYG. LAW § 81.02 provides:

> The court may appoint a guardian for a person if the court determines:
>
> 1. that the appointment is necessary to provide for the personal needs of that person, including food, clothing, shelter, health care, or safety and/or to manage the property and financial affairs of that person; and
>
> 2. that the person agrees to the appointment, or that the person is incapacitated as defined in subdivision (b) of this section. In deciding whether the appointment is necessary, the court shall consider the report of the court evaluator, as required in paragraph five of subdivision (c) of section 81.09 of this article, and the sufficiency and reliability of available resources, as defined in subdivision (e) of section 81.03 of this article, to provide for

---

340. *Id.* at 509–10 (internal citations and quotation marks omitted).

personal needs or property management without the appointment of a guardian. Any guardian appointed under this article shall be granted only those powers which are necessary to provide for personal needs and/or property management of the incapacitated person in such a manner as appropriate to the individual and which shall constitute the least restrictive form of intervention, as defined in subdivision (d) of section 81.03 of this article.[341]

Normally, in a guardian-ward relation, in light of the ward's disabilities or impairments, the ward (or his or her family) has no choice but to repose trust and confidence in the guardian's superior knowledge and abilities. It goes without saying, against this backdrop, the risk of abuse on the part of the guardian is great.[342] Thus, the law imposes on the guardian a strict duty to act with the utmost good faith and honor. The guardian, essentially, may not act selfishly—the ward's interests must be put first.[343]

In *Matter of Jones*,[344] the New York Supreme Court surcharged the guardian for numerous violations of the duty to act loyally. The ward was born with devastating bodily deformities and he is confined to a specially equipped wheelchair. Accordingly, the ward's living quarters needed special alterations in order to allow him to have maximum independence. At trial, the Supreme Court found, inter alia, that the guardian: (1) unbeknownst to all parties, selected a business associate of his as contractor for the ward's home-alterations project, (2) rented from his business associate an unsuitable basement apartment as temporary housing for the ward and his family, (3) caused the ward to lose his Medicaid income by improperly depositing funds into a guardianship account instead of depositing them into the supplemental needs trust, (4) failed to oversee house renovations such that the alterations actually carried out did not accommodate the ward's special needs, and (5) wasted a great amount of moneys on ill-suited renovations and expenditures.

The Supreme Court, in imposing the surcharge explained that:

---

341. N.Y. Mental Hyg. Law § 81.02 (Consol. 2019).

342. *See, for example*, Nora McL. C. v. Peggy D., 764 N.Y.S.2d 128, 128 (App. Div. 2003).

343. James MM. v. June OO., 740 N.Y.S.2d 730, 732 (App. Div. 2002) ("Law Guardian has [a] statutorily directed responsibility to represent [a] child's wishes as well as to advocate the child's best interest, and, in cases where there is a conflict between the two, the Law Guardian may advocate for the disposition that, in his or her judgment, promotes the child's best interest. . . .") (internal quotation marks and citations omitted).

344. 929 N.Y.S.2d 200 (N.Y. Sup. Ct. 2011).

The hallmarks of a fiduciary relationship are uncompromised loyalty and fidelity on the part of the fiduciary and the repose of trust on the part of the ward/beneficiary.

   . . .

Movant occupied three fiduciary positions vis a vis Roy and his estate, as trustee, as guardian, and as counsel. It has long been held that a guardian is charged with the highest possible fiduciary responsibility toward his ward and will be judged under the strictest standards. Guardianship is a trust of the most sacred character. From the guardian the law exacts absolute fidelity and will be satisfied with nothing less.

A guardian is charged with this highest fiduciary responsibility because a ward, by virtue of incapacity, is absolutely reliant upon his or her guardian. The expansive powers delegated to guardians must be exercised with the soundest of judgment and it is solely the ward's best interest that must inform that judgment.[345]

c. Trustee-Beneficiary

Now, let us briefly recall that a *trust* is an arrangement whereby the *settlor* transfers legal title to certain assets to a *trustee* who is tasked with the responsibility to take custody and administer said property for the benefit of a third party, the *beneficiary*, who, in turn, holds equitable title to the subject property.[346] Thus, under traditional law, trust property's ownership is bifurcated: legally, the trustee is the owner of the asset placed into the trust and as such may freely deal with third parties but, simultaneously, the beneficiary who holds equitable title is entitled to distributions and generally to benefit from the administration of the trust property.[347]

Obviously, given the legal structure of a trust, the trustee may be tempted to take advantage of his or her authority at the expense of the beneficiary. Indeed, as mentioned above, the trustee appears vis-à-vis the public to be the full owner of the assets being administered. Therefore, to prevent misconduct, the law directs the trustee to act loyally and in good faith: the trustee is never allowed to subordinate the beneficiaries' interests to his or her own interests.[348] As a corollary, the trustee: (1) must act impartially, (2) must not commingle trust property with

---

345. *Id.* (internal citations and quotation marks omitted).
346. Robert H. Sitkoff & Jesse Dukeminier, Wills, Trusts, and Estates Ch 6 (Wolters Kluwer Law & Business, 10th ed. 2017); Restatement (Third) of Trusts § 2 (Am. Law Inst. 2003).
347. Robert H. Sitkoff, *An Agency Costs Theory of Trust Law*, 89 Cornell L. Rev. 621 (2004).
348. Sitkoff & Dukeminier, *supra* note 346.

other property, (3) must earmark trust assets, and (4) has a duty to account to the beneficiaries.[349]

In *City Bank Farmers Tr. Co. v. Cannon*,[350] guardians ad litem for infant beneficiaries objected to an accounting filed by the trustees and moved to surcharge the trustees for breach of fiduciary duty. Objectants asserted that losses on stock held in trust were incurred after the security issuer became affiliated with the trustees. Objectants further asserted that the trustees' divided loyalties prevented them from objectively making the determination of whether to retain or sell the stock at issue.

The Court of Appeals explained:

> The standard of loyalty in trust relations does not permit a trustee to create or to occupy a position in which he has interests to serve other than the interest of the trust estate. Undivided loyalty is the supreme test, unlimited and unconfined by the bounds of classified transactions. Undivided loyalty did not exist after affiliation of the trustee and the Bank because of the ownership by the trust of the shares of the Bank. The officers of the trustee responsible for the administration of the trust were under a duty with unremitting loyalty to serve both the interest of the Trust Company and the interest of the trust estate. These were conflicting interests insofar as the trust investment in the National City Bank shares required decision whether to hold or to sell the shares in a falling market. The sale of this large number of shares might have seriously affected the interests of the Trust Company by depressing the value of these shares in a rapidly deteriorating market. Consequently the trustee had conflicting interests to serve in deciding to sell or not to sell. We do not for a moment suggest that the trustee did not act in the utmost good faith. Both courts below so found. But that is not enough for when the trustee has a selfish interest which may be served, the law does not stop to inquire whether the trustee's action or failure to act has been unfairly influenced. It stops the inquiry when the relation is disclosed and sets aside the transaction or refuses to enforce it, and in a proper case, surcharges the trustee as for an unauthorized investment. It is only by rigid adherence to these principles that all temptation can be removed from one acting as a fiduciary to serve his own interest when in conflict with the obligations of his trust. The rule is designed to obliterate all divided loyalties which may creep into a fiduciary relationship and utterly to destroy their effect by making voidable any transactions in which they appear.
>
> In continuing to act as trustee and retaining the shares, the respondent Trust Company violated the rule of undivided loyalty and is accountable for the loss

---

349. *Id.*
350. 51 N.E.2d 674 (N.Y. 1943).

on the shares unless the donor by approving the investment and its retention has estopped the guardian ad litem and the infant remaindermen he represents from objecting to the investment.[351]

However, in this case, the court overruled the objections and declined to impose the surcharge only because: "The donor approved the investments and their retention in advance with full knowledge of the resulting divided loyalty and of her own power to remove the trustee or otherwise to revoke or amend the trust and do as she pleased with these shares. . . ."[352]

d. Principal-Agent

At common law, *agency* is a fiduciary relationship whereby one party (the agent) agrees to act under the direction (and on behalf) of another party (the principal).[353] Put differently, the agent is tasked with the responsibility to represent the principal in transacting business. As such, the agent is given authority to affect the principal's rights and obligations.

Needless to say, should the agent decide to represent adverse parties in matters substantially related to one another, it would be objectively impossible for the agent to fully protect the interests of all parties contemporaneously.[354] Indeed, in such a scenario, the agent would have to be unfaithful to one of the represented parties in order to carry out the assigned task.

To safeguard the principal against any possible misuse of the agent's authority, the law imposes strict fiduciary obligations on the agent, who is required to act loyally, honorably, and in good faith. Accordingly, among other things, fiduciary law directs the agent to disclose all possible (and actual) conflicts, account for secret profits, and refrain from usurping the principal's opportunities arising from the transactions in which the agent is involved.[355]

In sum, an agent is subject to liability for breach of fiduciary duty where (1) an agent-principal relationship exists, (2) the agent acts adversely to the principal's interests, and (3) the agent acts either in bad faith or in any way inconsistent with its agency to the principal.

---

351. *Id.* at 675-76 (internal citations omitted).
352. *Id.* at 677.
353. RESTATEMENT (THIRD) OF AGENCY § 1.01 (AM. LAW INST. 2006).
354. *See, for example*, New-York Cent. Ins. Co. v. Nat'l Prot. Ins. Co., 14 N.Y. 85, 92 (N.Y. 1856).
355. *See, for example*, Murray v. Beard, 7 N.E. 553 (N.Y. 1886), *see also* Sokoloff v. Harriman Estates Dev. Corp., 754 N.E.2d 184, 189 (N.Y. 2001).

Such is the import of the case *Lamdin v. Broadway Surface Advert. Corp.*[356] In *Lamdin*, plaintiff, director of sales, sued his employer for the balance of his salary. The employer contended that plaintiff's claim should fail because he had breached his fiduciary obligations by raking secret profits while in the employ of defendant. At trial, it emerged that defendant's customers had the option of paying for services either in cash or through a so-called letter of credit. Typically, letters of credit were later converted into actual cash through a broker who would buy said letters of credit at a discounted rate. Clearly, from a business standpoint, it was in the interest of the employer to get paid in cash as compared to via letters of credit.

As it turned out, the plaintiff/employee was paid an extra commission on the side by the letter-of-credit broker. Indeed, for every letter of credit sold to the broker, the employee would be paid an extra commission. Consequently, unbeknownst to the employer, plaintiff had an incentive to act adversely to the employer's interests and pursue noncash customers.

Trial court dismissed the employee's claim and the Appellate Division reversed. On further appeal, the Court of Appeals reinstated the trial court's order, explaining:

> [O]n the whole case we are of the opinion that the plaintiff in this instance fell below the standard required by the law of one acting as an agent or employee of another. He is prohibited from acting in any manner inconsistent with his agency or trust and is at all times bound to exercise the utmost good faith and loyalty in the performance of his duties. Not only must the employee or agent account to his principal for secret profits but he also forfeits his right to compensation for services rendered by him if he proves disloyal. . . . It is an elementary principle that an agent cannot take upon himself incompatible duties, and characters, or act in a transaction where he has an adverse interest or employment. In such a case he must necessarily be unfaithful to one or the other, as the duties which he owes to his respective principals are conflicting, and incapable of faithful performance by the same person.[357]

Moreover, under New York common law, a faithless servant (or employee) who: (1) acts adversely to the principal/employer, (2) with respect to the performance of his duties, (3) in a manner that permeates the services in a material and substantial part, and (4) where such conduct substantially violated the servant's obligations, is not entitled to compensation for the services rendered.

---

356. 5 N.E.2d 66 (N.Y. 1936).
357. *Id.* at 67 (internal citations and quotation marks omitted).

If the faithless servant was paid a salary or commission, then the principal is entitled to disgorgement of said remuneration.[358] To prevail on a faithless servant theory, the principal need not show the existence of actual damages.

In *Pure Power Boot Camp, Inc. v. Warrior Fitness Boot Camp, LLC*,[359] plaintiff, a former employer, brought suit against former employees for breach of fiduciary duty. According to plaintiff, former employees attempted to divert plaintiff's clientele inter alia by (1) stealing customers' files, (2) misappropriating know-how from plaintiff, (3) disparaging plaintiff in the eyes of clients, and (4) arranging a sudden and unexpected staff shortage at plaintiff's main facility. In other words, plaintiff argued that defendants opened a competing business and, while in plaintiff's employ, carried out a number of deceptive and deceitful tactics so as to steal clients from plaintiff.

As relevant here, in finding for plaintiff, the District Court explained:

> [A]s an additional measure of compensatory damages for Defendants' breach of their duty of loyalty to Pure Power, Plaintiffs contend that, pursuant to New York's faithless servant doctrine, they are entitled to the compensation Belliard and Fell earned while working as fitness instructors at Pure Power. Unlike a traditional breach of fiduciary duty claim, which requires a showing of actual damages, to prove a violation of New York's faithless servant doctrine, an employer is not obligated to show that it suffered . . . provable damage as a result of the breach of fidelity by the agent. . . . In determining whether an employee's conduct warrants forfeiture under the faithless servant doctrine, New York courts continue to apply two alternative standards. *See* Phansalkar [v. Andersen Weinroth & Co.], 344 F.3d [184] at 200-02 [(2d Cir. 2003)]. The first standard requires that "misconduct and unfaithfulness . . . substantially violate . . . the contract of service." *Id.* at 201 (quoting Turner v. Kouwenhoven, 2 N.E. 637, 639 (N.Y. 1885)). The second standard requires only that an agent "act . . . adversely to his employer in any part of [a] transaction, or omit . . . to disclose any interest which would naturally influence his conduct in dealing with the subject of [his] employment." *Id.* (quoting Murray v. Beard, 7 N.E. 553, 554 (N.Y. 1886)).

> Here, the Court concludes that forfeiture is appropriate under either standard.[360]

---

358. Feiger v. Iral Jewelry, Ltd., 363 N.E.2d 350 (N.Y. 1977); Phansalkar v. Andersen Weinroth & Co., L.P., 344 F.3d 184, 200 (2d Cir. 2003).

359. 813 F. Supp. 2d 489 (S.D.N.Y. 2011).

360. *Id.* at 524-25 (some internal quotations marks and citations omitted).

7. Misappropriation of Trade Secrets

The law's protection of trade secrets respects the privacy of inventors. The inventor of useful information has a tort remedy against anyone who wrongfully obtains and uses the trade secret the inventor has kept secret.[361] The rights within the trade secret include the right to exclude all uses of a trade secret and give the inventor an opportunity to obtain an advantage over competitors who do not know how to use said secret.[362] The owner of a trade secret, upon establishing the elements of the tort of misappropriation of trade secrets, can recover damages and usually is also entitled to injunctive relief.[363] A party seeking a preliminary injunction must demonstrate a likelihood of success on the merits, irreparable injury absent injunctive relief, and a balancing of the equities in its favor.[364]

A trade secret cause of action is a creation of state common law, which has gradually been standardized by the adoption in some states of the Uniform Trade Secrets Act (UTSA). New York, however, has not adopted a version of the UTSA, nor does New York have a statute governing trade secrets. New York derives its definition of a trade secret from section 757 of Restatement of torts, comment b, which provides that a trade secret is any formula, pattern, device, or compilation of information that is used in one's business, and which gives him an opportunity to obtain an advantage over competitors who do not know or use it.[365] A key distinction is that New York requires that the trade secret information be in "continuous use" to qualify for protection.[366] Misappropriation consists of the use or disclosure of a trade secret that was acquired through improper means (such as theft or bribery) or by breach of confidence (such as through employment).[367]

New York uses a multifactor balancing test to determine whether information qualifies as a trade secret.[368] The Restatement suggests that in deciding a trade secret claim, the following factors should be considered: "(1) the extent to which the information is known outside of [the] business; (2) the extent to which it is known by employees and others involved in [the] business; (3) the extent of measures taken by [the business] to guard the secrecy of the information; (4) the value of the information to [the business] and [its] competitors; (5) the amount of effort

---

361. Restatement of the Law, Torts § 757, cmt. e (Am. Law Inst. 1939).
362. *Id.* at cmt. b.
363. Restatement (Second) of Torts, *supra* note 306.
364. Pearlgreen Corp. v. Yau Chi Chu, 778 N.Y.S.2d 516, 517 (App. Div. 2004).
365. Ashland Mgmt. Inc. v. Janien, 624 N.E.2d 1007, 1013 (N.Y. 1993).
366. Lehman v. Dow Jones & Co., 783 F.2d 285, 298 (2d Cir. 1986) (applying New York law).
367. Restatement (Second) of Torts § 757 (Am Law Inst. 1977).
368. New York follows Restatement (Second) of Torts (Am. Law Inst. 1979).

or money expended by [the business] in developing the information; (6) the ease or difficulty with which the information could be properly acquired or duplicated by others."[369]

To recover damages on a cause of action for misappropriation of a trade secret, the plaintiff bears the burden of proving damages. Plaintiff must prove the existence of a legally protectable trade secret, that it had been misappropriated either by improper means or a confidential relationship, and that misappropriation was caused by the defendant, which resulted in unjust gain and harm to the plaintiff. The burden of proof for damages in trade secret matters must be proven with reasonable certainty.[370]

a. Common-Law Trademark Infringement

New York recognizes a common-law trademark infringement cause of action. The elements necessary to prevail on a common-law cause of action for trademark infringement mirror the elements set forth in the Lanham Act under federal law.[371] To prevail on a common-law trademark infringement claim, a plaintiff must demonstrate that (1) it has a valid and legally protectable mark, and (2) there is a likelihood of confusion arising from the defendant's use of a similar mark.[372] In an action for trademark infringement brought pursuant to either New York[373] or federal law,[374] it is necessary to show that the defendant's use of the trademark is likely to cause confusion or mistake, or to deceive; actual confusion need not be shown.[375]

II. STATUTORY

A. Statutory Trademark Infringement

New York State has a trademark registration statute that is codified in Section 360 of Article 24 of the New York General Business Law.[376] The statute provides for

---

369. RESTATEMENT, *supra* note 306, at cmt. b; *Ashland Mgmt.*, 82 N.Y.2d at 407.

370. *See, generally, Ashland Mgmt.*, 82 N.Y.2d 395.

371. *See* FragranceNet.com. Inc. v. FragranceX.com, Inc., 493 F. Supp. 2d 545, 548 (E.D.N.Y. 2007).

372. Am. Footwear Corp. v. Gen. Footwear Co., 609 F.2d 655, 664 (2d Cir. 1979) (applying New York law).

373. N.Y. GEN. BUS. LAW § 360-k (Consol. 2018).

374. 15 U.S.C.S. § 1114(1)(a) (LexisNexis 2018).

375. Allied Maint. Corp. v. Allied Mech. Trades, Inc., 369 N.E.2d 1162, 1165 (N.Y. 1977).

376. N.Y. Gen. Bus. Law § 360 *et seq.*

registration of trademarks, service marks, certification marks, and collective marks. The mark must be in use to be eligible for registration in New York, as New York does not authorize intent to use applications.

The elements of a cause of action against a person who uses the mark without the registrant's consent pursuant to Section 360-k of Article 24 of the New York General Business statute are as follows:

> (a) use, without the consent of the registrant, any reproduction, counterfeit, copy, or colorable imitation of a mark registered under this article in connection with the sale, distribution, offering for sale, or advertising of any goods or services on or in connection with which such use is likely to cause confusion or mistake or to deceive as to the source of origin of such goods or services; or (b) reproduce, counterfeit, copy or colorably imitate any such mark and apply such reproduction, counterfeit, copy or colorable imitation to labels, signs, prints, packages, wrappers, receptacles, or advertisements intended to be used upon or in connection with the sale or other distribution in this state of such goods or services; shall be liable in a civil action by the registrant for any and all of the remedies provided in section three hundred sixty-l of this article, except that under this subdivision the registrant shall not be entitled to recover profits or damages unless the acts have been committed with the intent to cause confusion or mistake or to deceive.[377]

Remedies available for trademark infringement under the New York statute are injunctive relief, destruction of infringing products, damages and disgorgement of profits, where the infringing acts: (1) are committed with the intent to cause confusion or mistake or to deceive, or (2) consist of counterfeits or imitation.[378] Where the infringing acts were committed with knowledge or bad faith, the court has discretion to award both (1) up to three times damages and profits, and (2) reasonable attorneys' fees.[379]

1.   Confusion About a Product

A person may commit a tort by intentionally causing confusion about another's product by false or confusing statements. This can occur if one party states a product or goods or services are associated with one company while knowing it is associated with a different one.

---

377. *Id.* at § 360-k.
378. *Id.* at § 360-m.
379. *Id.* at § 360-m.

2. Injurious Falsehood

When a person makes a false statement or communication of fact to a third person that degrades the quality of another's good or services thus injuring that party and causing damage, the tort of injurious falsehood occurs. Injurious falsehood is substantiated on the matter that those who are unjustly harmed should be justly compensated.[380] One who publishes a false statement harmful to the interest of another is subject to liability for pecuniary loss if he or she (1) intends the publication of the statement to result in harm to the interests of the other having a pecuniary value, or either recognizes or should recognize that it is likely to do so; and (2) knows that the statement is false or acts in reckless disregard of its truth or falsity.[381]

To establish a cause of action for injurious falsehood, a plaintiff must demonstrate that a defendant maliciously made false statements with the intent to harm the plaintiff, or made such statements recklessly and without regard to their consequences; and that a reasonably prudent person would or should have anticipated that damage to the plaintiff would result.[382] The plaintiff must show that the defendant recognized or should have recognized the statement would cause harm.

3. Unfair Competition

Unfair competition is a blanket term that covers a variety of unfair tactics. It exists when the total impression a product gives to the consumer results in confusion as to the origin of the product. The impression of a product includes its packaging, size, shape, color, design, wording, any decorative indicia, and name. A common form is that of trademark infringement. The purpose of a trademark is to identify the maker of the product. A trademark is a word, phrase, or symbol that is used to identify a manufacturer or sponsor of a good or provider of a service.[383] It is the owner's way of preventing others from duping customers into buying a product they mistakenly believe is sponsored by the trademark owner. A trademark "inform[s] people that trademarked products come from the same source."[384]

---

380. Andrews v. Steinberg, 471 N.Y.S.2d 764, 769 (N.Y. Sup. Ct. 1983).
381. RESTATEMENT (SECOND) OF TORTS § 623A (Am. Law Inst. 1977).
382. N. State Autobahn, Inc. v. Progressive Ins. Grp. Co., 953 N.Y.S.2d 96, 107 (App. Div. 2012).
383. N.Y. GEN. BUS. LAW § 360(a) (LexisNexis 2018).
384. New Kids on the Block v. News Am. Publ'g, Inc., 971 F.2d 302, 305 n.2 (9th Cir. 1992).

B. Statutory Eviction Laws

An eviction is a court proceeding a landlord can use to evict a tenant from a rented apartment, house, condominium, or co-op. A tenant with a valid lease is protected from eviction so long as that tenant does not violate any substantial terms of the lease. In New York, a tenant can be evicted for not paying rent or violating the lease. However, a landlord must give formal notice in both regulated and unregulated apartments of their intention to obtain legal possession of the apartment. A landlord may then commence an eviction proceeding against that tenant called a summary proceeding.

There are two types of summary proceedings: (1) nonpayment proceeding and (2) holdover proceeding. A nonpayment proceeding serves to evict a tenant who fails to pay the agreed-upon rent and to recover back rent. The parties continue to have a landlord-tenant relationship and the lease is still in effect until the entry of a final judgment of possession and the issuance of a warrant of eviction, which then cancels the agreement and the landlord-tenant relationship.[385]

A rent demand is a jurisdictional condition precedent to the commencement of a nonpayment proceeding. The burden is on the landlord to prove that a proper demand for rent was made upon the tenant prior to the commencement of the nonpayment proceeding. Additionally, although an eviction terminates the landlord-tenant relationship, the parties to a lease are not foreclosed from contracting as they please. Where a lease provides that a landlord is under no duty to mitigate damages after its reentry by virtue of its successful prosecution of a summary proceeding, and that the tenant remains liable for damages, the tenant remains liable for all rent obligations arising under the lease for the balance of the contracted term.[386] Conversely, in a holdover proceeding, the relationship between the landlord and the tenant has been terminated prior to the commencement of the summary proceeding, by either the expiration of the lease or the termination of the lease based upon a tenant default. A holdover proceeding is when a tenant significantly violates a substantial obligation of the lease, either for illegal purposes or committing a nuisance, and so on, or stays beyond the lease term without permission.[387]

Landlords are prohibited from evicting tenants for retaliatory reasons, such as a tenant reporting the landlord to the housing code for violations. In many areas in New York, tenants have little protection from retaliation, especially when a landlord commences an ejectment or summary proceeding against them. Section 223-b

---

385. N.Y. Real Prop. Acts. Law. § 749(3) (LexisNexis 2018).

386. H.L. Realty, LLC v. Edwards, 15 N.Y.S.3d 413 (App. Div. 2015).

387. N.Y. Real Prop. Acts. Law § 711 (LexisNexis 2018).

of the New York Real Property Law protects tenants against retaliatory measures taken by a landlord. A tenant will prevail if the court finds that the landlord retaliated for a protected tenant act; and second, that they "would not otherwise have" commenced the action.[388] The tenant will bear the burden of proof on both of these issues. For the first element, the tenant only needs to demonstrate that he engaged in protected acts and that the landlord subsequently brought the action.[389] The second evidentiary element—retaliatory motive—will be the crucial and problematic issue in cases arising under section 223-b. The tenant must demonstrate that, *but for* their protected activities, the landlord would not have instituted the eviction proceeding.[390]

C. Americans with Disabilities Act—Federal and State

1. *Federal Statutory Framework*

The Americans with Disabilities Act (ADA) is a federal statute that prohibits discrimination on the basis of disability in employment, state and local government, public accommodations, commercial facilities, transportation, and telecommunications. The law defines the term "disability" as a person who has a physical or mental impairment that substantially limits a major life activity, has a history of such impairment, or is regarded as having such impairment.[391] The ADA is divided into several sections, or titles, each of which addresses a separate area of protection for the disabled. Title I prohibits discrimination in employment.[392] Title II prohibits discrimination against disabled individuals in connection with the provision of public services and governmental entities.[393] Title III prohibits discrimination against disabled individuals in the provision of public accommodations by various nongovernmental entities.[394] Another part of the ADA is designed to permit disabled individuals to communicate effectively using telecommunication networks.[395] Finally, there is a catchall section that contains general rules, including a provision ensuring that state and the new federal law does not preempt local laws providing greater protection to the disabled than the ADA.[396]

---

388. *Id.* § 223-b(4).
389. *Id.*
390. *Id.* (Emphasis added).
391. 42 U.S.C.S. § 12102(2) (LexisNexis 2018).
392. *Id.* §§ 12111-17.
393. *Id.* §§ 12131-65.
394. *Id.* §§ 12181-89.
395. 47 U.S.C.S. §§ 225, 611 (LexisNexis 2018).
396. 42 U.S.C. §§ 12201-12213 (LexisNexis 2018).

A plaintiff suing for disability discrimination under the ADA bears the initial burden of establishing a *prima facie* case.[397] If the plaintiff succeeds in establishing a *prima facie* case of disability discrimination, the burden shifts to the employer to demonstrate that the employee's proposed accommodation would have resulted in undue hardship.[398] The elements in proving a *prima facie* case vary based on the Title.

To establish a *prima facie* case of Title I discriminatory discharge under the ADA, an employee bears the burden of demonstrating that (1) he was an "individual who has a disability" within the meaning of the statute, (2) the employer had notice of his disability, (3) he could perform the essential functions of the job with reasonable accommodation, and (4) the employer refused to make such accommodation.[399] If the plaintiff succeeds in establishing a *prima facie* case of disability discrimination, the burden shifts to the employer to demonstrate that the employee's proposed accommodation would have resulted in undue hardship.[400]

A plaintiff states a claim for relief under Title II if he alleges: (1) that he has a qualifying disability; (2) that he is being denied the benefits of services, programs, or activities for which the public entity is responsible, or is otherwise discriminated against by the public entity; and (3) that such discrimination is by reason of his disability.[401]

To state a claim for relief under Title III, the plaintiffs must allege: (1) that they are disabled within the meaning of the ADA; (2) that defendants own, lease, or operate a place of public accommodation; and (3) that defendants discriminated against them by denying them a full and equal opportunity to enjoy the services defendants provide.[402]

2. New York State Statutory Framework

New York State disability discrimination claims are governed by the same legal standards as federal ADA claims.[403] The state has passed the New York State Human Rights Laws (NYSHRL), which are intended to safeguard workers with

---

397. Parker v. Columbia Pictures Indus., 204 F.3d 326, 332 (2d Cir. 2000).

398. *Id.*

399. *See* Stone v. City of Mount Vernon, 118 F.3d 92, 96–97 (2d Cir.1997), *cert. denied,* 522 U.S. 1112 (1998); *Parker,* 204 F.3d at 332.

400. *See Stone,* 118 F.3d at 97; *Parker,* 204 F.3d at 332.

401. Hale v. King, 642 F.3d 492, 499 (5th Cir. 2011).

402. *See* 42 U.S.C. § 12182(a); Molski v. M.J. Cable, Inc., 481 F.3d 724, 730 (9th Cir. 2007); Powell v. Nat'l Bd. of Med. Exam'rs, 364 F.3d 79, 85 (2d Cir.2004); Stan v. Wal–Mart Stores, Inc., 111 F.Supp.2d 119, 124 (N.D.N.Y.2000); Camarillo v. Carrols Corp., 518 F.3d 153, 156 (2d Cir. 2008).

403. Rodal v. Anesthesia Grp. of Onondaga, P.C., 369 F.3d 113, 117 (2d Cir. 2004).

disabilities from employment discrimination. The statute defines disability as a physical, mental, or medical impairment resulting from anatomical, physiological, genetic, or neurological conditions that prevents the exercise of a normal bodily function or is demonstrable by medically accepted clinical or laboratory diagnostic techniques or a record of such an impairment or a condition regarded by others as such an impairment.[404] This provides broader protection and allows for the impairment to be diagnosed medically or be just something that prevents a normal bodily function.[405] The ADA Amendments Act of 2008 provides a medical element "major bodily function"[406] as a subelement to the category of major life activities, which provides broader protection like that under the NYSHRL.

Additionally, the New York City Human Rights Law states that it is an unlawful discriminatory practice for an employer, because of actual or perceived disability, to refuse to hire or employ or to bar or to discharge from employment such person or to discriminate against such person in compensation or in terms, conditions, or privileges of employment.[407] It further provides that an employer bears the obligation to make reasonable accommodations to enable a person with a disability to satisfy the prerequisites of a job where the disability is known to the employer. However, it is an affirmative defense if the plaintiff could not perform the essential requisites of the job even with a reasonable accommodation.[408] The NYCHRL provides a definition for disabilities as any physical, medical, mental, or psychological impairment or a history of such impairment that includes impairment of any system of the body, and includes those who are recovering or have recovered from alcoholism, drug addiction, or other substance abuse and is currently free of such abuse.[409]

D. Racketeer Influenced and Corrupt Organizations Act—Federal and State

1. *Federal Statutory Framework*

The Racketeer Influenced and Corrupt Organizations Act[410] (RICO), is a federal statute that imposes criminal or civil liability upon those who engage in prohibited

---

404. N.Y. Exec. Law § 292 (Consol. 2018).
405. *Id.* § 292(21).
406. 122 Stat. 3553, §4(a)(3)(2) (2008).
407. N.Y.C. Civ. Rights Law § 8-107(1).
408. *Id.* § 8-107(15).
409. *Id.* § 8-107(16).
410. 18 U.S.C.S. §§ 1961 *et seq.* (LexisNexis 2018).

activities as addressed within the statute.[411] This section focuses on civil RICO liability. Section 1962(c) makes it "unlawful for any person employed by or associated with any enterprise engaged in, or the activities of which affect, interstate or foreign commerce, to conduct or participate, directly or indirectly, in the conduct of such enterprise's affairs through a pattern of racketeering activity. . . ."[412] The material elements of a civil RICO cause of action are (1) a RICO enterprise, (2) the enterprise conducted the criminal act through a pattern of racketeering activity, and (3) the existence of definitive damages.[413]

a. RICO Enterprise

With respect to the first element, a RICO "enterprise" is defined to include "any individual, partnership, corporation, association, or other legal entity, and any union or group of individuals associated in fact although not a legal entity."[414] As the Supreme Court has explained:

> The enterprise is an entity, for present purposes a group or persons associated together for a common purpose of engaging in a course of conduct . . . [It] is proved by evidence of an ongoing organization, formal or informal, and by "evidence" that the various associates function as a continuing unit . . . The enterprise is not the "pattern of racketeering activity;" it is an entity separate and apart from the pattern of activity in which it engages. The existence of an enterprise at all times remains a separate element which must be proved.[415]

Although an enterprise can be either formal or informal, there are still some organizational structure requirements: (1) the existence of a hierarchy or organizational structure of an alleged enterprise, and (2) the constituent members of the alleged enterprise must function as a unit.[416] An enterprise can be a group or individuals; however, that group or those individuals must be "associated together for a common purpose of engaging in a course of conduct."[417] The plaintiff must demonstrate that the organization contained a continuing unit that functions on

---

411. H. J. Inc. v. Northwestern Bell Tel. Co., 492 US 229, 232 (1989).

412. 18 U.S.C.S. § 1962(c) (LexisNexis 2018).

413. *Id.* §§ 1962(c) and 1964(c).

414. *Id.* § 1961(4); 101 McMurray, LLC v. Porter, No. 10-cv-9037, 2012 U.S. Dist. LEXIS 41219 (S.D.N.Y.) (March 23, 2012).

415. United States v. Turkette, 452 U.S. 576, 583 (1981); *accord,* First Capital Asset Mgmt., Inc. v. Satinwood, Inc., 385 F. 3d 159, 173 (2d Cir. 2004).

416. *See* Eaves v. Designs for Finance, Inc., 785 F. Supp. 2d 229 (S.D.N.Y. 2011).

417. *Turkette,* 452 U.S. at 583.

the basis of some framework.[418] Commissions of felonies by a group of persons with no infrastructure to assist the continuing relationship of an enterprise does not constitute an enterprise.[419] The enterprise must be separate and distinct from the pattern of activity in which it engages, but it does not have to be wholly unrelated.[420]

An association-in-fact enterprise must have a structure, comprised of at least three structural features: a purpose, relationships among those associated with the enterprise, and longevity sufficient to permit these associates to pursue the enterprise's purpose.[421] An association-in-fact enterprise is "a group of persons associated together for a common purpose of engaging in a course of conduct."[422]

The existence of an enterprise may be inferred from the evidence showing that persons associated with the enterprise engaged in a pattern of racketeering activity. As the Supreme Court has recognized, the evidence used to prove the pattern of racketeering activity and the evidence establishing an enterprise "may in particular cases coalesce."[423]

b.   Pattern of Racketeering Activity

With respect to the second element, a civil RICO claim for relief also requires that there be a "pattern of racketeering activity."[424] The "pattern of racketeering activity" element will be sustained when a defendant has conducted the activities of an enterprise "through" a pattern of racketeering activity. To satisfy this element, a plaintiff must plead facts establishing that (1) the defendant "was enabled to commit the predicate offenses <u>solely</u> by virtue of his position in the enterprise or involvement in or control over the affairs of the enterprise," or (2) "the predicate offenses are related to the activities of that enterprise."[425] A pattern of racketeering activity requires a plaintiff to plead at least two predicate acts of racketeering

---

418. Prudential Ins. Co. v. United States Gypsum, 711 F Supp. 1244 (D.N.J. 1989).

419. Robinson v. Kidder, Peabody & Co., 674 F. Supp. 243 (E.D. Mich.1987).

420. *Prudential Ins. Co.*, 711 F. Supp. 1244.

421. Boyle v. United States, 556 U.S. 938, 945–47 (2009). The Supreme Court noted, however, that "[a]lthough an association-in-fact enterprise must have these structural features, it does not follow that a district court must use the term 'structure' in its jury instructions. A trial judge has considerable discretion in choosing the language of an instruction so long as the substance of the relevant point is adequately expressed."

422. *Id.* (citing *Turkette*, 452 U.S. at 583).

423. *Id.*

424. 18 U.S.C.S § 1961(5) (LexisNexis 2018).

425. United States v. Daidone, 471 F.2d 371, 375 (2d Cir. 2006).

within ten years.[426] A "pattern" is established for RICO purposes where the predicate acts "themselves amount to, or . . . otherwise constitute a threat of *continuing* racketeering activity" and "are related."[427] The Supreme Court has explained that predicate acts extending over a few weeks or months and threatening no future criminal conduct do not satisfy the pattern requirement.[428]

A plaintiff in a RICO action must allege either an open-ended pattern of racketeering activity (i.e., past criminal conduct coupled with a threat of future criminal conduct) or a closed-ended pattern of racketeering activity (i.e., past criminal conduct extending over a substantial period of time).[429] Courts have held that two years is a minimum duration for closed-ended continuity, but the "mere fact that predicate acts span two years is insufficient, without more to support a finding of a closed-ended pattern."[430] "Courts have uniformly and consistently held that schemes involving a single, narrow purpose and one or few participants directed towards a single victim do not satisfy the RICO requirement of a closed or open pattern of continuity."[431]

Alleged RICO schemes involving a single victim and a natural termination point—such as a single real estate deal—establish neither the "open-ended" or "closed-ended" continuity necessary to allege a "pattern."[432]

"Courts have imposed a heightened pleading requirement on RICO claims because such assertion has been found to be an unusually potent weapon—the litigation equivalent of a thermonuclear device."[433] A plaintiff must plead the alleged predicate acts with particularity.[434] [A]ll of the concerns that dictate that fraud be

---

426. 18 U.S.C.S. § 1961(5) (LexisNexis 2018).

427. H.J. Inc. v. Northwestern Bell Tel. Co., 492 U.S. 229, 239–240 (1989).

428. *Id.* at 240–241.

429. *First Capital Asset Mgmt., Inc.,* 385 F. 3d at 180.

430. *Id.* at 181.

431. Evercrete Corp. v. H-Cap Ltd., 429 F. Supp. 2d 612, 624–625 (S.D.N.Y. 2006).

432. United States v. Aulcino, 44 F. 3d 1102, 113 (2d Cir. 1995) (No pattern alleged where "a defendant had a piece of property the sale of which, even if by fraudulent means, provide a natural end to his project."); Bernstein v. Misk, 948 F. Supp. 228, 237 (E.D.N.Y. 1997) (Alleged acts of mail and wire fraud committed in connection with an isolated real estate venture which has been, or will be terminated, posed no threat of continued criminal conduct); Gross v. Waywell, 628 F. Supp. 2d 475, 494 (S.D.N.Y. 2009) (Allegations of RICO violations involving "a limited number of participants or victims, a discrete scheme with a narrow purpose or a single property . . . are generally insufficient to demonstrate closed-ended continuity.")

433. Krog Corp. v. Vanner Grp., Inc., 52 Misc. 3d 1225(A) (Cnty. Ct. 2016); *see* Besicorp Ltd. v. Kahn, 736 N.Y.S.2d 708, 712 (App. Div. 2002).

434. *Besicorp Ltd.,* 736 N.Y.S.2d at 713.

pleaded with particularity exist with even greater urgency in civil RICO actions.[435] "[T]he complaint [must] specify the statements it claims were false or misleading, give particulars as to the respect in which plaintiff . . . contend[s] the statements were fraudulent, state when and where the statements were made, and identify those responsible for the statements," as well as "allege facts that give rise to a strong inference of fraudulent intent."[436]

"A claim of . . . wire fraud must specify the content, date, and place of any alleged misrepresentations and the identity of the persons making them . . . [t]he cases are legion that a RICO complaint cannot be predicated on innocuous business communications, absent some factual basis for inferring the sender's intent to defraud the recipient via a scheme to defraud."[437]

c.   Definitive Injury

With respect to the third element of the federal statute, RICO limits a private civil action to any "person injured in his business or property by reason of a violation of section 1962 of the chapter."[438] The Second Circuit has held that, ". . . as a general rule, a cause of action does not accrue under RICO until the amount of damages becomes clear and definite."[439]

2.   *New York State Civil Forfeiture Statutory Framework*

a.   CPLR Article 13-A

Article 13-A of the New York Civil Practice Law and Rules provides a statutory mechanism for civil forfeiture.[440] Civil forfeiture involves the state's seizure of property without compensation because of the conviction and commission of a crime. The civil forfeiture of property under Article 13-A is predicated on the commission of a "specified felony offense" as set forth in and defined at CPLR Section 1310 (4-b).[441] An action under CPLR Article 13-A is typically brought by a "claiming authority" to recover property that constitutes the proceeds or

---

435. Plount v. Am. Home assurance Co., 668 F. Supp. 204, 206 (S.D.N.Y. 1987).
436. Moore v. PaineWebber, Inc., 189 F.3d 165, 173 (2d Cir. 1999).
437. Cont'l Kraft Corp. v. Euro-Asia Dev. Grp., Inc., No. 97-CV-0619, 1997 U.S. Dist. LEXIS 14672, at **12-14 (E.D.N.Y. Sept. 8, 1997).
438. 18 U.S.C.S. § 1964(c) (LexisNexis 2018).
439. First Nationwide Bank v. Gelt Funding Corp., 27 F.3d 763, 768 (2d Cir. 1994), *cert. denied*, 513 U.S. 1079 (1995).
440. CPLR § 1310 *et seq.*
441. *Id.* at § 1310(4-b).

substituted proceeds of a crime against a "criminal defendant" or "non-criminal defendant."[442]

To prevail on a "pre-conviction forfeiture crime" cause of action for civil forfeiture under CPLR Section 1311(b) the claiming authority must (1) obtain a felony conviction, (2) prove by a preponderance of the evidence that the property that is the subject of the action constitutes the proceeds or substituted proceeds of the defendants' criminal acts, and (3) prove by a preponderance of the evidence that defendants knew or should have known that the proceeds were obtained through the commission of a crime or that they fraudulently obtained their interest in the proceeds as part of a scheme to avoid forfeiture.[443]

(1)   Felony Conviction

To establish the first element, if the action is not grounded upon the conviction of a pre-conviction forfeiture crime, "it shall be necessary in the action for the claiming authority to prove the commission of a pre-conviction forfeiture crime by clear and convincing evidence."[444] The issuance of a prior preliminary injunction under Article 13-A which restrained the use of the criminal defendants assets, has been held to be sufficient proof to establish the first element.[445]

(2)   The Property

The second element—proceeds or substituted proceeds of a crime—requires the claiming authority to demonstrate that the defendant has some forfeitable interest in the property to be recovered.[446] Proceeds of a crime are defined as property obtained through the commission of certain specified felonies, including any appreciation in the value of such property.[447] Substituted proceeds of a crime are defined as property obtained by the sale or exchange of proceeds of a crime, and any gain realized by such sale or exchange.[448] The claiming authority must establish that the property is the proceeds or substituted proceeds of a crime by a preponderance of the evidence.[449]

---

442. *Id.* at §§ 1310 and 1311.
443. Morgenthau v. A.J. Travis Ltd., 708 N.Y.S.2d 827 (N.Y. Sup. Ct. 2000).
444. CPLR § 1311(b).
445. *Morgenthau*, 708 N.Y.S.2d 827.
446. Dillon v. Hawthorne, 526 N.Y.S.2d 733 (Cnty. Ct. 1988).
447. CPLR § 1310(2).
448. *Id.* at § 1310(3).
449. *Morgenthau*, 708 N.Y.S.2d 827.

(3) Defendant's Knowledge

The third element—knowledge that the proceeds were obtained by the commission of a crime or fraudulently obtained interest—may be established by relying upon "badges of fraud."[450] Badges of fraud are circumstances so commonly associated with fraudulent transfers that their presence gives rise to an inference of intent.[451] These circumstances include a close relationship between the parties, inadequacy of consideration, retention of control of the property after the conveyance and intra-family transfers made without any signs of tangible consideration.[452] A defendant's diversion of assets when engaged in a criminal enterprise has been held to be a knowing participation in a scheme to avoid maintaining accounts that could have been attached.[453]

b. CPLR Article 13-B

Article 13-B of the CPLR provides for certain additional civil remedies for enterprise corruption. The provisions of Article 13-B involve a separate civil proceeding from Article 13-A, the purpose of which is to sever the connection of the defendant from the enterprise by means of certain specified injunctive relief set forth at CPLR Section 1353.[454]

---

450. *Id.*
451. *Id.*
452. *Id.*
453. *Id.*
454. CPLR § 1353 *et seq.*

5 | Use of Burden of Proof in Discovery

OUTLINE

INTRODUCTION

Discovery is the stage of litigation at which you discover the other side's contentions and proof. It is also the stage where you establish what your proof is going to be on your cause of action or defense. In essence, you are lining up your proof and seeing what the other side has. Success—or failure—in an action can hinge on a party's discovery plan. This stage of litigation, like all the others, is extremely well suited to marry the concepts of the burden of proof and discovery.

What must you discover during discovery? Simply stated, a lawyer must discover (and catalogue) what evidence exists for each element of the causes of action and each element of any affirmative defenses that have been raised in the complaint. As a best practice, a litigator should actually begin to make lists and file folders full of evidence on each cause of action or affirmative defense. Most fact patterns end up being chronological or transactional. That is to say, fact patterns develop either in a strict chronological manner or by transaction. For example, a breach of contract cause of action would be *chronological*:

- Day 1: You sign the contract.
- Day 20: The goods are delivered.
- Day 60: There is an objection to the quality of the goods.
- Day 65: There is a demand letter.

A real estate closing would be *transactional*—the real estate deed closes today, the title report shows there are defects in the title, the transaction cannot close, and the parties sue each other.

During discovery, a litigator should first focus on the elements of the cause of action or defense, together with facts that can be used against the other side, such as dishonesty, character flaws, or anything else that could be useful in a courtroom (because, absent summary judgment, that is ultimately where the case is heading). When asking for discovery, a litigator should *only* request items related to his own burden of proof and the adversary's burden of proof.

Motion practice concerning discovery issues, therefore, is often an integral part of a successful litigation plan. As a result, the successful attorney must consider the burdens of proof related to various discovery motions. The type of burden will vary depending on the nature and substance of the motion sought in connection with discovery.

An underlying burden on any discovery motion is compliance with the court's rules. For example, Sections 202.7(a) and (c) of the Uniform Rules for the New York State Trial Courts requires the submission of a "good faith" affirmation setting forth that counsel has conferred with opposing counsel in a good faith effort to resolve the issues at hand, along with details surrounding their communication. It is important for a practicing attorney to diligently check all of the rules of the court pertaining to discovery and discovery motions, including the rules of the particular judge assigned to the case.

Judges may also institute their own rules requiring premotion conferences, letters, and calls to chambers, as well as other pretrial practices. For example, some judges require a premotion letter and/or conference before a party makes any discovery-related motion.[1]

An attorney cannot possibly succeed on a discovery motion without complying with all of the court's rules, including the judge's rules.[2] Complying with such rules should be considered an element of making the motion, along with the other elements necessary to satisfy the applicable burden of proof.

I. PICKING THE RIGHT DISCOVERY DEVICE FOR THE BURDEN OF PROOF

Effectively planning a discovery strategy is key to successful litigation practice. When the litigator has planned ahead, determined whether his case is transactional or chronological, and has thoroughly researched his client's and his adversary's burden of proof, the litigator knows what kinds of documents and testimony he needs to obtain. Specifically, tailored document demands directed to a party, coupled with depositions seeking only the testimony relevant to establish the litigator's causes of action or defenses, should enable the litigator to obtain the documents and testimony that he has determined he needs. The litigator may determine that a nonparty is in possession, custody or control of the documents or information he desires—in such case, nonparty discovery will also be warranted.

Focused on Article 31 of the New York Civil Practice Law and Rules (CPLR), the litigator is armed with an arsenal of devices to utilize to obtain those documents and information he has determined necessary to his action—depositions upon oral questions, depositions upon written questions (without the state), interrogatories, demands for addresses, discovery and inspection of documents or property, physical and mental examinations of persons, and requests for admissions.[3] Additionally, the litigator has a tool under CPLR §§ 3120 and 2305 to subpoena a nonparty for records and compel the nonparty to testify at a deposition.[4] However,

---

1. *See, for example*, STATE OF NEW YORK UNIFIED COURT SYSTEM, RULES OF THE JUSTICES 43 (2020), https://www.nycourts.gov/LegacyPDFS/courts/1jd/supctmanh/Uniform_Rules.pdf (last visited February 22, 2020).
2. *See, for example*, Congregation Beth Shalom of Kingsbav v. Yaakov, 13 N.Y.S.3d 518, 520 (App. Div. 2015) (noting that the New York Supreme Court was correct in denying party's motion to strike for failure to "submit an affirmation of good faith pursuant to 22 NYCRR 202.7(a)(2)").
3. CPLR § 3102(a).
4. Note, however, that a subpoena directed to a person who does not reside in the State of New York in an action pending in the State of New York will not be effective to compel the production

these requests cannot be overly broad under CPLR § 3120 and must be pled with reasonable specificity.[5]

A.   Obtaining Discovery from Parties

When addressing the use of discovery devices to obtain information from the other party, the burden of proof is arguably the greatest consideration. Naturally, the more information gathered at this stage of litigation from parties the greater the likelihood of success at trial, or even avoiding trial by a motion for summary judgment.

CPLR § 3101(a) requires "full disclosure" between parties "of all matter[s] *material and necessary* to the prosecution or defense of an action, *regardless of the burden of proof.*"[6] This means any and all information that is useful, within the realm of reason to request, and is "sufficiently related to the issues 'which will assist preparation for trial by sharpening the issues and reducing delay and prolixity'," must be disclosed by either side.[7] However, under CPLR §§ 3101(b) and (c), respectively, any privileged matter or attorney work-product is not subject to discovery. In determining what is *material and necessary*, the court has broad discretion.[8] Naturally, as what may constitute material and necessary can vary broadly depending on the claims at issue, satisfaction of the term is determined on a case-by-case basis, as illustrated by some of the cases below. Additionally, although parties are free to choose their own discovery devices, courts have held that, in general, "a party must complete one discovery device before invoking [another]."[9]

As noted above, and pursuant to CPLR § 3102(a), the available "disclosure devices" are depositions, interrogatories, demands for addresses, discovery and

---

of things or testimony. *See* N.Y. Jud. Law § 2-b. For a discussion on obtaining disclosure for an out-of-state nonparty, *see* the discussion that follows in section I.C.

5. Julius Blum, Inc. v. Allied Hardware, Inc., 655 N.Y.S.2d 594, 594 (App. Div. 1997) (using the term "reasonable particularity").

6. Emphasis added.

7. Brooks v. Hausauer, 379 N.Y.S.2d 306, 307 (App. Div. 1976) (quoting Allen v. Crowell-Collier Publ'g Co., 235 N.E.2d 430, 432 (N.Y. 1968)).

8. Manhattan Med. Imaging PC v. State Farm Ins. Co., No. 022680/07, 2007 N.Y. Misc. LEXIS 8567, at * 4 (Civ. Ct. Nov. 15, 2007) ("There are many circumstances where it is necessary to balance the need for information to establish a claim or a defense against the burdens of providing the requested information. In this regard, CPLR § 3103(a) provides that '[t]he court may at any time on its own initiative' limit, condition or regulate the use of any discovery device to 'prevent unreasonable annoyance, expense, embarrassment, disadvantage, or other prejudice.'").

9. Zlatnick v. Gov't Emps. Ins. Co., 768 N.Y.S.2d 582, 586 (Civ. Ct. 2003).

inspection of documents or property, physical and mental examinations of persons, and requests for admissions. Each will be discussed in turn.

1. Depositions

A deposition is the under-oath, out-of-court testimony of a witness. Like a trial, the questions and responses of the attorney and witness are memorialized by a certified court reporter. CPLR §§ 3106–3117 and 3119 govern the rules on depositions. Generally, a party must answer deposition questions that are given within reason. Importantly, an adverse party's deposition can always be used at trial.[10] However, more important than using a deposition as a discovery tactic, are the types of questions an attorney will ask of the deposed party.

Notwithstanding advising the witness of her duty to tell the truth, and general procedural preparation, background questions are addressed first. After preliminary instructions and information are completed, the lawyer then asks more fact-based questions at the heart of the claim(s). Questions should focus on obtaining knowledge about each and every fact the other side could possibly use against your client and each and every fact your client knows.[11] This not only helps you build your case or find weaknesses in the other side's argument, but also allows the possibility to use deposition testimony in the future to supplement a motion for summary judgment. "[T]he standard governing the appropriate scope of questioning at a deposition is not based on admissibility at trial, but on whether the questioning relates to the controversy and will assist in trial preparation."[12]

An example of how to use deposition questions skillfully is set forth in *Quinones v. Caballero*.[13] The case dealt with a minor's capacity to use a deposition for summary judgment purposes, but the principle behind it focused on the burden of proof. In this case the deposition testimony of a twelve-year-old girl helped win her case. The case dealt with a suit to recover personal injury damages among other damages resulting from the young girl's fall on defendant's snow-covered sidewalk.[14] When the defendant could not recall whether or not snow removal services were implemented at the site of her fall, the plaintiff's sworn deposition

---

10. CPLR § 3117(a).

11. T. Jeff Wray, Depositions That Win Cases: A Defense Perspective 71, https://www .americanbar.org/content/dam/aba/events/labor_law/basics_papers/elst/wray.authcheckdam.pdf (last visited Dec. 4, 2018).

12. Hildebrandt v. Stephan, 978 N.Y.S.2d 774, 779 (Sup. Ct. 2013).

13. 802 N.Y.S.2d 831 (Sup. Ct. 2005).

14. *Id.* at 833.

testimony was used for summary judgment on this "undisputed evidence" that the sidewalk at the time of her fall was covered in snow.[15] The relevant portion of the deposition was as follows:

> Q. When you got out of school that day, was it still snowing or had it stopped?
> A. It was still snowing. (Affirmation of Keith E. Ford, exhibit D, at 18.)

✳ ✳ ✳ ✳ ✳

> Q: Let's go back to when you were walking to school. It wasn't snowing out then?
> A: No. (*Id.* at 12.)
> Q: When you were walking to school that morning, did you walk over the area where you fell later that day?
> A: No, 'cause it was covered with snow . . .
> Q: You indicated there were parts where the snow was pushed away.
> A: In the middle was like a skinny part in the middle you could walk through.
> Q: Like a path?
> A: Yes.
> Q: Was that path in the area where you fell?
> A: No. (*Id.* at 15–16.)[16]

Undoubtedly, the lawyer's understanding of which questions to ask (and how they addressed the material elements of each cause of action) played a part in the plaintiff's success.

2.   Interrogatories

CPLR §§ 3130–3133 discuss the use, scope, and service of interrogatories. In general, "any party may serve upon any other party written interrogatories."[17] Normally, interrogatories are answered by a client in conjunction with their counsel.[18] Answers to interrogatories are nonbinding but they can be used as admissions in evidence.[19] Additionally, interrogatories are to be answered "[w]ithin twenty days

---

15. *Id.* at 838.
16. *Id.* at 834.
17. CPLR § 3130(1).
18. CPLR § 3130 (Advisory Committee Notes).
19. *Id.*

after service," unless a party objects.[20] In the event of an objection, a party must specify the grounds for the objection.[21]

In contrast to depositions, interrogatories are limited in their use.[22] They are impermissible in wrongful death actions "predicated solely" on negligence,[23] and medical malpractice.[24] They are, however, allowed in strict products liability cases.[25]

Choosing and forming questions is vital in establishing the burden of proof for your causes of action. In line with CPLR § 3101, the information requested from interrogatories must be "material and necessary" to the claim, which varies depending on the claim at issue. For example, in *Allen v. Crowell-Collier Publishing Company*, an older New York Court of Appeals case, the cause of action was based on retirement and severance pay.[26] The plaintiffs, who were discharged company nonunion employees, sought information regarding the company's retirement and severance pay practices.[27] The plaintiffs submitted interrogatories seeking information, among other things, about the company's past and current practices regarding retirement and severance pay at the defendant's various plants and offices.[28] The reasoning behind this questioning concerned uniformity of these forms of payment among the plants to determine whether or not union and nonunion employees were treated differently.[29] The defendants contended these interrogatories were *not* "material or necessary" within the meaning of CPLR § 3103, but the court disagreed.[30] The court held that the term "material and necessary" was not synonymous with "indispensable," rather noting the test was one of "usefulness and reason," and was to be interpreted liberally to require disclosure."[31] In this case, the plaintiffs'

---

20. CPLR § 3133(a).

21. *Id.*

22. CPLR § 3130(a).

23. *Id.; Compare* Allen v. Minskoff, 344 N.E.2d 386, 389 (N.Y. 1976) (holding interrogatories under CPLR 3130 are prohibited) *with* Rothholz v. Chrysler Corp., 309 N.Y.S.2d 834, 837 (Sup. Ct. 1970) (disallowing the use of interrogatories in a wrongful death action under CPLR § 3120, however allowing interrogatories pursuant to other claims in the case because statutory preclusion as to those claims not identified).

24. CPLR § 3130(a); *for example*, Josephson v. Cohen, 395 N.Y.S.2d 84, 84 (App. Div. 1997) (citing statutory provision).

25. CPLR § 3130(a); *for example*, Ribley v. Harsco Corp., 394 N.Y.S.2d 740, 741 (Sup. Ct. 1977) (holding interrogatories for strict products liability are not prohibited under CPLR § 3130).

26. 235 N.E.2d 430 (N.Y. 1968).

27. *Id.* at 431.

28. *Id.*

29. *Id.*

30. *Id.*

31. *Id.* at 432.

information request was "material and necessary to the prosecution of their action"—knowing whether or not the defendant's severance pay practices were effective at the time of their employment.[32] Additionally, with the defendant not maintaining burdensome or privileged information, the court found that this information required answers as the complaint stated the defendant "established and announced" its policies.[33]

3.   Demand for Addresses

CPLR § 3118 is relatively succinct, stating:

> A party may serve on any party a written notice demanding a verified statement setting forth the post office address and residence of the party, of any specified officer or member of the party and of any person who possessed a cause of action or defense asserted in the action which has been assigned. The demand shall be complied with within ten days of its service.

This discovery device is fairly straightforward. Importantly, the "[t]he demand should not be used in a burdensome or harassing manner."[34] If a party does not comply with this request when all procedural guidelines are followed, a motion to compel can be used to disclose this information.[35] For a discussion on motions to compel, see section II.A of this chapter.

4.   Request for Production of Documents

CPLR § 3120 governs the "[d]iscovery and production of documents and things for inspection, testing, copying or photographing." Notably, electronic documents and ESI—electronically stored information—are included in this provision as well.[36] Like other discovery devices, the burden of proof standard under CPLR § 3120 is "material and necessary." In contrast, due to recent changes made to the Preamble, under the Commercial Division Rules, which applies in certain cases, the burden of proof is "proportionality."[37]

---

32. *Id.* at 433.
33. *Id.*
34. Weinstein, Korn & Miller, CPLR Manual § 20.14 (David L. Ferstendig ed., LexisNexis Matthew Bender).
35. *Id.*
36. Delta Fin. Corp. v. Morrison, 819 N.Y.S.2d 908, 912 (Sup. Ct. 2006) (holding both current and deleted electronic documents are subject to discovery).
37. 22 NYCRR 202.70(g) (Preamble).

Notwithstanding certain procedural requirements for service and description in the statute, subsection 1 of CPLR § 3120 provides:

1. After commencement of an action, *any party may serve on any other party a notice* or on any other person a subpoena duces tecum:
    (i) to produce and permit the party seeking discovery, or someone acting on his or her behalf, to inspect, copy, test or photograph any designated documents or any things which are in the possession, custody or control of the party or person served; or
    (ii) to permit entry upon designated land or other property in the possession, custody or control of the party or person served for the purpose of inspecting, measuring, surveying, sampling, testing, photographing or recording by motion pictures or otherwise the property or any specifically designated object or operation thereon.

When it comes to the production of these documents, both parties—the party seeking document production and the party opposing its production—have respective burdens. As a general rule:

the party seeking the production of documents has the burden of establishing that the production of the demanded material will lead to the discovery of *evidence relevant to the case* while the party opposing discovery has the burden of establishing that the material is *irrelevant, privileged and/or confidential.*[38]

Unsurprisingly, the former portion of this principle alludes to the language in CPLR § 3101(a) and the latter portion of this principle goes hand in hand with the exceptions laid out in CPLR §§ 3101(b) and (c). Notably, a majority of the cases dealing with this discovery device concern a motion to compel demonstrating these documents are in fact relevant and necessary.[39] For a general discussion on motions to compel, see section II.A of this chapter.

---

38. Lipco Elec. Corp. v. ASG Consulting Corp., No. 8775/01, 2004 N.Y. Misc. LEXIS 1337, at *10 (Sup. Ct. Aug. 18, 2004) (emphasis added).

39. *See, for example*, MBIA Ins. Corp. v. Countrywide Home Loans, Inc., 895 N.Y.S.2d 643, 648 (Sup. Ct. 2010) (denying lender's motion to compel in a mortgage action, noting "[m]erely because discovery might be relevant does not consequently entitle [a party] to that discovery"); Home Equity Mortg. Tr. Series 2006-5 v. DLJ Mortg. Capital, Inc., No. 653787/2012, 156016/2012, 2012 N.Y. Misc. LEXIS 3441, at *9 (Sup. Ct. July 28, 2014) (denying defendant's motion to compel "Directing Certificate holders' investment strategies" because defendant's demand was irrelevant for the breach of contract claim).

5. *Request for Physical (or Mental) Examinations*

Physical and mental examinations are also permissible. Under CPLR § 3121, requests are only granted when "the mental or physical condition or the blood relationship of a party, or of an agent, employee or person in the custody or under the legal control of a party, is *in controversy*."[40] A condition is placed in controversy when a party "affirmatively asserts the condition either by way of counterclaim or to excuse the conduct complained of by the plaintiff."[41] "The initial burden of proving that a party's physical condition is *in controversy* is on the party seeking the information and it is only after such an evidentiary showing that discovery may proceed under the statute."[42] Like other discovery devices discussed, whether or not a mental or physical condition is placed in controversy is determined by the factual circumstances. For example, *Cannistra v. County of Putnam* was a personal injury case where the defendant failed to remember certain circumstances surrounding the accident that took place.[43] The Supreme Court of New York, Appellate Division, Second Department, held that the defendant did not put his physical condition in controversy.[44]

In contrast, in *Constatine v. Diello*, the court held the driver's physical condition, namely his eyesight, was in controversy.[45] The administratrix in this case appealed the lower court's decision vacating her notice for the defendant's eye examination.[46] The Appellate Division, Fourth Department, overturned the decision, holding the administratrix's proof sufficient establishing that the defendant driver's eye condition was placed in controversy.[47] This case dealt with the decedent's administratrix alleging the intestate's death was caused by the driver hitting the deceased while the deceased was walking or running across a highway.[48] At the hearing, the driver testified that his view was unobstructed and that the accident happened in daylight.[49] An eye test taken at the hearing revealed the driver's vision was impaired.[50] The court noted:

> The requirement of CPLR 3121 (subd. [a]) that the examination be allowed only
> if the physical condition of the party is in controversy does not, of course, mean

---

40. Emphasis added.
41. Cannistra v. Cty. of Putnam, 526 N.Y.S.2d 841, 842 (App. Div. 1988).
42. Dillenbeck v. Hess, 536 N.E.2d 1126, 1131–32 (N.Y. 1989).
43. *Cannistra,* 526 N.Y.S.2d at 842.
44. *Id.*
45. 264 N.Y.S.2d 153, 155 (App. Div. 1965).
46. *Id.* at 154.
47. *Id.* at 155.
48. *Id.* at 154.
49. *Id.*
50. *Id.* at 155.

that the movant must prove his case on the merits in order to meet the requirements for a physical examination but he must *produce sufficient information to satisfy the court* that such condition is in controversy.[51]

In this case, the sufficient information was the results at the hearing. In contrast, in the personal injury case, the presumably insufficient information was the defendant's inability to recall the events that took place. Therefore, as with much of the language concerning discovery, it seems that "sufficient information" is a term to be determined based on specific facts and circumstances.

6. Request for Admissions

CPLR § 3123 governs requests for admissions. The goal of admissions is "to avoid the time and expense involved in calling witnesses to prove facts over which there can be no reasonable dispute."[52] The scope of requests is usually kept to those pieces of information that are "easily provable" and "uncontroverted."[53] Requests for admission may not be used by a party in lieu of other discovery devices and "may not be employed to request admission of material issues or ultimate or conclusory facts."[54] Unlike a pleading, a request for admission is only deemed admitted "for the purpose of the pending action."[55] If a party does not reasonably answer the requests for admission, penalties can be imposed.[56] For a general discussion of penalties, see section II of this chapter.

An attorney has a variety of discovery devices available to obtain information from parties. Due their use limitations in some circumstances, an attorney must be savvy when choosing discovery device(s) to use to obtain relevant information that will inevitably help in establishing the elements of the causes of action for summary judgment and trial.

B. New York Commercial Division Rules

By way of background, the Commercial Division rules apply to a certain subsection of cases, as identified in Section 22 of the New York Codes, Rules and Regulations

---

51. *Id.* (emphasis added).
52. CPLR § 3123 (Expert commentary notes).
53. Meadowbrook-Richman, Inc. v. Cicchiello, 709 N.Y.S.2d 521, 522 (App. Div. 2000).
54. Lewis v. Hertz Corp., 597 N.Y.S.2d 368, 369 (App. Div. 1993).
55. CPLR § 3123(b).
56. *Id.* § 3123(c).

(NYCRR) 202.70. These include cases with varying monetary thresholds, ranging from $50,000 to $500,000, depending on the county and where certain "principal claims involve or consist of" a myriad of disputes, among them breach of contract, *Uniform Commercial Code* transactions, or commercial real property transactions.[57] Furthermore, certain cases, such as those involving landlord-tenant matters, are barred from being heard by the Commercial Division, irrespective of the monetary threshold.[58]

In December 2015, the Federal Rules of Civil Procedure (Rules 26(b)(1) and 37(e)) were amended to introduce and highlight the importance of proportionality.[59] Parallel amendments were made at state levels. In New York, "proportionality" in discovery was recognized by an amendment to the Preamble of the Commercial Rules effective December 1, 2015.[60] Specifically, in New York the goal was to "thwart abuse specifically in ESI" and "emphasize the applicability of the proportionality standard in all discovery matters."[61] Although comments from The City Bar expressed concern about the insufficient definition of "proportionality,"[62] ultimately the proposed change was adopted.[63] However, proportionality was not per se a new introduction to the Commercial Division Rules. Proportionality was previously adopted "as a guide in managing electronic discovery."[64] In pertinent part, the Preamble now reads: "The Commercial Division is mindful [of the need to] encourage proportionality in discovery[.]"[65]

---

57. 22 N.Y. C.R.R. § 202.70(a) (Consol. 2018) [hereinafter NYCRR].

58. *Id.* § 202.70(c).

59. American Bar Association, The 2015 Amendments to the FRCP, Part II: Rule 26, Proportionality, Judicial Intervention, and Mastering the Discovery Juggernaut 7–8 (2015), https://www.americanbar.org/content/dam/aba/multimedia/cle/materials/2016/01/ce1601frc.authcheckdam.pdf (last visited Dec. 4, 2018).

60. Ira B. Warshawsky, *The Rules of The Commercial Division – an Overview of Changes Throughout the Last Decade, Part 1, National Arbitration and Mediation*, Nat'l Arb. & Mediation (Nov. 2016), https://www.namadr.com/publications/the-rules-of-the-commercial-division-an-overview-of-changes-throughout-the-last-decade-part-1/.

61. William Gyves, *Host of Rule Changes Go into Effect Today in the New York Commercial Division*, Kelley Drye (Dec. 1, 2015), https://www.kelleydrye.com/News-Events/Publications/Client-Advisories/Host-of-Rule-Changes-Go-Into-Effect-today-in-the-N.

62. N.Y. City Bar, Report by The Council on Judicial Administration, Committee on State Courts of Superior Jurisdiction and Committee on Litigation: Comments on Pending Proposals From the Commercial Division Advisory Council (2015), https://www2.nycbar.org/pdf/report/uploads/20072926-CommentsonPendingProposalsfromtheCommercialDivisionAdvisoryCouncil.pdf (last visited Dec. 4, 2018).

63. Warshawsky, *supra* note 60.

64. Gyves, *supra* note 61.

65. 22 NYCRR § 202.70(g).

In 2016, *Ambac Assurance Corp. v. First Franklin Financial Corporation* referenced the adoption of this new standard in the Commercial Division Rules.[66] This case dealt with fraudulent inducements regarding residential mortgage backed securities.[67] The defendants in this case moved to compel the plaintiffs "to produce documents related to Ambac's loss mitigation activity," which Ambac opposed.[68] Referencing CPLR § 3101(a) regarding the motion to compel case, the court touched upon underlying "material and necessary" burden of proof standard.[69] The court then went on to discuss the defendant's specific discovery request, which dealt with ESI. Discussing relevant cases and the material and necessary standard yet again, the court went on to conclude:

> Defendants' concede that if this court were to grant their discovery request into all of Ambac's transactions, which number in the many hundreds, that they will likely assert that Ambac should have invested its money differently so as to purchase additional First Franklin bonds. [. . .] This would lead to multiple minitrials in order to determine the reasonableness of the loss mitigation strategy used for each of the transactions that Ambac engaged in. This type of inquiry is not material and necessary as to whether Ambac's loss mitigation strategies were reasonable in this particular Transaction. *Nor are these requests within the spirit of the commercial rules which encourage "proportionality in discovery" to effectively resolve matters.*[70]

Indeed, proportionality "has become the new black."[71]

For a discussion of proportionality in nonparty discovery, *see* sections I.C and D of this chapter.

C. Obtaining Discovery from Nonparties

What needs to occur when an attorney reasonably believes that an outside person, or "nonparty" to the subject action possesses information that is material to either his or her prosecution or defense of a case? CPLR § 3101(a)(4) allows for a party

---

66. *See* section II.C of this chapter where this case is used as an illustration.
67. Ambac Assurance Corp. v. First Franklin Fin. Corp., No. 651217/2012, 2016 N.Y. Misc. LEXIS 2592, at *1 (Sup. Ct. July 8, 2016).
68. *Id.*
69. *Id.* at 4–10.
70. *Id.* at 10–11 (emphasis added).
71. Vaigasi v. Solow Mgmt. Corp., No. 11 Civ. 5088 (RMB) (HBP) 2016 U.S. Dist. LEXIS 18460, at *41 (S.D.N.Y. Feb. 16, 2016).

to seek information from nonparties that may have such pertinent information. Specifically, CPLR § 3101(a)(4) states:

> Generally, there shall be full disclosure of all matter material and necessary in the prosecution or defense of an action, regardless of the burden of proof; by (4) any other person, upon notice stating the circumstances or reasons such disclosure is sought or required.

Although parties to a cause of action do not require the issuance of a subpoena to compel testimony or document requests, nonparty witness information is secured through the use of subpoenas during the discovery phase. CPLR §2301, which governs the relevant scope of the request to a party, lists two primary types of subpoenas: (1) a subpoena that requests the presence of a party to testify either in a trial or deposition setting, also known more formally as a *subpoena ad testificandum*; and (2) a subpoena of records (also known more formally as a *subpoena duces tecum*) that requests documents or other tangible materials relevant to the case and are practicable to produce.

Perhaps the most important factor, at least to develop in recent years, in connection with the ability to subpoena a third party—either for testimonial or document production purposes—is *relevancy*. The pivotal New York Court of Appeals case of *Matter of Kapon v. Koch* [hereinafter *Kapon*] clarified the relevancy requirements for subpoenaing a third party in compliance with the CPLR.[72] However, it is important to understand the prior standard eventually overruled by *Kapon*.

The "special circumstances" rule that followed the 1984 amendment to CPLR § 3101(a)(4) instituted a more liberal standard for third-party discovery in the notable First Department case of *Slabakis v. Drizin*.[73] The purpose of this liberal sentiment was to "give effect to the strong policy favoring full disclosure[s]" for parties' ability "to adequately prepare for trial."[74] However, that liberal sentiment toward third-party subpoena discovery was not agreed upon in the Second Department in *Dioguardi v. St. John's Riverside Hosp.*, where it was held that 1984 amendments did not favor such a liberal policy as *Slabakis* favored.[75]

---

72. 11 N.E.3d 709 (N.Y. 2014).
73. 485 N.Y.S.2d 270 (App. Div. 1985).
74. *Id.* at 271, 272 (holding that an attorney's need to depose a third-party witness in order to sufficiently prepare for trial was an adequate "special circumstance").
75. Dioguardi v. St. John's Riverside Hosp., 533 N.Y.S.2d 915, 916 (App. Div. 1988).

The desire of a party to subpoena a third party under the mere *relevancy* standard was held to be insufficient under *Dioguardi*.[76] Therefore, the burden on the party seeking to subpoena a third party required an additional factor such as the evidence sought "cannot be obtained from other sources."[77] The Second Department would later deny to extend *Dioguardi* in *Kooper v. Kooper* due to the legislative changes that took place to CPLR § 3101(a)(4).[78] What was required under Kooper was "in assessing whether the circumstances or reasons for a particular demand warrant discovery from a nonparty, those circumstances and reasons need not be shown to be 'special circumstances.'"[79] Furthermore, the court declined to list the circumstances that would properly call for a nonparty subpoena as the burden of determining what is reasonable in terms of discovery requests was placed on the trial courts, which must "balance [the] competing interests" of the parties.[80] The court in *Kooper* did note that "[a]s a matter of [public] policy, nonparties ordinarily should not be burdened with responding to subpoenas for lawsuits in which they have no stake or interest unless the particular circumstances of the case require their involvement."[81]

Since the 1984 amendment there was a split among the appellate divisions, with the First[82] and Fourth[83] Departments adopting a "material and necessary" standard in determining the scope of nonparty subpoenas. Meanwhile, the Second[84] and Third[85] continued with their "special circumstances" standard. This division posed a problem, and thus the New York Court of Appeals finally addressed the matter in *Kapon* in 2014.

Kapon involved a California action for fraud where a party sought to subpoena a New York-based nonparty.[86] Respondent Koch sought to subpoena deposition testimony and records from the petitioner for his California action under CPLR § 3119, also known as the Uniform Interstate Deposition and Discovery

---

76. *Id.*
77. *Id.*
78. Kooper v. Kooper, 901 N.Y.S.2d 312, 322 (App. Div. 2010) (declining to apply "special circumstances test").
79. *Id.*
80. *Id.*
81. *Id.* at 323.
82. *See, for example*, Velez v. Hunts Point Multi-Serv. Ctr., Inc., 811 N.Y.S.2d 5 (Sup. Ct. 2006).
83. Hauzinger v. Hauzinger, 842 NY.S.2d 646 (App. Div. 2007), *aff'd on other grounds*, 892 N.E.2d 849 (N.Y. 2008).
84. *See, for example*, *Kooper*, 901 N.Y.S.2d 312.
85. *See, for example*, Am. Heritage Realty LLC v. Strathmore Ins. Co., 957 N.Y.S.2d 495 (App. Div. 2012).
86. 11 N.E.3d 709 (N.Y. 2014).

Act.[87] However, the petitioner sought to quash the subpoenas under CPLR § 2304 and—in the alternative—sought a protective order under CPLR § 3103 for failing to state with particularity why the disclosure was sought.[88] A fuller discussion of such discovery-related motions can be found later in this chapter.

The Supreme Court denied the motions to quash the subpoenas, and allowed the petitioner "to object to . . . and decline to answer questions" that would put confidential information at risk of being disclosed.[89] Subsequently, the First Department Appellate Division affirmed the Supreme Court decision ruling that it "providently exercised its discretion in denying petitioners' motion, since petitioners failed to show that the requested testimony was irrelevant to the prosecution of the California action."[90]

The Court of Appeals disagreed not only with the lower courts, but also the petitioners' argument that CPLR § 3101(a) calls for the subpoena to bear the initial burden showing an actual need for disclosure on a motion to quash.[91] What the Court of Appeals went on to hold was CPLR § 3101(a)(4) imposed "no requirement that the subpoenaing party demonstrate that it cannot obtain the requested disclosure from any other source," therefore "so long as the disclosure sought is relevant to the prosecution or defense of an action, it must be provided by the nonparty."[92]

In simple terms, the Court of Appeals agreed with the material and necessary standard set forth by the First and Fourth Appellate Divisions and rebuffed the special circumstances standard of the Second and Third Appellate Divisions.[93] A word of caution issued by the *Kapon* court was that while a nonparty subpoena may not always rise to the requirements under CPLR § 3101(a)(4) nonparty subpoenas, an attorney can satisfy this (material and necessary) requirement by attaching the pleading to the subpoena.[94]

Following the *Kapon* decision, courts were left with the task of exercising their independent discretion in ruling on motions to quash subpoenas issued to third

---

87. *Id.* at 712.
88. *Id.*
89. *Id.*
90. *Id.*
91. *Id.* at 713.
92. *In re Kapon*, 11 N.E.3d at 714 [hereinafter *Kapon*].
93. The court in *Kapon* also held that the subpoena in question satisfied the "material and necessary" notice requirements under CPLR 3101(a)(4). *Id.* at 715 n.3.
94. Furthermore, this is not the only means to satisfy the requirements under the statute. The *Kapon* court deemed that the burden a party has in issuing a nonparty subpoena is to provide sufficient information that would allow the third party to "challenge the subpoenas on a motion to quash." *Id.* at 715.

parties. In *Ferolito v. Arizona Beverages USA, LLC*, the plaintiff issued subpoenas dueces tecum to nonparties in connection with a business dissolution.[95] The nonparties objected citing that the information sought by the plaintiff contained trade secrets and sought to dismiss the subpoena.[96] The First Department affirmed (in part) the lower court's decision to allow the subpoena. The court held that the subpoena at issue had properly satisfied the notice requirements under *Kapon* as it sought to determine the relationship between the nonparties and defendants.[97] Further, the nonparties had successfully met their initial burden of showing that a portion of the information sought did amount to a disclosure of trade secrets in further compliance with *Kapon*.[98]

This case, one of the first notable decisions following *Kapon*, shows the initial burden that a party must meet in order to comply with CPLR § 3101(a)(4) requirements. However, what it also shows is that *Kapon* did not have a significant impact only on the contents of a nonparty subpoena, but on (more importantly) the burden that the subpoenaed party must meet in order to quash a party's request for testimony or records.

What happens when the attorney during the course of discovery wants to dispose a nonparty that does not reside within the State of New York? There is a broad answer in the form of the Uniform Interstate Depositions and Discovery Act (UIDDA) commissioned in 2007 by the Uniform Law Commission.[99] The UIDDA was enacted in 2007 as an "efficient and inexpensive" means to depose or otherwise compel nonresident parties and nonparties to cooperate in discovery.[100] However, states that have enacted these procedures must still comply with the rules of the state where the subpoenaed party is located.[101] New York is one of the states that adopted the UIDDA under CPLR § 3119, which states in part:

> (b) Issuance of subpoena. (1) to request issuance of a subpoena under this section, a party must submit an out-of-state subpoena to the county clerk in the county in which discovery is sought to be conducted in this state. A request for the issuance of a subpoena under this section does not constitute an appearance in the courts of this state.

---

95. 990 N.Y.S.2d 218, 219 (App. Div. 2014).
96. *Id.* at 220.
97. *Id.*
98. *See id.*
99. *Interstate Discovery and Depositions Act Summary*, Unif. Law Comm'n, http://www.uniformlaws .org/ActSummary.aspx?title=Interstate%20Depositions%20and%20Discovery%20Act (last visited Dec. 4, 2018).
100. *Id.*
101. *Id.*

The notable case of *Kapon* is also the standard in New York in connection with CPLR § 3119.[102] As discussed above, *Kapon* involved a California action seeking to properly subpoena a nonparty residing within New York. According to the *Kapon* court, UIDDA "provides a streamlined mechanism for disclosure in New York for use in an action that is pending in another state or territory within the United States."[103]

However, it is important to know the other possible means of obtaining nonparty testimony from a nonresident of New York. There are three notable methods to obtaining nonresident nonparty witness cooperating during the discovery phase: (1) stipulation under CPLR §§ 2104 (generally) and 3106, (2) subpoena under CPLR § 3119, and (3) use of a commission.

The first method, stipulation, is a normal means of obtaining nonparty cooperation under CPLR § 3106. A stipulation is an agreement or requirement between parties that is not subject to consideration when made in connection with judicial proceedings.[104] Although a stipulation appears to be an ideal method to obtain nonparty witness, nonparty witnesses can be uncooperative.[105] In those instances, the obvious next step would be to compel the testimony or supply of information from a material nonparty (nonresident) witness.[106]

The second method, subpoenas under CPLR § 3119, is much more commonplace among practitioners. Although *Kapon* is the standard for subpoenas

---

102. It should also be noted that *Kapon* was the first New York Court of Appeals dealing with CPLR § 3119 in connection with subpoenaing a nonresident nonparty for an out of state action.

103. *Kapon*, 11 N.E.3d at 712. Also, as previously stated under *Kapon* the burden of proof for subpoenaing a nonparty is "material and necessary." However, because not every state has adopted the UIDDA Act in a similar manner as New York, it is imperative that the attorney check with the local rules of the state where the person resides to ensure the subpoena is proper.

104. *Stipulation*, BLACK'S LAW DICTIONARY (10th ed. 2014).

105. *See, for example*, Desideri v. Brown, 584 N.Y.S.2d 815, 815 (App. Div. 1992) (affirming motion to compel nonparty witness); Desai v. Blue Shield of Ne. N.Y., Inc., 513 N.Y.S.2d 562, 563 (App. Div. 1987) (reversing protective order requiring defendant not to answer questions); Boatswain v. Boatswain, 778 N.Y.S.2d 850, 853 (Sup. Ct. 2004) (noting information sought by nonparty relevant to the action).

106. It is important to know that the vast majority of law practitioners might not even consider a stipulation as a viable, or rather worthwhile, endeavor to obtain a witness's cooperation in obtaining testimony or desired discovery material. Further, *stipulation(s)* are more likely to be used within the context of CPLR § 3102(b) as a means to disclose information (both tangible and electronically stored information) between parties. There are few instances where parties sought to use stipulations to obtain discovery from nonresidents. *See, for example, Boatswain*, 778 N.Y.S.2d at 850; however, success is unlikely. The enactment of CPLR § 3119 provided a more streamlined process for obtaining information from nonresident nonparties, but it is still worth noting that stipulations were, at least in the past, attempted under these circumstances.

generally under CPLR § 3119, it is important to note a preceding case out of the second department—*Hyatt v. State of California Tax Board.*[107] In *Hyatt*, the California Tax Board subpoenaed a New York resident for records in connection with its appeals process.[108] The Tax Board had a California judge issue the subpoena and utilized local New York counsel to serve the subpoena, as authorized by CPLR § 3119(b)(4).[109] Hyatt sought to quash the subpoenas, citing that the California Tax Board lacked the proper authority to issue such subpoenas, and in the alternative sought a protective order citing a common-interest privilege.[110] The Second Department affirmed the lower court's ruling to modify the subpoena requests, limiting the scope to nonproprietary information.[111]

An important caveat to take away from that particular case was the choice of law that a subpoena would operate under when served from another state. The court in *Hyatt* had the question of whether the Supreme Court had properly applied New York law in connection with the common interest privilege.[112] Hyatt, the plaintiff, argued on the trial level that Nevada law applied to the subpoena request and common-interest privilege because that is where he resided.[113] However, both the Supreme Court and Second Department disagreed, stating that New York had the greatest interest in the subpoena request. The Second Department reasoned that:

> to determine which state's privilege law should apply, New York courts apply an interest analysis. '[T]he law of the jurisdiction having the greatest interest in the litigation will be applied and . . . the facts or contacts which obtain significance in defining State interests are those which relate to the purpose of the particular law in conflict.'[114]

---

107. 962 N.Y.S.2d 282 (App. Div. 2013).
108. *Id.* at 285.
109. *Id.* at 292.
110. *Id.* at 287.
111. *See id.* at 294–97 (holding that the Supreme Court was correct in limiting the scope of the subpoenas to the "audit" years in question and affirmed the protective order for certain information pertaining to the prosecution and defense of his patents).
112. The *common interest privilege*, also known as the *joint-defense privilege* is the rule that a defendant can assert the attorney-client privilege to protect a confidential communication to a code-fendant's lawyer if the communication was related to the defense of both defendants. *Common-Interest Privilege*, BLACK'S LAW DICTIONARY (10th ed. 2014).
113. *Hyatt*, 962 N.Y.S.2d at 295. Further, it is worth noting that Hyatt's alleged residency in Nevada was disputed in part because of his move from California mid-year in 1991 and immediate challenge of an income-based tax assessment. *See id.* at 292.
114. *Id.* (quoting Miller v. Miller, 237 N.E.2d 877, 879 (N.Y.1968); *see* Edwards v. Erie Coach Lines Co., 952 N.E.2d 1033, 1036 (N.Y. 2011); Schultz v. Boy Scouts of Am., 480 N.E.2d 679, 684 (N.Y. 1985); First Interstate Credit Alliance v. Andersen & Co., 541 N.Y.S.2d 433, 434 (Sup. Ct. 1989).

The *Hyatt* court reasoned New York had the greatest interest because the corporate records were based and created in New York, and parties to the lawsuit sought to depose New York-based attorneys.[115]

A development following *Hyatt* was the New York Court of Appeals case of *Ambac Assurance Corporation v. Countrywide Home Loans*.[116] There, Ambac sought the discovery of communications pertaining to the merger of Countrywide Home Loans with Bank of America.[117] Ambac believed that these communications were necessary to prove their cause of action for fraud in an effort to evade creditors, while Bank of America argued that these documents fell within the common-interest privilege.[118] The Court of Appeals reiterated that New York courts have a tradition of rejecting efforts to expand the common-interest doctrine to communications "that do no concern *pending* or *reasonably anticipated litigation.*"[119] Thus, the Court of Appeals ruled—in split decision—the litigation limitations placed on the common-interest doctrine outweighed any rationale for expanding this exception, and in further continuance of the "narrow construction that New York courts have traditionally applied."[120]

Although this may not appear to be substantially related to nonresident nonparties, it is important to remember disclosure under CPLR § 3119 must take into account the concept of both common interest and—more important—attorney-client privileged material. A practitioner must take into account the content of the sought-after material during discovery.

The third and final means to obtain out-of-state discovery material—by commission—is a lesson in the history of New York litigation practices. Now that you have an understanding of the current process to obtain a nonparty subpoena (nonresidents), it is important to also understand the process that existed prior to New York's enactment of the UIDAA. When a party to a cause of action sought to obtain documents or testimony from a New York resident (and/or nonparty), they would do so through a CPLR § 3102 commission, or an order obtained through special proceeding.

This was, and still is, a multistep process that must be followed under the CPLR. The failure of any out-of-state attorney to comply with these procedures

---

115. *Hyatt*, 962 N.Y.S.2d at 295.
116. 57 N.E.3d 30 (N.Y. 2016).
117. *Id.* at 32–33.
118. *See id.*
119. *Id.* at 37 (emphasis added).
120. *Id.* at 40.

would result in denial of his subpoena request.[121] First, the out-of-state attorney seeking to obtain documents or testimony would obtain an order (commission) from his local court.[122] For example, in *In re Deliotte* [hereinafter *Deliotte*], parties to a Michigan lawsuit issued a subpoena to a nonparty by attaching a Michigan subpoena to a proposed New York order compelling requesting documents.[123] However, this was not the proper means to begin such a request, as the attorneys failed not only to comply with the CPLR 3101 notice requirement, but also overlooked the use of a motion (or notice) to obtain discovery under CPLR § 3120(b).[124] The public policy requirements of using this particular procedure allowed for the subpoenaed party to "make a reasoned judgment" as to whether he should comply with the motion or seek a protective remedy.[125]

The second step is to commence a special proceeding in New York to determine whether the issued request is to the satisfaction of the New York courts.[126] Should the subpoena be approved by a New York court, the court will issue an order allowing for the issuance of the out-of-state subpoena. The subpoena can be carried either through the court itself or through the clerk of the county where the requested discovery is to occur.[127]

This is not an overly complicated procedure but, as shown by *Deloitte* above, an applicant seeking disclosure in New York should take special care to follow all procedures. It must be that noted that, should an applicant seek disclosure of only documents from a New York resident (nonparty), then the application is comparable to a subpoena duces tecum under CPLR § 3120. In contrast, should an applicant seek the testimony of a New York nonparty resident, then this is equated to CPLR § 3106(1)(i).[128] The problem with such a procedure was the failure of the statute to adequately provide a remedy for when a witness ignored the issued subpoena. As we saw in *Deloitte*, the failure of an applicant to follow the proper procedure will

---

121. *See, for example, In re* Welch, 706 N.Y.S.2d 597 (Sup. Ct. 2000) (holding that the out-of-state subpoenas issued to New York residents were fatally defective under CPLR § 3102); *In re* Deloitte, 552 N.Y.S.2d 1003, 1005 (Sup. Ct. 1990).

122. CPLR § 3102(e).

123. *In re Deloitte*, 552 N.Y.S.2d at 1004.

124. *See id.* at 1005.

125. *See id.*

126. *See* CPLR § 3102(e).

127. *Id.*

128. CPLR § 3106(b) states in part: "[W]here the person to be examined is not a party or person who at the time of taking the deposition is an officer, director, member or employee of a party, he shall be served with a subpoena. Unless the court orders otherwise, on motion with or without notice, such subpoena shall be served at least twenty [20] days before the examination. . . ."

lead to an (almost) automatic dismissal. Now the question becomes, what happens when an applicant has their subpoena request approved but not necessarily by a New York court, but the witness of whom testimony is sought still objects?

This was the situation in *Ayliffe & Companies v. Canadian Universal Insurance Company*, where the applicant had a commission from a California court.[129] The Appellate Division was faced with the question of whether an ex parte subpoena—drafted in pursuit of disclosure under CPLR § 3102(e)—was available without a prior order.[130] The First Department did not address this issue with any particularity but focused more on whether disclosure was warranted.[131] It addressed the scope of a court's inquiry in connection with objections raised by witnesses subpoenaed to testify. Specifically, the court will determine: "(1) whether the witnesses' fundamental rights are preserved; (2) whether the scope of the inquiry fall within the issues of the pending out-of-State action; and (3) whether the examination is fair [all while affording the other jurisdiction the widest possible latitude]."[132] Of course, the court will use its discretionary powers under CPLR § 3103(a)[133] to quash those CPLR § 3102 subpoenas if they are overly broad or as a means to prevent harassment.[134] Naturally, these steps and defenses are unnecessary when a New York witness is cooperative and the attorney can secure a stipulation—without leave of any New York court under CPLR § 328(b).[135]

D. Nonparty Discovery and the Commercial Division Rules

Similar to the changes in the Commercial Division Rules that affected both party and nonparty discovery, in 2014 changes specifically applicable to *nonparty*

---

129. 564 N.Y.S.2d 297 (App. Div. 1990).
130. *Id.*
131. *Id.*
132. *Id.*
133. The court—under CPLR § 3103(a)—"[M]ay at any time on its own initiative, or on motion of any party or of any person from or about whom discovery is sought, make a protective order denying limiting, condition or regulating the use of any disclosure device. [Further], [s]uch order shall be designed to prevent unreasonable annoyance, expense, embarrassment, disadvantage, or other prejudice to any person or the courts."
134. *See, for example, In re* Kirkland & Ellis, 670 N.Y.S.2d 753, 756 (Sup. Ct. 1998) (noting subpoenas that are overly broad in their requests and/or seek privileged material created in anticipation of litigation may be quashed).
135. CPLR § 328(b) states that service in connection with a proceeding in a tribunal outside the state may be made within the state without a court order. *See Boatswain*, 778 N.Y.S.2d at 852.

discovery were enacted. Effective September 2, 2014, the chief administrative judge of the Courts of New York adopted Rule 11-c and Appendix A to section 202.70(g) of the Commercial Division Rules. Rule 11-c titled "Discovery of Electronically Stored Information from Nonparties," reads:

> Parties and *nonparties* should adhere to the Commercial Division's Guidelines for Discovery of Electronically Stored Information ("ESI") from *nonparties*, which can be found in Appendix A to these Rules of the Commercial Division.[136]

Appendix A, lengthier than its Rule 11-c counterpart, is titled "Guidelines for Discovery of Electronically Stored Information ("ESI") from Non-Parties." Broken down into multiple sections, the applicable provision dealing with proportionality is section III under the "Guidelines" heading. This section lays out various "proportionality factors." Section III states in full:

> III. A party seeking ESI discovery from a nonparty should reasonably limit its discovery requests, taking into consideration the following *proportionality factors*:
>
> A. The importance of the issues at stake in the litigation;
>
> B. The amount in controversy;
>
> C. The expected importance of the requested ESI;
>
> D. The availability of the ESI from another source, including a party;
>
> E. The "accessibility" of the ESI, as defined in applicable case law; and
>
> F. The expected burden and cost to the nonparty.[137]

Although currently cases do not address the proportionality factors set forth in Appendix A, a fairly recent New York Surrogate's Court case drew a parallel between the Uniform Rules, Commercial Division Rules, and nonparty discovery ESI, specifically in Nassau County.[138]

---

136. N.Y. COURTS, ADMINISTRATIVE ORDER OF THE CHIEF ADMINISTRATIVE JUDGE OF THE COURTS 1 (2014), https://www.nycourts.gov/LegacyPDFS/RULES/comments/orders/AO133-14.pdf (last visited Dec. 4, 2018) (emphasis added).

137. *Id.* at 2 (emphasis added).

138. *See* Tener v. Cremer, 931 N.Y.S.2d 552, 554 (App. Div. 2011) ("The Uniform Rules addressing the discovery of ESI are fairly recent. They took effect in 2009. However, the Rules of the Commercial Division of the Supreme Court have addressed discovery of ESI for some time. Rule 8 (b) of the rules contains requirements similar to those in the Uniform Rules (22 NYCRR 202.70 [g]). The Commercial Division for Supreme Court, Nassau County has built on Commercial Division rule 8 (b) to develop the most sophisticated rules concerning discovery of ESI in the State of New York. That court also publishes in-depth guidelines for the discovery of ESI (the Nassau Guidelines).

II. BURDEN OF PROOF IN DISCOVERY-RELATED MOTIONS

A. Motion to Compel

When the desired disclosure is not forthcoming from either the party or the non-party to whom the demand was made, a litigator must swiftly move to compel the requested production. Before making the motion, of course, check the rules applicable to your action to determine if, in addition to making a good faith effort to obtain the disclosure without court involvement,[139] you need to first request a premotion conference with the court or for any other requirements that must be met prior to making your motion to compel.

Relevant to a motion to compel is the scope of the disclosure demanded, and the moving party must understand the potential limits of this scope. CPLR § 3101(a), governing the scope of disclosure by parties, provides as follows:

> Generally. There shall be full disclosure of all matter material and necessary in the prosecution or defense of an action, regardless of the burden of proof, by: (1) a party, or the officer, director, member, agent or employee of a party;

The statutory terms "material and necessary" are to be interpreted liberally.[140] Consequently, the only showing that a party seeking disclosure need make is that the evidence sought may lead to the disclosure of admissible proof.[141] This means that in addition to requiring disclosure of all evidence that is relevant to a case, CPLR § 3101 also requires the disclosure of all information *reasonably calculated to lead to* relevant evidence.[142]

After receiving demands for such evidence and information, the receiving party has a duty to respond to said demands. When a party fails to respond to

---

While aimed at parties, the Nassau Guidelines are appropriate in cases, such as this, where a non-party's data is at issue.").

139. 22 N.Y.C.R.R. § 202.7.

140. *See, for example*, Riverside Capital Advisors, Inc. v. First Secured Capital Corp., 739 N.Y.S.2d 281, 282 (App. Div. 2002); Liverano v. Devinsky, 717 N.Y.S 2d 629, 630 (App. Div. 2000).

141. *See, for example*, Prink v. Rockefeller Ctr., Inc., 398 N.E.2d 517, 520 n.1 (N.Y. 1979) (discussing standard for disclosure); Montgomery v. Taylor, 713 N.Y.S.2d 188, 189 (App. Div. 2000).

142. *See* Bigman v. Dime Savs. Bank, 545 N.Y.S.2d 721, 723 (App. Div. 1989) ("any matter which may lead to the discovery of admissible proof is discoverable."); *see also* Reid v. Soults, 30 N.Y.S.3d 669, 670 (App. Div. 2016) ("The Supreme Court improvidently exercised its discretion in finding that the subject videotape compilation and its sources were irrelevant to the claims in this case. The videotape contains footage that is relevant to the plaintiff's pecuniary loss claim and the life expectancy of the decedent.")

discovery demands, the party seeking the discovery has a remedy pursuant to CPLR § 3124:

> If a person fails to respond to or comply with any request, notice, interrogatory, demand, question or order under this article, except a notice to admit under section 3123, the party seeking disclosure may move to compel compliance or a response.

The court has broad discretion in the control of the disclosure process, and the exercise of that discretion is guided by the test of "usefulness and reason."[143] In deciding a motion to compel, the court's role is to determine whether the requested documents are "material and necessary" to the prosecution or defense of the action as that phrase is used in CPLR § 3101(a).[144] Remember, "'material and necessary is interpreted *liberally* to require disclosure, upon request, of any facts bearing on the controversy which will assist in the preparation for trial," even at this point in the process.[145] Although the scope of disclosure is interpreted liberally, courts must also "balance the parties' competing interests" when ruling on a motion to compel.[146]

In construing CPLR § 3101(a) liberally, courts have acknowledged that "[p]retrial disclosure extends not only to admissible proof but also to testimony or documents which may lead to the disclosure of admissible proof."[147] Consistent with this liberal interpretation of the permissible scope of discovery, documents and information are considered *material* within the meaning of CPLR § 3101(a) so long as they are being sought "in good faith for possible use as evidence-in-chief or rebuttal or for cross-examination," or may otherwise enter the case as admissible evidence.[148] For example, in *Rega*, the defendants sought to compel the

---

143. McMahon v. Aviette Agency, Inc., 753 N.Y.S.2d 605, 606 (App. Div. 2003).

144. *See* Flowers v. Lyell Metal Co., Inc., 665 N.Y.S.2d 482, 482 (App. Div. 1997) (ordering defendant Harris to produce photographs pursuant to the causes of action as plaintiff "demonstrated a substantial need" pursuant to CPLR § 3103(d)(2)).

145. Anonymous v. High Sch. for Envtl. Studies, 820 N.Y.S.2d 573, 578 (App. Div. 2006) (emphasis added); *see* Polygram Holding, Inc. v. Al Cafaro, 839 N.Y.S.2d 493, 494 (App. Div. 2007) ("What constitutes 'material and necessary' should be construed *liberally* to require disclosure of any facts bearing on the controversy which assist by sharpening the issues and reducing delay.") (emphasis added).

146. Accent Collections, Inc. v. Cappelli Enters, Inc., 924 N.Y.S.2d 545, 547 (App. Div. 2011).

147. Fell v. Presbyterian Hosp., 469 N.Y.S.2d 375, 377 (App. Div.1983); *see also* People v. Greenberg, 851 N.Y.S.2d 196, 205 (App. Div. 2008) (noting documents considered to be "material and necessary" under CPLR § 3101 constitutes "a category long held to be broader than that of evidence admissible at trial").

148. Rega v. Avon Prods., Inc., 854 N.Y.S.2d 688, 688 (App. Div. 2008) (*quoting* Allen v. Crowell-Collier Publ'g Co., 235 N.E.2d 430, 432 (N.Y. 1968)).

plaintiff's medical records in a personal injury matter and the plaintiff opposed, seeking a protective order.[149] The court granted the defense motion to compel because the plaintiff had made his injuries sustained in the accident an issue, thus "material" within the scope of CPLR 3101(a).[150]

For documents and information to be considered *necessary* within the meaning of CPLR § 3101(a), "it is not required that it be indispensable but only that it be needful."[151] Regarding the parties' respective burdens on a motion to compel, "the party seeking discovery has the burden of establishing that the production of the demanded material or information will lead to admissible evidence," which is not a high burden to meet.[152] Once the moving party has met its burden, "the party opposing the discovery has the burden of establishing that the material is irrelevant, privileged and/or confidential."[153] In the case of *Alumil Fabrication, Inc. v. F.A. Alpine Window Manufacturing Corporation*, the defense moved to compel deposition testimony from a third-party witness, and plaintiff opposed the motion by stating that the request was improper and unnecessary.[154] The court disagreed, and held that the defendant had shown that the deposition was necessary to support its defense.[155]

Notably, "the party seeking to prevent disclosure has a *heavy burden*, especially where the materials sought are relevant."[156] "[T]here is a *strong presumption* of disclosing all relevant material" with the provision of CPLR § 3101 (a)(1) being accorded a liberal interpretation in favor of disclosure.[157] Courts have held that the requested documents are to be specifically designated.[158] Even when a privilege is asserted, and the court agrees the privilege is legitimate and protectable, it may limit the extent of that privilege in its interpretation of relevant law.

For example, in the criminal context, a Fifth Amendment privilege is often seen as "effectively bar[ring the moving party] from pursuing the discovery she seeks

---

149. *Rega*, 854 N.Y.S.2d 688 at 688.

150. *Id.*

151. Robinson v. Meca, 632 N.Y.S.2d 728, 730 (App. Div. 1995).

152. United States Luggage Co., L.P. v. Vormittag Assocs., Inc., 799 N.Y.S.2d 164, 164 (Sup. Ct. 2004).

153. *Id.*

154. *See* Alumil Fabrication, Inc. v. F.A. Alpine Window Mfg. Corp. 53 N.Y.S.3d 554 (App. Div. 2017).

155. *Id.* at 555.

156. Marten v. Eden Park Health Servs., Inc., 680 N.Y.S.2d 750, 752 (App. Div. 1998) (emphasis added).

157. Coddington v. Lisk, 671 N.Y.S.2d 826, 827 (Sup. Ct. 1998) (emphasis added).

158. *See, for example*, Nitz v. Prudential-Bache Sec., 477 N.Y.S.2d 479, 480 (App. Div. 1984) (upholding Special Term's exclusion of records other than those pertaining to commodity training).

through other discovery methods that do not involve . . . testimony."[159] However, the United States Supreme Court has ruled that the Fifth Amendment privilege only extends to "the person asserting the privilege" and is limited to testimony and not to discoverable documents.[160] The burden of demonstrating that particular items are exempt from discovery falls upon the party asserting the exemption. The combination of the court's broad discretion, along with the presumption that most information will lead to the admissible evidence, often provides a way for evidence to enter, even where evidence is protected by privilege. It is often subject to an exception that could allow for its entry.[161]

The broad discretion of the court and its liberal interpretation are not without limits. Although liberally construed, the movant has the burden to set forth an argument that it is not engaging in a mere "fishing expedition."[162] Hence, merely presenting hypothetical speculation that the discovery might point to something is improper.[163] For example, courts have been reluctant to allow broad access to social media posts merely because a party uses social media.[164] Mere speculation that a party's social media posts *may* contradict a claim can also be improper grounds for a motion to compel.[165] But when the movant can connect the discovery sought to the specific and particular claim, a motion to compel is proper. For example, in a medical malpractice case where defendants sought the medical records of an infant plaintiff's siblings to show that other factors were unlikely to have contributed to the plaintiff's injuries (e.g., genetic factors), a motion to compel would likely be granted.[166] There, a court could easily determine the records were "material and necessary."[167]

---

159. Crocker C. v. Anne R., 2016 N.Y. Misc. LEXIS 3356, at *38 (Sup. Ct. Sept. 19, 2016).

160. United States v. Doe, 465 U.S. 605, 610 (1984) (citing Fisher v. United States, 425 U.S. 391, 397 (1976)); *Crocker C.*, 2016 N.Y. Misc. LEXIS 3356, at *37 (citing *United States v. Doe*, 465 U.S. at 610).

161. Allsbrook v. McCrory's Inc., 440 N.Y.S.2d 325, 326 (App. Div. 1981); *see United States v. Doe*, 465 U.S. at 610 (citing *Fisher*, 425 U.S. 391 at 396; *Crocker C.*, 2016 N.Y. Misc. LEXIS 3356, at *37.

162. Forman v. Henkin, 22 N.Y.S.3d 178, 180 (App. Div. 2015).

163. *See, for example, id.* at 181 (noting more than just plaintiff's previous use of Facebook to post photos and send messages is required to allow for further discovery).

164. *See, for example,* Tapp v. N.Y. Urban Dev. Corp., 958 N.Y.S.2d 392, 393 (App. Div. 2013) (noting reluctance in the context of having "the court conduct an in camera inspection of the account's usage").

165. *For example,* Pecile v. Titan Capital Grp., 979 N.Y.S.2d 303, 305 (App. Div. 2014); *see, for example,* Richard v. Hertz Corp., 953 N.Y.S.2d 654, 656 (App. Div. 2012) (requiring the movant show relevancy of the posts to the claim).

166. *See, for example,* Kaous v. Lutheran Med. Ctr., 30 N.Y.S.3d 663, 667 (App. Div. 2016) (affirming lower court's order in a medical malpractice case requiring plaintiff to provide defendants with authorizations for medical releases for pregnancies and genetic testing).

167. *See id.* (discussing interpretation standard for material and necessary).

CPLR § 3126 sets forth *possible* nondisclosure penalties. It is important to note that the list is not exhaustive. The text states, "the court may make such orders with regard to the failure or refusal as are just."[168] However, three specific penalties are mentioned. One, the court could deem relevant issues as resolved for the party bringing the order.[169] Two, it can prohibit the "disobedient party" from introducing evidence, witnesses, or any other testimonial proof in support of their "claims or defenses."[170] Third, the court can strike out portions of the pleadings, stay the proceeding until compliance is met, dismiss the action partially or in its entirety, and even enter a default judgment "against the disobedient party."[171]

According to the Court of Appeals, compliance with court orders requires both timely and meaningful responses.[172] However, parties are often faced with the substantial risk of not receiving disclosures prior to the deadline for filing a note of issue—a document filed with the clerk, noting the case is ready for trial.[173] Unfortunately, New York Departments handle timely disclosures differently. In the First[174] and Fourth[175] Departments, penalties under CPLR § 3126 may be sought post note of issue. In contrast, in the Second Department,[176] a note of issue is a sufficient defense to a discovery sanction. Despite this inconsistency, if a party is in noncompliance with a discovery order, a variety of standard forms are available corresponding with the particular discovery sanction sought.

---

168. CPLR § 3126.
169. *Id.* § (1).
170. *Id.* § (2).
171. *Id.* § (3).
172. *See* Kihl v. Pfeffer, 722 N.E.2d 55, 58 (N.Y. 1999) ("[W]e underscore that compliance with a disclosure order requires both a timely response and one that evinces a good-faith effort to address the requests meaningfully.")
173. *See* CPLR § 3402.
174. *See, for example,* Magee v. The City of N.Y., 662 N.Y.S.2d 18, 18 (App. Div. 1997) (striking defendant's answer for failure to comply with discovery order); *see also* 1–25 LexisNexis Answer Guide New York Civil Disclosure § 25.03 (2017) (to avoid waiver or dismissal, "care must be taken to avoid a dismissal for failing to timely file a note of issue and certificate of readiness—and to avoid waiving disclosure as a result of a filing made while discovery remains to be completed—by taking steps to obtain judicial approval of post-note of issue disclosure.").
175. *See, for example,* Hill v. Sheehan, 545 N.Y.S.2d 868, 868 (App. Div. 1989) (striking defendant's answer for failure to comply with discovery order); *see also* 1-25 LexisNexis Answer Guide New York Civil Disclosure § 25.03 (2017).
176. *See, for example,* Siragusa v. Teal's Express, Inc., 465 N.Y.S.2d 321, 323 (App. Div. 1983) (denying motion to vacate note of issue and dismiss the complaint).

The Court of Appeals rarely deals with disclosure issues because of its limited jurisdiction, but there have been instances where complaints have been dismissed because of nondisclosure. For example, *Kihl v. Pfeffer* dealt with a preliminary conference order. The parties sent interrogatories to be responded to within thirty days.[177] The plaintiff did not respond to the defendant's interrogatories and the defendant moved to either compel a response or strike the complaint.[178] Opposing the motion, the defendant served its answers to the interrogatories.[179] However, the defendant pressed on with the motion, claiming inadequate responses.[180] After some back and forth to resolve the issue as to whether the order was actually served, upon the Court of Appeals' review, the court ultimately sided with the defendant and dismissed the complaint.[181]

Despite the variations among departments as to when sanctions can be implemented, CPLR § 3126 is liberal and arguably harsh in imposing possible sanctions and remedies for parties' noncompliance. However, it is a good reminder that it is almost always in a party's best interest to comply with court orders—otherwise, a variety of so-called "just" measures could be implemented.

B. Motion for Protective Order or Order of Confidentiality

When a party has moved to compel disclosure from another party in the action, it should be anticipating that the nonmovant will contemporaneously move for a protective order. Certainly, even absent any motion to compel disclosure, a litigator may need to move for a protective order to protect his client from having to produce certain evidence. For example, it is well settled that, upon a proper showing, a party is entitled to a confidentiality order to protect itself, as well as trade and business secrets.[182] CPLR § 3103 expressly provides that a protective

---

177. *Kihl*, 722 N.E.2d at 57.
178. *Id.*
179. *Id.*
180. *Id.*
181. *Id.* at 58.
182. *See, for example*, N.Y. Tel. Co. v. Pub. Serv. Comm'n, 436 N.E.2d 1281, 1283 (N.Y. 1982) ("Numerous decisions in this and other jurisdictions demonstrate the variety of protective means that have been fashioned to maintain the confidentiality of trade secret information that is the subject of litigation."); *In re* Verizon N.Y., Inc. v. N.Y. State Pub. Serv. Comm'n, 23 N.Y.S.3d 446, 449–50 (App. Div. 2016) (discussing the legislative history regarding trade secrets and applying to the facts of the case); Curtis v. Complete Foam Insulation Corp., 498 N.Y.S.2d 216, 217 (App. Div. 1986) (noting "the liberal discovery rules are modified when trade secrets are sought to be discovered").

order may, under certain circumstances, be granted by the court. CPLR 3103(a) states, in relevant part:

> The court may at any time on its own initiative, or on motion of any party or of any person from whom discovery is sought, make a protective order denying, limiting, conditioning, or regulating the use of any disclosure device. Such order shall be designed to prevent unreasonable annoyance, expense, embarrassment, disadvantage, or other prejudice to any person or the courts.

The moving party must demonstrate that it would be prejudiced by reason of the disclosure of the evidence.[183] A court has the ultimate control and supervising authority over the scope of discovery through use of the protective order.[184]

The court has broad discretion in supervising disclosure.[185] A protective order will only be issued if a factual showing is made of prejudice, annoyance, or privilege.[186] The burden of demonstrating a basis for a protective order is on the moving party.[187] However, the showing must consist of more than merely "conclusory

---

183. *See, for example*, Brignola v. Pei-Fei Lee, M.D., P.C., 597 N.Y.S.2d 250 (App. Div. 1993) ("Given that defendants have not demonstrated how the presence of plaintiffs' expert would cause undue annoyance, embarrassment, expense, disadvantage or prejudice, we find that Supreme Court erred in granting a protective order precluding the expert's attendance at defendant's deposition."); Carella v. King, 603 N.Y.S.2d 219, 220 (App. Div. 1993) (affirming order denying defendant's cross-motion for a protective order as defendant's reasons did not amount to prejudice); Scalone v. Phelps Mem'l Hosp. Ctr., 591 N.Y.S.2d 419, 423 (App. Div. 1992) (noting standard in wrongful death actions); Jamaica Wellness Med., P.C. v. USAA Cas. Ins. Co., 16 N.Y.S.3d 444, 448 (Civ. Ct. 2015) (holding plaintiffs were not entitled to a protective order because the subpoena was not unduly restrictive or prejudicial); *see also* Vivitorian Corp. v. First Cent. Ins. Co., 610 N.Y.S.2d 604, 605 (App. Div. 1994) (denying protective order and holding "accident reports prepared in the regular course of business operations or practices are discoverable, even if made solely for the purpose of litigation"); Koump v. Smith, 250 N.E.2d 857, 865–866 (N.Y. 1969) (holding disclosure invalid as the requested disclosure was for an issue not in controversy).
184. *In re* Pioneer Elecs. Corp., 393 N.E.2d 478, 479 (1979) ("Our court will not disturb the determinations made by that court [for a protective order] in the absence of a demonstration that as a matter of law there has been an abuse of discretion."); Boylin v. Eagle Telephonics, 515 N.Y.S.2d 273, 273 (App. Div. 1987) (citing In re *Pioneer Elecs. Corp.*); *Jamaica Wellness Med. P.C.*, 16 N.Y.S.3d at 450 (citing *Boylin*).
185. *See Brignola*, 597 N.Y.S.2d at 251 ("Trial courts are vested with broad discretion to issue appropriate protective orders to limit discovery.")
186. *Id.*; *Carella*, 603 N.Y.S.2d at 220; *see* Slater v. Edcomm, Inc., No. 652635/11, 2016 N.Y. Misc. LEXIS 3198, at *10 (N.Y. Sup. Ct. Sept. 6, 2016) ("[A protective] order shall be designed to prevent unreasonable annoyance, expense, embarrassment, disadvantage, or other prejudice to any person or the courts.").
187. Parker v. Parker, 773 N.Y.S.2d 518, 523 (Sup. Ct. 2003); *see also* Blum v. N.Y. Stock Exch., N.Y.S.2d 225, 226 (App. Div. 1999) (holding in the context of a confidentiality agreement plaintiff satisfied its burden).

allegations."[188] Once the moving party has made such a showing, then the party opposing the protective order has the burden to demonstrate that the discovery should be ordered and the "exceptions" to withhold the particular evidence "are unavailable."[189]

Protective orders are frequently sought to prevent disclosure of confidential personal information, such as medical records, psychological records, and social service records. Patients are generally entitled to their medical records for purposes of litigation.[190] This is true both when litigation has begun, as well as when litigation is only contemplated.[191] However, the Court of Appeals has advised that, even if a patient consents to release of her records, a treating doctor should be able to move for a protective order to "protect a patient, third party, or the doctor, or hospital, from potential injury."[192] When a doctor makes such a motion, though, there is a strong presumption against granting it.[193] Thus, this presumption can only be rebutted under exceptional circumstances, such as imminent and serious physical or psychological damage to the patient.[194]

One type of protective order, a confidentiality order, may be entered where a party demonstrates a legitimate concern for exposure of trade or business secrets.[195] "The initial showing required to support an assertion that trade secrets would be revealed through discovery is minimal," and is thus a low threshold burden requirement.[196] A statement made by the attorney for the party seeking the order that a document contains trade secrets is legally insufficient.[197] Once

188. Fuhs v. Fuhs, 517 N.Y.S.2d 828, 829 (App. Div. 1987).
189. Quirino v. N.Y.C. Transit Auth., 303 N.Y.S.2d 991, 997 (Sup. Ct. 1969); *see* Garcia v. Brooklyn Union Gas Co., 417 N.Y.S.2d 443, 446–47 (Sup. Ct. 1979).
190. Wheeler v. Comm'r of Soc. Servs., 662 N.Y.S.2d 550, 553 (App. Div. 1997).
191. *Id.* at 553–54.
192. Cynthia B. v. New Rochelle Hosp. Med. Ctr., 458 N.E.2d 363, 368 (N.Y. 1983).
193. *Id.* at 369.
194. *Id.*
195. *For example*, Camenos v. F.W. Woolworth Corp., 650 N.Y.S.2d 3, 4 (App. Div. 1996) (mandating confidentiality order as defendant "adequately demonstrated concern for its trade secrets"); Finch, Pruyn & Co. v. Niagara Paper Co., 643 N.Y.S.2d 773, 776 (App. Div. 1996) (holding while the lower court was correct in denying a protective order, the plaintiff was entitled to confidentiality order as defendant met its burden for establishing the material at issue constituted a trade secret); *see also* Bristol, Litynski, Wojcik, P.C. v. Town of Queensbury, 562 N.Y.S.2d 976, 977 (App. Div. 1990) (setting forth twofold analysis for granting an order of confidentiality); Jackson v. Dow Chem. Co., 624 N.Y.S.2d 675, 676 (App. Div. 1995) (citing and explaining *Bristol's* two-step analysis).
196. *Jackson*, 624 N.Y.S.2d at 676; *see Bristol*, 562 N.Y.S.2d at 977 ("[T]he initial showing required of the [movant] was minimal[.]"); Linderman v. Pa. Bldg. Co., 734 N.Y.S.2d 67, 68 (App. Div. 2001) (applying to facts of the case).
197. *In re* Estate of Seviroli, 800 N.Y.S.2d 357, 357 (Sur. Ct. 2005).

such an assertion is made and the burden is met, the party seeking disclosure must show that the trade or business secret is "indispensable to the ascertainment of truth and cannot be acquired in any other way."[198] Any protective order issued to protect trade secrets must be specific.[199]

A counterpart, or extension of an order of confidentiality, is a sealing motion. However, as a general rule, confidentiality (and sealing) is the exception.[200] Importantly, marking documents as "confidential" or "private" does not factor into or control a court's finding of whether or not a record should be sealed.[201] This is because on the whole the public is entitled to access, to "inspect and copy" all court documents.[202] The Supreme Court of New York, Appellate Division, First Department, noted in *Danco Laboratories, Ltd. v. Chemical Works of Gideon Richter, Ltd.,* "[e]specially where issues of major public importance are involved, the interests of the public as well as the press in access to court recordings 'weigh heavily' in favor of release."[203]

Additionally, New York has had a "long recognition that 'civil actions and proceedings should be open to the public in order to ensure that they are conducted efficiency, honestly, and fairly.'"[204] Specifically, the "[n]ews media and the public" have a right "to access judicial proceedings and a common-law right to inspect items filed or admitted into evidence."[205] This is true not only under common law,[206] the

---

198. Curtis v. Complete Foam Insulation Corp., 498 N.Y.S.2d 216, 217 (App. Div. 1986).

199. *In re Estate of Seviroli*, 800 N.Y.S.2d at 357.

200. *In re* Will of Hofmann, 727 N.Y.S.2d 84, 85 (App. Div. 2001).

201. Mosallem v. Berenson, N.Y.S.2d 575, 579 (App. Div. 2010).

202. Danco Labs., Ltd. v. Chem. Works of Gedeon Richter, Ltd., 711 N.Y.S.2d 419, 423 (App. Div. 2000).

203. *Id.* at 425.

204. MBIA Ins. Corp. v. Countrywide Home Loans, Inc., No. 602825/08, 2013 N.Y. Misc. LEXIS 367, at *4 (Sup. Ct. Jan. 3, 2013) (quoting *Mosallem*, 905 N.Y.S.2d at 578)).

205. Coopersmith v. Gold, 594 N.Y.S.2d 521, 526 (Sup. Ct. 1992) .

206. *For example*, Gryphon Domestic VI, LLC v. APP Int'l Fin. Co., B.V., 814 N.Y.S.2d 110, 113 (App. Div. 2006); *In re* Application of Nat'l Broad. Co., 635 F.2d 945, 949 (2d Cir. 1980) ("The existence of the common law right to inspect and copy judicial records is beyond dispute."); *see* Globe Newspaper Co. v. Superior Court, 457 U.S. 596, 615 (1982) ("Massachusetts does not deny the press and the public access to the trial transcript or to other sources of information about the victim's testimony. Even the victim's identity is part of the public record, although the name of a 16-year-old accused rapist generally would not be a matter of public record. Mass. Gen. Laws Ann., Ch. 119, § 60A."); *see also* Richmond Newspapers v. Virginia, 448 U.S. 555, 580 (1980) (holding right to attend criminal trials as an implicit guarantee of the First Amendment); *see also* Associated Press v. Bell, 510 N.E.2d 313, 314 (N.Y. 1987) (vacating order closing courtroom to the public); Hearst Corp. v. Clyne, 409 N.E.2d 876, 879 (N.Y. 1980) (same); Newsday, Inc. v. Sise, 518 N.E.2d 930, 933 n.4 (N.Y. 1987) (rejecting petitioner's claim to access juror's names and addresses under the common law claim of right to access to judicial records and constitutional right to criminal

New York State constitution,[207] statutes,[208] and civil rights laws,[209] but also under the First,[210] Sixth,[211] and Fourteenth[212] Amendments to the United States Constitution. However, this right to inspect and copy is not absolute.[213] As a result, "[a] sealing order is not 'an unconstitutional restriction of freedom of the press.'"[214] Because of this presumed right of public access, the Supreme Court of New York, Appellate Division, First Department, has shied away particularly from authorizing sealing of court records, allowing it in "strictly limited circumstances," for example, where a business' competitive advantage or trade secrets are at issue, as mentioned above in reference to granting confidentiality orders.[215]

The statute governing the sealing of court records, Section 22 NYCRR 216.1, states:

(a) Except where otherwise provided by statute or rule, a court shall not enter an order in any action or proceeding sealing the court records, whether in whole or in part, except upon a written finding of *good cause*, which shall specify the grounds thereof. In determining whether *good cause* has been shown, *the court shall consider the interests of the public as well as of the parties.* Where it appears necessary or desirable, the court may prescribe appropriate notice and opportunity to be heard. (emphasis added).

(b) for purposes of this rule, "court records" shall include all documents and records of any nature filed with the clerk in connection with the action. Documents obtained through disclosure and not filed with the clerk shall remain subject to protective orders as set forth in CPLR 3103(a).

   Due to this presumption of allowing the public access to all court documents, *the burden of proof is* on "the party seeking to seal court records . . . to demonstrate compelling circumstances to justify restricting public access."[216]

---

proceedings); Richmond Newspapers v. Virginia, 448 U.S. 555, 580 (1980) (holding right to attend criminal trials as an implicit guarantee of the First Amendment).

207. N.Y. CONST. art I, § 8; *see also Richmond Newspapers*, 448 U.S. at 580 (1980) (holding right to attend criminal trials as an implicit guarantee of the First Amendment).

208. *See* N.Y. JUD. LAW § 4; *see Coopersmith*, 594 N.Y.S.2d 521, 526 (Sup. Ct. 1992) (holding burden of proof for good cause to seal the record not met).

209. *See* N.Y. CIV. RIGHTS LAW § 12.

210. U.S. CONST. AMEND. I.

211. U.S. CONST. AMEND. VI.

212. U.S. CONST. AMEND. XIV.

213. *Coopersmith*, 594 N.Y.S.2d at 523.

214. *Id.* at 527 (quoting Danziger v. Hearst Corp., 107 N.E.2d 62, 64 (N.Y. 1952)).

215. Mosallem v. Berenson, 905 N.Y.S.2d 575, 580 (App. Div. 2010).

216. *Mosallem*, 905 N.Y.S.2d at 579; *see* Mancheski v. Gabelli Grp. Capital Partners, 835 N.Y.S.2d 595, 598 (App. Div. 2007) ("A finding of 'good cause' presupposes that public access to the documents

The term *good cause* goes hand in hand with *compelling interest*. As stated in *Mancheski v. Gabelli Group Capital Partners*, "[a] finding of 'good cause' presupposes that public access to the documents at issue will likely harm to a compelling interest of the movant."[217] The term "good cause" is not defined outright in the statute. Although "good cause" is a term of art, in the sealing context it is a "well[-]established legal phrase."[218] Almost impossible to define in absolute terms, "it generally signifies a sound basis or legitimate need to take judicial action."[219] The courts exercise their prudent discretion to determine whether or not a compelling interest exists.[220]

Courts take into account and balance "the potential harm for and embarrassment to the litigants and public alike."[221] for example, *Coopersmith v. Gold* dealt with a medical malpractice claim against the defendant psychiatrist for alleged illegal sexual conduct.[222] The court held that good cause was established because the "details of the allegations if publicized extensively might taint potential jurors and lead to identification of some or all of the proposed witnesses."[223] Therefore, the court reasoned "confidentiality is essential at this stage of the proceedings and the records and transcript of the oral argument are directed to be sealed by the County Clerk, not to be opened except upon order of the court."[224] In this case, the compelling interest was loud and clear.

In contrast, the court in *Mosallem v. Berenson* reversed and vacated a sealing order by the lower court because compelling circumstances were not present.[225] In this case, the vice president of a corporation, Mosallem, was convicted of federal crimes; allegations existed that senior executives in the company were engaged in the cover up.[226] The press had a continuing interest in the documents that brought forth the prosecution, requesting case files.[227] In vacating the sealing order, the court indicated that no compelling circumstances were given "as

---

at issue will likely result in harm to a compelling interest of the movant."); *Danco Labs., Ltd.*, 711 N.Y.S.2d at 425 (App. Div. 2000) (finding good cause).

217. *Mancheski*, 835 N.Y.S.2d at 598.

218. *Coopersmith*, 594 N.Y.S.2d at 529–30 (quoting *In re* Alexander Grant & Co. Litig., 820 F.2d 352, 356 (11th Cir. 1987)).

219. *Coopersmith*, 594 N.Y.S.2d at 530 (*quoting In re Alexander*, 820 F.2d at 356).

220. *Id.* at 530.

221. *Id.*; *see also In re Alexander*, 820 F.2d at 356.

222. *See* 594 N.Y.S.2d at 523.

223. *Id.* at 524.

224. *Id.*

225. 905 N.Y.S.2d 575, 582 (App. Div. 2010).

226. *Id.* at 579.

227. *Id.* at 577.

to why the documents were so confidential or sensitive that public access to them should have been restricted." For one, the court attributed a lack of compelling circumstances because no facts were established alleging specific harm, showing the harm "outweighs the importance of public access to the records."[228] Additionally, no evidence was put forth indicating that the documents contained trade secrets or other revelations that might have harmed the corporation's competitive standing.[229] The court also remarked on the defendant's failure to take prompt action:

> [a]lthough not determinative, defendant's failure to take prompt action undermines their claims that the documents contain confidential business information, would invade federal grand jury secrecy or would cause unspecified harm to their business reputations.[230]

Furthermore, the court remarked "how Mosallem may have come to be in possession of the documents [did] not warrant granting sealing motion."[231] The court closely examined Rule 216.1(a) to explain:

> There is nothing in Rule 216.1(a) that addresses whether a court can consider a litigant's wrongful conduct or bad faith in determining whether public access should be restricted. Some useful guidance can be gleaned from analogous principles governing admissibility of wrongfully obtained evidence. New York follows the common-law rule that the admissibility of evidence is not affected by the means through which it is obtained. Thus, in the absence of some constitutional, statutory, or decisional authority requiring the suppression of otherwise valid evidence (*see e.g.* CPLR 4506), such evidence is admissible in a civil action even if obtained by wrongful means.[232] (Internal citations omitted.)

In the limited circumstances where a court grants a sealing motion, "a document need not be withheld from the public in its entirety as '[r]edaction is a viable option, predicated upon the required level of need.'"[233] Under 216.1(a) the precise areas where redaction should occur has to be pointed out, otherwise violating

---

228. *Id.* at 580.
229. *Id.*
230. *Id.* at 580–581.
231. *Id.* at 581.
232. *Id.*
233. *MBIA Ins. Corp.*, 2013 N.Y. Misc. LEXIS 367, at *7 (quoting *Danco Labs., Ltd.*, 711 N.Y.S.2d at 425.

Rule 216.1.[234] For example, *Danco Laboratories., Ltd. v. Chemical Works of Gedeon Richter, Ltd.* dealt with a sealing order about possible distribution and sale of a "controversial" abortion pill.[235] The court affirmed and modified the lower court's sealing order because good cause for limited protection existed; both parties agreed "its disclosure purportedly will reveal trade secrets and the identities of persons who then may be targeted for harassment or violence."[236] However, the Supreme Court of New York, Appellate Division, First Department, found the lower court's failure to target the areas where redaction should occur violated state law.[237] Nevertheless, the appellate court ordered the appropriate redaction and appointed a special referee to handle motions that could arise about future redaction of trade secret information or identities.[238]

Ultimately, the burden of proof for a sealing order boils down to a few simple elements—establishing good cause and putting forth compelling interests that outweigh the public's right to access court documents. As case law indicates, it is not an easy standard to meet, as confidentiality orders are seldom granted.

C. Motion to Quash

A motion for a protective order is the preferred method to protect a party from improper disclosure but the CPLR also allows *any person* served with a subpoena to challenge its validity. CPLR § 2304 specifically states that:

> A motion to quash, fix conditions or modify a subpoena shall be made promptly in the court in which the subpoena is returnable. If the subpoena is not returnable in a court, a request to withdraw or modify the subpoena shall first be made to the person who issued it and a motion to quash, fix conditions or modify may thereafter be made in the Supreme Court. Reasonable conditions may be imposed upon the granting or denial of a motion to quash or modify.

A motion to quash a subpoena is the exclusive vehicle to test the validity, sufficiency, and propriety of the subpoena.[239] Such a motion is generally limited in scope to challenging the subpoena's demands, the need therefor and whether

---

234. *Danco Labs., Ltd.*, 711 N.Y.S.2d at 425.
235. *Id.* at 421.
236. *Id.*
237. *Id.* at 426.
238. *Id.*
239. Ayubo v. Eastman Kodak Co., 551 N.Y.S.2d 944, 945 (App. Div. 1990) (regarding a personal injury action involving a subpoena for business records seeking information on similar claims made against defendant).

the issuer can obtain the same disclosure elsewhere, and its validity or jurisdiction of the issuing authority.[240] Should a motion to quash be granted, "it results in completely voiding the process," and "thus saving the needless expenditure of litigation effort."[241]

For nonjudicial subpoenas, or a subpoena "not returnable in court," a request to withdraw or modify should be made to the party issuing the subpoena prior to challenging it. There is conflicting authority in New York as to whether this is a necessary step to be able to file the motion.[242] In any event, the Uniform Rules for the New York State Trial Courts require a good faith effort to resolve any issue prior to filing a motion with the courts.[243]

On a motion to quash a subpoena, the movant bears the burden of proving that the materials sought are utterly irrelevant to any proper inquiry.[244] "However, this broadly stated standard, while consistent with a policy favoring the production of information, should not serve as an excuse for a court to abdicate its responsibility to determine whether the materials sought are in fact relevant to a legitimate subject of inquiry."[245] The issuer of the subpoena remains obligated to tailor any document requests with specificity so that the recipient can reasonably ascertain what documents to produce.[246] Applying the "utterly irrelevant" standard, a subpoena which "does not merely call for the files of specific officers of the company or for documents regarding limited or specifically defined subjects" may be "patently overbroad, burdensome, and oppressive" and therefore "unenforceable."[247]

The court should grant a motion to quash when the "futility of the process to uncover anything legitimate is inevitable or obvious . . . or where the

---

240. *See* Brunswick Hosp. Ctr., Inc. v. Hynes, 420 N.E.2d 51 (N.Y. 1981); Santangello v. People, 344 N.E.2d 404 (N.Y. 1976).

241. *Santangello*, 344 N.E.2d at 406.

242. Rubino v. 330 Madison Co., LLC, 958 N.Y.S.2d 587, 588 (Sup. Ct. 2013); *see, for example, id.* (denying a motion to quash because no request to withdraw or modify the subpoena was made prior to filing the motion); Brooks v. City of N.Y., 678 N.Y.S.2d 479, 480 (Sup. Ct. 1998) (allowing a motion to quash despite a lack of request to withdraw as the subpoena was made within a court action).

243. 22 N.Y.C.R.R. § 202.7(c).

244. *See Kapon*, 11 N.E.3d 709, 711 (N.Y. 2014); *see also* Velez v. Hunts Point Multi-Serv. Ctr., Inc., 811 N.Y.S.2d 5, 16 (Sup. Ct. 2006) (reversing and allowing access to records as the moving party did not meet the burden to show the requested records were irrelevant).

245. *In re* Reuters Ltd., 662 N.Y.S.2d 450, 453 (App. Div. 1997); *In re* Brodsky 891 N.Y.S.2d 590, 600 (Sup. Ct. 2009).

246. *In re Reuters Ltd.*, 662 N.Y.S.2d at 453.

247. *Id.* at 456.

information sought is 'utterly irrelevant to any proper inquiry.'"[248] A party may not use a subpoena as an alternative or to further pretrial discovery,[249] but a party may demand the production of specific documents or evidence—"[t]he purpose of a subpoena *duces tecum* is 'to compel the production of specific documents that are relevant and material to facts at issue in a pending judicial proceeding.'"[250]

A subpoena *duces tecum* may be challenged on the ground that the subpoena is overbroad, burdensome, or oppressive.[251] "In light of the elimination of the 'special circumstances' standard from the statute governing the scope of disclosure from a nonparty, on a motion to quash a subpoena *duces tecum* or for a protective order, in assessing whether the circumstances or reasons for a particular demand warrant discovery from a nonparty, those circumstances and reasons need not be shown to be 'special circumstances.'"[252] Any request for the delivery of documents that is not specific to a relevant time span or, alternatively, a request seeking the delivery of "all" documents is overly broad and burdensome by definition. A a result, it should either be modified or quashed completely. A moving party demanding "all" documents has not met its burden of demonstrating the necessary relevance of its demands.[253]

D. Motion for an Order of Contempt

Any time an order of the court has been violated, a motion for an order of contempt is proper. In the discovery context, a natural opportunity may arise once your motion to compel disclosure has been granted and the court has issued an order compelling your adversary to produce certain documents by a particular date. When that date has come and gone, a motion for an order of contempt is proper.

---

248. Myrie v. Shelley, 655 N.Y.S.2d 66, 67 (App. Div. 1997) (quoting Anheuser-Busch Inc. v. Abrams, 520 N.E.2d 535, 538 (N.Y. 1988)); *see also* Ayubo v. Eastman Kodak Co., 551 N.Y.S.2d 944, 946 (App. Div. 1990).

249. *See* Fox v. Namani, 622 N.Y.S.2d 842, 843 (Sup. Ct. 1994) (quoting "utterly irrelevant" language).

250. *Myrie*, 655 N.Y.S.2d at 67 (App. Div. 1997) (quoting People v. Robinson, 449 N.Y.S.2d 321, 322 (App. Div. 1982)).

251. La Belle Creole Int'l, S. A. v. Att'y Gen. of N.Y, 176 N.E.2d 705, 707–08 (N.Y. 1961) (involving an investigation by the attorney general to determine whether application should be made to enjoin a foreign corporation from committing fraudulent or illegal acts).

252. *Kooper*, 901 N.Y.S.2d at 320.

253. *See, for example*, Chu v. Green Point Sav. Bank, 646 N.Y.S.2d 28, 29 (App. Div. 1996); Glickman v. Glickman, No. 5897/08 2008 N.Y. Misc. LEXIS 10605, at *14 (Sup. Ct. 2008).

The Court of Appeals has used a five-part test in order for the movant to prevail on a motion for civil contempt.[254] To prevail on a civil contempt claim, the movant must demonstrate that (1) a lawful order was in effect, (2) the order clearly expressed an unequivocal mandate, (3) it must appear with reasonable certainty that the order has been disobeyed, (4) the party to be held in contempt must have had knowledge of the order, and (5) the rights of a party to the litigation must be prejudiced.[255] The party moving for civil contempt has the overall burden of proof to establish, by clear and convincing evidence, that the court order or subpoena has been violated.[256] When the party moving for contempt has satisfied its burden, the burden shifts to the opposing party.[257]

The party moving to hold an opposing party in contempt must show that each of the five elements of contempt is present. Importantly, the Court of Appeals has held that willfulness is not a required element of civil contempt.[258] For an order to be lawful, and thus satisfy the first element of civil contempt, the court must be within its authority to issue such an order. For example, in *El-Dehdan*, the court's order that directed the defendant to deposit certain funds from the transfer of properties was authorized by the Domestic Relations Law as well as by statute and, as such, the court was within its authority to issue the subject order.[259]

A clear order from the court requiring a party to take or refrain from an action satisfies the second element of civil contempt.[260] A court order must be very clear, and the action must violate the words of the order to qualify for the third element of contempt. When the action or inaction complained of is not clearly proscribed in a court order, such action cannot be the basis for contempt.[261]

It must be shown that the party in violation of a court order possessed actual knowledge of the order in order to be found in contempt.[262] Service of an order on

---

254. McCormick v. Axelrod, 453 N.E.2d 508, 512–13 (N.Y. 1983); *see* El-Dehdan v. El-Dehdan, 978 N.Y.S.2d 239, 245 (App. Div. 2013) (noting guidance set forth in N.Y. Jud. Law § 750 *et seq.*).
255. *McCormick*, 453 N.E.2d 508 at 512–13; Riccelli Enters., Inc. v. State of N.Y. Workers' Comp. Bd., 38 N.Y.S.3d 316, 318 (App. Div. 2016).
256. Yalkowsky v. Yalkowsky, 461 N.Y.S.2d 54, 55 (App. Div. 1983).
257. *Id.*
258. El-Dehdan v. El-Dehdan, 41 N.E.3d 340, 349–50 (N.Y. 2015).
259. *Id.* at 349.
260. *Id.*
261. *See* Kinney v. Simonds, 714 N.Y.S.2d 151, 152 (App. Div. 2000) (noting an order to "entertain counseling" is not a clear and explicit mandate to participate in counseling); *Nelson v. Nelson*, 598 N.Y.S.2d 609, 612 (App. Div. 1993) (noting an order that one party *should* consult with the other is not a clear and explicit mandate to do so).
262. Dotzler v. Buono, 40 N.Y.S.3d 846, 848 (App. Div. 2016).

a party's attorney does not grant the party actual knowledge of the order until the party actually receives it.[263] Actual knowledge of the order is an *indispensable* element of a contempt proceeding.[264] With that said, service of the order is not always necessary to impute actual knowledge on a party in violation of a court order.[265]

The last element of contempt, prejudice, is satisfied when the moving party shows that disobedience of the order "defeats, impairs, impedes, or prejudices the rights of a party."[266] A contention that the degree to which the order was disobeyed was *de minimis* may be insufficient to defeat a finding of prejudice. The possibility that some prejudice may result from the disobedience can satisfy this element.[267]

To hold a party in civil contempt for disobeying a subpoena, "[i]t is not necessary that such disobedience be deliberate; rather the mere act of disobedience, regardless of its motive, is sufficient to sustain a finding of civil contempt if such disobedience defeats, impairs, impedes, or prejudices the rights of a party."[268]

Judiciary Law sections 750 and 751, respectively, give the court the power to punish for criminal contempt and lay out appropriate punishments. Judiciary Law section 753 gives the court the power to punish for civil contempt. Although this book focuses on the burden of proof in a civil trial, it would be remiss not to briefly mention criminal contempt. In contrast to civil contempt, criminal contempt punishments can only be enforced for certain enumerated acts.[269] Important to note is that any acts noted in this section, such as "willful disobedience" to a court's "lawful mandate" are also punishable as misdemeanors.[270] Unfortunately, for the person charged with criminal contempt, one punishment does not bar the other.[271]

---

263. *Id.*

264. Orchard Park Cent. Sch. Dist. v. Orchard Park Teachers Ass'n, 378 N.Y.S.2d 511, 518 (App. Div. 1976).

265. People *ex rel.* Stearns v. Marr, 74 N.E. 431, 434 (N.Y. 1905).

266. Great Neck Pennysaver, Inc. v. Cent. Nassau Publ'ns Inc., 409 N.Y.S.2d 544, 546 (App. Div. 1978).

267. *Great Neck Pennysaver, Inc.* 409 N.Y.S.2d at 546; *Yalkowsky*, 461 N.Y.S.2d at 56 (App. Div. 1983).

268. *Great Neck Pennysaver Inc.* 409 N.Y.S.2d at 546 (emphasis added); see also *El-Dehdan*, 978 N.Y.S.2d at 242.

269. *Compare* N.Y. JUD. LAW § 750(A) ("[a] court of record has power to punish for a criminal contempt, a person guilty of any of the following acts, and no others") *with id.* § 753(8) (indicating a catchall provision: "[i]n any other case, where an attachment or any other proceeding to punish for a contempt, has been usually adopted and practiced in a court of record, to enforce a civil remedy of a party to an action or special proceeding in that court, or to protect the right of a party.")

270. *See id.* § 750(A)(3); *see* People v. Meakim, 30 N.E. 828 (N.Y. 1892).

271. *Meakim*, 30 N.E. at 831.

Section 750 lays out the appropriate remedies for criminal contempt:

> Except as provided in subdivisions (2), (3) and (4), punishment for a contempt, specified in section seven hundred fifty, *may be by fine, not exceeding one thousand dollars, or by imprisonment, not exceeding thirty days, in the jail of the county where the court is sitting, or both,* in the discretion of the court. (Emphasis added.)

When fines are the imposed remedy, they are to be paid into the public treasury, not to the party seeking contempt.[272] One impermissible method of punishment is imposing costs in proceedings.[273]

For civil contempt, the Judiciary Law allows punishments by either fine, imprisonment, or both.[274] For example, a fine can be ordered where a party has disobeyed an injunction.[275] Also, although proving damages is usually in a party's best interest for greater recovery, a party can still recover a remedy without doing so. In a recent 2015 case the Second Department held "[w]here no actual damages are shown, the amount of a fine for a civil contempt cannot exceed $250."[276] This cap is only for *each* disobedient act; therefore, where "multiple acts of disobedience" occur, a party may recover a maximum of $250 per "act" as determined by the court.[277]

E.   Motion to Strike a Pleading

A party's failure to fully comply with a discovery demand may warrant the striking of its answer. The court enjoys the right to strike a party's pleading for failing to comply with discovery. Specifically, CPLR § 3126 provides, in pertinent part, as follows:

> If any party . . . refuses to obey an order for disclosure or willfully fails to disclose information which the court finds ought to have been disclosed, pursuant to this article, the court may make such orders with regard to the failure or refusal as are just, among them:
>
> . . .

---

272. Wilwerth v. Levitt, 28 N.Y.S.2d 257, 258 (App. Div. 1941).
273. Boon v. McGucken, 22 N.Y.S. 424 (App. Div. 1893).
274. N.Y. JUD. LAW § 753(A) ("A court of record has power to punish, by fine and imprisonment . . .").
275. Friendly Ice Cream Corp. v. Great E. Mall, Inc., 381 N.Y.S.2d 368 (App. Div. 1976).
276. Weissman v. Weissman, 18 N.Y.S. 3d 59, 61 (App. Div. 2015) (quoting Vider v. Vider, 925 N.Y.S.2d 189, 192 (App. Div. 2011).
277. Town Bd. of Town of Southampton v. R.K.B. Realty, LLC, 936 N.Y.S.2d 228, 232 (App. Div. 2012) (quoting People v. Metro. Police Conference, 647 N.Y.S.2d 11, 12 (App. Div. 1996)).

3. an order striking out the pleadings or parts thereof, or staying further proceedings until the order is obeyed . . . or rendering a judgment by default against the disobedient party.[278]

Although a demonstration of willful, contumacious, or bad-faith conduct is necessary to successfully strike a pleading under CPLR § 3126, the court may infer such conduct from the party's actions.[279] A party's repeated failure to respond in whole or in part to discovery demands "constitute[s] the type of dilatory and obstructive conduct which [could justify] striking their answer."[280] Blatant failure to comply with duties to the court creates an opportunity for recompense for the party complying with court rules in the form of this just remedy. This remedy is not automatic. The moving party has the additional burden of demonstrating malicious intent, ill will, or bad faith motivating its adversary's failure.

The intentional destruction of evidence will result in an assumption that the destroyed evidence is relevant, and warrants the striking of the pleading.[281] The filing of unnecessary motions, particularly if they are numerous and voluminous, in violation of a court order to complete disclosure is a clear example of the type of action that a court will find sufficient to strike a pleading.[282] The failure to produce a witness who has necessary testimony has also been the basis for striking the portion of a pleading that relies on that witness's testimony.[283]

To compel production, courts may issue conditional orders to strike, or to outright dismiss a pleading. In the event the order is not complied with, the party in violation of the order must both show a reasonable excuse for noncompliance and offer an affidavit of merit.[284] The Court of Appeals has held that once a conditional order is issued, if it is disobeyed and such a showing cannot be made, the order is self-executing and it is an error to allow the action to proceed without the full preclusive effect of the order.[285]

---

278. *See* Zletz v. Wetanson, 490 N.E.2d 852, 853 (1986) (noting dismissal is appropriate where "a party . . . disobeys a court order and by his conduct frustrates the disclosure scheme provided by the CPLR").

279. Garnett v. Hudson Rent a Car, 685 N.Y.S.2d 463, 463 (App. Div. 1999); Hudson v. City of N.Y, 700 N.Y.S.2d 67, 68 (App. Div. 1999); Cano v. BLF Realty Holding Corp., 663 N.Y.S.2d 202, 203 (App. Div. 1997).

280. Ortiz v. Weaver, 590 N.Y.S.2d 474, 475 (App. Div. 1992).

281. UMS Solutions., Inc. v. Biosound Esaote, Inc., 44 N.Y.S.3d 93, 95 (App. Div. 2016).

282. Arts4All, Ltd. v. Hancock, 863 N.Y.S.2d 193, 194 (App. Div.), *aff'd* 918 N.E.2d 945 (N.Y. 2009).

283. Crooke v. Bonofacio, N.Y.S.3d 28, 29 (N.Y. App. Div. 2017).

284. Fiore v. Galang, 478 N.E.2d 188, 189 (N.Y. 1985).

285. Gibbs v. St. Barnabas Hosp., 942 N.E.2d 277, 281 (N.Y. 2010).

It is important to note that the sanction of striking a pleading is drastic, and should not be employed unless the moving party makes a "clear showing that the failure to comply with discovery demands is willful, contumacious, or in bad faith."[286] For example, the Appellate Division, Second Department, affirmed the lower court's denial of the motion to strike in the case of A.F.C., concluding that:

> The Supreme Court properly declined to dismiss the complaint, finding that the plaintiff substantially complied with outstanding discovery requests and that its conduct was not willful, contumacious, or done in bad faith. . . .[287]

A variety of discovery motions are available for parties to obtain or keep out relevant information. Each motion encompasses its own burden of proof and ramifications for noncompliance. Understanding when, why, and how to utilize these motions can assist a party in creating the burden of proof needed later on down the road—at trial, or even on appeal.

---

286. A.F.C. Enters., Inc. v. N.Y.C. Sch. Constr. Auth., 822 N.Y.S.2d 775, 775 (App. Div. 2006); *see also In re* W.O.R.C. Realty Corp. v. Assessor, 823 N.Y.S.2d 407, 409 (App. Div. 2006) ("Contrary to the contentions of the appellants, it was not clearly demonstrated that the petitioner's discovery defaults were willful, contumacious, or done in bad faith as to warrant the extreme sanction of dismissing the petitions pursuant to CPLR [§] 3126(3).").
287. *A.F.C. Enters., Inc.*, 822 N.Y.S.2d at 775.

6 | Use of Burden of Proof in Dispositive Motions

INTRODUCTION

Article 32 of the Civil Practice Law and Rules (CPLR) sets forth several motions for accelerated judgments in an action without the necessity of a full trial. These motions include a pre-answer motion to dismiss under CPLR § 3211, a motion for summary judgment under CPLR § 3212, a motion for summary judgment in lieu of complaint under CPLR § 3213, and, finally, a motion for a default judgment under CPLR § 3215.

The motion to dismiss permits a party to file a motion, prior to issue being joined with the filing of an answer, for judgment dismissing one or more causes of action asserted against them.[1] A motion for summary judgment permits a party to seek judgment on either its causes of action or affirmative defenses without a trial in front of the fact finder.[2] The motion for summary judgment is only available after issue has been joined, and upon a showing that there is no triable issue of fact and that the movant is entitled to judgment as a matter of law.[3]

A motion for summary judgment in lieu of complaint provides for an expedited procedure for judgment where the action is predicated upon an instrument for the payment of money only.[4] In this scenario, the plaintiff may serve with the summons a notice of motion for summary judgment and the supporting papers in lieu of a complaint.[5] A motion for summary judgment in lieu of complaint is ideal in situations where there is an unpaid promissory note, guaranty, or bounced check. A motion for a default judgment permits a party to enter a judgment upon a party who has failed to appear or otherwise answer a complaint, plead, or proceed to trial.[6] Common among the above motions is that the procedure permits the entry of judgment without any trial on the merits.

I. MOTION TO DISMISS

A. CPLR § 3211(a)(7)

As explained in the previous chapters of this book, the basic structure of a legal norm is typically shaped thus: *if a number of legally operative facts occurred in the real world, then a certain legal effect results.* To put this concept in mathematical

---

1. CPLR § 3211(a).
2. *Id.* § 3212.
3. *Id.* § 3212(a), (b).
4. *Id.* § 3213.
5. *Id.*
6. *Id.* § 3215.

terms: xyz = A + B + C. Where *A*, *B*, and *C* represent distinct propositions of fact, *xyz* represents a legal effect. Naturally, should a dispute concerning the occurrence of certain propositions of fact comprising a transaction or occurrence ensue, the competent court of law will probably be asked to intervene and settle the matter.

The proponent, who wants the court to intervene and bring about the legal effect set forth by the law, ought to explicitly request such intervention in writing. By the same token, the proponent must provide the court with an outline of the transaction or occurrence that allegedly took place. This document, which may take several forms (*e.g.*, complaint, answer, and so on), is generically called a *pleading*.

Going back to our terminology, the previous point can be put as follows: the party who wants to obtain the *xyz* relief ought to file a *pleading* with the competent court of law alleging (and subsequently proving) that the *A*, *B*, and *C* propositions of fact took place sometime in the past.

Needless to say, if the proponent fails to allege in the *pleading* all relevant facts which, under the applicable law, comprise a cause of action, then the relief prayed for cannot be granted.[7] At common law, the procedure through which a court could do away with a claim where the proponent failed to plead all relevant facts comprising a cognizable cause of action was called a *demurrer*.[8] When a party to a lawsuit filed a demurrer seeking dismissal of a cause of action, the court's inquiry was limited to the four corners of the pleading. Therefore, any circumstance beyond the face of the pleading could not be considered in adjudicating the motion.

In New York, the CPLR has somewhat broadened the scope of the old common law demurrer. In fact, CPLR § 3211(a)(7) provides: "A party may move for judgment dismissing one or more causes of action asserted against him on the ground that: the pleading fails to state a cause of action."[9] Furthermore, CPLR § 3211(c) clarifies that "[u]pon the hearing of a motion made under subdivision (a) or (b), either party may submit any evidence that could properly be considered on a motion for summary judgment."[10]

Similar to a demurrer, on a CPLR § 3211(a)(7) motion, the court will dismiss a cause of action if, after viewing the complaint's allegations in the light most favorable to the nonmoving party, it appears either that (1) the nonmovant failed to allege all relevant propositions of fact comprising the cause of action, or (2) the nonmovant lodged a nonexistent cause of action. On such a motion,

---

7. CPLR § 3211(a)(7).
8. Higgitt, Practice Commentary, McKinney's Cons Laws of NY, Book 7B, CPLR C3211:22.
9. CPLR§ 3211(a)(7); *id.* § 3211(e) states that a motion to dismiss is to be made "[a]t any time before service of the responsive pleading."
10. *Id.* § 3211(c).

the allegations of the pleading "must be accepted as true," the court must liberally "accord the plaintiff the benefit of every possible favorable inference," and should "determine only whether the facts as alleged fit within any cognizable legal theory."[11]

However, by way of contrast with the old common-law demurrer, per CPLR § 3211(c), on a motion to dismiss, the parties are allowed (but not required) to submit affidavits or other evidentiary materials either in support of or in opposition to the motion.[12] Where evidence is tendered in support of (or in opposition to) a CPLR § 3211(a)(7) motion, "the court must determine whether the proponent of the pleading has a cause of action, not whether the proponent has stated one."[13]

In other words, on a motion to dismiss, evidentiary materials may be used as a *shield* or a *sword*. First, the party opposing a motion to dismiss may seek to prevent dismissal of a cause of action by submitting evidentiary materials. Indeed, the nonmovant may amplify his or her (defective) pleading by producing affidavits or other evidentiary materials which, considered together with the facially insufficient pleading, show the existence of a cognizable cause of action.[14] The purpose of this rule is to allow the nonmovant to "preserve inartfully pleaded, but potentially meritorious claims."[15]

In addition, extrinsic evidentiary materials may occasionally be used as a sword to attack a facially sufficient pleading. In other words, where evidence unequivocally shows either that (1) a pleaded fact is not a fact at all,[16] or (2) a pleaded proposition of fact is flatly unbelievable, then an apparently well-pleaded cause of action may be dismissed.[17] However, courts are generally reluctant to dismiss a seemingly well-pleaded cause of action. Indeed, it has been said that, although CPLR § 3211(a)(7) permits the proponent of a claim to submit affidavits, "it does not oblige" the proponent "to do so on penalty of dismissal," and the proponent "will not be penalized because he has not made an evidentiary showing in support of his complaint."[18] On the other hand, allegations in the complaint that are "bare legal conclusions, as well as factual claims [that are] either inherently incredible

---

11. Teng Fang Jiang v. Bldg. No. One, LLC, 2014 N.Y. Misc. LEXIS 5199, at *2 (N.Y. Sup. Ct. Oct. 15, 2014).
12. CPLR § 3211(c).
13. Zurich Depository Corp. v. Iron Mtn. Info. Mgt., Inc., 879 N.Y.S.2d 143, 145 (App. Div. 2009).
14. African Diaspora Mar. Corp. v. Golden Gate Yacht Club, 968 N.Y.S.2d 459, 464 (App. Div. 2013).
15. Shah v. Exxis, Inc., 31 N.Y.S.3d 512, 514 (App. Div. 2016).
16. Guggenheimer v. Ginzburg, 372 N.E.2d 17, 21 (N.Y. 1977).
17. M & B Joint Venture, Inc. v. Laurus Master Fund, Ltd., 853 N.Y.S.2d 300, 303 (App. Div. 2008).
18. Sokol v. Leader, 904 N.Y.S.2d 153, 155 (App. Div. 2010).

or flatly contradicted by documentary evidence, are not presumed to be true and [are not] accorded every favorable inference."[19]

Such is the import of the case of *Rovello v. Orofino Realty Co.*,[20] wherein the Court of Appeals of New York clarified to what extent extrinsic evidentiary materials may be considered on a motion to dismiss. In *Rovello*, plaintiff purchaser sued the defendant seller for specific performance of a contract under which the defendant agreed to sell inter alia the outstanding stock of a corporation.[21] The plaintiff alleged that the relevant part of said agreement was never performed. Defendant moved to dismiss for failure to state a claim.[22] In support of the motion, Defendant submitted affidavits to the effect that the plaintiff failed to tender the down payment as provided by the contract of sale.[23] Conversely, the plaintiff's affidavits failed to address said issue altogether.[24]

The trial court denied the motion and on appeal, a divided panel of the Appellate Division reversed and dismissed the cause of action.[25] On further appeal, the Court of Appeals reversed and reinstated the trial court's order.[26] To that end, the Court of Appeals said:

> The mere fact that, judged on the complaint and affidavits alone, plaintiff could not withstand a motion for summary judgment under CPLR 3212, which requires disclosure of all the evidence on the disputed issues, cannot be controlling. Of course, CPLR 3211 allows plaintiff to submit affidavits, but it does not oblige him to do so on penalty of dismissal, as is the case under CPLR 3212 when defendant has made an evidentiary showing that refutes the pleaded cause of action. If plaintiff chooses to stand on his pleading alone, confident that its allegations are sufficient to state all the necessary elements of a cognizable cause of action, he is at liberty to do so and, unless the motion to dismiss is converted by the court to a motion for summary judgment, he will not be penalized because he has not made an evidentiary showing in support of his complaint.
> . . .
> On the other hand, affidavits may be used freely to preserve inartfully pleaded, but potentially meritorious, claims. . . . In sum, in instances in which a motion to

---

19. *M & B Joint Venture*, 853 N.Y.S.2d at 303 (citing Biondi v. Beekman Hill Hous. Apartment Corp., 692 N.Y.S.2d 304, 308 (App. Div. 1999)).
20. Rovello v. Orofino Realty Co., Inc., 357 N.E.2d 970 (N.Y. 1976).
21. *Id.* at 971, 973.
22. *Id.*
23. *Id.* at 973.
24. *Id.* at 971–973.
25. *Id.* at 970, 973; Rovello v. Orofino Realty Co., Inc., 378 N.Y.S. 2d 740, 741 (App. Div. 1976).
26. *Rovello*, 357 N.E.2d at 970, 973.

dismiss made under CPLR 3211 (subd [a], par 7) is not converted to a summary judgment motion, affidavits may be received for a limited purpose only, serving normally to remedy defects in the complaint, although there may be instances in which a submission by plaintiff will conclusively establish that he has no cause of action. It seems that after the amendment of 1973 affidavits submitted by the defendant will seldom if ever warrant the relief he seeks unless too the affidavits establish conclusively that plaintiff has no cause of action.[27]

In *Miglino v. Bally Total Fitness of Greater N.Y., Inc.,*[28] the plaintiff, as executor of the decedent's estate, brought a wrongful death suit against the defendant, the owner and operator of a health club. In support of his common law and statutory causes of action sounding in negligence, plaintiff alleged that when the decedent collapsed at the defendant's health club, defendant's employees failed to administer CPR and to defibrillate decedent.[29]

Defendant filed a motion to dismiss for failure to state a claim.[30] In support of the motion, defendant submitted evidentiary materials to the effect that the health club's employees fulfilled the limited duties imposed on health clubs when patrons suffer from a coronary incident.[31] Namely, the defendant's affidavits showed that defendant called 911, broadcast an announcement summoning medical personnel, and made available to the victim an employee trained in CPR and in operating a defibrillator unit.[32] On this record, the trial court denied the motion, noting that the defendant's affidavits made out a "strong, but not conclusive showing that the plaintiff does not have a cause if action."[33] The Appellate Division affirmed.[34] The Court of Appeals also affirmed, stating:

> Here, the complaint asserts that Bally did not "employ or properly employ life-saving measures regarding [Miglino]" after he collapsed. Bally's motion is supported by affidavits that contradict this claim, by purporting to show that the minimal steps adequate to fulfill a health club's limited duty to a patron apparently suffering a coronary incident—i.e., calling 911, administering CPR and/or relying on medical professionals who are voluntarily furnishing emergency

---

27. *Id.* at 972.
28. Miglino v. Bally Total Fitness of Greater N.Y., Inc., 985 N.E.2d 128 (N.Y. 2013).
29. *Id.* at 128–30.
30. *Id.* at 130.
31. *Id.* at 129–30.
32. *Id.*
33. Miglino v. Bally Total Fitness of Greater N.Y., Inc., 2010 N.Y. Misc. LEXIS 6797, at *5 (N.Y. Sup. Ct. 2010).
34. *Miglino,* 985 N.E.2d at 128.

care—were, in fact, undertaken. But, as noted before, this matter comes to us on a motion to dismiss, not a motion for summary judgment. As a result, the case is not currently in a posture to be resolved as a matter of law on the basis of the parties' affidavits, and Miglino has at least pleaded a viable cause of action at common law.[35]

Miglino's (apparently) broad language seems to imply that, on a CPLR § 3211(a)(7) motion, affidavits may be used only for preventing summary dismissal of a defective (but potentially meritorious) complaint.[36] Thus, an argument that *Rovello* has been implicitly overruled by *Miglino* could hypothetically be made. However, in *Liberty Affordable Hous., Inc. v. Maple Court Apartments*,[37] the Fourth Department clarified that:

> Indeed, given its unqualified citation to *Rovello*, *Miglino* is properly understood as a straightforward application of *Rovello*'s long-standing framework. *Miglino* was "not currently in a posture to be resolved as a matter of law on the basis of the parties' affidavits" . . . because the evidentiary submissions were insufficiently conclusive, not because they were categorically inadmissible in the context of a CPLR 3211(a)(7) motion. We therefore conclude that the court properly considered defendant's evidentiary submissions in evaluating the motion to dismiss at bar.[38]

B. CPLR § 3211(a)(1)

As explained above, the proponent of a cause of action argues that, because a certain set of legally operative facts occurred in the real world, the competent court should intervene and carry out the legal effect set forth by the law against the wishes of the nonmoving party. Obviously, before a court of law may take steps to afford the proponent whatever relief he or she prayed for, the propositions of fact upon which proponent's case rests must be authenticated.

Theoretically, there are three avenues through which a court may ascertain what the real-world state of affairs is, namely: (1) through experience, (2) by direct observation, and (3) by evaluating evidence. As has been explained in the first chapter of this book, in our modern justice system, judges and jurors ought

---

35. *Id.* at 134.

36. *Id.*; CPLR § 3211(a)(7).

37. Liberty Affordable Hous., Inc. v. Maple Court Apartments, 998 N.Y.S.2d 543, 545 (App. Div. 2015).

38. *Id.* at 547. *See also* Basis Yield Alpha Fund (Master) v. Goldman Sachs Grp., Inc., 980 N.Y.S.2d 21 (App. Div. 2014).

not to have prior direct knowledge of the events underlying the pending lawsuit. From the above, it follows that courts may authenticate the propositions of fact upon which proponent's claims rest only by considering the evidence[39] submitted by litigants.

It goes without saying, when human beings are to evaluate evidence tending to show the occurrence (or nonoccurrence) of a certain event, different assessments of the credibility of the evidence may result. Reasonable people may weigh the same piece of evidence differently or, alternatively, different pieces of evidence similarly.

Indeed, whenever the evidence tendered at trial is such that reasonable minds may differ as to the weight the evidence should be assigned, a triable issue of fact arises. If such an issue of material fact arises, then the case has to be submitted to the decider of fact (generally, the jury) for deliberations. By way of contrast, when the judge ascertains that reasonable minds may *not* differ as to the credibility to assign the evidence, the case may be taken away from the jury and decided as a matter of law.

Now, let us recall that the proponent of a claim who bears the burden of production must make out a *prima facie* case, that is, produce sufficient evidence on each element of the cause of action, or else be defeated as a matter of law. Once the proponent makes out such a *prima facie* showing, the burden of production shifts to the opponent who will lose the case unless the opponent: (1) impeaches the proponent's proof, (2) introduces rebuttal evidence, or (3) makes out a *prima facie* showing of an affirmative defense. Subsequently, if the opponent makes out a *prima facie* showing of a defense, the burden of production may shift back to the proponent.

There are several procedural devices through which the judge may decide a case as a matter of law. One such procedural device is dismissal under CPLR § 3211(a)(1).[40] Section 3211(a)(1) provides that "[a] party may move for judgment dismissing one or more causes of action asserted against him on the ground that . . . a defense is found upon documentary evidence."[41]

As a matter of semantics, an item of *documentary evidence* may be defined as an object capable of establishing the truth of a past event.[42] In other words, a tangible object qualifies as an item of *documentary evidence* if, by observing

---

39. In limited circumstances, the court may take judicial notice of widely known facts.
40. CPLR § 3211(a)(1).
41. *Id.*
42. *Documentary Evidence*, Ballentine's Law Dictionary (3d ed. 1998); *see also* Curtis v. Bradley, 31 A. 591 (Conn. 1894).

or touching it, reasonable people could conclude that a past event did (or did not) occur. Logically, tangible objects are inherently somewhat more reliable than other kinds of evidence because of their durable and immutable character.

If a *prima facie* showing is neutralized by *strong* documentary evidence it is unlikely that the adversary will be able to rebut such evidence. Accordingly, the judge may dismiss a cause of action where the opponent effectively neutralizes the proponent's *prima facie* showing by producing documentary evidence tending to disprove the elements of their adversary's causes of action. In fact, as a result of said documents production, the burden of going forward with the evidence shifts back to the proponent. Thus, dismissal is warranted if the proponent fails to meet his or her burden of production.

Under CPLR § 3211(a)(1), the court may dismiss a claim as a matter of law when the opponent tenders documents that (1) definitively "dispose of [the] plaintiff's claim,"[43] (2) utterly disprove proponent's factual contentions,[44] and (3) are "unambiguous, authentic, and undeniable. . . ."[45] The Second Department clarified that "[n]either affidavits, deposition testimony, nor letters are considered 'documentary evidence.'"[46] Conversely, "[m]aterials that clearly qualify as 'documentary evidence' include 'documents reflecting out-of-court transactions such as mortgages, deeds, contracts, and any other papers, the contents of which are essentially undeniable.'"[47]

In *Eisner v. Cusumano Constr., Inc.*,[48] plaintiff brought suit against defendant construction company claiming damages for an alleged breach of contract. Defendant filed a pre-answer motion to dismiss under CPLR § 3211(a)(1) alleging that plaintiff—in violation of the written contract—did not provide notice of the alleged breach, failing to afford the defendant an opportunity to cure said breach.[49] Essentially, the defendant argued that plaintiff failed to comply with a condition precedent set forth in the contract.[50] Indeed, the defendant attempted to prove said defense by submitting evidence (i.e., the contract, certain affidavits, and

43. Bronxville Knolls v. Webster Town Ctr. P'ship, 634 N.Y.S.2d 62 (App. Div. 1995).
44. Ozdemir v. Caithness Corp., 728 N.Y.S.2d 824 (App. Div. 2001).
45. Granada Condo. III Ass'n v. Palomino, 913 N.Y.S.2d 668, 669 (App. Div. 2010) (citing Fontanetta v. John Doe 1, 898 N.Y.S.2d 569 (App. Div. 2010)).
46. *Id.* (citing Suchmacher v. Manana Grocery, 900 N.Y.S.2d 686 (Mem.) (App. Div. 2010)).
47. Midorimatsu, Inc. v. Hui Fat Co., 951 N.Y.S.2d 570, 682 (App. Div. 2012) (citing *Fontanetta*, 898 N.Y.S.2d at 574 (quoting Siegel, Practice Commentaries, McKinney's Cons. Laws of N.Y., Book 7B, CPLR C3211:10)).
48. Eisner v. Cusumano Constr., Inc., 18 N.Y.S.3d 683 (App. Div. 2015).
49. *Id.* at 684.
50. *Id.*

text messages).[51] The Supreme Court granted the motion to dismiss and an appeal ensued.[52] The Second Department reversed, stating:

> On a pre-answer motion to dismiss pursuant to CPLR 3211, the pleading is to be afforded a liberal construction and the plaintiff's allegations are accepted as true and accorded the benefit of every possible favorable inference.
>
> . . .
>
> In order for evidence submitted in support of a CPLR 3211(a)(1) motion to qualify as documentary evidence, it must be unambiguous, authentic, and undeniable. Judicial records, as well as documents reflecting out-of-court transactions such as mortgages, deeds, contracts, and any other papers, the contents of which are essentially undeniable, would qualify as documentary evidence in the proper case. However, neither affidavits, deposition testimony, nor letters are considered documentary evidence within the intendment of CPLR 3211(a)(1).
>
> Here, the affidavits and text messages relied upon by the Supreme Court in concluding that the plaintiff failed to comply with the alleged condition precedent were not essentially undeniable, and did not constitute documentary evidence. Furthermore, the documentary evidence that was submitted by the defendants in support of their motion did not conclusively establish that the plaintiff failed to comply with the subject provision of the parties' agreement, and proof of the existence of that contract provision did not, without more, conclusively establish a defense as a matter of law.[53]

In *Weston v. Cornell University*,[54] the plaintiff, a professor, brought suit against his employer for breach of contract. The plaintiff claimed she was wrongfully terminated by defendant Cornell University, despite the fact that she had been offered a tenured position.[55] Cornell filed a motion to dismiss under CPLR § 3211(a)(1) claiming that, although the first paragraph of the written employment offer stated the university was extending an offer for a tenured position, the document's second paragraph qualified that statement, making clear that the employer did not actually guarantee tenure.[56] Indeed, defendant argued that the offer's second paragraph set forth a mere promise that Cornell University would process plaintiff's application for tenure.[57] The Supreme

---

51. *Id.* at 683, 685.
52. *Id.* at 683–684.
53. *Id.* at 685–686 (internal citations and quotation marks omitted).
54. Weston v. Cornell Univ., 868 N.Y.S.2d 364 (App. Div. 2008).
55. *Id.* at 363–364.
56. *Id.*
57. *Id.*

Court granted the motion to dismiss and an appeal ensued.[58] The Third Department reversed, stating:

> On a motion pursuant to CPLR 3211 (a)(1), it is well settled that dismissal is warranted only if the documentary evidence conclusively establishes a defense and resolves every factual issue as a matter of law. Here, the issue raised by defendant's motion is whether the written offer clearly and unambiguously establishes that plaintiff was not assured that her employment would be protected by tenure and, thus, she would have no claim for breach of contract. In determining whether a contract's provisions are ambiguous, a court must determine as a matter of law whether they lack a definite and precise meaning and provide a reasonable basis for a difference of opinion.[59]

In other words, if the documentary evidence is ambiguous such that reasonable minds may differ as to its interpretation, a triable issue of fact for the jury arises and dismissal is not warranted.

C.   CPLR § 3211(b)

Generally speaking, the party asserting a defense argues that the claimant is not entitled to the relief prayed for because certain events occurred in the real world such that, under the applicable law, the adversary's claim is neutralized. To put it differently, the litigant asserting a defense contends that—notwithstanding the purported truthfulness of the claimant's assertions of fact—additional events took place and that the legal effect of such additional events is to negate the relief the adversary claimed to be entitled to.

In mathematical terms, the previous point can be stated as follows: typically, the proponent of a cause of action argues that he or she is entitled to the xyz legal effect because the propositions of fact A, B, and C took place (i.e., xyz = $A + B + C$); the opponent, who seeks to ward off the proponent's attack, counters asserting that the xyz legal effect is neutralized because the events D and E occurred in addition to the facts A, B, and C (i.e., non-xyz = [A + B + C] + [D + E]).

Therefore, an opponent who wants to assert a defense ought to file a pleading (generally, the answer) alleging that the propositions of fact upon which his or her defense is based actually took place in the real world. Needless to say, if the opponent fails to allege all elements of the defense, then said defense will fail. To this end,

---

58. *Id.*
59. *Id.* at 365 (internal citations and quotations mark omitted).

CPLR § 3211(b) provides that "[a] party may move for judgment dismissing one or more defenses, on the ground that a defense is not stated or has no merit."[60] Such a motion may be directed at any defense except mere denials.[61] Essentially, a CPLR § 3211(b) motion mirrors a motion to dismiss pursuant to CPLR § 3211(a)(7).[62] Thus, the above discussion relating to CPLR § 3211(a)(7) is largely applicable to a motion to dismiss a defense.[63]

On a motion to dismiss a defense brought under CPLR 3211(b), "the plaintiff bears the burden of demonstrating that the affirmative defense is 'without merit as a matter of law.'"[64] By way of example, in *Staropoli v. Agrelopo, LLC*,[65] a personal injury case, the plaintiff, as executor of the decedent's estate, brought suit inter alia against the driver and the owner of the vehicle that allegedly caused the accident at issue. The owner of the vehicle asserted an affirmative defense contending that the driver was not an authorized user under the terms of the loan agreement pursuant to which the vehicle had been originally loaned to the driver's wife.[66] Accordingly, the vehicle's owner submitted documentary evidence *prima facie* showing that the driver was an *unauthorized* user.[67] Essentially, the owner of the vehicle argued that, under N.Y. Vehicle & Traffic Law § 388, they could not be held vicariously liable.[68]

The driver moved to strike the affirmative defenses pursuant to CPLR § 3211(b) and the trial court denied the motion.[69] On appeal, the Second Department affirmed, stating:

> Pursuant to CPLR 3211(b), a "party may move for judgment dismissing one or more defenses, on the ground that a defense is not stated or has no merit." In reviewing a motion to dismiss an affirmative defense, the court must liberally construe the pleadings in favor of the party asserting the defense and give that party the benefit of every reasonable inference. In addition, if there is any doubt as to the availability of a defense, it should not be dismissed.

---

60. CPLR § 3211(b).
61. Chi. Dressed Beef Co. v. Gold Medal Packing Corp., 254 N.Y.S.2d 717, 717-18 (App. Div. 1964).
62. CPLR §§ 3211(a)(7), (b).
63. *Id.*
64. Mazzei v. Kyriacou, 951 N.Y.S.2d 557, 559 (App. Div. 2012) (citing Greco v. Christofferson, 896 N.Y.S.2d 363 (App. Div. 2010) (quoting Vita v. New York Waste Servs., LLC, 824 N.Y.S.2d 177, 178–79 (App. Div. 2006)).
65. Staropoli v. Agrelopo, LLC, 24 N.Y.S.3d 722 (App. Div. 2016).
66. *Id.* at 722–724.
67. *Id.* at 724–725.
68. *Id.*
69. *Id.*

Here, the loaner car agreement . . . that Phillips executed with Westbury prior to receiving the vehicle generally allowed the appellant, as her spouse, to drive the vehicle. However, such permission was conditioned upon other terms within the agreement. Among these terms were Phillips's agreement that she would not allow the loaner vehicle to be operated by "anyone who is not a qualified and licensed driver" or by "anyone whose driver's license in any state has been revoked or suspended within the previous 3 years, even if he or she now possesses a valid driver's license." The evidence submitted by Westbury, and, in particular, its submission of an extract of the appellant's driver license record from the New York State Department of Motor Vehicles, provided substantial evidence to rebut the presumption . . . . Accordingly, the appellant was not entitled to dismissal of the subject affirmative defenses, since such defenses were not "without merit as a matter of law."[70]

II. SUMMARY JUDGMENT

A. Summary Judgment Motions

A motion for summary judgment is to be made only after the pleadings are complete. It can only be made, with a few exceptions, once a complaint is served by plaintiff and an answer to that complaint is served on plaintiff by defendant. The expression is that the "pleadings have to be closed," meaning that the complaint and the answer have been served. The movant carries the burden of proof to show there are no genuine material issues of fact and that the movant is entitled to judgment as a matter of law.

The rules associated with summary judgment are fairly straightforward. The proponent of a motion for summary judgment carries the initial burden of production of evidence as well as the burden of persuasion. The moving party must tender sufficient evidence to demonstrate: (1) the absence of a material issue of fact, and (2) that it is entitled to judgment as a matter of law.

Failure to make that initial showing requires denial of the motion, regardless of the sufficiency of the opposing papers. If the movant does not come forward with enough proof to establish that there are no issues of material fact, then the motion is denied no matter what the nonmoving party says.

Once the moving party has made a *prima facie* showing of entitlement of summary judgment, the burden of production shifts to the opponent, who must now go forward and produce sufficient evidence in admissible form to establish the

---

70. *Id.* (internal citations omitted).

existence of a triable issue of fact or demonstrate an acceptable excuse for failing to do so. The burden of persuasion always remains with the moving party.

The court's main function on a motion for summary judgment is issue finding rather than issue determination. Because summary judgment is a drastic remedy, it should not be granted where there is any doubt as to the existence of a triable issue. Thus, when the existence of an issue of fact is even arguable or debatable, summary judgment should be denied. In reviewing a motion for summary judgment, the court must accept as true the evidence presented by the nonmoving party and deny the motion if there is "even arguably any doubt as to the existence of a triable issue."[71]

Summary judgment, in its most basic definition, asks the court to dispose of actions in which there is no genuine issue as to any material fact and the movant is entitled to judgment as a matter of law, prior to trial.[72] In *Crawford-El v. Britton*, the Supreme Court characterized summary judgment as "the ultimate screen to weed out truly unsubstantial lawsuits prior to trial."[73] The goal of summary judgment is largely to achieve judicial efficiency. Despite the well-articulated rule framed in the CPLR, satisfying the requirements of summary judgment as the moving or nonmoving party can prove challenging. The burden of proof on the moving party to achieve summary judgment is significant, as is the subsequent burden on the nonmoving party. Deconstructing the summary judgment provision is essential to successfully navigating through the requirements of a motion for summary judgment.

In New York, summary judgment (CPLR § 3212) is a procedural device aimed to more efficiently and quickly resolve civil cases and empowers the court to assess a party's causes of action or defenses prior to trial.[74] Because an order of summary judgment ultimately bankrupts a party of its day in court, it is considered a drastic remedy.[75]

Rule 3212(b) outlines the supporting proof required by, and the grounds of relief for, either the moving or nonmoving party as follows:

> A motion for summary judgment shall be supported by affidavit, by a copy of the pleadings and by other available proof, such as depositions and written admissions.

---

71. Baker v. Briarcliff Sch. Dist., 613 N.Y.S.2d 660, 661-62 (App. Div. 1994) (citing Hourigan v. McGarry, 484 N.Y.S.2d 243, 244 (App. Div. 1984)).

72. MBIA Ins. Corp. v. J.P. Morgan Sec. LLC, 997 N.Y.S.2d 99 (N.Y. Sup. Ct. 2014).

73. Crawford-El v. Britton, 523 U.S. 574, 600 (1998).

74. CPLR § 3212.

75. Rotuba Extruders, Inc. v. Ceppos, 385 N.E.2d 1068, 1072 (N.Y. 1978) (quoting Moskowitz v. Garlock, 259 N.Y.S.2d 1003, 1004 (App. Div. 1965)).

The affidavit shall be by a person having knowledge of the facts; it shall recite all the material facts; and it shall show that there is no defense to the cause of action or that the cause of action or defense has no merit. . . . The motion shall be granted if, upon all the papers and proof submitted, the cause of action or defense shall be established sufficiently to warrant the court as a matter of law in directing judgment in favor of any party. Except as provided in subdivision (c) of this rule the motion shall be denied if any party shall show facts sufficient to require a trial of any issue of fact.[76]

"Summary judgment is the procedural equivalent of a trial. . . ."[77] A party can move for summary judgment to resolve an entire action, or move for partial summary judgment to dismiss specific causes of action or defenses.[78] "In considering a motion for summary judgment, the function of the court is not to determine issues of fact or credibility, but merely to determine whether such issues exist."[79] The motion "must be denied if any doubt exists as to a triable issue or where a material issue of fact is arguable."[80]

1. Pretrial Resolution: Undisputed Material Facts

A New York court is authorized to grant summary judgment only where the moving party has demonstrated that there are *no material issues of fact* for a particular cause of action and it can be decided as a matter of law.[81] Once the movant has established that there are no issues of material fact, and only questions of law remain, the court may decide the motion without a trial based solely upon the parties' summary judgment evidence. The movant bears the burden of proof and is required to submit sufficient evidentiary proof of the elements of the alleged cause of action or defense to justify a court ordering judgment in its favor.[82]

a. What Is a Material Fact?

The elements of the specific cause of action alleged influence whether a fact is material. For example, in a defamation action against a public figure, one element that plaintiff must prove is that the defendant made the defamatory statement with actual malice. Actual malice is therefore a material fact. If the defendant

---

76. CPLR § 3212(b).
77. Rivers v. Birnbaum, 953 N.Y.S.2d 232, 244 (App. Div. 2012).
78. CPLR § 3212(e).
79. *Rivers*, 953 N.Y.S.2d at 232 (citing Gitlin v. Chirinkin, 949 N.Y.S.2d 712 (App. Div. 2012)).
80. *Id.* (quoting Dykeman v. Heht, 861 N.Y.S.2d 732 (App. Div. 2008)).
81. CPLR § 3212(b); Brill v. City of New York, 814 N.E.2d 431, 433 (N.Y. 2004).
82. *See* Zuckerman v. New York, 404 N.E.2d 718, 719-21 (N.Y. 1980).

moves for summary judgment, in order to defeat the motion, the plaintiff must submit evidentiary proof of actual malice. If the plaintiff fails to do so, defendant's motion for summary judgment will be granted and the action dismissed.[83]

b. Who Can Move for Summary Judgment and When the Motion Can Be Made

Any party may move for summary judgment in any action on any cause of action or defense.[84] A party may move for summary judgment after issue has been joined and an answer to the complaint has been filed.[85] Pursuant to CPLR § 3212(a), a party may initially move for summary judgment only after the defendant has served an answer.[86] Parties generally move for summary judgment after discovery is finished, and after the note of issue and certificate of readiness are filed to avoid a potential denial of the motion due to outstanding discovery.[87]

2. *The Movant's Burden*

The proponent of a motion for summary judgment pursuant to CPLR § 3212 carries the initial burdens of proof, production of evidence, and persuasion.[88] The moving party must make a *prima facie*[89] showing of sufficient evidence in admissible form to demonstrate as a matter of law the absence of a material issue of fact.[90] "Failure to make [that initial] showing requires denial of the motion, regardless of the sufficiency of the opposing papers."[91]

Conversely, the exposing of a defect in the nonmovant's evidence does not help satisfy the movant's lofty burden of proof. Pointing out a gap in the opposition's

---

83. *See* Friends of Animals, Inc. v. Associated Fur Mfrs., 390 N.E.2d 298, 298-99 (N.Y. 1979).
84. CPLR § 3212(a).
85. *Id.*
86. *Id.*
87. Lindbergh v. SHLO 54, LLC, 9 N.Y.S.3d 105, 107 (App. Div. 2015) (A "note of issue" is filed in New York state court confirming that (1) a case is trial ready and (2) that parties have completed all necessary discovery); CPLR § 3402(a); *see* Caban v. Mastrosimone, 10 N.Y.S.3d 615, 616 (App. Div. 2015).
88. CPLR § 3212; Alvarez v. Prospect Hosp., 501 N.E.2d 572, 574 (N.Y.1986).
89. *Prima facie* is a Latin term meaning "at first sight" or "at first look." This refers to the standard of proof under which the party with the burden of proof need only present enough evidence to create a rebuttable presumption that the matter asserted is true. A *prima facie* standard of proof is relatively low. It is far less demanding than the preponderance of the evidence, clear and convincing evidence, and beyond a reasonable doubt standards that are also commonly used.
90. *MBIA Ins. Corp.*, 997 N.Y.S.2d 99.
91. Weingrad v. New York Univ. Med. Ctr., 476 N.E.2d 642, 643-44 (N.Y. 1985) (citing Redemption Church of Christ of Apostolic Faith, Inc. v. Williams, 444 N.Y.S.2d 305, 306-07 (App. Div. 1981)).

proof, as opposed to "affirmatively demonstrating the merit of" its own motion for summary judgment, is simply insufficient.[92] Once the moving party establishes proof in evidentiary form, the burden shifts to the nonmovant, who must subsequently fully divulge proof to establish the cause of action.[93] In addition, evidence "merely casting doubt on the credibility of [an] expert" is insufficient to substantiate a cause of action.[94]

3.   Admissible Evidence

The movant must demonstrate entitlement to summary judgment by the "tender of evidentiary proof in admissible form."[95] The requirement that the proof be admissible is predicated upon the notion that a successful motion will deprive a party of a trial and result in an immediate judgment.[96] The burden of proof requires admissible evidence; thus, admissibility becomes one of the prongs of summary judgment in New York. What is admissible under New York law is detailed within CPLR Article 45.

a.   Affidavits and Exhibits

CPLR § 3212(b) provides that a summary judgment motion be supported by affidavits of persons having knowledge of the facts, copies of the pleadings, and other proof, such as depositions and written admissions.[97] Affidavits and exhibits submitted in support of the motion should set out the facts necessary to decide the motion. For the movant to obtain summary judgment on a cause of action or defense, the affidavits and exhibits must demonstrate that the cause of action has merit and there is no defense.[98] Conversely, for a movant to obtain summary judgment dismissing a cause of action or defense, the affidavits and exhibits must demonstrate that the cause of action or defense has no merit.[99]

In commercial litigation, the movant is required to submit a statement of material facts that the movant contends are not in dispute. The party opposing

---

92. *See* Vittorio v. U-Haul Co., 861 N.Y.S.2d 726, 727 (App. Div. 2008); Corrigan v. Spring Lake Bldg. Corp., 804 N.Y.S.2d 412, 412-13 (App. Div. 2005).
93. *See* Burton v. Ertel, 483 N.Y.S.2d 854 (App. Div. 1985); Piccolo v. DeCarlo, 456 N.Y.S.2d 171, 172-73 (App. Div. 1982).
94. *See* Cusano v. General Elec. Co., 489 N.Y.S.2d 622, 624 (App. Div. 1985).
95. *Friends of Animals, Inc.*, 390 N.E.2d at 299.
96. *Id.*
97. CPLR § 3212(b) (Consol. 2019).
98. *Id.*
99. *Id.*

summary judgment is then required to submit an opposing statement identifying the issues in dispute that must be tried.[100]

b. Depositions

Deposition transcripts submitted in support of a summary judgment motion must be in admissible form and comply with the requirements set out in the CPLR, including CPLR § 3116.[101] The questions and the answers must be usable in the motion context, as if it were trial testimony where the rules of evidence apply to the use of testimony as well.

4. Opposing the Motion and Shifting the Burden of Production

Once the moving party has made a *prima facie* showing of entitlement to summary judgment, the burden of production shifts to the opponent, who must now come forward and produce sufficient evidence in admissible form to establish the existence of a triable issue of fact or demonstrate an acceptable excuse for failing to do so.[102] If the movant fails to successfully make a *prima facie* showing of entitlement to summary judgment as a matter of law, then the opposing "party bears no burden to otherwise persuade the court against summary judgment."[103] Essentially, if the movant does not successfully meet its burden of proof, the burden never shifts to the opposing party to demonstrate the existence of triable material issues of fact.[104]

In reviewing a motion for summary judgment, the court "must accept as true the evidence presented by the nonmoving party," and must deny the motion "if there is even arguably any doubt as to the existence of a triable issue."[105] The burden of production imposed upon the opponent is the duty to come forward with affirmative and admissible proof that establishes the existence of genuine, triable issues of fact, which plainly indicate a need to proceed to trial.[106] It is imperative that the party opposing summary judgment raise and lay bare

---

100. 22 N.Y.C.R.R. § 202.70(g) (Lexis 2019).

101. Marks v. Robb, 935 N.Y.S.2d 593, 595 (App. Div. 2011); CPLR § 3116.

102. Zuckerman v. New York, 404 N.E.2d 718 (N.Y. 1980).

103. *See* William J. Jenack Estate Appraisers and Auctioneers, Inc. v. Rabizadeh, 5 N.E.3d 976, 980 (N.Y. 2013) (citing Vega v. Restani Const. Corp., 965 N.E.2d 240 (N.Y. 2012)).

104. *See* Lewis Family Farm, Inc. v. Adirondack Park Agency, 882 N.Y.S.2d 762 (App. Div. 2009).

105. *Baker*, 613 N.Y.S.2d at 661–662 (App. Div. 1994) (quoting *Hourigan*, 484 N.Y.S.2d at 244).

106. Zolin v. Roslyn Synagogue, 545 N.Y.S.2d 846, 847 (App. Div. 1989).

its proof, and demonstrate the existence of material questions of fact that the movant "is entitled to litigate."[107] New York courts have ruled that reliance upon the hope that cross-examination, for example, will establish the opponent's case, is a wholly insufficient means of raising an issue of fact.[108] Issue finding is fundamental to defeating a motion for summary judgment: "[w]hile it is true that where the moving party offers factual evidence sufficient to justify summary relief, the burden falls upon the opposing party to come forth with evidentiary facts to offset the movant's proof. . . . It is equally established that issue-finding, rather than issue-determination, is the key to a motion for summary judgment."[109]

The opponent of a motion for summary judgment may, in certain instances, rely upon inadmissible evidence to oppose summary judgment,[110] provided it can demonstrate a reasonable explanation for not submitting admissible evidence.[111] The opponent may even rely on hearsay evidence, provided it is not the only evidence submitted.[112]

The burden of opposing a motion can be satisfied by a tender of deposition testimony showing the movant's inability to prove an element of the relevant cause of action.[113] Attestations of privilege on behalf of the party moving for summary judgment do not serve to relieve the movant from its burden of presenting sufficient evidence to establish there are no material issues of fact. Only the party opposing summary judgment may escape the high burden of proof by providing a satisfactory explanation for its failure to meet the strict requirement of presenting proof in admissible form.[114] The movant's substantial burden includes the obligation to demonstrate the absence of genuine issues of material fact on *every* relevant issue raised by the pleadings, including affirmative defenses.[115]

---

107. Fargnoli v. Icovelli, 470 N.Y.S.2d 862, 863 (App. Div. 1983).
108. Badman v. Civil Serv. Emps. Ass'n, 458 N.Y.S.2d 385 (App. Div. 1982).
109. Graney Dev. Corp. v Taksen, 404 N.Y.S.2d 180, 182 (App. Div. 1978); *see* Blake v. Gardino, 315 N.Y.S.2d 973 (App. Div. 1970); Sillman v. Twentieth Century-Fox Film Corp., 144 N.E.2d 387, 392 (N.Y. 1957); Van Opdorp v. Merchants Mutual Ins. Co., 390 N.Y.S.2d 279 (App. Div. 1976); Milstein v. Montefiore Club of Buffalo, Inc., 365 N.Y.S.2d 301 (App. Div. 1975).
110. *See Zuckerman*, 404 N.E.2d at 719–721; *Friends of Animals, Inc.*, 390 N.E.2d at 299.
111. *Friends of Animals, Inc.*, 390 N.E.2d at 299.
112. Feinberg v. Sanz, 982 N.Y.S.2d 133, 136 (App. Div. 2014); Rugova v. Davis, 976 N.Y.S.2d 61, 62 (App. Div. 2013).
113. *See* Wiwigac v. Snedaker, 723 N.Y.S.2d 248 (App. Div. 2001).
114. *See* Finkelstein v. Cornell Univ. Med. Coll., 702 N.Y.S.2d 285 (App. Div. 2000).
115. *See* Aimatop Rest., Inc. v. Liberty Mut. Fire Ins. Co., 425 N.Y.S.2d 8 (App. Div. 1980).

5. Conclusory Allegations

Summary judgment may not be defeated by mere surmise, conjecture, suspicion,[116] or speculation. The burden of production imposed upon the opponent demands more than mere conclusions, expressions of hope, repetition, or incorporation by reference of the allegations asserted in the pleadings, whether verified or unverified.[117]

New York law holds that conclusory allegations may not establish the existence of a triable issue of fact.[118] In 2014, the Appellate Division, Second Department, after the plaintiff established its *prima facie* entitlement to judgment as a matter of law by showing that the defendant in fact executed the instruments in question, found that the defendant's conclusory allegations of fraud were insufficient to defeat the plaintiff's entitlement to summary judgment.[119] Conclusory allegations are generally an ineffective strategy to oppose summary judgment. In *Unifirst Corp. v. Tristate Indus. Uniform*, the Fourth Department held that conclusory allegations are insufficient to raise a factual issue on a summary judgment motion.[120] Defendant Tristate—seeking summary judgment in an unfair competition matter—met its burden of proof by demonstrating "in admissible form that [they] did not remove confidential information [or] trade secrets," nor "unlawfully interfere with the relationships of [*Unifirst* and] its customers."[121] However, Unifirst, the party opposing summary judgment, did not meet its burden of proof because it failed to submit admissible evidence "establishing that there were unresolved material questions of fact requiring a trial."[122] The court held that Unifirst's "conclusory allegations" against Tristate were "insufficient to raise a factual issue," and thus summary judgment in favor of Tristate was upheld.[123]

In a tort action to recover damages for medical malpractice, the Second Department held that general, conclusory allegations of negligence maintained

---

116. *See* Shaw v. Time-Life Records, 341 N.E.2d 817, 821 (N.Y. 1975) (quoting Shapiro v. Health Ins. Plan of Greater New York, 163 N.E.2d 333, 337 (N.Y. 1959)); Vacca v. Gen. Elec. Credit Corp., 451 N.Y.S.2d 869, 871 (App. Div. 1982) (quoting *Shapiro*, 163 N.E.2d at 337).

117. *See* NYP Holdings, Inc. v. McClier Corp., 921 N.Y.S.2d 35, 38 (App. Div. 2011), Marinelli v. Shifrin, 688 N.Y.S.2d 72 (1st Dep't 1999); Ladonne Sales v. Crimmen, 490 N.Y.S.2d 661 (App. Div. 1985).

118. *See* Sun Convenient, Inc. v. Sarasamir Corp., 999 N.Y.S.2d 432, 435 (App. Div. 2014).

119. *Id.*

120. *See* Unifirst Corp. v. Tri-State Indus. Uniform, 613 N.Y.S.2d 102 (App. Div. 1994).

121. *Id.* at 103.

122. *Id.*; *Zuckerman*, 404 N.E.2d at 718–720.

123. *Unifirst Corp.*, 613 N.Y.S.2d at 103.

by the plaintiff's expert witness were unsupported by evidence necessary to establish the essential elements of malpractice.[124] In *Waterman v. Weinstein Memorial Chapel*, the Second Department again rejected conclusory allegations made in a failed effort to preclude summary judgment.[125] There, the conclusory allegations were made in opposition to the motion for summary judgment, yet nonetheless proved ineffective.[126] The Second Department routinely finds that conclusory allegations are ineffective in opposing summary judgment.[127] Even when the conclusory allegations are submitted in an affidavit, the court rejects the merit of such proof.[128] "[A] motion for summary judgment may not be defeated by the assertion of mere conclusory allegations, expressions of hope or unsubstantiated assertions."[129] It is "incumbent upon the defendant . . . to demonstrate the existence of a bona fide defense by evidentiary facts, and not one based upon conclusory allegations."[130]

6. *Premature Motion Burden, Where Further Discovery Will Disclose Relevant Evidence to Oppose Motion*

A party opposing summary judgment, who contends the motion is premature, must substantiate that further discovery would likely lead to the disclosure of relevant evidence necessary to justify opposition to the motion, and that the likelihood of such evidence will present a triable issue of fact.[131] The opposing party may even contend that the existence of the relevant evidence essential to justify opposition to the motion is solely within the knowledge and control of the moving party.[132]

7. *Motions for Summary Judgment in Lieu of Complaint*

The CPLR provides for an expedited procedure for obtaining a judgment without the necessity of filing a complaint when the action is predicated upon an

---

124. Rosado v. Lutheran Med. Ctr., 608 N.Y.S.2d 506, 507 (App. Div. 1994).

125. Waterman v. Weinstein Mem'l Chapel, 853 N.Y.S.2d 623, 624 (App. Div. 2008).

126. *Id.* at 623–625.

127. *See* V. Savino Oil & Heating Co., Inc. v. Rana Mgmt. Corp., 555 N.Y.S.2d 413 (App. Div. 1990).

128. *Id.*

129. *Id.*

130. Layden v. Boccio, 686 N.Y.S.2d 763 (App. Div. 1998).

131. *See* Williams v. Spencer-Hall, 979 N.Y.S.2d. 157 (App. Div. 2014); Desena v. City of New York, 828 N.Y.S.2d 188 (App. Div. 2007).

132. *See* Cueva v. 373 Wythe Realty, Inc., 976 N.Y.S.2d 516 (App. Div. 2013).

instrument for the payment of money only.[133] CPLR § 3213 provides, in relevant part, as follows:

> When an action is based upon an instrument for the payment of money only or upon any judgment, the plaintiff may serve with the summons a notice of motion for summary judgment and the supporting papers in lieu of a complaint. . . . If the motion is denied, the moving and answering papers shall be deemed the complaint and answer, respectively, unless the court orders otherwise.[134]

A plaintiff may file a summons and a motion for summary judgment in lieu of a complaint under CPLR § 3213, if the matter "is based upon an instrument for the payment of money only or upon any judgment."[135] The question whether the dispute involves an "instrument for the payment of money only" is determined by reference to the document at issue and whether any extrinsic evidence, beyond proof of nonpayment and the instrument itself, is necessary to establish a *prima facie* case for liability.[136]

"[A] document comes within CPLR § 3213 if a prima facie case would be made out by the instrument and a failure to make the payments called for by its terms."[137] However, "[t]he instrument does not qualify if outside proof is needed, other than simple proof of nonpayment or a similar de minimis deviation from the face of the document."[138] It has been difficult for the courts to lay down a clear rule as to which documents qualify for CPLR § 3213 review without answering the separate questions whether, on the one hand, the matter involves an instrument for payment of money only, and whether, on the other hand, summary judgment in the instant matter is appropriate. New York courts that have found a matter to satisfy the "money only" provision of CPLR § 3213 have often settled the question by finding that "[i]n the instant action, no proof other than the instrument sued upon and the affidavit of non-payment is needed to establish a prima facie case."[139]

---

133. *See* CPLR § 3213.

134. *Id.*

135. *Id.*

136. Weissman v. Sinorm Deli, Inc., 669 N.E.2d 242 (N.Y. 1996); Craven v Rigas, 896 N.Y.S.2d 504 (App. Div. 2010).

137. *Weissman*, 669 N.E.2d at 245 (internal quotation marks omitted).

138. *Id. See* Ro & Ke, Inc. v. Stevens, 878 N.Y.S.2d 394 (App. Div. 2009); Stallone v. Rostek, 809 N.Y.S.2d 920 (App. Div. 2006).

139. Council Commerce Corp. v. Paschilides, 459 N.Y.S.2d 463 (App. Div. 1983); *see also* Technical Tape, Inc. v. Spray Truck Inc., 517 N.Y.S.2d 147 (App. Div. 1987); Seaman-Andwall Corp. v. Wright Mach. Corp., 295 N.Y.S.2d 752 (App. Div. 1968).

Once it is demonstrated that the action was properly brought under CPLR § 3213, the standard for summary judgment is the same as that under CPLR § 3212.[140] A plaintiff commencing an action under CPLR § 3213 may establish entitlement to summary judgment by demonstrating that there are no triable issues of fact.[141] Pursuant to CPLR § 3213, the plaintiff would demonstrate no triable issues of fact by presenting the instrument upon which money is owed and proof of nonpayment by defendant.[142] To defeat such a showing, a defendant must present admissible evidence that raises triable issues of fact that would preclude liability.[143] Even if the instrument itself and proof of nonpayment present a *prima facie* case for liability under CPLR § 3213, affidavits that raise triable issues of fact with respect to a bona fide affirmative defense may properly defeat summary judgment.[144] Similarly, if the instrument by its terms references other agreements as to which triable issues of fact exist, summary judgment under CPLR § 3213 would be inappropriate.[145]

The summary judgment in lieu of complaint process provides a litigant with a speedy and efficient resolution to matters that qualify as instruments for the payment of money only.

B. Motion for Default Judgment

With regard to a motion for a default judgment, the burden of proof is set forth in CPLR § 3215(f), which provides in pertinent part as follows:

> on any application for judgment by default, the applicant shall file *proof of service of . . . a summons and notice . . . and proof of the facts constituting the claim, the default and the amount due by affidavit made by the party.* . . . Proof of mailing the notice required by subdivision (g) of this section, where applicable, shall also be filed.[146]

The applicable burden of proof on a motion for default judgment is set forth in CPLR § 3215(f), which requires that the movant "file proof of service . . . and proof of the facts constituting the claim, the default and the amount due

---

140. CPLR § 3213.
141. *Id.*
142. Dresdner Bank AG v. Morse/Diesel, Inc., 499 N.Y.S.2d 703 (App. Div. 1986).
143. *Seaman-Andwall Corp.*, 295 N.Y.S.2d at 754–755.
144. *See, for example*, Silvestri v. Iannone, 689 N.Y.S.2d 241 (App. Div. 1999); Silber v. Muschel, 593 N.Y.S.2d 306 (App. Div. 1993).
145. *Technical Tape, Inc.*, 517 N.Y.S.2d. at 149–150.
146. CPLR § 3215(f) (emphasis added).

by affidavit made by the party."[147] Accordingly, "where service is proper and a plaintiff makes out the facts of its entitlement to judgment, a plaintiff is entitled to a default judgment when defendant fails to appear."[148] With regard to the movant's burden to make out its entitlement to judgment, "the application for default must be supported by either an affidavit of a person with knowledge, or a verified complaint."[149]

However, a party will fail to meet its burden of proof on a default judgment where (1) declaratory relief requested affects the rights of other parties not alleged to be in default,[150] (2) the pleadings alone fail to establish that the plaintiff has a right to a declaratory judgment against the defendant,[151] and (3) the precise issue presented by plaintiff's motions had already been decided against it in another action. In the context of a declaratory judgment action, "[a] default judgment in a declaratory judgment action will not be granted on the default and pleadings alone for it is necessary that plaintiff establish a right to a declaration against . . . a defendant."[152]

C. Motion to Amend Pleading

Generally, leave to amend a pleading pursuant to CPLR § 3025(b) should be freely granted where the proposed amendment is not palpably insufficient or patently devoid of merit and will not prejudice or surprise the opposing party.[153] The Appellate Division, Second Department, has acknowledged that leave to amend should be freely given provided the amendment is not palpably insufficient, does not prejudice or surprise the other side, and is not patently devoid of merit.[154] In exercising its discretion, the court should consider how long the amending party

---

147. *Id.*

148. Ostroy v. Six Sq. LLC, 902 N.Y.S.2d 823 (App. Div. 2010).

149. *Id.*; Wolf v. 3540 Rochambeau Assoc., 650 N.Y.S.2d 161 (App. Div. 1996).

150. Merchants Ins. Co. of New Hampshire, Inc. v. Long Island Pet Cemetery Inc., 616 N.Y.S.2d 299 (App. Div. 1994).

151. *Id.*

152. *Id.* at 300 (citing Levy v. Blue Cross & Blue Shield, 508 N.Y.S.2d 660, 662 (App. Div. 1986); Dole Food Co., Inc. v. Lincoln Gen. Ins. Co., 885 N.Y.S.2d 657 (App. Div. 2009).

153. G.K. Alan Assoc., Inc. v. Lazzari, 840 N.Y.S.2d 378 (App. Div. 2007); Trataros Constr., Inc. v. New York City Hous. Auth., 823 N.Y.S.2d 534 (App. Div. 2006); Surgical Design Corp. v. Correa, 819 N.Y.S.2d 542 (App. Div. 2006); Melendez v. Bernstein, 815 N.Y.S.2d 702 (App. Div. 2006).

154. Spodek v. Neiss, 961 N.Y.S.2d 251 (App. Div. 2013); *see also* Santori v. Metro. Life, 784 N.Y.S.2d 117 (App. Div. 2004); Zacher v. Oakdale Islandia Ltd. P'ship, 621 N.Y.S.2d 376 (App. Div. 1995); Sotomayer v. Princeton Ski Outlet Corp., 605 N.Y.S.2d 296 (App. Div. 1993); Goldstein v. Barco of California, Inc., 486 N.Y.S.2d 688 (App. Div. 1985).

was aware of the facts upon which the motion was predicated, whether a reasonable excuse for the delay was offered, and whether prejudice resulted therefrom.[155] In addition, where a party has been guilty of an extended delay in moving to amend, it must submit an affidavit establishing a reasonable excuse for the delay; otherwise the motion to amend must be denied.[156]

As to the issue of prejudice, the nonmoving party will be prejudiced by the amendment when he "has been hindered in the preparation of his case or has been prevented from taking some measure in support of his position."[157] Specifically, prejudice exists where an amendment seeks "to add [a] new theor[y] of liability that [was] not readily discernible from the allegations in" the original pleading.[158]

Finally, case law is clear that the movant must make some evidentiary showing that the proposed amendment has merit and "a court must examine the underlying merit of the proposed claims, since to do otherwise would be wasteful of judicial resources."[159]

D. Motion for a Preliminary Injunction or Temporary Restraining Order

1. *Motions for Preliminary Injunction*

Courts regard the motion for a preliminary injunction to be one of the most potent pretrial motions available and "one of the most drastic tools in the arsenal of judicial remedies."[160] Consequently, courts warn the preliminary injunction remedy is one that should not be granted routinely or with ease.[161] CPLR §§ 6301

---

155. Surgical Design Corp., Appellant, v. Jamir Correa, et al.; *see also,* Auwarter v. Malverne Union Free School Dist., 715 N.Y.S.2d 852 (App. Div. 2000); Surlak v. Surlak, 466 N.Y.S.2d 461, 471 (App. Div. 1983); Haller v. Lopane, 759 N.Y.S.2d 504, 506 (App. Div. 2003).

156. Reape v. City of New York, 708 N.Y.S.2d 131, 133 (App. Div. 2000); Volpe v. Good Samaritan Hosp., 623 N.Y.S.2d 330 (App. Div. 1995); Perricone v. City of New York, 464 N.Y.S.2d 839, 842 (App. Div. 1983).

157. RCLA, Inc. v. 50-09 Realty, LLC, 852 N.Y.S.2d 211 (App. Div. 2008) (quoting Loomis v. Civetta Corinno Constr. Corp., 429 N.E.2d 90 (N.Y. 1981).

158. Morris v. Queens-Long Is. Med. Group, P.C., 854 N.Y.S.2d 222 (App. Div. 2008).

159. Toscano v. Toscano, 754 N.Y.S.2d 888 (App. Div. 2003); *see also* Reape v. City of New York, 708 N.Y.S.2d 131, 133 (App. Div. 2000); *Volpe,* 623 N.Y.S.2d 330.

160. Hanson Trust PLC v. ML SCM Acquisition, Inc., 781 F.2d 264, 273 (2d Cir. 1986); *see* JSG Trading Corp. v. Tray–Wrap, Inc., 917 F.2d 75, 80 (2d Cir. 1990).

161. Medical Soc'y of the State of New York v. Toia, 560 F.2d 535, 538 (2d Cir. 1977); Wandyful Stadium, Inc. v. Town of Hempstead, 959 F.Supp. 585, 591 (E.D.N.Y. 1997).

and 6312 govern the granting of a preliminary injunction.[162] The party seeking a preliminary injunction bears the burden of proof[163] and must demonstrate: "(1) a likelihood of ultimate success on the merits; (2) irreparable injury absent the granting of the preliminary injunction; and (3) that a balancing of equities favors his position."[164]

"The purpose of a preliminary injunction is to maintain the status quo and prevent the dissipation of property that could render a judgment ineffectual."[165] "The existence of a factual dispute will not bar the granting of a preliminary injunction if one is necessary to preserve the status quo and the party to be enjoined will suffer no great hardship as a result of its issuance."[166] The decision to grant a request for a preliminary injunction rests in the sound discretion of the court.[167]

a. Likelihood of Success

To establish the likelihood of success, the movant must make a clear showing of the right to relief.[168] "It is enough if the moving party makes a *prima facie* showing on his right to relief; the actual proving of his case should be left to the full hearing on the merits."[169] It is not for the court to determine finally the merits of an action

---

162. CPLR § 6301 ("A preliminary injunction may be granted in any action where it appears that the defendant threatens or is about to do, or is doing or procuring or suffering to be done, an act in violation of the plaintiff's rights respecting the subject of the action, and tending to render the judgment ineffectual, or in any action where the plaintiff has demanded and would be entitled to a judgment restraining the defendant from the commission or continuance of an act, which, if committed or continued during the pendency of the action, would produce injury to the plaintiff.")

163. *Id.* § 6312(a) ("on a motion for a preliminary injunction the plaintiff shall show, by affidavit and such other evidence as may be submitted, that there is a cause of action, and either that the defendant threatens or is about to do, or is doing or procuring or suffering to be done, an act in violation of the plaintiff's rights respecting the subject of the action and tending to render the judgment ineffectual; or that the plaintiff has demanded and would be entitled to a judgment restraining the defendant from the commission or continuance of an act, which, if committed or continued during the pendency of the action, would produce injury to the plaintiff.")

164. Gambar Ents., Inc. v. Kelly Servs., Inc., 418 N.Y.S.2d 818, 824 (App. Div. 1979). *See also* Picotte Realty, Inc. v. Gallery of Homes, Inc., 412 N.Y.S.2d 47, 48 (App. Div. 1978); Albini v. Solork Assocs., 326 N.Y.S.2d 150, 151 (App. Div. 1971).

165. Ying Fung Moy v. Hohi Umeki, 781 N.Y.S.2d 684, 686 (App. Div. 2004); *see also* Olympic Tower Condo. v. Cocoziello, 761 N.Y.S.2d 179, 180 (App. Div. 2003).

166. Mr. Natural, Inc. v. Unadulterated Food Prods., Inc., 544 N.Y.S.2d 182, 183 (App. Div. 1989).

167. *Ying Fung Moy,* 781 N.Y.S.2d at 686.

168. Butterman v. Physicians' Reciprocal Insurers, 631 N.Y.S.2d 488 (N.Y. Sup. Ct. 1995).

169. Gambar Enters. v. Kelly Servs., Inc., 418 N.Y.S.2d 818, 825 (App. Div. 1979); *see also* McLaughlin, Piven, Vogel, Inc. v. W.J. Nolan & Co., 498 N.Y.S.2d 146, 153 (App. Div. 1986); Parkmed Co. v. Pro-Life Counselling, Inc., 457 N.Y.S.2d 27, 29 (App. Div. 1982).

upon a motion for preliminary injunction; rather, the purpose of the interlocutory relief is to preserve the *status quo* until a decision is reached on the merits.[170]

Factual disputes do not necessarily bar the granting of a preliminary injunction. On the occasion where safeguarding the *status quo* is paramount, and the opposing party will not suffer a great hardship, a factual dispute will likely not preclude preliminary injunction.[171] However, if the facts upon which a moving party relies to demonstrate "likelihood of success" are in dispute, a preliminary injunction will likely not be granted on the basis that a factual dispute of such a nature requires a full and final determination on the merits, which goes beyond the scope of a preliminary injunction.[172]

b. Irreparable Harm

Irreparable harm has been defined as "that which cannot be repaired, restored, or adequately compensated in money, or where the compensation cannot be safely measured."[173] That injury must be "imminent, not remote or speculative."[174] The risk of further economic harm by loss of good will and patronage is sufficient to demonstrate irreparable harm.[175]

The judicial definition of irreparable harm materially elevates the movant's burden of proof, because the moving party must demonstrate that he is truly without a remedy other than the court's action to impose interlocutory relief. It is well-settled law in New York that where damages are compensable with money, such harm is not irreparable.[176] Courts have held that damage to a corporation's reputation constitutes irreparable injury because the consequences of this type of harm are incalculable and, thus, monetary damages are inadequate.[177] Loss of employment does not constitute irreparable harm because it merely inflicts severe hardship, not irreparable harm, as the courts consider back pay and reinstatement compensable with money and adequate relief.[178]

---

170. Hoppman v. Riverview Equities Corp., 226 N.Y.S.2d 805 (App. Div. 1962); Peekskill Coal & Fuel Oil Co. v. Martin, 108 N.Y.S.2d 30 (App. Div. 1951).

171. Melvin v. Union Coll., 600 N.Y.S.2d 141 (App. Div. 1993).

172. *Id.* at 142–143; Blueberries Gourmet, Inc. v. Aris Realty Corp., 680 N.Y.S.2d 557 (App. Div. 1998).

173. Bisca v. Bisca, 437 N.Y.S.2d 258, 261 (N.Y. Sup. Ct. 1981) (quoting WILLIAM Q. DEFUNIAK, HANDBOOK OF MODERN EQUITY 32 (2d ed. 1956)).

174. Golden v. Steam Heat, Inc., 628 N.Y.S.2d 375, 377 (App. Div. 1995).

175. People v. Anderson, 529 N.Y.S.2d 917, 924 (App. Div. 1988).

176. *See* Scotto v. Mei, 642 N.Y.S.2d 863 (App. Div. 1996).

177. Klein, Wagner & Morris v. Lawrence A. Klein, P. C., 588 N.Y.S.2d 424 (App. Div. 1992).

178. Armitage v. Carey, 375 N.Y.S.2d 898 (App. Div. 1975).

c. Balancing of the Equities

Balancing of the equities—the final element to be considered—requires the movant to demonstrate "that the irreparable injury to be sustained . . . is more burdensome [to the petitioner] than the harm caused to respondent through imposition of the injunction."[179] Equities dictate the establishment of an injunction where there is "no assurance that the plaintiff will be able to stay in business pending trial" without the injunction.[180]

When balancing the equities, the court must "weigh the relative hardship that may be imposed upon each of the parties by the issuance or denial of the preliminary injunction."[181] If the balance appears to favor the nonmoving party, that is to say, the nonmovant will suffer comparative harm significantly greater than the harm suffered by the movant, the preliminary injunction is likely denied. Where the balance appears to favor the moving party, the granting of preliminary injunction is expected.

d. Undertaking

In the event that the court grants a preliminary injunction, the movant will be required to post a bond in an amount sufficient to cover any damages that the enjoined party might sustain if it were subsequently determined that the movant was not entitled to injunctive relief. CPLR § 6312(b) provides, in relevant part, as follows:

> [P]rior to the granting of a preliminary injunction, the plaintiff shall give an undertaking in an amount to be fixed by the court, that the plaintiff, if it is finally determined that he or she was not entitled to an injunction, will pay to the defendant all damages and costs which may be sustained by reason of the injunction. . . .[182]

The successful applicant for a preliminary injunction must be prepared to post a monetary undertaking and must have the financial ability to do so, or the injunction will not issue.

---

179. Nassau Roofing & Sheet Metal Co. v. Facilities Dev. Corp., 418 N.Y.S.2d 216, 218 (App. Div.), *appeal dismissed*, 48 N.Y.2d 654 (N.Y. 1979); *McLaughlin, Piven, Vogel, Inc.*, 498 N.Y.S.2d at 152.
180. *Mr. Natural, Inc.*, 544 N.Y.S.2d at 183.
181. Western N.Y. Motor Lines, Inc. v. Rochester-Genesee Reg. Trans. Auth., 340 N.Y.S.2d 252, 259 (N.Y. Sup. Ct. 1973).
182. CPLR § 6312(b).

2. Motion for Temporary Restraining Order

CPLR §§ 6301 and 6313 govern the basis for the issuance of a temporary restraining order.[183] Section 6313, the authorizing provision, provides that "if, on a motion for a preliminary injunction, the plaintiff shall show that immediate and irreparable injury, loss or damages will result unless the defendant is restrained before a hearing can be had, a temporary restraining order may be granted without notice."[184] The CPLR continues: "[a] temporary restraining order may be granted pending a hearing for a preliminary injunction where it appears that immediate and irreparable injury, loss or damage will result unless the defendant is restrained before the hearing can be had."[185] The mandated statutory showing is limited to "immediate and irreparable injury." Put somewhat differently:

> The object of a[n] . . . interlocutory injunction is to prevent irreparable injury pending the final ascertainment of the right, but not to determine the right itself. Thus, when the nature and purpose of a temporary injunction order are considered, it is evident that the court should give greater weight and consideration to the danger threatened and the consequences thereof, having first determined that the plaintiff, on his or her own papers, has established prima facie his or her right to the ultimate relief or judgment demanded, than to questions concerned with the probability of the plaintiff being able to prove his or her case; for the very purpose of a [temporary] injunction is to preserve the *status quo* until a final determination can be had.[186]

In seeking immediate and temporary relief within the pending period, the burden upon the movant for a temporary restraining order is to demonstrate a clear sense of urgency and imminent harm. Any delay in seeking a temporary restraining order may undermine the movant's claim.[187] Because a temporary restraining order may be granted *ex parte*, rather than on notice as required for a preliminary injunction, a higher burden of proof is placed on the moving party before this extreme relief is granted.[188]

---

183. *Id.* §§ 6301, 6313.
184. *Id.* § 6313(a).
185. *Id.* § 6301.
186. Bisca v. Bisca, 437 N.Y.S. 2d 258, 261–262 (N.Y. Sup. Ct. 1981); *see* Long Is. Daily Press Publ'g Co. v. Tomitz, 176 N.Y.S.2d 215 (N.Y. Sup. Ct. 1958) (emphasis added); *see also* Yonkers Racing v. Catskill Regional Off-Track Betting Corp., 532 N.Y.S.2d 407, 408 (App. Div. 1988).
187. *See* Seabury Constr. Corp. v. Dept. of Envtl. Prot. N.Y., 607 N.Y.S.2d 1017 (N.Y. Sup. Ct. 1994).
188. CPLR §§ 6301, 6313.

Although a temporary restraining order is deliberately urgent, and carries with it a higher burden of proof, it is nonetheless a provisional remedy granted during the pendency of a preliminary injunction motion. Though the stated purpose of a temporary restraining order is to preserve the *status quo*, the court may grant a temporary restraining order even if doing so potentially disturbs the existing conditions.[189] New York courts further instruct that even where the granting of a temporary restraining order would be commensurate with the preliminary injunctive relief sought, that fact alone does not bar the likelihood of receiving the provisional relief afforded by a temporary restraining order.[190]

E.   Motion to Reargue and Motion to Renew

A motion for leave to reargue a prior motion pursuant to CPLR § 2221(a) is appropriately granted upon a showing by the movant that the court overlooked or misapprehended the facts or law, or for some reason mistakenly arrived at its earlier decision.[191] Section 2221(d)(2) provides that a motion to reargue shall be predicated upon matters of fact or law allegedly overlooked or misapprehended by the court in determining the prior motion.[192] A motion to reargue is addressed to the sound discretion of the court and may be granted only upon a showing that the court: (1) overlooked or misapprehended the relevant facts, (2) overlooked or misapprehended the relevant law, or (3) for some reason mistakenly arrived at its earlier decision.[193] Reargument is not designed to afford the unsuccessful party successive opportunities to reargue issues previously decided or to present arguments different from those originally asserted.[194]

It is axiomatic in this state that a motion for leave to reargue pursuant to CPLR § 2221 is addressed to the sound discretion of the court and may be granted only upon a showing that "the court overlooked or misapprehended the facts or law[,] or for some reason mistakenly arrived at its earlier decision."[195] It is equally

---

189. 2207 Pavilion Assoc., LLC. v. Plato Foufas & Co., 856 N.Y.S.2d 27 (N.Y. Sup. Ct. 2007).
190. *Id.*
191. Swenning v. Wankel, 528 N.Y.S.2d 130, 131 (App. Div. 1988); James v. Nestor, 502 N.Y.S.2d 27, 28 (App. Div. 1986).
192. CPLR § 2221(d)(2).
193. William P. Pahl Equip. Corp. v. Kassis, 588 N.Y.S.2d 8 (App. Div. 1992); Schneider v. Soloway, 529 N.Y.S.2d 1017 (App. Div. 1988).
194. *William P. Pahl Equip. Corp.*, 588 N.Y.S.2d at 11; Pro Brokerage, Inc., v. Home Ins. Co., 472 N.Y.S.2d 661 (App. Div. 1984).
195. Swenning v. Wankel, 528 N.Y.S.2d 130, 131 (App. Div. 1988), *see also* Bliss v. Jaffin, 573 N.Y.S.2d 687, 688 (App. Div. 1991); James v. Nestor, 502 N.Y.S.2d 27, 28 (App. Div. 1986).

well settled that a motion to renew under CPLR § 2221 is properly used to draw the court's attention to new or additional facts that, although in existence at the time of the original motion, were not known to the party seeking renewal and, therefore, were not placed before the court.[196] Importantly, a motion for resettlement pursuant to CPLR § 2221 is one designed solely to correct errors or omissions as to form, or for clarification which may not be used to effect a substantive change in or to amplify the prior decision of the court.[197]

---

196. Being v. Wynward, 522 N.Y.S.2d 511, 524 (App. Div. 1987), *app. dismissed*, 524 N.E.2d 879 (N.Y. 1988); Bassett v. Bando Sangsa Co., Ltd., 478 N.Y.S.2d 298, 299 (App. Div. 1984); 300 West Realty Co. v. City of New York, 471 N.Y.S.2d 858, 860 (App. Div. 1984).
197. Elson v. Defren, 726 N.Y.S.2d 407, 411 (App. Div. 2001).

7 | Trial Preparation Based on the Burden of Proof

OUTLINE

INTRODUCTION

Trial is the phase of litigation where the team shows up on the field and begins to utilize all the prior efforts directed at discovery; all the prior efforts at identifying and understanding the burden of proof, production, and persuasion. Trial is game day, when all the pieces come together and when winning and losing come into focus. There is a reality to reflect on.

The reality is that you have been focused on the burden of proof from the outset, so by the time the trial occurs you know exactly what is coming. You have zeroed in on the burden of proof during the discovery phase and have obtained the discovery you need to prove your cause of action or defense. To the extent that there has been motion practice, you have zeroed in on the case law and/or statutes and generated elements of the cause of action or defense and are ready to educate your judge on that subject. In the world of trial preparation, you have poised yourself to excel.

You have more work to do before you walk into that courtroom, though. The first thing you do is pick your team from your law firm. You need the person who, besides assisting you in the courtroom, watches the judge and jury for any clues, concerns, or issues. While examining, cross examining or answering a judge's question, you must try to stay in touch with the room—but to think that you can do everything all at once, each time, is a little much.

All judges who try cases have their own predilections and likes and you need to identify what your trial judge wants and how he or she wants it served up. Generally, you need to prepare exhibit lists and books, jury instructions, proposed *voir dire* questions (for a jury trial), a pretrial memorandum of law, and a trial binder. You also need to decide how to order your proof for presentation purposes because, in addition to everything else, you need the judge and the jury to be interested in your presentation so that none of them get disinterested, fall asleep, lose interest, or get bored and hold it against you. Order your proof and make a plan as to how to present it to the judge/jury. Organizing your presentation in terms of which witnesses to call and when and what documents and discovery responses (if any) you want to use, will help you with everything else.

The next step is to begin drafting your pretrial memorandum with a brief statement of the facts and, of course, the burden of proof. Use the pretrial memorandum as an opportunity to alert the judge to the proof you intend to offer. If the case is a jury trial, then at this time, prepare a draft of any proposed jury instructions, the most important of which is the burden of proof on the cause of action or defense. You will have to serve the pretrial memorandum on your adversary, so this can be tricky; you do not want to give away too much.

Then, line up your exhibits and exhibit books. You already decided early on that your case was either chronological or transactional and in discovery you lined up your documents accordingly. Now you need to pick the documents you want to use, decide whether and what the admissibility issues are, and who you can use to get the document in evidence. All of this could modify your initial outline of the presentation. With this arsenal, you then need to prepare exhibit binders for use in the courtroom: one copy for the judge, one copy for the witness, one copy for each adversary, and one for yourself. Exhibit binders require indexes and some judges even ask for a particular color of binder depending on whether you are plaintiff or defendant. Some judges also require counsel to agree to as much on admissibility as they can. Most judges require a list of documents to which there is an objection with the specific objection noted. You, as trial counsel, also need to check those binders to be sure the documents are correctly identified, and there are no sloppy copies or messy papers. It is your proof; you need to take ownership of it.

Now that you have your exhibit binders set up, prepare your trial binder. The next sections of this chapter are the categories that should go in your trial binder: voir dire questions, *in limine* motions, openings, plaintiff's case, motion at close of plaintiff's case, defendant's case, motions at the close of defendant's case, summation/closing argument, and rebuttal (if any).

I. *VOIR DIRE*

Voir dire, from the French meaning "to see, to speak," is a topic that will arise only in the context of a jury trial.[1] When your case is trial ready, you will report to the trial assignment part of the courthouse, and until a jury is picked and a trial judge assigned, that is where you (and your boxes of evidence) will go. On the appointed day, the judge in the trial part will call your case and instruct you to go pick a jury. You are looking for jurors who you think can understand the burden of proof (by their education and background), and vote with you for the result.

Voir dire is the method by which the jury is selected. The trial court has the responsibility of balancing the competing considerations of fairness to the defendant, judicial economy, and avoidance of embarrassment to potential jurors.[2] Thus, the trial judge has broad discretion to determine the method of jury selection.[3] The trial judge's rulings will not be overturned absent a showing of an abuse of discretion. The purpose of *voir dire* is to ensure the jury is fair, impartial, and unbiased by excluding those who show prejudice or bias.[4] Thus, when selecting the jury, counsel should select the type of jurors who will not only be able to follow and understand the elements of the claim or defenses but also be sympathetic to your case. Although the right to examine prospective jurors is not absolute, it is a statutory right that may be asserted as long as the statute remains in force.[5]

To ensure an efficient selection process, the trial judge should preside at the commencement of *voir dire* and its opening.[6] The trial judge determines whether supervision of *voir dire* should continue after it has commenced, and whether

---

1. *Voir Dire*, BLACK'S LAW DICTIONARY (4th ed. 2011).
2. 47 AM. JUR. 2D *Jury* § 171 (2017).
3. *Id.*; *see, for example*, 22 N.Y.C.R.R. § 202.33 (2017) (hereinafter NYCRR).
4. 73A N.Y. JUR. 2D *Jury* § 87 (2017).
5. *Id.*
6. 22 NYCRR § 202.33(e).

to preside over part or all of the remainder of the *voir dire*.[7] Additionally, on the application of any party, a judge shall be present during the examination of jurors.[8] Further, the methods of jury selection "[are] left to the sound discretion of the trial court."[9] That discretion includes whether the courtroom is to be open or closed during jury selection. Any claim made against the court in regard to the closure to the public or press during certain parts of jury selection need to be weighed against competing interests, such as the right of the accused to a fair trial.[10]

Generally, eight jurors, including two alternates, are selected.[11] Prior to questioning, all prospective jurors are to complete a background questionnaire supplied by the court.[12] Questionnaires are to be made available to counsel and upon completion of jury selection or removal of a prospective juror, returned to the jurors or discarded by court staff.[13] During *voir dire*, each counsel may state the contentions of his client and identify the parties, attorneys, and witnesses likely to be called.[14] However, counsel may not read from any pleadings or inform potential jurors of the amount of money at issue.[15]

Mechanically, there are few ways in New York that juries are picked.[16] One is "White's method" and another is the "Struck method."[17] Regardless of which method is used, questioning of the prospective jurors is conducted first by counsel for the plaintiff(s) and then by counsel for the defendant(s).[18] In each round the exercise of challenges alternates between the parties, with each party exercising one challenge at a time.[19]

Under the White's method of jury selection,

> Prior to the identification of the prospective jurors to be seated in the jury box, counsel shall ask questions generally to all of the jurors in the room to determine whether any prospective juror in the room has knowledge of the subject matter, the parties,

---

7. *Id.*
8. CPLR § 4107; *see, for example*, 73A N.Y. Jur. 2d *Jury* § 88 (2017).
9. *See In re* Daily News, L.P., 6 N.Y.S.3d 19, 23 (App. Div. 2015) (citing United States v. Wecht, 537 F.3d 222, 242 (3rd Cir. 2008)).
10. *Id.* at 24.
11. 22 NYCRR § 202.33 App. E (A)(2).
12. *Id.* App. E (A)(3).
13. *Id.*
14. *Id.* App. E (A)(4).
15. *Id.*
16. *See* 22 NYCRR § 202.33(f).
17. *Id.* § 202.33(f)(1) (White's method, set forth in subdivision (g)); *id.* § 202.33(f)(2) (Struck method set forth in subdivision (g)).
18. *Id.* App. E (B)(3); *id.* App. E (C)(3).
19. *Id.* App. E (B)(5); *id.* App. E (C)(5).

their attorneys or the prospective witnesses. A response from a juror that requires elaboration may be the subject of further questioning of that juror by counsel on an individual basis. Counsel may exercise challenges for cause at this time.[20]

Cause exists where the potential juror is in the employ of a party to the action or in any manner interested.[21] Here, the court must hear and decide whether to grant or deny challenges for cause and has broad discretion to do so.[22] Another ground for a challenge is if the potential juror is related to a party.[23] In such instance, the potential juror will only be disqualified if the party related to the juror raises the objection before the case is opened; any other party must raise the objection no later than six months after the verdict.[24] However, objections and challenges for cause should be made as "unobtrusively" as possible and counsel should make every effort to settle disputes without court assistance.[25]

Those jurors eliminated for cause are dismissed and then the jury box gets filled with six jurors. The lawyers then question all six. In other words, after counsel has asked general questions to the group of prospective jurors, they are questioned in rounds. Each round consists of: "(1) seating prospective jurors in the jury box; (2) questioning of the seated prospective jurors; and (3) removal of seated prospective jurors upon exercise of challenges."[26] The first round begins initially with the seating of six prospective jurors.[27] Here, undesignated alternates are used and additional prospective jurors equal to the number of alternate jurors are seated as well.[28]

In each round, the questioning of the seated prospective jurors shall be conducted first by counsel for the plaintiff, then by counsel for the remaining parties.[29] Within each round, challenges for cause are to be exercised by any party prior to the exercise of peremptory challenges.[30] Upon replacement of a prospective juror removed for cause, questioning reverts to the plaintiff.[31]

---

20. *Id.* App. E (B)(1).
21. CPLR § 4110(a) ("employ of a party to the action . . ."); *id.* § 4110(b) (juror relationship).
22. *Id.* § 4108.
23. *Id.* § 4110(b).
24. *Id.*
25. 22 NYCRR § 202.33 App. E (A)(8).
26. *Id.* App. E (B)(2).
27. *Id.*
28. *Id.*
29. *Id.* App. E (B)(3).
30. *Id.*
31. *Id.*

During *voir dire,* counsel for each party may seek to exclude potential jurors for cause, on consent, or by exercising peremptory challenges.[32] Peremptory challenges are a form of challenge exercised by counsel to remove jurors without cause.[33] Thus, an attorney may object to the qualifications of a juror through a challenge unless the parties stipulate to excuse him.[34] Such challenge is tried and determined by the court.[35]

Both the plaintiff and defendant each have a total of three peremptory challenges plus one peremptory challenge for every two alternate jurors.[36] Counsel must exercise peremptory challenges outside the presence of the panel of prospective jurors or against a list or ballot, so that jurors remain unaware of which side is excusing jurors.[37] Additionally, counsel must avoid discussing legal concepts, such as the burden of proof, which is left to the court.[38]

After questioning and the exercise of challenges for cause or on consent, peremptory challenges are exercised one at a time.[39] Thus, once there are six cause-free jurors in the box, peremptory challenges shall be exercised.[40] In the first round, peremptory challenges are exercised in the order in which parties are listed in the case caption.[41] In subsequent rounds, the peremptory challenges are to be exercised one at a time by removing a juror's name from a list or ballot from a board that gets passed back and forth between both parties until no other peremptory challenges are exercised.[42] A second, single peremptory challenge may be exercised within the round only after all counsel has either exercised or waived their first peremptory challenges.[43]

Alternatively, an attorney may waive the making of a peremptory challenge.[44] Once waived, an attorney may not thereafter exercise a peremptory challenge

---

32. *See, generally,* Ann Pfau, Implementing New York's Civil Voir Dire Law and Rules (Jan. 2009), http://www.nycourts.gov/publications/pdfs/ImplementingVoirDire2009.pdf.

33. *Peremptory challenge,* Wex Dictionary, http://www.law.cornell.edu/wex/peremptory challenge (last visited Feb. 11, 2019) ("[W]ithout the need for any reason or explanation - unless the opposing party presents a prima facie argument that this challenge was used to discriminate on the basis of race, ethnicity, or sex.")

34. CPLR § 4108.

35. *Id.*

36. CPLR § 4109.

37. 22 NYCRR § 202.33 App. E (A)(5).

38. *Id.* App. E (A)(6).

39. *Id.* App. E (B)(4).

40. *See, generally,* Pfau, supra note 32.

41. 22 NYCRR § 202.33 App. E (B)(4).

42. *Id.*

43. *Id.*

44. *Id.*

within that round, but may do so in subsequent rounds.[45] This process shall continue until no other peremptory challenges are exercised.[46]

The only limitations with respect to peremptory challenges can be found in the Supreme Court decision of *Batson v. Kentucky*.[47] In their decision the court held that it was unconstitutional for a party to exercise peremptory challenges in an effort to remove members of the jury pool based on race. Later decisions held that additional cognizable groups, including those based on gender and sexual orientation, fit under the *Batson* ruling.[48] During the course of jury selection, the judge can override your preemptory challenge and require the juror to remain. If the judge believes you are going in that direction, then outside of the presence of the jury, the judge will ask you why you used your challenge—and you'd better have a good reason.

At the end of each round, seated jurors who remain unchallenged shall be sworn and removed from the room.[49] The challenged jurors are replaced and a new round commences.[50] After the selection of six jurors, designated jurors are selected. Designated jurors are selected in the same manner as described above.[51]

The Struck method is a little different from White's method. Under the Struck method,

> Unless otherwise ordered by the Court, selection of jurors shall be made from an initial panel of 25 prospective jurors, who shall be seated randomly and who shall maintain the order of seating throughout the *voir dire*. If fewer prospective jurors are needed due to the use of designated alternate jurors or for any other reason, the size of the panel may be decreased.[52]

Counsel must first ask general questions to the prospective jurors as a group "to determine whether any prospective juror has knowledge of the subject matter, the parties, their attorneys or the prospective witnesses."[53] If a juror's response

---

45. *Id.* App. E (B)(5) ("In subsequent rounds, the first exercise of peremptory challenges shall alternate from side to side.").
46. *Id.*
47. 476 U.S. 79 (1986).
48. *See, for example*, SmithKline Beecham Corp. v. Abbott Labs., 740 F.3d 471 (9th Cir. 2014) (applying *Batson* in the context of sexual orientation); J.E.B. v. Alabama *ex rel.* T.B., 511 U.S. 127 (1994) (applying *Batson* to groups based on gender); Edmonson v. Leesville Concrete Co., 500 U.S. 614 (1991) (applying *Batson* in a civil case).
49. 22 NYCRR § 202.33 App. E (B)(6).
50. *Id.*
51. *Id.* App. E (B)(7).
52. *Id.* App. E (C)(1).
53. *Id.* App. E (C)(2).

requires further elaboration he or she may be subject to further questioning.[54] At this time, challenges for cause may be exercised.[55]

Once counsel has completed the general questioning of the prospective jurors, in an action with one plaintiff and one defendant, counsel for the plaintiff proceeds first with the questioning of prospective jurors and "counsel may be permitted to ask follow up questions."[56] Where a case has multiple parties, questioning shall be conducted in the order in which the parties' names appear in the case caption.[57] As soon as it becomes apparent, counsel should exercise a challenge for cause and at the end of the period, "all challenges for cause must have been exercised by respective counsel."[58]

After both parties exercise challenges for cause, "the number of prospective jurors remaining shall be counted."[59] If the jurors remaining are less than the total number of jurors needed, including alternates, plus the maximum number of peremptory challenges allowed by the court or statute that may be exercised (the "jury panel number"), additional prospective jurors shall be added.[60] This process is to be repeated until the number of prospective jurors, not subject to challenge for cause, equals or exceeds the jury panel number.[61]

Once all prospective jurors in the panel have been questioned and all challenges for cause have been made, the plaintiff shall then exercise its peremptory challenges by "alternately striking a single juror's name from a list or ballot passed back and forth between or among counsel until all challenges are exhausted or waived."[62]

In cases where there are multiple plaintiffs and/or defendants, peremptory challenges are to be exercised by counsel in the order in which their names appear in the caption, unless the order, in the opinion of the court, would unduly favor one side.[63] If this occurs, the court, after consulting with the parties, shall specify the order in which peremptory challenges are to be exercised balancing the interests of the parties.[64] Counsel who waives a challenge may not thereafter exercise a peremptory challenge.[65]

---

54. *Id.*
55. *Id.*
56. *Id.* App. E (C)(3).
57. *Id.*
58. *Id.*
59. *Id.* App. E (C)(4).
60. *Id.*
61. *Id.*
62. *Id.* App. E (C)(5).
63. *Id.*
64. *Id.*
65. *Id.*

Like White's method, each side can challenge a juror "for cause" or by using a preemptory challenge.[66] "For cause" means the juror is employed by a party,[67] related within the sixth degree of consanguinity of a party,[68] is an employee of an insurance company issuing policies of insurance for personal injury or property damage and other reasons that arise.[69] A preemptory challenge is one in which you do not need to state a reason for their exclusion, as long as it is not based on one of the cognizable groups discussed above.[70]

At the completion of peremptory challenges, trial jurors, including alternates when nondesignated alternates are used, are selected in the order in which they have been seated from the remaining prospective jurors on the panel.[71] Counsel must select designated alternates in the same manner as above, but with an initial panel of not more than ten prospective alternates, unless otherwise directed by the court.[72] The first six jurors remaining on the list or on the board are the jury and the next two are the alternates; where the alternates are nondesignated, the first eight jurors become the jury.[73]

With respect to the length of time allotted to question potential jurors, in *Horton v. Associates in Obstetrics & Gynecology*, the Appellate Division imposed a 30-minute time limit.[74] Counsel was still allowed to use peremptory challenges thereafter. The court held that trial judges are authorized to impose time limits for the questioning of prospective jurors during *voir dire* and found that such limitation does not deprive a party of proper legal representation.[75] Thus, when conducting *voir dire*, the trial judge may set time limits for questioning of prospective jurors, which may consist of a general period for the completion of the questioning.[76]

Once the jury is selected, the jurors go back to the jury pool area, and the lawyers go back to the trial assignment part to await the availability of a trial

---

66. CPLR § 4110.
67. *Id.* § 4110(a).
68. *Id.* 4110(b).
69. *Id.* § 4110(a).
70. *Id.* App. E (C)(5).
71. *Id.* App. E (C)(6).
72. *Id.* App. E (C)(7).
73. *Id.*
74. 645 N.Y.S.2d 354, 354–55 (App. Div. 1996).
75. *Id.*
76. 22 NYCRR § 202.33(d) ("Time limitations. The trial judge shall establish time limitations for the questioning of prospective jurors during the voir dire. At the discretion of the judge, the limits established may consist of a general period for the completion of the questioning, a period after which attorneys shall report back to the judge on the progress of the voir dire, and/or specific time periods for the questioning of panels of jurors or individual jurors.").

judge. If the case is in the commercial part, the lawyers go to the trial judge in the commercial part who had the case all along.

II. MOTIONS *IN LIMINE*

"A motion *in limine* [is a pretrial tool that typically] challenges evidence which is [alleged] to be inadmissible, immaterial, or [unduly] prejudicial, or [that] requests a limitation on the use of evidence," or which seeks court permission to do something at trial that a party desires.[77] "*In limine*," which is Latin for "on the threshold," suggests that the request to preclude evidence should be made before the trial starts.[78] According to Black's Law Dictionary, a motion *in limine* is defined as "[a] pre-trial request that certain inadmissible evidence not be referred to or offered at trial."[79] This is the stage of civil litigation where each side can ask the court to rule on some aspect of the trial before the trial begins. Often these motions are made before jury selection; and in the commercial part, ruled on well before jury selection. The genesis behind the rule is that the ruling will impact how one or both sides proceed at the trial itself.

Motions *in limine* are not specifically authorized by any New York statute, but courts have found authority pursuant to their "inherent power"[80] under the New York Civil Practice Law and Rules (CPLR) § 4011, to admit or exclude evidence.[81] The function, generally, of a motion *in limine* is "to permit a party to obtain a preliminary order before . . . trial excluding the introduction of anticipated inadmissible, immaterial, or prejudicial evidence or limiting its use. Its purpose is to prevent the introduction of such evidence to the trier of fact, in most instances a jury."[82] As such, if the court should find that the evidence produced by the parties is otherwise inadmissible, immaterial or prejudicial, the court should exclude such information. If the court finds otherwise, such evidence is admissible and can be

---

77. Drago v. Tishman Constr. Corp. of N.Y., 777 N.Y.S.2d 889, 893 (Sup. Ct. 2004) (citing State v. Metz, 671 N.Y.S.2d 79, 83 (App. Div. 1998)).
78. *Motion In Limine*, WEX LEGAL DICTIONARY, https://www.law.cornell.edu/wex/motion_in_limine (last visited Feb. 11, 2019) ("A pretrial motion asking that certain evidence be found inadmissible, and that it not be referred to or offered at trial."); *in limine*, Merriam-Webster's, https://www.merriam -webster.com/dictionary/in%20limine ("*[O]n the threshold*: as a preliminary matter—used for motions regarding the admissibility of evidence brought up at a pretrial hearing.") (emphasis added).
79. *Motion in limine*, BLACK'S LAW DICTIONARY (10th ed. 2014).
80. People v. Michael M., 618 N.Y.S.2d 171, 175 (Sup. Ct. 1994); *see* Sci. Applications Int'l Corp. v. Envtl. Risk Sols., LLC, 964 N.Y.S.2d 62, 62 (Sup. Ct. 2012) ("The Court has authority to grant a motion *in limine* to exclude evidence in advance of trial.")
81. MBIA Ins. Corp. v. Countrywide Home Loans, Inc., 958 N.Y.S.2d 647, 647 (Sup. Ct. 2010).
82. *Metz*, 671 N.Y.S.2d at 83 (emphasis omitted).

used. Although less common, motions *in limine* may also be used to request the trial court allow something that a party desires.[83]

A. Burden of Proof on a Motion *in Limine*

It has been said that there are three types of motions *in limine*:

1. A prohibitive motion *in limine* seeking an order definitively barring the opponent from offering or mentioning the precluded evidence in any manner during the trial.
2. A conditional motion seeking a ruling requiring the opposing party to refrain from offering, or in any manner mentioning before the jury, evidence constituting the subject matter of the ruling, without first notifying the court and counsel of its intention to offer such evidence and without first obtaining the court's resolution of admissibility out of the hearing of the jury.
3. A motion *in limine* seeking a ruling permitting the introduction of evidence.[84]

The first and second categories listed above, prohibitive and conditional motions, are the more commonly made motions *in limine*, directed to the preclusion of evidence rather than the admission of evidence. On a prohibitive or conditional motion *in limine*, the movant's burden is to establish that the evidence sought to be excluded "is actually inadmissible, irrelevant, immaterial, and/ or unduly prejudicial, before the opponent is called upon to justify introduction of the evidence."[85] The trial judge ultimately has discretion to grant or deny the motion *in limine*.[86] A litigant must point to specific pieces of evidence that it seeks to be regarded as inadmissible and provide explanation as to why.

The party moving to preclude evidence must effectively meet the burden of demonstrating that the subject evidence is inadmissible; and the admissibility of evidence requires a threshold showing of relevance and necessity. Evidence is considered relevant if it has any "tendency in reason to prove any material fact."[87] All

---

83. *See, for example*, People v. Santana, 600 N.E.2d 201 (N.Y. 1992); Reed v. Reed, 734 N.Y.S.2d 806 (Sup. Ct. 2001); People v. Franks, 761 N.Y.S.2d 459 (Nassau Cty Ct. 2003) (expert testimony); People v. Coulter, 697 N.Y.S.2d 498 (Nassau Dist. Ct. 1999).

84. People v. L. B. Smith, Inc., 437 N.Y.S.2d 574, 579 (Sup. Ct. 1981).

85. Van Wert v. Randall, 950 N.Y.S.2d 726, 726 (Sup. Ct. 2012).

86. Louzon v. Ford Motor Co., 718 F.3d 556, 560 (6th Cir. 2013).

87. People v. Alvino, 519 N.E.2d 808, 812 (N.Y. 1987) (quoting People v. Lewis, 506 N.E.2d 915, 916 (1987)).

evidence that is considered relevant is admissible at trial unless an exclusionary rule would be violated in doing so.[88] Thus, the movant's burden on a prohibitive or conditional motion *in limine* is to establish that the disputed evidence is not relevant or necessary to the case or that an exclusionary rule applies and precludes admission. The opposing party's burden is to show that the disputed evidence must be admitted because it is, in fact, relevant and necessary to the issue and that no exclusionary rule applies.

The third category of motions *in limine*, although less common than the prohibitive or conditional motion, is the motion that seeks permission to introduce a piece of evidence the party desires.[89] In such a case, the proponent's burden is the exact opposite of the movant on a prohibitive or conditional motion—the proponent must establish the admissibility, relevance, and necessity of the evidence.[90]

At its core, the moving party's burden is to prove why the disputed evidence should be precluded (if on a prohibitive or conditional motion) or admitted (on a motion seeking to admit evidence). For example, if the movant's motion to preclude evidence is predicated on prejudice, the movant must establish and prove the prejudice that would result from the introduction of the disputed evidence.

An effective motion *in limine* can preclude evidence that your adversary needed in order to meet its burden of proof.[91] It is not the judge's responsibility to ensure that the foundation evidence is offered.[92] If necessary, the objector may move to include the evidence if he has been deprived the opportunity of making a *prima facie* case due to an *in limine* ruling.

B. Why Make a Motion *in Limine*?

Motions *in limine* can be beneficial to both the court and the moving party. They often create trial efficiency and allow the hearing judge to understand the merits of the case before it begins. If successful, a motion *in limine* to preclude evidence can serve to "sav[e] the parties and the court from significant litigation time . . . [and] significantly streamline the action without compromising either party from proving its case."[93] Precluding evidence before the case commences prevents the

---

88. *Id.*
89. *See, for example,* People v. Franks, 761 N.Y.S.2d 459, 460 (Cnty. Ct. 2003); People v. Coulter, 697 N.Y.S.2d 498, 499 (Dist. Ct. 1999).
90. *Franks,* 761 N.Y.S.2d at 462 (Cnty. Ct. 2003) (showing acceptance in the relevant scientific community in a sexual conduct case regarding expert testimony).
91. Endervelt v. Slade, 618 N.Y.S.2d 520, 522 (Sup. Ct. 1994).
92. *See* Huddleston v. United States, 485 U.S. 681, 690, n.7 (1988).
93. MBIA Ins. Corp. v. Countrywide Home Loans, Inc., 30 Misc. 3d 1201(A), 1201A (Sup. Ct. 2010).

adverse party from mentioning the object of the motion from the outset. This way, the precluded evidence will not be referenced during opening statements, *voir dire*, or during the trial itself, as it is not an easy task to "unring a bell."[94]

Motions *in limine* are filed when the mere mention of a piece of evidence at trial would be so unfairly prejudicial or irrelevant that it would create an improper bias.[95] The purpose of the motion is to prevent the introduction of such evidence to the trier of fact.[96] In many cases, the motion is appropriate for precluding demonstrative evidence,[97] findings of administrative bodies,[98] and hearsay.[99] In all, *in limine* motions are powerful tools that can curtail your adversary's presentation and prevent them from meeting their burden of proof.

Although there are many advantages to motions *in limine*, they may have the adverse effect of alerting the opposing party to weaknesses in one's argument or highlighting the importance the moving party places on the disputed evidence. Additionally, because motions *in limine* are considered advisory rulings, they are not appealable until after the trial is over—or at least until that ruling can actually be said to have involved the merits[100] or affected a substantial right of a party.[101] Moreover, because it is possible that the judge who heard and decided the motion *in limine* will not be the same judge at trial, the trial judge may actually reconsider the *in limine* rulings made by the motion judge and take a different position than the motion judge did.[102]

---

94. *See* People v. Griffin, 671 N.Y.S.2d 34, 36 (App. Div. 1998); David Finley & Julie Kay Baker, NEW YORK MOTIONS IN LIMINE, § 1:1 DESCRIPTION AND PURPOSE OF MOTION (2016 ed.) ("The primary advantage of the motion is to avoid the futile attempt of trying to undo the harm done where jurors have been exposed to damaging evidence, even where stricken by the court. This scenario has been described as the obviously futile attempt to 'unring the bell.'").

95. *Metz*, 671 N.Y.S.2d at 83.

96. *Id.*

97. People v. Estrada, 486 N.Y.S.2d 794 (App. Div. 1985).

98. Staatsburg Water Co. v. Staatsburg Fire Dist., 531 N.Y.S.2d 876, 527 N.E.2d 754 (1988).

99. Dehn v. Kaplan, 516 N.Y.S.2d 480 (App. Div. 1987).

100. *See* CPLR § 5701(a)(iv).

101. *Id.*; *see, for example*, Rondout Elec., Inc. v. Dover Union Free Sch. Dist., 758 N.Y.S.2d 394, 397 (App. Div. 2003) (noting the motion is considered the "functional equivalent" of a motion for summary judgment; however, the order may be appealable); Chateau Rive Corp., v. Enclave Dev. Assocs., 725 N.Y.S.2d 215 (App. Div. 2001); Brennan v. Mabey's Moving & Storage, Inc., 640 N.Y.S.2d 686 (App. Div. 1996); Hargrave v. Presher, 221 A.D.2d 677, 632 N.Y.S.2d 886 (App. Div. 1995) (Mikoll, J., dissenting); *see also*, section II.F titled "Nonappealable Motions *in Limine*."

102. Kelly v. Metro-North Commuter R.R., 902 N.Y.S.2d 78, 79 (App. Div. 2010) ("A motion court's evidentiary ruling before trial does not foreclose a related application to the trial court.")

C. Subjects of the Motion

There are many subjects to consider on a motion *in limine*. You may ask the court to exclude evidence that was not produced during discovery,[103] to preclude a witness from testifying who was not identified by a party during discovery,[104] or to preclude the offer of any evidence concerning an issue that a party has waived or that is not at issue.[105] Experts and expert testimony are frequently the subjects of motions *in limine*. For example, you may ask the court that an expert be precluded from testifying because the expert testimony is not at all necessary or helpful to the court.[106] Experts may also be excluded because the process they utilized is flawed;[107] the expert never looked at the underlying business or material records and instead relied on a summary, for example.

These instances may all be recognized as evidence that is not relevant to any issue in the case, that is extremely prejudicial or not useful, or in violation of the rules of evidence. The potential relief sought is the instruction to refrain from specified conduct or from mentioning prohibited material. If the court determines that evidence is admissible, then the weight to be given to that evidence is for the trier of fact to decide.[108] There is no limit on the subject of a motion *in limine*. Certain types of evidence, however, are more likely than others to receive consideration by the hearing judge. Most commonly, motions *in limine* seek to preclude evidence or testimony that would be considered irrelevant, immaterial, misleading, and of no probative value[109] or that would be unfairly prejudicial.[110] Evidence may fall under any of these categories if it is irrelevant to the issues of the case, if the matters were already resolved on summary judgment, or if it would unfairly influence the jury. In criminal cases, a common example of this is the introduction of past criminal convictions to the jury. Trial courts often find that evidence of a defendant's prior convictions might lead the jury to unfairly

---

103. *See* Getty v. Zimmerman, 830 N.Y.S.2d 409, 410 (App. Div. 2007).

104. Brown v. United Christian Evangelistic Ass'n, 704 N.Y.S.2d 621, 622 (App. Div. 2000) ("[I]n the event that the plaintiff does not provide further information and attempts, nevertheless, to introduce at trial the testimony of witnesses whose addresses were not previously disclosed, the appellants may seek preclusion of that evidence at that time.")

105. *See, for example,* Gray v. Jaeger, 851 N.Y.S.2d 872, 872 (App. Div. 2008) (no evidence may be introduced on issues deemed admitted by defendant's answer).

106. *See, for example*, Vail v. KMart Corp., 807 N.Y.S.2d 399 (App. Div. 2006).

107. *See, for example*, Wolf *ex rel.* Ginsburg v. Bakert, 808 N.Y.S.2d 921 (Sup. Ct., Nassau County 2005).

108. People v. Middleton, 429 N.E.2d 100, 104 (N.Y. 1981).

109. *Vail*, 807 N.Y.S.2d at 401.

110. Van Dusen v. Mcmaster, 814 N.Y.S.2d 438, 438–49 (App. Div. 2006).

conclude that his past behavior is relevant to the issue of whether he committed the offense *sub judice*.

Evidence introduced as "expert opinion" by nonexperts is often the subject of a motion *in limine* seeking to preclude evidence. In most cases, an expert can be anyone with strong knowledge on the subject matter at issue. Still, instances such as using a police report as "expert opinion," for example, are often subject to objection, as a party can easily argue that it does not illustrate expert testimony.[111]

Unreliable hearsay is given significant attention when preclusion is sought via a motion *in limine*.[112] Opinion evidence must be based on facts in the record or personally known to the witness, the two limited exceptions being that an expert may rely on out-of-court material if it is of a kind accepted in the profession as reliable in forming a professional opinion or if it comes from a witness subject to full cross-examination at trial.[113] When, instead, the opinion evidence has no foundation, a motion *in limine* to preclude evidence based on unreliable hearsay is likely to receive positive consideration from the court.

Two popular decisions are often cited to illustrate the wide variety of purposes for asserting a motion *in limine*. In *MBIA Insurance Corporation v. Countrywide Home Loans, Inc.*, plaintiff moved for an order allowing the use of statistical sampling to prove a *prima facie* case of fraud and breach of contract, as well as to prove damages.[114] The motion was made far before trial commenced and the trial court granted it before discovery had concluded.[115] In reaching its determination, the court relied on the motion's permissive manner, and the fact that it was not precluded by New York statutes, codes, or common law.[116]

In *Schron v. Grunstein*, plaintiff moved *in limine* to preclude the defendant from using parol evidence to demonstrate that a loan agreement and an option agreement should be read together.[117] The trial court granted the motion, despite the fact that the order had the potential to curtail discovery.[118] However, this

---

111. *See, for example*, Hatton v. Gassler, 631 N.Y.S.2d 757, 758 (App. Div. 1995) ("[T]he [police report] contained a police officer's conclusions as to the cause of the accident even though the officer was not an eyewitness to the accident and his conclusions were not based upon a 'postincident expert analysis of observable physical evidence.'"); Murray v. Donlain, 433 N.Y.S.2d 184, 192 (App. Div. 1980).

112. *See* Hambsch v. New York City Transit Authority, 469 N.E.2d 516, 517 (N.Y. 1984).

113. *Id.*

114. *See* MBIA Ins. Corp. v Countrywide Home Loans, Inc., 958 N.Y.S.2d 647 (Sup. Ct. 2010).

115. *Id.* at 647.

116. *Id.*

117. 917 N.Y.S.2d 820, 826–827 (Sup. Ct. 2011).

118. *Id.* at 827.

decision came quite close to the overuse of a motion *in limine* producing unintended consequences, as warned against in *Scalp & Blade, Inc. v. Advest, Inc.*[119]

D.   When a Motion *in Limine* Is Denied

Evidence should be excluded on a motion in *limine* only when the evidence is clearly inadmissible on all potential grounds. If the motion *in limine* seeking the exclusion of evidence is denied, the movant must thereafter object when his adversary produces that evidence in order to preserve the record on appeal.[120] If, at this point, the party who sought to preclude the evidence still cannot meet its burden to establish its inadmissibility, the court will affirm its decision to deny the motion *in limine*. If the party does not object to the questionable evidence offered, the decision cannot be appealed based on the judge's advisory motion *in limine* ruling.[121] It is important to remember that even when a motion *in limine* is not granted, an advocate must still raise objections or make offers of proof at trial to protect the record.[122]

Although in most cases a motion in *limine* ruling cannot be appealed, there are some issues that are. An interlocutory appeal can be taken to the appellate division if the order of the motion in *limine* "involves some part of the merits"[123] or "affects a substantial right of a party."[124] Additionally a motion in *limine* can be appealed on the grounds that the order limits the scope of issues to be tried.[125] Just remember, if the motion in *limine* is based on the merits of the controversy and if granting or denying such motion would substantially affect one of the parties then it is appealable.[126]

When a motion *in limine* lacks the necessary specificity with respect to the evidence to be excluded, the court may reserve judgment on the motion until trial when admission of particular pieces of evidence is in an appropriate factual context. As the court in *Wechsler v. Hunt Health Systems, Ltd.* made clear, "[a] district court is well within its discretion to deny a motion *in limine* that fails to identify the evidence with particularity or to present arguments with specificity."[127]

---

119. 765 N.Y.S.2d 92 (App. Div. 2003).
120. Metz, 671 N.Y.S.2d at 79.
121. Winograd v Price, 800 N.Y.S.2d 649 (App. Div. 2005).
122. *See* Weatherbee Constr. Corp. v. Miele, 705 N.Y.S.2d 222 (App. Div. 2000).
123. CPLR § 5701(a)(2)(iv).
124. *Id.* § 5701(a)(2)(v).
125. *See* Parker v. Mobil Oil Corp., 793 N.Y.S.2d 434, 436 (App. Div. 2005).
126. *Id.* at 436.
127. Weschler v. Hunt Health Sys., Ltd., 2003 WL 21998980, at *3 (internal quotations omitted).

E.   When an *in Limine* Ruling Is Violated

If a court grants a motion *in limine* and the adverse party violates the ruling by introducing the prohibited evidence at trial, then the movant on the *in limine* motion bears the burden of proving that he was substantially prejudiced by that violation.[128] Otherwise, it may not be a reversible error.

For the violation to be considered a reversible error, the party must establish that the error was so egregious that it denied him of his right to due process or fair trial.[129] Generally, when evidence is improperly used at trial, the judge may instruct a jury to ignore the remarks,[130] direct the party to refrain from such remarks or risk reversal,[131] or, in severely prejudicial cases, call for a mistrial.

F.   Nonappealable Motions *in Limine*

When a motion *in limine* results in a failure to fully develop evidence, depriving the nonmoving party of the opportunity of presenting all relevant material, it is considered more akin to a motion for summary judgment. In such a case, it must be considered whether the judge abused his discretion in precluding evidence that was necessary for a party to prove a *prima facie* case. In fact, motions *in limine* are sometimes looked down upon because they can be considered "an inappropriate attempt at a disguised summary judgment."[132] New York courts, therefore, may be reluctant to grant a motion *in limine* where it would have been better presented as a motion for summary judgment.[133]

If a motion rests solely on the presumption that the opposing party would not be able to develop a *prima facie* case, it should not be decided *in limine* when if true it would likely defeat the purpose of any evidentiary rulings. This tactic is comparable to getting two bites of the apple. If permissible, any motion *in limine* would be proper so long as the movant accompanied the motion with the argument that the evidence in dispute is irrelevant. In this case, any matter could potentially be raised *in limine*. Therefore, the motion will not likely be considered if it appears in the form of a rephrased summary judgment motion.

---

128. *See* Ohler v. United States, 529 U.S. 753 (2000).
129. *Id.*
130. *See* People v. Galloway, 430 N.E.2d 885, 887 (N.Y. 1981).
131. People v. Mott, 465 N.Y.S.2d 307, 310 (App. Div. 1983).
132. Schron v. Grunstein, 917 N.Y.S.2d 820, 823 (Sup. Ct. 2011).
133. Downtown Art Co. v. Zimmerman, 648 N.Y.S.2d 101, 101 (App. Div. 1996); Carrasquillo v. N.Y.C. Dep't of Educ., 960 N.Y.S.2d 313, 313 (App. Div. 2013).

Generally, no appeal lies from a pretrial adjudication of the admissibility of evidence.[134] Often, the granting of a motion *in limine* will restrict a party from proving its case, thus limiting the amount in damages that could be recovered. When the order goes a step further than limiting damages, and instead grants a party's partial summary judgment motion, then the motion *in limine* was mislabeled.[135] When an *in limine* ruling "limits the issues to be tried . . . clearly involves the merits of the controversy and affects a substantial right" the decision is appealable.[136] "Unlike a summary judgment motion, which is designed to eliminate a trial in cases where there are no genuine issues of material fact, a motion *in limine* is designed to narrow the evidentiary issues for trial and to eliminate unnecessary trial interruptions."[137] If a motion *in limine* impermissibly limits the scope of issues being tried, then it is appealable.[138]

In *Scalp & Blade v. Advest, Inc.*, the defendants moved *in limine* just before trial commenced. They sought to preclude plaintiffs from offering evidence of additional profits, which would have supported the plaintiff's demand for lost appreciation of damages.[139] The trial court granted defendant's motion and plaintiffs appealed.[140] The Fourth Department ruled that the *in limine* order was appealable because it was the "functional equivalent of a motion for partial summary judgment dismissing the complaint."[141] The court found that the motion clearly involved "the merits of the controversy" and reversed the lower court in a decision shedding considerable pretrial guidance on substantive trial issues.[142] Trial preparation requires disciplined planning well in advance of the trial date and the motion *in limine* is one tool that can be very effective when made part of the early stages of such.

In other words, a motion *in limine* is an advisory ruling and therefore is not appealable. However, when a party misuses a motion *in limine* and asserts it as the procedural equivalent of a motion for partial summary judgment, the court will decide that motion. Such an order involves some part of the merits of the case and, therefore, is appealable.[143]

---

134. Vesperman v. Wormser, 725 N.Y.S.2d 361, 362 (App. Div. 2001).
135. *See* Roundout Elec., Inc. v. Dover Union Free Sch. Dist., 758 N.Y.S.2d 394, 397 (App. Div. 2003).
136. *Id.*; Scalp & Blade, Inc. v. Advest, Inc., 765 N.Y.S.2d 92 (App. Div. 2003).
137. Bradley v. Pittsburgh Bd. of Educ., 913 F.2d 1064, 1069 (3d Cir. 1990).
138. Innovative Transmission & Engine Co., LLC, v. Massaro, 879 N.Y.S.2d 856, 857 (App. Div. 2009).
139. *Scalp & Blade*, 765 N.Y.S.2d at 93.
140. *Id.* at 95.
141. *Id.* at 96.
142. *Id.*
143. *See* CPLR § 5701(a)(2)(iv).

Motions *in limine* are not required to "be made in writing [or to comply] with CPLR § 2214."[144] In fact, there is little regulation governing pretrial motions, as they are a somewhat recent phenomenon. In 1966, a New York court stated, "[c]oncededly, there is no statutory authorization for the consideration of a pretrial motion to suppress evidence in a civil action."[145] Although a motion *in limine* is not bound by any particular formal requirements in New York, pursuant to the Commercial Division rules, the motion should be provided to the court ten days before jury selection.[146] Certain judges provide for their own preferred timing and restrictions on motions *in limine*. There are also specific instances where a motion *in limine* to preclude evidence should be made even further in advance. For example, where a motion is made on the admissibility of scientific data or expert opinion on such, "early presentation" is preferred.[147] Otherwise, it is common for a judge to hear a motion *in limine* and wait to make a decision until more of the case has unfolded. A well-timed and precise motion will allow the judge to make a well-informed decision on whether the disputed evidence is necessary to the case or not.

III. OPENING STATEMENTS

A party has a right to make an opening statement at trial when the case is to be tried by jury.[148] The right to make an opening statement in a jury trial is regarded as substantial, the denial of which may be grounds for requiring a new trial.[149] In 1889, the Court of Appeals held that the purpose of an opening statement was as follows:

> The object of the pleadings is to define the issue between the parties and when issue of fact is tried before a jury they cannot appreciate the evidence, as it is given, unless they know the nature of the issues to be decided. Hence it is customary and proper for counsel, in opening, to tell the jury what the issues are as well as what they expect to prove.[150]

---

144. Drago v. Tishman Constr. Corp., 777 N.Y.S.2d 889, 894 (Sup. Ct. 2004) (quoting Wilkinson v. British Airways, 740 N.Y.S.2d 294, 296 (App. Div. 2002)); CPLR § 2214 (providing guidelines for notice and timing of motions).
145. Van Guilder v. Fallsburgh, 269 N.Y.S.2d 562, 562 (App. Div. 1966).
146. 22 NYCRR 207.70, Rule 27. These rules are applicable only to the branches of the Commercial Division located in Albany, Erie, Kings, Monroe, Nassau, New York, Onondaga, Queens, Suffolk, and Westchester counties.
147. *Drago*, 777 N.Y.S.2d at 894.
148. CPLR § 4016.
149. 4 Carmody-Wait 2d § 1302 (2017).
150. Tisdale v. Del. & Hudson Canal Co., 22 N.E. 700, 701 (N.Y. 1889).

The party with the burden of proof typically opens first. This rule is not absolute and the court has discretion to alter who goes first.[151] The burden of proof is determined based on the pleadings (amended and supplemental) as they stand at commencement of trial.[152] Before a party delivers its opening statement, the court in its discretion may limit the parties' time for making their opening statements.[153] The plaintiff has the right, but not the obligation, to make an opening statement.[154] A plaintiff's opening statement should set forth the evidence he or she intends to present to prove the elements of his causes of action.

A defendant's opening statement should set forth the burden of proof required for each cause of action and why the plaintiff will fail to meet this burden. A defendant's opening statement should also set forth the evidence the defendant intends to present to prove the elements of his affirmative defenses.

Although the right to deliver an opening statement exists in jury trials, it is not an absolute right in nonjury trials. Denial of opening statements should not warrant a reversal on appeal.[155] Often a trial judge in a bench trial will dispense with the opening statements and direct parties to proceed with their proof.

Before the case gets submitted to the jury, the judge charges the jury. The jury charge is typically issued at the close of the evidence and after closing arguments. A jury can be charged at an earlier time during the trial if the court reasonably directs.[156] Any party may file written requests that the court instruct the jury on the law as set forth in the requests.[157] The court, outside of the jury's presence, shall inform counsel of its proposed action on the requests prior to their arguments to the jury, but the jury will typically be charged after the arguments are heard.[158] A party must object to the giving or failure to give an instruction before

---

151. CPRL § 4011.

152. WEINSTEIN, KORN & MILLER, NEW YORK CIVIL PRACTICE: CPLR ¶ 4016.05 (David L. Ferstendig ed., LexisNexis Matthew Bender) (hereinafter WEINSTEIN, NEW YORK CIVIL PRACTICE); *see, for example*, De Vito v. Katsch, 556 N.Y.S.2d 649, 651–652 (App. Div. 1990).

153. WEINSTEIN, NEW YORK CIVIL PRACTICE ¶ 4016.02.

154. Reyes v. City of N.Y., 656 N.Y.S.2d 379, 381 (App. Div. 1997) (Goldstein, J., dissenting).

155. 4 N.Y. PRAC., COM. LITIG. IN NEW YORK STATE COURTS § 4016 (4th ed.); *see, for example*, Lohmiller v. Lohmiller, 528 N.Y.S.2d 586, 588 (App. Div. 1988) (holding that the denial of an opening statement was not reversible error where the court trying the divorce action was familiar with the parties' contentions raised prior to trial and had presided over open court stipulation as to certain facts); *In re* Saggese v. Steinmetz, 921 N.Y.S.2d 360, 361 (App. Div. 2011) (holding denial of an opening statement was a harmless error where the court was fully familiar with the facts of the case, the parties, and their arguments from prior court appearances).

156. CPLR § 4110-b.

157. *Id.*

158. *Id.*

the jury retires to consider its verdict and state the matter to which he objects and grounds of his objection.[159]

Proposed jury charges should be prepared prior to trial and should walk the jury through the elements of each cause of action (including counterclaims) and defense such that the jury can be guided as to whether the burden of proof has been satisfied by a particular party. As the trial progresses, proposed jury charges can be revised based on the evidence and testimony elucidated at trial.

IV. PROOF AT TRIAL

After both parties present their opening statements, the party bearing the burden of proof is obligated to complete his *prima facie* case before the opposing party must present his proof.[160]

Just like most theatre performances, a trial is essentially a staged representation of real life. In fact, under the supervision of a judge, each litigant, in turn, goes "on stage" and puts up a presentation for the benefit of the audience, that is, the finder of fact. At the end of the performance, pursuant to the instructions given by the judge, the audience decides which presentation was more convincing and a verdict in favor of one of the litigants will be rendered.

Generally speaking, at trial, each litigant will (1) argue that certain legally operative facts occurred in the real world at some time in the past such that—under the applicable law—a legal effect is triggered; and (2) pray the court to intervene in carrying out said effect against the wishes of the other party, if necessary.

Now, for the sake of exposition, let us momentarily indulge in a metaphor that, in our opinion, sheds light on how a typical trial actually works. Suppose that, after the discovery phase has ended, the parties involved in the lawsuit marshal all their items of proof (i.e., depositions, documents, records, and so on) and put them into two different buckets, one for the plaintiff and one for the defendant. Suppose further that each litigant physically carries his or her evidence bucket to the courthouse where a trial is scheduled to take place.

Once in the courthouse, the litigants enter the designated courtroom where the judge informs them that the finder of fact will be allowed to see, hear, or touch *only* whatever evidence is placed into the courtroom's bucket. Conversely, whatever remains in the litigants' own buckets will be completely disregarded by the court.

---

159. *Id.*
160. Roberts v. St. Francis Hosp., 470 N.Y.S.2d 716, 718 (App. Div. 1983); Yeomans v. Warren, 448 N.Y.S.2d 889, 890 (App. Div. 1982); *see also* Seguin v. Berg, 21 N.Y.S.2d 291, 293 (App. Div. 1940).

Logically, being so instructed, the litigants in our example will want to pour the contents of their buckets over into the courtroom's bucket so as to allow the decider of fact to see, hear, or touch proof that allegedly shows their entitlement to relief. However, at this point, the judge promptly intervenes forbidding such pouring over until the judge ascertains that the items about to be put into the courtroom's bucket are relevant, competent, authentic, and otherwise in compliance with all the rules governing the admissibility of evidence. Ultimately, the judge, who in this respect acts as a gatekeeper, is tasked with the duty of making sure the evidence shown to the finder of fact meets certain threshold levels of reliability.

Clearly, the courtroom's bucket in our example represents the *official record* of the proceedings, whereas the parties' own buckets represent the collection of proof the attorneys gathered during their pretrial investigation of the matter at issue.[161]

An *official record* can be defined as an accurate and complete account of a series of acts or occurrences kept in a permanent form by the clerk of the court.[162] Such records generally include the "information collected by officers and employees of the [court] as well as information provided to the [court] by others who are required . . . to file or deposit such information with the [court]."[163]

An ancient Latin maxim best captures those concepts. It runs thus: *Quod non est in actis non est in mundo*—that is, whatever is not placed into the record does not exist in the real world.

Parenthetically, recall that a legal norm establishing a cause of action is typically structured thus: if certain relevant facts occurred, then a legal effect is triggered. At trial, neither the finder of fact nor the judge has firsthand knowledge of the subject matter of the parties' contentions. Obviously, before a court may authoritatively cause the legal effect set forth by the law to come about against the wishes of the nonmoving party, it ought to verify that the relevant facts underlying the cause of action occurred. Thus, at trial, the parties will attempt to "reenact" past events so as to convince the audience, that is, the fact finder, that those legally operative propositions of fact actually took place in the past somewhere outside the courtroom.

As has been explained in the previous chapters of this book, legal norms provide that the party bearing the burden of production ought to present *enough* evidence so as to be able to potentially convince a reasonable finder of fact that the events underlying the proponent's claim occurred, or else be defeated as a matter of law.

---

161. *Official Record*, The Wolters Kluwer Bouvier Law Dictionary Desk Edition.
162. *Id.*
163. *Id.*

In other words, to authenticate his or her contentions, the proponent of a cause of action must tender evidence into the record so as to allow a reasonable finder of fact to ascertain whether the proponent is entitled to the relief prayed for. Obviously, if the proponent of a cause of action fails to get his or her evidence admitted at trial, then the finder of fact will not be able to see, hear, or touch those items of proof. Therefore, in this scenario, the proponent's claim will be rejected as a matter of law because a reasonable jury would not find for the proponent without at least some proof of every element of the cause of action.

To illustrate this point, let us assume for a moment that the plaintiff is suing the defendant for battery claiming nominal damages. In New York, a *prima facie* case for battery is made out when the plaintiff establishes the following elements: (1) the alleged tortfeasor made bodily contact with the victim, (2) such bodily contact was made with intent, and (3) the contact was offensive in nature.[164]

As to a battery cause of action, the plaintiff shoulders the burden of proof and the burden of production. The plaintiff must prove the elements of the tort by a preponderance of the evidence. In other words, the plaintiff has to go first and tender sufficient evidence showing the existence of each element of the cause of action. Sufficient evidence means proof that would provide a reasonable jury with at least one rational avenue to conclude that each proposition of fact comprising the *prima facie* case for battery *more likely than not* occurred.

Thus, in our example the plaintiff has to tender proof that would convince a hypothetical reasonable jury there is at least a fifty-one percent chance the plaintiff was offensively touched with intent by the alleged tortfeasor. At the outset, before the finder of fact may see, hear, or touch such proof, the plaintiff must persuade the judge to admit said evidence into the record.

The quantum of evidence a litigant should attempt to introduce into the record at trial depends on what standard of proof applies to the cause of action being tried. By way of example, if the clear-and-convincing-evidence standard applies to the cause of action at bar, then the propounder should seek to introduce into the record stronger (or more) evidence as compared to proof that would be needed had a preponderance standard applied.

An item of proof can be defined as an event that is caused to come about in the courtroom for the benefit of the finder of fact because of its ability to represent or reproduce a real-world occurrence that allegedly happened in the past. By way of example, evidence *par excellence* is live testimony. A witness is called to the stand, where he or she is asked certain questions on the record tending to elicit statements regarding events the witness perceived with his or her senses.

---

164. *See, for example*, Zgraggen v. Wilsey, 606 N.Y.S.2d 444, 445 (App. Div. 1994).

As a matter of policy, to make sure the evidence tendered at trial meets certain threshold levels of reliability, the law imposes a number of restrictions and limitations on the kind, form, and content of proof that may be relied upon by litigants.

Generally speaking, all relevant evidence is admissible in court except where a specific rule bars its admission.[165] Relevant evidence means "evidence having any tendency to make the existence of any fact that is of consequence to the determination of the action more probable or less probable than it would be without the evidence."[166] For example, evidence may be excluded by the hearsay rule, by the best evidence rule, or for lack of a proper foundation or predicate. Moreover, the Court of Appeals, citing Richardson on evidence, stated: "even if the evidence is proximately relevant, it may be rejected if its probative value is outweighed by the danger that its admission would prolong the trial to an unreasonable extent without any corresponding advantage; or would confuse the main issue and mislead the jury; or unfairly surprise a party; or create substantial danger of undue prejudice to one of the parties. . . ."[167]

Now, let us recall for a moment our battery case. The plaintiff, who bears the burden of production, must go first and prove that she was offensively touched with intent by the defendant. Suppose that, to meet such burden, she calls a witness to the stand that testifies the witness saw the defendant punching the plaintiff and that, as a result of the bodily contact, the plaintiff fell. Suppose further that the plaintiff authenticates and introduces into the record a series of letters sent by the defendant to the effect that defendant repeatedly threatened the plaintiff he would punch her as soon as possible.

Clearly, the plaintiff made out a *prima facie* case. At this point, if the defendant wants to avoid the direction of a verdict for the plaintiff he must either impeach or rebut the plaintiff's evidence; that is, unless he is able to *prima facie* establish an affirmative defense.

First, the defendant may attempt to impeach, that is, undermine the credibility, of the plaintiff's evidence. By way of example, during cross-examination the defendant may confront the plaintiff's witness with a prior inconsistent statement made by the witness concerning the incident at issue. Moreover, the defendant may ask

---

165. Ando v. Woodberry, 168 N.E.2d 520, 521 (N.Y. 1960) ("In view of the fact that Mr. Nichols' plea of guilty to the charges leveled against him—failing to signal and making an improper turn—is relevant to the issue of his negligence in turning off Fifth Avenue, we must simply decide whether there is any justification for excluding it. Two possible grounds of exclusion suggest themselves; the first, that such testimony is hearsay and, the second, that its introduction violates public policy.")

166. *See, for example,* People v. Davis, 371 N.E.2d 456, 460 (N.Y. 1977) (citing Unif. R. of Evid., Rule 401, 1974).

167. *Id.* at 460 (quoting secondary sources).

the witness about an alleged motive to fabricate the testimony. Furthermore, the defendant may confront the witness with the witness's felony conviction for a crime involving moral turpitude or, alternatively, ask the witness about a prior bad act he or she allegedly committed that would badly reflect on the witness's credibility. The defendant could call another witness to the stand who is willing to testify that in their community the plaintiff's witness has a reputation for lying. Finally, the defendant may ask the witness about his or her alleged sensory impairment that would prevent the witness from accurately perceiving the incident at issue.

Second, the defendant may rebut, that is, attempt to negate, the plaintiff's evidence. By way of example, the defendant may call another witness to the stand who is willing to testify that the witness saw the incident at issue and that the defendant did not punch the plaintiff. Moreover, the defendant may produce another witness willing to testify that on the day of the incident the defendant was thousands of miles away from the scene and could not possibly be responsible for the punch at issue.

V. MOTION AT THE CLOSE OF PLAINTIFF'S EVIDENCE

A court may enter "judgment as a matter of law" on a particular claim.[168] "Any party may move for judgment with respect to a cause of action or issue, on grounds that the moving party is entitled to judgment as a matter of law, after the close of the evidence presented by an opposing party with respect to the cause of action or issue or at any time on the basis of admissions."[169] Counsel must specify the grounds for the motion and such motion does not waive the right to a jury trial or to present further evidence even if it is made by all parties.[170] Remember that most courts prefer disposition of cases on their merits, rather than oral application while the jury is waiting.[171]

A court cannot grant a motion for judgment as a matter of law unless the party has been fully heard on an issue. Additionally, the evidence must be viewed in the light most favorable to the nonmoving party and not provide any rational basis for a jury to find in the nonmoving party's favor.[172] Further, a court will not

---

168. CPLR § 4401.
169. *Id.*
170. *Id.*
171. *See* Murray v. Brookhaven Mem'l Hosp. Med. Ctr., 902 N.Y.S.2d 576 (App. Div. 2010).
172. *See* Hoberg v. Shree Granesh, LLC, 926 N.Y.S.2d 578, 580 (App. Div. 2011) (quoting Szczerbiak v. Pilat, 686 N.E.2d 1346, 1348 (N.Y. 1997).

grant a motion by plaintiff for judgment as a matter of law, absent admissions fatal to a defendant's position at trial, until the defendant has put on their case.[173] A judgment granting such motion is a judgment on the merits of a case unless the judgment specifies otherwise.[174]

The plaintiff must present admissible evidence establishing the elements of its causes of action. After the plaintiff rests his or her case, the defendant may make a motion for judgment as a matter of law pursuant to CPLR § 4401.[175] The defendant's motion shall state that the plaintiff has not presented sufficient evidence satisfying its burden of proof and as a result, the defendant is entitled to judgment as a matter of law.[176] The only way a CPLR § 4401 motion can be granted after the plaintiff's case in chief is if they failed to establish a *prima facie* case or failed to establish a specific issue upon which the application is made.[177] If such motion is denied, the defendant will then proceed to put forth his or her case. A plaintiff shall not attempt to make such motion prior to the defendant's case. Any attempt shall result in the motion being denied.[178]

VI. DEFENDANT'S CASE

At the close of the evidence by the plaintiff, the defendant puts forth his or her evidence. The defendant must put forth all relevant evidence to help establish that the plaintiff has not met its burden of proof and/or any affirmative defenses to the plaintiff's cause(s) of action. Remember that the defendant does not bear the burden of proof in the case. So, if he does not present any evidence or witnesses that does not necessarily mean that the trier of fact must find against him, since he holds no burden to disprove the cause of action brought by the plaintiff.

The defendant's trial job is to prevent evidence of the plaintiff's causes of action from coming in, and getting into evidence all of the evidence needed to establish an affirmative defense to eliminate one of the elements of the cause of action. In *Lorenz Diversified Corp. v. Falk*, the plaintiff sued on a promissory note and established by proof the existence of the note and defendant's default in payment thereunder.[179] Plaintiff presented a *prima facie* showing at trial of

---

173. Griffin v. Clinton Green S., LLC, 948 N.Y.S.2d 8, 11 (App. Div. 2012) (referring to CPLR § 4401).
174. 8A CARMODY-WAIT 2D § 59:22 (2017).
175. CPLR § 4401.
176. *Id.*
177. *See* Georgetti v. United Hosp. Med. Ctr., 611 N.Y.S.2d 583, 584 (App. Div. 1994).
178. 105 N.Y. JUR. 2D *Trial* § 281.
179. Lorenz Diversified Corp. v. Falk, 844 N.Y.S.2d 370 (App. Div. 2007).

the burden of proof. The defendant's turn came and he failed to controvert the evidence offered by the plaintiff concerning the default and the note, and further failed to offer evidence that the note was paid in full. The defendant's defense was that he had paid cash for the note to Felix Shiffman. The defendant, however, did not call Shiffman to the stand, and instead asked the court to draw an adverse inference against the plaintiff because the plaintiff did not call him. The burden of proof on payment rests with the defendant—not the plaintiff—and that is why the Second Department entered judgment in plaintiff's favor.[180]

VII. MOTION AT CLOSE OF DEFENDANT'S CASE

At the close of the defendant's case a plaintiff may make a motion for judgment as a matter of law pursuant to CPLR § 4401.[181] The statute states that a party can move for the motion upon the close of the evidence presented by the opposing party.[182] A court is correct in granting a CPLR § 4401 motion for a judgment as a matter of law when the trial court finds that, based on the evidence presented, there is no rational process by which the trier of fact could find for the nonmoving party.[183] When the court is entertaining a CPLR § 4401 motion it must view the evidence in the light most favorable to the nonmoving party, affording that party every favorable inference that reasonably may be drawn from the evidence.[184] A plaintiff's motion for judgment as a matter of law shall state that the defendant has failed to rebut the plaintiff's claims and/or put forth any evidence supporting, if any, its affirmative defense and, as a result, the plaintiff is entitled to judgment as a matter of law.

In *Godlewska v. Niznikiewicz*, a medical malpractice case, a motion for judgment as a matter of law was granted against the plaintiff and the action dismissed at the close of the plaintiff's case.[185] The plaintiff offered expert testimony that a defendant-doctor departed from good and accepted medical practices in failing to diagnose and treat the plaintiff, but did not offer testimony connecting this departure to the plaintiff's surgery. *Brenner v. Dixon* was a personal injury action by

---

180. *Id.*
181. CPLR § 4401.
182. *Id.*
183. *See* Szczerbiak v. Pilat, 686 N.E.2d 1346, 1348 (N.Y. 1997); Blum v Fresh Grown Preserve Corp., 54 N.E.2d 809, 809–811 (N.Y. 1944); Figueroa v. City of N.Y., 954 N.Y.S.2d 485, 485 (App. Div. 2012).
184. Gomez v. Casiglia, 890 N.Y.S.2d 81 (App. Div. 2009).
185. Godlewska v. Niznikiewicz, 779 N.Y.S.2d 79 (App. Div. 2004).

plaintiff who was riding a bicycle and was hit by the defendant's car.[186] The trial court had dismissed the plaintiff's complaint at the close of the plaintiff's case. The basis for dismissal was the plaintiff's admission that he failed to signal he was turning left before hitting into defendant's car. The Appellate Division, however, reinstated on the basis that the plaintiff had offered photographs showing the road where the accident took place was wide, and the plaintiff's testimony that before he turned, he looked back and saw the defendant's car "well down [the] road."[187] The plaintiff also testified that he had begun his left turn and had already crossed the double yellow line before the defendant's car hit him—inferring that the defendant had time to see the plaintiff. The case was reinstated as the jury could naturally have found for the plaintiff. In *Red Apple Supermarkets, Inc. v. Hudson Towers Hous. Co.,* a trial court granted the defendant's motion for judgments after its case.[188] The plaintiff grocery store sued the defendant landlord for negligence. Apparently, the wires leading to the power source burnt, leaving the grocery store without power; the merchandise was ruined and the store lost sales. The trial court granted the defendant's motion for judgment after its case based on the plaintiff's failure to establish that the defendant caused the wires to burn. The Appellate Division affirmed.[189]

VIII. MOTION DURING TRIAL FOR CONTINUANCE OR NEW TRIAL

Another trial motion often utilized during trial is a motion for continuance or a new trial. At any time during the trial, the court, on motion of any party, may order a continuance or a new trial in the interest of justice.[190] Whether a new trial or continuance is granted is left to the discretion of the trial court.[191] The common grounds for a CPLR § 4402 motion include (1) witness unavailability, (2) need for additional evidence, (3) illness, (4) surprise, and (5) new counsel.[192]

It is an abuse of discretion for a trial court to deny a continuance during trial "where the application complies with every requirement of law and is not made

---

186. Brenner v. Dixon, 951 N.Y.S.2d 635 (App. Div. 2012).

187. *Id.* at 637.

188. Red Apple Supermarkets, Inc. v. Hudson Towers Hous. Co., 869 N.Y.S.2d 779 (App. Div. 2009).

189. *Id.*

190. CPLR § 4402.

191. *See, for example,* Taveras v. Martin, 863 N.Y.S.2d 475, 476 (App. Div. 2008) ("The court did not improvidently exercise its discretion in denying the appellant's request for a mistrial.").

192. CPLR § 4402.

merely for delay, evidence sought is material, and need for continuance does not result from failure to exercise due diligence."[193]

IX. CLOSING ARGUMENT

Each party has a right to present a closing argument. At the close of all the evidence on the issues tried, an attorney for each party having a separate right may make a closing argument.[194] A denial of this right during a jury trial is usually grounds for a reversal.[195] The party with the burden of proof, usually the plaintiff, has the right to open first, and therefore has the right, under the inverse rule, to close last.[196] Plaintiff may also choose to close first but reserve some of its time for rebuttal.

Although CPLR § 4016 expressly authorizes the inverse order, courts may not apply it where it will be unjust to the defendant. Where strict adherence to the inverse rule under CPLR § 4016 results in unfairness, the court has discretion to depart from it. An example is where the burden of proof has shifted during trial.[197] This can occur where a defendant voluntarily withdraws its responses to allegations in the complaint and proceeds with affirmative defenses or where admissions, directed verdicts, or other events similarly shift the burden of proof, because the sequence of opening and closing statements is initially based on a pretrial determination as to the burden of proof.[198] CPLR § 4016 further states

---

193. *In re* Tripp, 957 N.Y.S.2d 389, 391 (App. Div. 2012) (declined to grant continuance after considering "'the merit or lack of merit of the action, extent of the delay,' the number of adjournments granted, the 'lack of intent to deliberately default or abandon the action' and the length of the pendency of the proceeding.") (quoting Belsky v. Lowell, 497 N.Y.S.2d 945, 947 (App. Div. 1986)); Canty v. McLoughlin, 791 N.Y.S.2d 625, 625 (App. Div. 2005) (holding error for the court to deny a defendant's request for an adjournment of proof to 9:30 a.m. the next morning to present a witness after plaintiff rested at 3:30 p.m.).

194. CPLR § 4016.

195. *See, for example,* Ross v. Manhattan Chelsea Assocs., 598 N.Y.S.2d 502, 503–504 (App. Div. 1993) (holding the court committed reversible error when it denied defendant's counsel the right to summation on the issue of liability where the jury's finding on liability certainly affected defendant's interests regarding unresolved cross-claims); Phillips v. Chevrolet Tonawanda Div. of Gen. Motors Corp., 352 N.Y.S.2d 73, 74 (App. Div. 1974) (holding reversible error to deny a third-party defendant the opportunity to address the jury in summation); Kappa Frocks, Inc. v. Alan Fabrics Corp., 32 N.Y.S.2d 985, 986 (App. Div. 1942) (stating that the privilege of opening and closing in a jury trial is a substantial and important right); *see also* WEINSTEIN, NEW YORK CIVIL PRACTICE ¶ 4016.02.

196. 4 N.Y. PRAC., COM. LITIG. IN NEW YORK STATE COURTS § 46:6 (4th ed.); *see also* N.Y. C.P.L.R § 4016.

197. 4 N.Y. PRAC., COM. LITIG., *supra* note 196 at § 46:6 (4th ed.).

198. *Id.*

that in personal injury and wrongful death cases, a party shall be allowed to reference a specific dollar amount that they believe represents the appropriate compensation.[199] Nevertheless, the court shall instruct the jury at the conclusion of closing statements that (1) the attorney's reference to such specific dollar amount is permitted as argument, (2) the attorney's reference to a specific dollar amount is not evidence and should not be considered by the jury as evidence, and (3) the determination of damages is solely for the jury to decide.[200]

Plaintiff's counsel's closing argument should restate the burden of proof and discuss how the evidence he presented met each element required for the cause of action. Counsel's closing argument should also argue facts and reasonable inferences and how they apply to the law.

Defendant's counsel's closing argument should discuss how the plaintiff has failed to meet his burden of proof with respect to the elements required for his claim. Further defendant's counsel should discuss the applicable law with respect to the affirmative defenses and how, as a result, his client should not be found liable.

The permissible scope of a summation is not discussed in CPLR § 4016. However, the purpose of a closing argument is to draw reasonable inferences from the evidence admitted and assist the jury in fairly arriving at a verdict based on the law and the evidence, although it is an error for counsel to appeal to the passions of the jury.[201] Thus, in his summation, counsel must refer only to facts that are already admitted in evidence.[202]

It is within the court's discretion to limit the parties' time for making their closing statements.[203] However, such limitations cannot be severe, as it will constitute an abuse of discretion if it prevents making effective summations.[204]

During counsel's closing argument, he must only refer to facts already admitted in evidence.[205] He may clarify and reiterate issues in the case by reference to the parties' claims, cross claims, counterclaims, and defenses.[206] However, distinct from opening statements, parties may go beyond stating the issues and enjoy a fair

---

199. CPLR § 4016(b).

200. *Id.*

201. 75 Am. Jur. 2d *Trial* § 444 (2017).

202. 4 N.Y. Prac., Com. Litig., *supra* note 196 at § 46.7 (4th ed.).

203. *Id.; see*, CPLR § 4011; Weinstein, New York Civil Practice ¶ 4016.02.

204. 4 N.Y. Prac., Com. Litig. *supra* note 196 at §46.4 (4th ed.).

205. *Id.; see* Cattano v. Metro. S. R. Co., 66 N.E. 563, 565 (N.Y. 1903) (holding that "[a]ppeals to prejudice or passion, and the statement of facts neither proved nor presumed, have no place in a trial conducted according to the rules of the common law.").

206. 4 N.Y. Prac. Com. Litig. *supra* note 196 at §46.7 (4th ed.).

right to comment on the evidence.[207] Counsel may not refer to matters that would unfairly prejudice the jury against an opponent or other party.[208]

Last, counsel, in its closing argument, may not assume the court's role by instructing the jury on the law.[209] An incorrect statement by counsel of the law or burden of proof may warrant a new trial.

X. USE OF BURDEN OF PROOF IN POST-TRIAL MOTIONS

CPLR § 4404 addresses post-trial motions for judgment and new trials.[210] Under CPLR § 4404(a), "after a trial of a cause of action or issue triable of right by a jury . . . any party [may move to] 'set aside a verdict . . . and direct that judgment . . . as a matter of law [be entered]' or it may order a new trial . . . where the verdict is contrary to the weight of the evidence, in the interest of justice or where [at least five-sixth of the members of the jury][211] cannot agree after [deliberating] for as long as deemed reasonable by the court."[212] Where there is no jury, CPLR § 4404(b) authorizes "the court [to] set aside its decision or any judgment entered. . . ."[213] The court "may make new findings of fact or conclusions of law . . . [issue] a new decision . . . or it may order a new trial. . . ."[214] The movant must raise by a single motion every ground for post-trial relief then available.[215] The court may act either upon motion of a party or *sua sponte*.

The motion authorized by CPLR § 4404 encompasses different kinds of post-trial relief. In fact, on the one hand, the movant may seek that judgment as a matter of law be directed—this is sometimes referred to as judgment notwithstanding

---

207. *Id.*

208. *Id.*

209. *Id.*; *see* Williams v. Brooklyn E. R. Co., 26 N.E. 1048, 1050 (N.Y. 1891) ("It may be observed . . . that it is the function of the judge to instruct the jury upon the law, and where counsel undertake to read the law to the jury, the judge may properly interpose to prevent it.")

210. CPLR § 4404.

211. *Id.* § 4404(a); *see id.* § 4113(b).

212. *Id.* § 4404(a).

213. *Id.* § 4404(b).

214. *Id.*

215. CPLR § 4405. A post-trial motion has to be made before the judge who presided at the trial within fifteen days after the decision, verdict, or discharge of the jury. The court may deny the motion if it is made more than fifteen days after the decision without good cause for the delay. *Id*; Turco v. Turco, 985 N.Y.S.2d 261, 267 (App. Div. 2014) ("The plaintiff moved pursuant to CPLR 4404 (b), inter alia, to set aside certain portions of the decision and for a new trial. Since the motion was not made within 15 days after the decision, and the plaintiff failed to demonstrate good cause for the delay, the Supreme Court providently exercised its discretion in denying the motion as untimely.")

the verdict. On the other hand, the movant may ask the court to order a new trial. Needless to say, the legal bases for directing a verdict as opposed to granting a new trial are different.[216] Thus, for the sake of exposition, it seems necessary to highlight those differences.

Parenthetically, recall that whoever lodges a claim generally bears the burden of proof, the burden of production, and the burden of persuasion. Let us further recall that the burden of proof is permanently assigned to one of the litigants by the substantive law. Conversely, the burden of production may shift between the parties during trial. If the proponent tenders sufficient evidence on each one of the causes of action's elements making out a *prima facie* showing, then the opponent must neutralize the other party's evidence or else be defeated as a matter of law. There are several procedural devices through which an interested party may move for judgment as a matter of law. One such procedural device is a motion for post-trial relief under CPLR § 4404.[217]

The standard for granting a post-trial motion for judgment as a matter of law mirrors the standard established under CPLR § 4401 for granting motions at the close of the evidence. Under both provisions, the movant has to show that the jury's verdict for the nonmovant is (or would be) utterly illogical because the evidence tendered is insufficient as a matter of law. Evidence is insufficient when the record shows there are no rational avenues through which a reasonable decider of fact could find in favor of the nonmoving party.[218]

As has been explained in previous sections of this chapter, adjudicating whether the evidence is insufficient for a rational decider of fact to find for the propounder

---

216. *See, for example,* Cohen v. Hallmark Cards, Inc., 382 N.E.2d 1145, 1147 (N.Y. 1978) ("The Appellate Division decision did not turn on the factual question whether the jury determination was against the weight of the evidence. Rather, it was based on the legal issue whether there was sufficient evidence to support the factual finding that Hallmark acted knowingly. Although these two inquiries may appear somewhat related, they actually involve very different standards and may well lead to disparate results. Whether a particular factual determination is against the weight of the evidence is itself a factual question. In reviewing a judgment of Supreme Court, the Appellate Division has the power to determine whether a particular factual question was correctly resolved by the trier of facts. If the original fact determination was made by a jury, as in this case, and the Appellate Division concludes that the jury has made erroneous factual findings, the court is required to order a new trial, since it does not have the power to make new findings of fact in a jury case.")
217. CPLR § 4404.
218. Mirand v. City of N.Y., 637 N.E.2d 263, 266 (N.Y. 1994) ("Where, as here, a jury verdict is set aside on the ground that, as a matter of law, it is not supported by *sufficient* evidence, and the Appellate Division reverses, the matter is reviewable, the relevant inquiry being whether 'there is simply no valid line of reasoning and permissible inferences which could possibly lead rational [people] to the conclusion reached by the jury on the basis of the evidence presented at trial.'") (emphasis in original) (internal quotations omitted).

entails making a legal determination, namely, establishing whether the party bearing the burden of production failed to lift it. Therefore, such determination is in the exclusive purview of the judge.

Let us recall that once the burden of production has been effectively met, and provided that such burden did not shift to the other party during trial, the case is generally submitted to the jury for deliberations. After the case is submitted for deliberations, only the burden of proof and the burden of persuasion come into play. When deliberating, the finder of fact ought to consider the evidence (i.e., the jury has to weigh the convincing force of the evidence) and determine whether one party's proof preponderates over that of the other. Subsequently, having weighed the evidence, the decider of fact must find for either the plaintiff or defendant pursuant to the instructions given by the judge. If the decider of fact finds the evidence to be in equipoise, the burden of proof rule will determine which party loses.

Generally speaking, weighing the convincing force of the evidence entails making a factual determination. As such, making this assessment is in the jury's purview.[219] However, under CPLR § 4404, the judge is empowered to set aside the verdict and to grant a new trial where the verdict is deemed to be against the weight of the evidence.[220]

In fact, the judge is tasked with the responsibility of supervising the jury so as to confirm that lay jurors' findings of fact are based on a fair interpretation of the evidence presented.[221] A verdict is deemed contrary to the weight of the evidence, and thus not allowed to stand, when the evidence offered by the movant so overwhelmingly preponderates over the other party's proof that the verdict rendered for the nonmovant is likely the result of passion, prejudice, and/or patent mistake.[222]

---

219. *See, for example*, Frances G. v. Vincent G., 536 N.Y.S.2d 138, 139 (App. Div. 1988).

220. *Cohen*, 382 N.E.2d at 1148 ("as was noted above, the Appellate Division has authority to review findings of fact made by the jury, and to decide whether such determinations are in accord with the weight of the evidence.").

221. *See, for example*, Ford v. Southside Hosp., 785 N.Y.S.2d 474, 475 (App. Div. 2004).

222. *See, for example*, Provenzano v. Peters, 661 N.Y.S.2d 41, 41–42 (App. Div. 1997) ("The power of the trial court to set aside a jury verdict pursuant to CPLR 4404 (a) is a broad one intended to ensure that justice is done. Under this section, a trial court has discretion to set aside a verdict which is clearly the product of substantial confusion among the jurors. Upon appellate review, a trial court's exercise of discretion must be accorded great respect. Here, the handwritten gratuitous comment from the jury at the end of the verdict sheet was inconsistent with its answers to the interrogatories posed by the court and thus demonstrated that there was substantial confusion among the jurors as to the burden and quantum of proof applied during deliberations. Accordingly, under the circumstances of this case, we conclude that the trial court did not improvidently exercise its discretion in setting aside the verdict and ordering a new trial.") (internal citations omitted); Triggs v. Kelly, 582 N.Y.S.2d 548, 549 (App. Div. 1992) ("[A] motion to set aside a verdict as against the

To be sure, the judge may not set aside a verdict only because he or she views the verdict as unjust or simply because the judge would have decided the case differently.[223] In other words, when it comes to weighing the evidence, the judge is merely a gatekeeper, so to speak, who must purely ascertain whether the finder of fact reached its decision through a fair line of reasoning.[224]

To sum up, the judge may vacate the verdict and order a new trial where he or she determines that although the jury reached a (logically) possible decision, the fact finder impermissibly did so through a capricious or irrational process such that the interpretation given the evidence seems unfair, albeit rationally conceivable.

The interplay between the concepts of insufficiency of the evidence warranting the direction of a verdict, and contrariness of the verdict to the weight of the evidence warranting *vacatur* and a new trial is best explained by reference to the case of *Killon v. Parrotta*[225] decided by the Court of Appeals.

In *Killon*, the plaintiff, a friend of the defendant's wife, called the defendant on the phone and threatened him.[226] Thereafter, the defendant drove twenty miles to the plaintiff's house to confront him.[227] During the twenty-mile drive, the defendant placed several phone calls to his wife, presumably to alert her of his intentions.[228] After the defendant reached the plaintiff's house, a physical altercation ensued.[229] The plaintiff suffered injuries resulting from the battery.[230]

At trial, the defendant claimed he had acted in self-defense.[231] The plaintiff countered alleging that the self-defense justification was not available because the defendant was the initial aggressor.[232] Indeed, the defendant testified that he saw the plaintiff exiting his home with a maul-hammer in hand and that, as a result

---

weight of evidence must be viewed in a light most favorable to the prevailing party. Whether a jury verdict should be set aside on this ground does not involve a question of law but rather a discretionary balancing of many factors. A verdict should not be set aside as against the weight of evidence unless the jury could not have reached the verdict on any fair interpretation of the evidence.") (internal citations omitted).

223. *See, for example,* Durkin v. Peluso, 585 N.Y.S.2d 137, 138 (App. Div. 1992) ("[T]his power does not imply that a trial court can freely interfere with any verdict that it finds unsatisfactory or with which it disagrees. . . .")
224. *See, for example,* Sanford v. Jonathan Woodner Co., 758 N.Y.S.2d 399, 401 (App. Div. 2003).
225. 65 N.E.3d 41 (N.Y. 2016); *see also* Harrison v. Harrison, 607 N.Y.S.2d 204 (App. Div. 1993) (noting the effects of setting aside a verdict against the weight of the evidence).
226. *Killon v. Parrotta*, 65 N.E.3d 41, 42 (N.Y. 2016).
227. *Id.*
228. *Id.*
229. *Id.* at 42–43.
230. *Id.* at 43.
231. *Id.* at 42.
232. *Id.*

of the injured party's conduct, he retrieved a bat from his truck before approaching the plaintiff.[233] The defendant further testified that the plaintiff encouraged his dog to attack him and contemporaneously swung the maul-hammer's handle at him.[234] Thus, the defendant stated that he did swing the bat at the plaintiff but he did so in response to the adversary's initial aggression.[235]

The plaintiff, though, testified that when the defendant approached his property he told him to leave.[236] By way of contrast with the defendant's version, the plaintiff further testified that he threw the maul-hammer on the floor as the defendant was approaching.[237] A witness who was present at the scene testified that when the defendant exited his truck he was already carrying the bat.[238] The jury found for the defendant.[239]

On appeal, the Appellate Division found that "no fair interpretation of the evidence [sustained] the verdict. . . ."[240] as a result, the court ordered a new trial and concluded as a matter of law that the defendant was the initial aggressor.[241] On retrial, the judge refused to instruct the jury on self-defense because of the Appellate Division's conclusion.[242] The second jury awarded damages.[243]

On appeal from retrial, the Appellate Division affirmed.[244] On further appeal, in which both "Appellate Division [orders were] brought up for review," the Court of Appeals vacated and remanded for retrial.[245] Essentially, the Court of Appeals explained that if the Appellate Division finds that "no fair interpretation of the evidence [sustains] the verdict . . ." then the appropriate relief is retrial.[246] On the other hand, if the Appellate Division intends to direct judgment as a matter of law, then the court must find that the jury's verdict was *utterly irrational* as there were no logical avenues through which the jury could have found the way it did.[247]

---

233. *Id.* at 42–43.
234. *Id.* at 43.
235. *Id.*
236. *Id.*
237. *Id.*
238. *Id.*
239. *Id.*
240. *Id.* at 44.
241. *Id.*
242. *Id.*
243. *Id.*
244. *Id.*
245. *Id.* at 46.
246. *Id.* at 44–46.
247. *Id.*

Here, according to the Court of Appeals, the Appellate Division's order entered on appeal from the first jury's verdict was erroneous because the wrong test was applied: the Appellate Division had determined that the jury returned a verdict against the weight of the evidence and having so established impermissibly stated that the plaintiff was not the initial aggressor as a matter of law.[248] The Court of Appeals also indicated that given the conflicting versions of the events, indeed there was *a* rational avenue for the jury to infer that the plaintiff was the initial aggressor.[249]

The Court of Appeals put the point thus:

> Where the Appellate Division determines that a verdict is against the weight of the evidence, the remedy is to remit for a new trial. By contrast, where the Appellate Division intends to hold that a jury verdict is insufficient as a matter of law, it must first determine that the verdict is "utterly irrational. . . ." To conclude that a verdict is utterly irrational, requiring vacatur of the verdict, the Court must determine that "there is simply no valid line of reasoning and permissible inferences which could possibly lead [a] rational [person] to the conclusion reached by the jury on the basis of the evidence presented at trial." When it can be said that "it would not be utterly irrational for a jury to reach the result it . . . determined . . . , the court may not conclude that the verdict is as a matter of law not supported by the evidence."[250]

In its 2012 order, although the Appellate Division examined the facts and determined that "the jury's conclusion that defendant was not the first to threaten the immediate use of physical force [wa]s unreachable on any fair interpretation of the evidence"—ostensibly a weight of the evidence review—the effect of that order was to hold as a matter of law that the defendant was the initial aggressor to whom the defense of justification was not available—a determination that could only be reached by concluding that the verdict was "utterly irrational." Yet, the Appellate Division did not use the utterly irrational test. The Appellate Division's error in not applying the proper test resulted in the defendant being improperly precluded from raising a justification defense on the retrial. The defendant should have been afforded a new trial on all the issues in the case, including consideration of his justification defense by the jury.[251]

---

248. *Id.*
249. *Id.*
250. *Id.* at 45 (internal citations omitted).
251. *Id.* (internal citations omitted).

In *Grassi v. Ulrich*,[252] the plaintiff was allegedly injured in a car accident.[253] At trial, the defendant conceded that the accident was caused by his negligence.[254] However, the defendant contended, and an expert testified, that the plaintiff's injuries resulted from a preexisting condition unrelated to the accident.[255] Plaintiff's expert opined differently.[256] The jury found for the defendant.[257] The trial court denied the plaintiff's motion to set aside the verdict as against the weight of the evidence.[258] An appeal ensued, and the Appellate Division, having found sufficient evidence to sustain the verdict, affirmed.[259] On further appeal, the Court of Appeals reversed, stating:

> The Appellate Division erred in curtailing its review of the denial of that motion after simply finding record evidence to support the jury's verdict. Having found sufficient evidence to support the verdict, the Court was then required to consider the conflicting medical evidence presented by plaintiff and determine whether "the evidence so preponderate[d] in favor of the [plaintiff] that [the verdict] could not have been reached on any fair interpretation of the evidence . . ."[260]

As has been explained above, weighing the convincing force of the evidence entails making a factual determination, which is in the purview of the finder of fact. By the same token, assessing whether a verdict is against the weight of the evidence is similarly a factual determination. However, making the latter determination is in the purview of the judge as supervisor of the finder of fact.

The Appellate Division, being part of the Supreme Court, as judge of the facts and of the law,[261] may assess whether a verdict is against the weight of the evidence as well.[262] However, great deference is generally given to the trial judge's determination in that assessing whether a verdict is against the weight of the evidence is discretionary in nature and it entails balancing many factors.[263] As such, the trial judge is in a better position than the Appellate Division to observe firsthand the conduct

---

252. 664 N.E.2d 499 (N.Y. 1996).
253. *Id.*
254. *Id.*
255. *Id.*
256. *Id.*
257. *Id.*
258. *Id.*
259. *Id.*
260. *Id.* at 499–500 (internal citations omitted).
261. CPLR § 5501(c).
262. *See, for example*, Gomez v. Doe, 647 N.Y.S.2d 27, 28 (App. Div. 1996).
263. *See, for example*, Szabo v. Super Operating Corp., 382 N.Y.S.2d 63, 67 (App. Div. 1976).

of the parties, witnesses, and jurors. A trial judge's determination will be reversed by the Appellate Division only when an abuse of discretion is found.[264]

Such is the import of the case *Mann v. Hunt*,[265] where the Third Department clarified that the trial judge stands in a better position than the Appellate Division to make the discretionary assessment that a verdict cannot stand as contrary to the weight of the evidence.

In *Mann*, the plaintiff was allegedly injured while sitting in a parked car when the defendant's car collided with a nearby vehicle which, in turn, struck the plaintiff's automobile.[266] The defendant did not dispute he negligently caused said collision to occur.[267] However, the defendant testified, and a few eye witnesses confirmed, that the plaintiff was not sitting in the parked car at the time of the accident.[268] Rather, according to the defendant and the defendant's eye witnesses, the plaintiff appeared some seven minutes later.[269]

On her part, the plaintiff testified, and witnesses confirmed, that the victim was indeed sitting in the parked car at the time of the accident.[270] A medical expert further testified that he examined the plaintiff and her bruises were consistent with the accident at issue.[271] On this record, the jury found for the defendant.[272]

The trial judge set aside the "jury['s] verdict for defendant" as "against the weight of the evidence" and the defendant appealed.[273] On appeal, the Appellate Division affirmed, stating:

> The semantic problem that adheres to the expression "against the weight of evidence" has never been given an entirely successful solution. It involves essentially a matter of judgment and appraisal with the standards stemming back deep in the soil of the experience of the profession.
>
> Everyone would admit that there are circumstances in which a trial judge's duty may require him to set aside a verdict which is too high, too low, or so wrong that it will not stand. The judge, indeed, has the active and continuous burden of supervising the work of the juries which report to him. But he will not interfere

---

264. *See, for example*, Straub v. Yalamanchili, 871 N.Y.S.2d 773, 774 (App. Div. 2009).
265. 126 N.Y.S.2d 823 (App. Div. 1953).
266. *Id.* at 825.
267. *Id.*
268. *Id.*
269. *Id.*
270. *Id.*
271. *Id.*
272. *Id.* at 826.
273. *Id.* at 824, 826.

just because he dislikes the verdict; or feels quite strongly he would have done something else; or even because he may think the verdict is unjust.

The point of interference is not fixed on the caprice of judicial individualism; it is rather arrived at by a synthesis of all the experience that the judge has had: in the beginning as a law student, in the later controversies of law practice, in the hearing of cases and the writing of decisions, in the sum of all that he has absorbed in the courtroom and in the library.

In the end it is an informed professional judgment; and although lawyers might differ greatly about how the components of the judgment are arranged and added up, there would be a very considerable agreement about the result to be reached in any case once the facts were thoroughly understood.

The problem presented by the term "against the weight of evidence", indeed, is very similar in its implications to the problem of what the profession has meant by the word "reasonable" applied to private conduct or official act. Therefore, while the rule is not easily, or at all, capable of being laid down in plain words as an infallible guide to decision and can be illustrated only imperfectly by opinions in past cases, it is a rule which the profession understands as the cumulative product of its own experience.

A court which reviews the weight of evidence as well as the law, as does an Appellate Division, must approach an appeal from a decision by a trial judge setting aside a verdict in the light of the nature of the duty and the subtle and not easily definable measure of responsibility which the judge exercises in decision.

The duty of the judge to supervise the reasonableness of the verdicts returned to him ought to be viewed liberally on appeal because the independence of mind with which that duty is exercised is ingredient to the sound health of the judicial process.

Even if the judges who look at the case on appeal would not themselves have set the verdict aside had they acted in the first instance, they should not find in this alone a ground for reversal. If the case comes within the area within which judicial interference would not be regarded by the profession as unreasonable, the exercise of the power thus to deal with the verdict ought to be upheld.[274]

In *Ruso v. Osowiecky*,[275] the plaintiff was injured when a "tractor-trailer operated by defendant" made contact with her car while driving on a three-lane highway.[276] At trial, testimonial evidence showed that on the day of the accident the "roadway was covered with an inch . . . of slushy snow."[277] A witness said that the tractor trailer operated by the defendant made contact with the plaintiff's

---

274. *Mann*, 126 N.Y.S.2d at 824–825 (internal citations omitted).
275. 681 N.Y.S.2d 661 (App. Div. 1998).
276. *Id.* at 662–663.
277. *Id.* at 663.

car, which was traveling in the center lane, after successfully pulling to the left lane and passing two other vehicles that were also traveling in the center lane.[278] Evidence further showed that after the collision at issue, the vehicles immediately following the plaintiff's car were "able to safely [come to a] stop."[279]

"The jury . . . found [that] both plaintiff and defendant [were] negligent but that only defendant's negligence was [the] proximate cause of [the accident]" and awarded damages.[280] The defendant moved "to set aside the verdict as against the weight of the evidence."[281] The trial court denied the motion and an appeal ensued.[282] The Appellate Division affirmed, saying:

> Initially, we reject defendants' contention that the jury's verdict was against the weight of the evidence. It is well settled that a jury verdict will be set aside as being against the weight of the evidence when the jury could not have reached the verdict by any fair interpretation of the evidence. Such a determination is discretionary and involves balancing many factors. The ultimate test is whether any viable evidence exists to support the verdict. Here, defendants contend that in the absence of any explanation for plaintiff's loss of control of her car, any fair interpretation of the evidence required some apportionment of negligence against plaintiff. We disagree. Defendant's pretrial testimony and his trial testimony contained inconsistencies; moreover, McClaney's testimony conflicted with defendant's version of the events leading up to the accident. Significantly, McClaney testified that although she was operating the car directly behind plaintiff, she was able to safely stop and avoid a collision with plaintiff's car. Although plaintiff may have negligently lost control of her car, both of the cars immediately behind her managed to avoid colliding with plaintiff. Notably, according to plaintiff, she has no memory of the accident because of her head injury.
>
> Viewing the evidence in a light most favorable to plaintiff, it could reasonably be concluded that it was defendant's decision to attempt to pass the cars that was the sole substantial factor which caused the accident. Upon our review of the record, a fair interpretation of the evidence would support the conclusion that defendant had ample opportunity to avoid the collision by slowing down and stopping behind McClaney's car instead of pulling into the left lane to pass. In our view, Supreme Court properly denied defendants' motion to set aside the verdict as against the weight of the evidence.[283]

---

278. *Id.*
279. *Id.*
280. *Id.*
281. *Id.*
282. *Id.*
283. *Ruso*, 681 N.Y.S.2d at 663 (internal citation omitted).

At common law, when a verdict was deemed to be excessive or inadequate as to the amount of damages awarded, a new trial on all issues, including liability, had to be granted. Conversely, in New York, courts are empowered to order a new trial on the question of damages only, provided that the issues of liability and damages are neither intertwined nor the result of a jurors' compromise.

The court must order a new trial on all questions when it appears that the jurors decided the amount of damages as a result of a compromise (i.e., a trade-off) as to the liability issue. Indeed, in a typical compromise situation, jurors who are skeptical about the liability question (impermissibly) agree to find such liability in exchange for a low damages award.[284]

Furthermore, as to the damages issue, should the court determine that the verdict rendered is either excessive or inadequate so as to warrant a new trial, it may nevertheless deny a motion for a new trial on the condition that the litigant other than the movant accepts a lower or higher amount of damages, respectively. The former order is usually called *remittitur* whereas the latter is called *additur*.[285]

In actions to recover for wrongful death, personal injuries, and damages to property, if the verdict "deviates materially from what would be reasonable compensation,"[286] an award of damages should be set aside and a new trial granted unless the nonmovant stipulates to a higher or lower amount as determined by the court. This standard has been interpreted to provide for a lower threshold to grant new trials as compared to the common law shock-the-conscience-of-the-court standard.[287]

---

284. *See, for example*, Figliomeni v. Bd. of Educ., N.E.2d 557, 560 (N.Y. 1975) ("In more modern practice, however, and in New York since 1951, it has come to be recognized that, where liability and damages are neither intertwined nor the result of a trade-off of a finding of liability in return for a compromise on damages, the court is empowered to limit the new trial to the issue of damages alone.")
285. *See, for example*, O'Connor v. Papertsian, 131 N.E.2d 883, 886 (N.Y. 1956) ("The power of the trial court to grant a new trial on the ground that the verdict is inadequate or excessive, is undisputed. Similarly the trial court may deny a motion for a new trial on condition that the party, other than the movant, stipulate to pay a greater amount or accept a lower amount, as the case may be. As we have said earlier, the Appellate Division is enabled to render the judgment which the trial court could or should have rendered upon the right of any or all of the parties and therefore can act as it did in the present case.") (internal citations and quotation marks omitted).
286. CPLR § 5501(c).
287. *See, for example*, Lauria v. N.Y.C. Dep't of Envtl. Prot., 600 N.Y.S.2d 603, 604 (App. Term 1993) ("It is noted that the standard of review evolved through the common law as to whether a verdict is excessive or inadequate has been that it 'shocks the conscience' of the court. The Legislature changed the standard in regard to the Appellate Division in 1986 by adding a sentence to CPLR 5501 (c). It states that 'the appellate division shall determine that an award is excessive or inadequate if it deviates materially from what would be reasonable compensation.' This apparently relaxes the 'shocks the conscience' standard to facilitate appellate changes in the verdict.") (internal citations omitted).

Furthermore, a new trial may be granted in the interest of justice. A verdict is not allowed to stand when the judge finds that error or misconduct during trial was prejudicial; this occurs when error or misconduct might have affected the outcome of the case.[288]

Generally speaking, a new trial in the interest of justice is warranted when the verdict is affected by misconduct of litigants, counsels, jurors, or judges;[289] errors in evidentiary rulings[290] or jury instructions;[291] newly discovered evidence;[292] and surprise.[293]

---

288. *See, for example*, Micallef v. Miehle Co., Div. of Miehle-Goss Dexter, 348 N.E.2d 571, 574 (N.Y. 1976) ("The Trial Judge must decide whether substantial justice has been done, whether it is likely that the verdict has been affected. . . .").

289. *See, for example*, Bainton v. Bd. of Educ., 292 N.Y.S.2d 229, 230 (App. Term 1968) ("It is undisputed that two of the jurors made separate and unauthorized visits to the scene of the accident. This was highly improper and so inherently prejudicial as to require a new trial."); Nugent v. Metro. S. R. Co., 61 N.Y.S. 476, 476 (App. Div. 1899) ("The object of a trial is to do justice, and whenever it is made to appear that one of the parties to the litigation has by fraud, connivance, conspiracy or any other dishonest act prevented his adversary from having a fair trial, then the court never hesitates to use the power which it possesses to rectify that wrong by vacating the judgment obtained and directing a new trial.")

290. *See, for example*, Perkins v. N.Y. Racing Ass'n, 378 N.Y.S.2d 757, 759 (App. Div. 1976) ("In addition, the trial court committed further error in excluding the testimony of one of the codefendants during plaintiffs' direct case on the ground that they had already read his deposition into evidence. This ruling was clearly erroneous, as plaintiffs had not thereby made that defendant their witness; nor had they adopted his testimony. They were, therefore, free to rebut it. Exclusion of this testimony was prejudicial to the plaintiffs' case, as the deposition was inadmissible against two defendants who were not parties to the action at the time the deposition was taken. For the foregoing reasons, a new trial is warranted in the interests of justice.") (internal citations omitted); *see also* Fox v. Tedesco, 789 N.Y.S.2d 742 (App. Div. 2005).

291. *See, for example*, Dobro v. Sloan, 368 N.Y.S.2d 621, 625–626 (App. Div. 1975) (affirming the grant of a new trial because "There were also errors in refusing to give to the jury charges offered by plaintiff from Pattern Jury Instructions relating to the burden of proof in a wrongful death action and to the effect that the jury might consider the fact of employment of a witness by a party in determining whether his testimony was in any way influenced by the employment relationship. The right to the first charge in an action of this kind is well established; the second requested instruction was appropriate because three witnesses called by defendant railroad were employed by it at the time of trial.") (internal quotations and citations omitted).

292. *See, for example*, Stoddard v. Stoddard, 37 N.Y.S.2d 605, 610 (Sup. Ct. 1942) ("The Courts have established certain requirements which must be met in a plea for a new trial on this ground: (a) the evidence must have been discovered since the trial; (b) it must be shown that such evidence could not have been discovered with proper diligence before the trial; (c) the evidence must be material; (d) it must be sufficiently cogent to render it reasonable to suppose that the conclusions of the Court or jury might have been otherwise had it been presented. So far as is reasonably possible, in the administration of justice, there should be finality to a trial; furthermore, parties and attorneys are supposed to prepare their cases for trial fully and when they fail so to do and are defeated, they cannot obtain the indulgence of the Court for another attempt.")

293. *See, for example*, Straub v. Yalamanchili, 871 N.Y.S.2d 773, 774 (App. Div. 2009) ("During the course of the trial here, defense counsel had ex parte conversations with Anthony Sanito and

By way of example, in *Packard v. State Farm General Insurance Co.*[294] the plaintiff submitted a claim to the defendant insurance company to recover damages for property loss due to a fire.[295] The insurance company rejected the claim, stating "that [the plaintiff had] fraudulently exaggerated the loss."[296] At trial, the defendant's counsel, when cross-examining the plaintiff, "asked questions [regarding] the cause of the fire."[297] "In the presence of the jury," the judge reprimanded counsel and declared that arson was not an issue being tried.[298] The jury found for the defendant.[299]

Upon a CPLR § 4404 motion, trial court ordered a new trial "in the interest of justice."[300] The Appellate Division affirmed and explained that:

> [W]e cannot say that Supreme Court abused its discretion in setting aside the verdict and ordering a new trial. On more than one occasion defense counsel referred to matters germane to the cause of the fire, an issue which should not have been raised. Supreme Court acknowledged that it amplified the errors by commenting that it was not an arson trial. Under the circumstances, Supreme Court was certainly empowered to order a new trial in the interest of justice.[301]

Last, it seems necessary to briefly mention motions under CPLR § 5015. It is well established in New York that courts retain inherent discretionary power to

---

Lowell Garner, both of whom treated plaintiff, without obtaining plaintiff's authorization under HIPAA. This was in clear violation of the law in effect at the time of trial and plaintiffs' counsel did not discover it until that time. Through these conversations, defense counsel obtained information that he otherwise did not have, which enabled him to elicit testimony that was not only favorable to his client, but that came as a complete surprise to plaintiffs and which they were unprepared to rebut.") (internal citations omitted); Kavanaugh v. Kuchner, 665 N.Y.S.2d 279, 279 (App. Div. 1997) ("In view of the discovery demands served by the defendants and the pretrial discovery order in this case, the trial court erred in allowing a witness who had never been disclosed to testify for the plaintiffs (see, CPLR 3101 [a]). Under the circumstances of this case, a new trial is warranted.")

294. 701 N.Y.S.2d 741 (App. Div. 2000); *see also* McCarthy v. Port of N.Y. Auth., 248 N.Y.S.2d 713, 717 (App. Div. 1964) ("The precedents make clear that there is no hard-and-fast rule for the granting of new trials in the interests of justice. When the attack is collateral, long-delayed, or merely reflects a disappointed or ill-prepared litigant's second thought, a new trial is always denied. Where, however, there is clear evidence of a gross fraud practiced upon the court, the court has power and exercises it to nullify its own verdict or judgment, thus fraudulently procured.")

295. *Packard*, 701 N.Y.S.2d at 742.

296. *Id.*

297. *Id.*

298. *Id.*

299. *Id.*

300. *Id.*; CPLR § 4404(a).

301. Packard v. State Farm General Insurance Co. 701 N.Y.S.2d 742–743 (App. Div. 2000).

vacate their judgments in the interest of substantial justice even after the time for filing a CPLR § 4404 motion has expired.[302]

CPLR § 5015 sets forth five grounds for *vacatur*, which "represent a codification of the principal grounds upon which courts have traditionally vacated default judgments as part of their 'inherent discretionary power.'"[303]

Those grounds, inter alia, include excusable default,[304] newly discovered evidence,[305] fraud or misrepresentation,[306] and lack of (personal or subject matter) jurisdiction.[307]

---

302. *See* Woodson v. Mendon Leasing Corp., 790 N.E.2d 1156, 1160 (N.Y. 2003); Lovelace v. RPM Ecosystems Ithaca, LLC, 988 N.Y.S.2d 523 (Sup. Ct., Tompkins County 2014), *aff'd* 14 N.Y.S.3d 815 (App. Div. 2015).

303. *Woodson*, 790 N.E.2d at 1160; Boyd v. Town of N. Elba, 813 N.Y.S.2d 247 (App. Div. 2006) (noting in addition to those five grounds, a court may vacate its own judgment "for sufficient reason and in the interests of substantial justice") (internal citations omitted).

304. *See, for example*, Gage v. Vill. of Catskill, 41 N.Y.S.3d 328, 329–30 (App. Div. 2016) ("Contrary to plaintiff's claim, this is not a case in which the excuse offered for the default is the insurer's delay in responding or interposing a defense on behalf of its insured. Rather, defendant's default was based upon its good faith, albeit mistaken, belief that its legal interests were being represented by SIC in the pending action, a belief that stemmed from SIC's involvement in the case from the time that the notice of claim was served and its appointment of counsel to represent defendant in the litigation that followed. Under these circumstances, Supreme Court providently exercised its discretion in finding that defendant demonstrated a reasonable excuse for its failure to appear in the action. Furthermore, defendant put forth a meritorious defense to the action, namely, that the piece of metal over which plaintiff tripped was a broken sign that had been erected by the state to control pedestrian traffic along a state highway that is not maintained by defendant. In view of the foregoing, we find no reason to disturb Supreme Court's vacatur of the default judgment.") (internal citations omitted).

305. *See, for example*, Ramos v. 1199 Hous. Corp., 774 N.Y.S.2d 346, 346–347 (App. Div. 2004) ("In 1991 the daughter of the plaintiff Dorca Diaz Ramos was murdered in her apartment. The assailant was not apprehended. The plaintiffs subsequently commenced this action against 1199 Housing Corporation . . . the owner of the building, which, in turn, impleaded Watchdog Patrols, Inc. . . . the security company it retained to provide security for the building. By order dated August 1, 1997, the Supreme Court granted the separate motions of 1199 and Watchdog for summary judgment dismissing the complaint and the third-party complaint, respectively. This Court affirmed that order, determining that the plaintiffs adduced no factual support for the contention that the assailant was an intruder who gained entry to the building by virtue of the alleged negligence of 1199. Consequently, no question of fact was raised as to whether the conduct of 1199 was a proximate cause of the occurrence. In June 2001 Richard Fontenez pleaded guilty to the crime, but his plea allocution provided no details of its circumstances. In or about June 2002 the plaintiffs moved pursuant to CPLR § 5015 (a) (2) to vacate the order dated August 1, 1997, on the ground of newly-discovered evidence. The Supreme Court improvidently exercised its discretion in granting the plaintiffs' motion since they failed to demonstrate that the new evidence would probably have led to a different result on the summary judgment motions.") (internal citations omitted); Evergreen Bank N.A. v. Dashnaw, 691 N.Y.S.2d 637, 639 (App. Div. 1999) ("While a court may vacate a prior order upon the ground of newly discovered evidence (CPLR 5015 [a] [2]), fraud, misrepresentation or other misconduct of an adverse party (CPLR § 5015 [a] [3]), modification of a prior order upon which it is based

(CPLR § 5015 [a] [5]) or in the interest of justice . . . defendants have not demonstrated that vacatur of the January 23, 1997 order is warranted on any of these grounds. In particular, the amended order is not 'newly-discovered evidence' within the meaning of CPLR § 5015 (a) (2). In order to vacate a prior judgment or order based upon newly discovered evidence, the movant has the burden of establishing that the new evidence would have produced a different result and that such evidence could not, despite due diligence, have been discovered earlier.") (internal citations omitted).
306. *See, for example*, Abacus Real Estate Fin. Co. v. P.A.R. Constr. & Maint. Corp., 513 N.Y.S.2d 743, 743–744 (App. Div. 1987) ("We find no error in the determination of the Supreme Court that the defendants failed to establish that the judgment against them was procured by fraud (see CPLR § 5015 [a] [3]). The defendants' contention that the plaintiff was seeking to recover an illegal brokerage commission is nothing more than a newly interposed theory of defense which could have been asserted prior to the entry of judgment. Equally unavailing is the defendants' contention that the judgment should have been vacated because Abacus Mortgage Investment Co. acted illegally in making a loan without first obtaining a license from the Superintendent of Banking as well as its argument that the court lacked jurisdiction to enter judgment.") (internal citations omitted); Country Wide Home Loans, Inc. v. Harris, 26 N.Y.S.3d 33, 34–35 (App. Div. 2016) ("The motion court properly granted Dunia's motion to vacate pursuant to CPLR 5015 (a) (3), even though Dunia only referenced CPLR 5015 and did not specify subdivision (a) (3) in his motion papers. The motion was made within a reasonable time, given that Dunia moved less than three months after entry of the judgment of foreclosure and sale, and there is no indication that he had actual notice of this action before entry of the judgment. Given that plaintiff knew of Dunia's fee interest since at least 2009, but neither joined him nor gave him notice of the instant action, the motion court properly vacated the judgment on the ground of extrinsic fraud.") (internal citations omitted).
307. Editorial Photocolor Archives, Inc. v. Granger Collection, 463 N.E.2d 365, 368 (N.Y. 1984) ("The fact that the preliminary injunction was issued, in effect upon defendant's default, is of no consequence. A judgment or order issued without subject matter jurisdiction is void, and that defect may be raised at any time and may not be waived."); Ismailov v. Cohen, 809 N.Y.S.2d 199, 201 (App. Div. 2006) ("Under the circumstances of this case, the Supreme Court improvidently exercised its discretion in denying the motion, in effect, for leave to renew. In support of his motion, Walker demonstrated that he was not served with process (*see* CPLR § 5015 [a] [4]). Thus, his 'default' was a nullity, as was the remedy the Supreme Court rendered in response, and vacatur of the judgment was required as a matter of law and due process even in the absence of a demonstration of a meritorious defense.") (internal citations omitted); In re Anna M., 940 N.Y.S.2d 121, 122–223 (App. Div. 2012) ("The Family Court denied the father's motion. without specifically addressing the issue of personal jurisdiction, the Family Court found that the father had notice of the petitioner's request for guardianship but failed 'to take action' and 'explain his delay' in moving to vacate the order of guardianship and opposing the petitions. The Family Court therefore determined that '[e]ven if there was a defect in service,' the 'doctrine of laches operate[d] to bar the father from vacating the guardianship order.'" This was error. CPLR § 5015 provides that "[t]he court which rendered a judgment or order may relieve a party from it upon such terms as may be just," upon the ground of, inter alia, "excusable default" (CPLR § 5015 [a] [1]) or "lack of jurisdiction to render the judgment or order" (CPLR 5015 [a] [4]). A court may not rule on the excusable nature of a defendant's default under CPLR § 5015 (a) (1) without first determining the jurisdictional question under CPLR § 5015 (a) (4). Where want of jurisdiction is the ground for a motion to vacate pursuant to CPLR § 5015, a default must be vacated once the movant demonstrates a lack of personal jurisdiction, and the movant is relieved of any obligation to demonstrate a reasonable excuse for the default and a potentially meritorious defense.") (internal citations omitted).

8 | Appeal Based on Burden of Proof

INTRODUCTION

In New York, the burden of proof likewise plays a significant role regarding appeals. As a preliminary matter, litigants must pay attention to the standard of review to be applied by the appellate court. Furthermore, there are limits as to which factual and legal matters the appellate court shall consider as part of the record on appeal and the appellate briefs submitted by the parties. Finally, the parties must pay close attention to the rules governing practice before the specific appellate court before which the appeal is pending. Each court has its own rules regarding certain requirements for the appeal to proceed.

I.   NEW YORK APPELLATE COURTS

The New York court system has three levels of appellate courts. Each court is governed by the New York Civil Practice Law and Rules (CPLR) and the rules promulgated by the specific court. A movant must be aware of what each court has the power to review and the procedures for taking an appeal.

A.   Court of Appeals

The Court of Appeals is the highest court in the state of New York. It is like the United States Supreme Court in that it is the court of last resort for appeals in the state. The source of the Court of Appeals' power comes from the New York Constitution.[1]

---

1. N.Y. CONST. art. VI, § 3; 1 NEW YORK APPELLATE PRACTICE § 11.01 (Lexis 2018).

The jurisdiction over civil cases can be found in CPLR §§ 5601, 5602.[2] The rules of the Court of Appeals can be found in 22 NYCRR § 500 *et seq.*

The Court of Appeals has no original jurisdiction over cases.[3] This court can only review questions of law that are brought under CPLR § 5501(b).[4] There is one exception applicable to civil cases where the Court of Appeals may review questions of fact. This situation is where "the appellate division, on reversing or modifying a final or interlocutory judgment in an action of a final interlocutory order in a special proceeding, finds new facts and a final judgment or a final order pursuant . . . is entered, but the right to appeal does not depend upon the amount involved."[5]

B. Appellate Division

The Appellate Division is the intermediate appellate court of New York State. The Appellate Division was created by the New York Constitution, under Article VI, § 4.[6] The Appellate Division was created to exercise "appellate jurisdiction in matter arising in the trial and special terms of the supreme court and in inferior courts."[7] The Appellate Division has jurisdiction to review both questions of law and fact.[8] The jurisdiction of the Appellate Division is over appeals from "a judgment or order of a court of original instance and on an appeal from an order of the supreme court, a county court or an appellate term determining an appeal."[9]

Under the New York Constitution, the Appellate Division is divided into four departments. The First Department has jurisdiction over the first judicial district.[10] The Second Department has jurisdiction over the second, ninth, tenth, and

---

2. *Id.*

3. Jefferson James Davis & Rachel M. Kane, 11 Carmody-Wait 2d § 71:2 (West November 2018 Update).

4. 1 New York Appellate Practice, *supra* note 1, § 11.02: The Finality Requirement for Review by the Court of Appeals. As will be discussed in later sections, CPLR § 5501 codifies the Scope of Review for the appellate courts of New York. Subsection (b) specifically states what the Court of Appeals can review. If it is not in the statute, the Court of Appeals is not permitted to hear it. Davis & Kane, *supra* note 3.

5. Davis & Kane, *supra* note 3 (citing N.Y. Const. art. VI, § 3(a)).

6. John A. Gebauer & Caralyn M. Ross, 11 Carmody-Wait 2d § 72:2 (West November 2018 Update).

7. *Id.*

8. CPLR § 5501(c) (LexisNexis 2018).

9. *Id.*

10. N.Y. Const. art. VI, § 4(a). The first judicial district covers Bronx and New York counties. *Id.* § 6(a). The rules for the First Department can be found at 22 NYCRR § 600 *et seq.*

eleventh judicial districts.[11] The Third Department has jurisdiction over the third, fourth, and sixth judicial districts.[12] The Fourth Department has jurisdiction over the fifth, seventh, and eighth judicial districts.[13]

C.   Appellate Term

The New York Constitution allows the Appellate Division to create separate Appellate Terms, which will have the power to "hear appeals in their judicial districts and/or counties other than appeals from the Supreme Court, Surrogate's Court, and Family Court, and appeals in felony criminal cases."[14] Only the First and Second Departments have created Appellate Terms.[15] The First Department created one for the first district.[16] The Second Department created two: one for the second and eleventh districts, and one for the ninth and tenth districts.[17] The Appellate Term's rules can be found in the NYCRR and in the Uniform Court Act.[18] The Uniform Court Act consists of the New York City Civil Court Act, the Uniform District Court Act, the Uniform City Court Act, and the Uniform Justice Court Act.[19] These acts are all basically the same, and "govern procedure in all the lower courts of the state."[20]

---

11. *Id.* The second judicial district covers Kings and Richmond counties. The ninth judicial district covers Dutchess, Orange, Putnam, Rockland, and Westchester counties. The tenth judicial district covers Nassau and Suffolk counties. The eleventh judicial district covers Queens county. *Id.* The rules for the Second Department can be found at 22 NYCRR § 700 *et seq.*

12. *Id.* The third judicial district covers Albany, Columbia, Greene, Rensselaer, Schoharie, Sullivan, and Ulster counties. The fourth judicial district covers Clinton, Essex, Franklin, Fulton, Hamilton, Montgomery, St. Lawrence, Saratoga, Schenectady, Warren, and Washington counties. The sixth judicial district covers Broome, Chemung, Chenango, Cortland, Delaware, Madison, Otsego, Schuyler, Tioga, and Tompkins counties. *Id.* The rules for the Third Department can be found at 22 NYCRR § 800 *et seq.*

13. *Id.* The fifth judicial district covers Herkimer, Jefferson, Lewis, Oneida, Onondaga, and Oswego counties. The seventh judicial district covers Cayuga, Livingston, Monroe, Ontario, Seneca, Steuben, Wayne, and Yates counties. The eighth judicial district covers Allegany, Cattaraugus, Chautauqua, Erie, Genesse, Niagara, Orleans, and Wyoming counties. *Id.* The rules for the Fourth Department can be found at 22 NYCRR § 1000 *et seq.*

14. 1 New York Appellate Practice, *supra* note 1, §12.01. This can be found under N.Y. Const. art. VI, § 8.

15. 1 New York Appellate Practice, *supra* note 1, §12.01.

16. *Id.*

17. *Id.*

18. *Id.* In the NYCRR, the rules for the Appellate Term will be found under the rules of the department the court is in. For the First Department, the rules are in 22 NYCRR § 640. For the Second Department, the rules are in 22 NYCRR §§ 730, 732.

19. *Id.* at n.20.

20. *Id.*

The Appellate Term has jurisdiction to review questions of law and fact in appeals from the Civil Court of the City of New York and from the Supreme Court, which have been transferred to the Civil Court by CPLR § 325(d).[21] Under the Uniform Court Act, the Appellate Term also has the power to "review any exercise of discretion by the court or judge below."[22]

II. TAKING AN APPEAL

A. Motion for a Stay

After a judgment or order has been entered by the court, the aggrieved party might wish to appeal. While the appeal is pending, this aggrieved party may worry that the party who won the judgment or order might take some action that could injure the aggrieved party. This could be selling the property that the judgment or order required the aggrieved party to convey or spending the money awarded by the court. To prevent these types of injuries from occurring, the aggrieved party may file a motion for a stay along with the appeal.

In civil actions, a stay is "an order to suspend all or part of a judicial proceeding or a judgment resulting from that proceeding."[23] The rules and procedures for stays are governed by CPLR § 5519 as well as the specific rules for each department of the appellate division and the court of appeals.[24] There are two types of stays under the CPLR that allow the proceedings to be stalled pending a decision of the appeal: stays that are automatically granted and stays that are granted at the discretion of the court.[25]

There are several situations where a stay of proceedings will be automatically granted under CPLR § 5519(a). For these situations, the movant must simply file and serve a notice of appeal and, depending on the situation, pay an undertaking to the clerk of court.[26] If the situation does fall under subsection (a), then the movant will need to seek an appeal through § 5519(c).[27] Automatic stays are applied to

---

21. 1 NEW YORK APPELLATE PRACTICE, *supra* note 1, § 12.01. *See also*, CPLR § 5501(d).

22. N.Y. CITY CIV. CT. ACT. § 1702(d); N.Y. UNIFORM DIST. CT. ACT § 1702(d); N.Y. UNIFORM CITY CT. ACT § 1702(d); N.Y. UNIFORM JUST. CT. ACT § 1702(d).

23. *Stay*, BLACK'S LAW DICTIONARY (10th ed. 2014).

24. 1 NEW YORK APPELLATE PRACTICE, *supra* note 1, § 6.01.

25. *Id.*

26. MARIANNE STECICH & RISA I. GOLD, 8 N.Y. PRACTICE, CIVIL APPELLATE PRACTICE § 9:3 (2d ed. 2018).

27. Dworetzky v. Ball, 374 N.Y.S.2d 430 (App. Div. 1975). *See also* Matter of State Farm Mut. Auto. Ins. Co. v. Pridhodko, 818 N.Y.S.2d 777 (App. Div. 2006); Governale v. Porsche-Audi of Bay

judgments or orders appealed from "which command a person to do an act."[28] Automatic stays will not be allowed if the judgment or order focuses on "future acts which are not expressly directed by the order or judgment appealed from . . ."[29]

One situation under this section of the CPLR allows the movant to only file a notice of appeal for an automatic stay to be applied. In this situation, the appellant must be the New York state government, a political subdivision of the state, or any agency or officer of the agency of the state.[30] The stay will be granted in any type of case and without a court order or an undertaking.[31] This automatic stay provision does not apply to orders that prohibit certain types of conduct, also known as prohibitory injunctions.[32]

There is a limitation to the automatic stay in the case where a government entity has revoked a small business's[33] license.[34] The stay in this situation will last for 15 days, and then the government entity must get an order from the court for an extended stay.[35] The stay may be extended through CPLR § 5519(e) if the government entity files a notice of appeal or motion for leave to appeal within five days after service of an order that is adverse to it with notice of entry.[36] The state may also be given an extended stay once those five days are up if the appeal is moved to the Court of Appeals.[37] This type of stay is only available to the government because there is a need to "stabilize the effect of adverse determinations on governmental entities and prevent disbursement of public funds pending an appeal."[38]

Ridge, Inc., 467 N.Y.S.2d 425 (App. Div. 1983); Deacon's Bench, Inc. v. Hoffman, 451 N.Y.S.2d 861 (App. Div. 1982).

28. Baygold Assocs., Inc. v. Congregation Yetev Lev of Monsey, Inc., 911 N.Y.S.2d 759, 761 (N.Y. Sup. Ct. 2010) (citing Matter of Pokoik v. Department of Health Servs. of County of Suffolk, 641 N.Y.S.2d 881 (App. Div. 1996)).

29. *Id.*

30. CPLR § 5519(a)(1).

31. WEINSTEIN, KORN & MILLER, CPLR MANUAL § 26.09[d] (David L. Ferstendig ed., LexisNexis Matthew Bender) (hereinafter "WEINSTEIN, CPLR MANUAL").

32. State v. Town of Haverstraw, 641 N.Y.S.2d 879 (App. Div. 1996). *See also* Matter of Village of Chestnut Ridge v. Town of Ramapo, 955 N.Y.S.2d 60 (App. Div. 2012).

33. Small business means "a corporation with no more than five stockholders and ten employees, a partnership with no more than five partners and ten employees, a proprietorship, or a natural person." WEINSTEIN, CPLR MANUAL § 26.09(d).

34. CPLR § 5519(a)(1).

35. STECICH & GOLD, *supra* note 26.

36. WEINSTEIN, CPLR MANUAL, *supra* note 31 at § 26.09[d].

37. *Id.* (citing Summerville v. City of New York, 767 N.E.2d 140 N.Y. 2002)).

38. *Summerville*, 767 N.E.2d at 144.

For the remaining situations where automatic stays are granted, the movant must file and serve the notice of appeal, as well as either pay an undertaking or take some other type of action. In the next two situations, a stay will be automatically granted in cases where there is a money judgment that is being appealed.[39] The order to pay money will be stayed if the movant pays an undertaking.[40] The court is responsible for setting how much the undertaking will be.[41] If the money judgment is to be paid in installments, the undertaking must also be paid in fixed installments which will be determined by the court.[42] The undertaking must include the amount the court has determined plus any post-judgment interest that will accrue during the pending appeal.[43] The undertaking is paid by the movant and will be held throughout the appeal.[44] If the judgment or order is reversed, the amount that was paid will be refunded to the movant.[45]

The CPLR also provides for automatic stays in the situations where the judgment or order directs the delivery of personal property[46] or an execution of an instrument.[47] In the case where a judgment or order directs the delivery of personal property, the movant has a choice between delivering the property to an officer designated by the court or paying a determined amount in an undertaking.[48] The purpose of this type of automatic stay is to "prevent the appellant from suffering an irreparable loss as a result of the appellant's having delivered personal property to the plaintiff as directed by the order of the trial court and then being unable to recover the property from the plaintiff if the trial court's determination is reversed on appeal."[49]

---

39. CPLR § 5519(a)(2)-(3).

40. *Id.* § 5519(a)(2); *see* Solow Mgt. Corp. v. Tanger, 887 N.E.2d 1121, 1124 (N.Y. 2008) ("the filing of an appeal bond pursuant to CPLR 5519 . . . requires that all enforcement actions be temporarily stated until there has been a determination as to the merits of the appeal.")

41. Stecich & Gold, *supra* note 26.

42. CPLR § 5519(a)(3).

43. HGCD Retail Servs., LLC. v. 44-45 Broadway Realty Co., 820 N.Y.S.2d 843, 843 (N.Y. Sup. Ct. 2006). In this case, the court's rationale was that an undertaking is submitted to "provide sufficient collateral to pay the judgment, and that would require taking into consideration the interest on such judgment." *Id.*

44. Stecich & Gold, *supra* note 26.

45. *Id.* (citing CPLR § 5519(d)).

46. CPLR § 5519(a)(4).

47. *Id.* § 5519(a)(5).

48. Stecich & Gold, *supra* note 26.

49. Wynyard v. Beiny, 782 N.Y.S.2d 593, 595 (N.Y. Surr. Ct. Bronx Co. 2004). In this case, the appellant wanted a stay on the sale of ACNY assets. The court held that since there was no court decree that directed the assets to be placed in the custody of an officer by the court, CPLR §5519(a)(6)

In cases where a judgment or order directs the execution of an instrument, the movant does not have to pay an undertaking if they execute and deposit the instrument in the office where the original judgment or order was entered.[50] If the judgment or order does not require execution of an instrument, then this section does not apply.[51]

Another situation where an automatic stay will be granted is if there is a judgment or order directing a party to convey or deliver real property.[52] In this case, the movant must pay an undertaking in a fixed amount and agree not to commit any waste of the property.[53] The movant must also agree that if the judgment or order is affirmed, then they will pay the value of the use and occupancy of the property.[54] If the judgement or order in this situation is for the sale of mortgaged property and a payment of a deficiency, "the undertaking must provide for the payment of a deficiency judgment."[55]

If a judgment or order requires the aggrieved party to perform the requirements of two or more of these situations, CPLR § 5519(a)(7) states that the aggrieved party must comply with the specific directions of each of the sections to obtain an automatic stay.[56] If the movant complies with one and not the other, the automatic stay will not be granted.[57]

The party seeking the stay of the proceedings has the burden of proving each of these elements.[58] A decision to lift the automatic stay is reviewed for abuse of

---

did not apply. The court also held that the appellants did not have an ownership interest in the assets so they would not suffer irreparable loss if they were sold. *Id.*

50. STECICH & GOLD, *supra* note 26.

51. *See* Novello v. 215 Rockaway, LLC, 2009 NY Slip Op 30915(U) at *5 (N.Y. Sup. Ct. Apr. 21, 2009). In *Novello*, the court held that since the order did not direct an execution of a contract of sale from the property, CPLR § 5519(a)(5) did not apply. *See also* Berle v. Buckley, 862 N.Y.S.2d 813 (N.Y. Sup. Ct. 2008). In *Berle*, the court held that the "Bill of Sale and assignment" that the respondent argued was the instrument being executed was not "the instrument that respondent implicitly was directed to execute" because it did not contain the "negotiated terms and conditions of the Buy-Sell Agreement." *Id.*

52. CPLR § 5519(a)(6).

53. STECICH & GOLD, *supra* note 26.; Jennings v. City of Glen Falls Indus. Dev. Agency, 780 N.Y.S.2d 672, 673 (App. Div. 2004) (holding that an automatic stay under CPLR § 5519(a)(6) did not arise because there was no evidence that the court approved an undertaking or that the plaintiff posted an appeal bond). *Id.*

54. STECICH & GOLD, *supra* note 26.

55. *Id.* (citing Brandywine Pavers, LLC. V. Bombard, 11 N.Y.S.3d 391 (App. Div. 2015)).

56. CPLR § 5519(a)(7); Maldonado v. N.Y. County Sheriff, 2006 U.S. Dist. LEXIS 64391, at *11 (S.D.N.Y. 2006).

57. Berle v. Buckley, 862 N.Y.S.2d 813 (N.Y. Sup. Ct. 2008).

58. Matter of Povoski v. Fischer, 2011 N.Y. Misc. LEXIS 5653 (N.Y. Sup. Ct. 2011).

discretion.[59] If a movant is seeking a discretionary stay and the court finds that the situation is covered by one of the automatic stay sections, the court will deny the discretionary stay.[60]

In the past, New York courts have held that only a defendant could post an undertaking for themselves; this changed with the passage of CPLR § 5519(b), which states that where a defendant who has a money judgment against them and is being defended by an insurance carrier under a liability insurance policy, that insurance company may post the undertaking and stay the proceedings.[61] The reason for this change was that insurance carriers occupy "a substantially different position than an unknown individual surety, who may be in collusion with the judgment debtor, or unavailable or insolvent at the conclusion of the appeal."[62] An insurance carrier is often considered more reliable than an individual, as the court recognized in *Kreitzer*.

The obligation to pay the undertaking in this situation falls on the insurance carrier.[63] The insurance carrier will post an undertaking that covers up to the amount of the policy limits.[64] To allow an insurance carrier to post more than the policy would "in effect, impermissibly increase the limits of the policy."[65] Because of this, the insurance carrier will only post up to the limit and the judgment will only be stayed up to that amount. The judgment will not be stayed for any amount in excess.[66]

If the amount of the judgment is more than the policy limits, the insurance carrier may obtain a stay by posting an undertaking up to the amount of the policy limit and taking three other actions. First, the insurance carrier must file with the clerk of the court that entered the judgment an undertaking and "a sworn statement of one of its officers, describing the nature of the policy and the amount of the coverage."[67] Next, the insurance carrier must serve "copies of these papers on the judgment creditor and his attorney."[68] Finally, the insurance company must

---

59. *In re* Sonnax Indus., 907 F.2d 1280, 1286 (2d Cir. 1990) (applying New York law) ("[W]e may overturn a denial of a motion to lift the automatic stay only upon a showing of abuse of discretion"). Abuse of discretion exists when a decision "rests on an erroneous finding of fact or makes an error of law." Almontaser v. N.Y.C. Dep't of Educ., 519 F.3d 505, 508 (2d. Cir. 2008) (applying New York law).
60. Sullivan v. Troser Mgt., Inc., 816 N.Y.S.2d 395, 395 (App. Div. 2006).
61. CPLR § 5519(b).
62. Kreitzer v. Chamikles, 434 N.Y.S.2d 123, 125 (N.Y. Sup. Ct. 1980).
63. 1 NEW YORK APPELLATE PRACTICE, *supra* note 1, § 6.03.
64. *Id.*
65. *Id.*
66. *Id.*
67. CPLR § 5519(b)(1).
68. *Id.* § 5519(b)(2).

mail or deliver to the insured defendant "written notice that the execution of the judgment is not stayed with respect to amounts above the coverage."[69] Once these have all been completed, the insurance carrier may obtain a stay as to the amount they posted in the undertaking. If the insured defendant wishes to receive a stay on the remaining amount, they will have to post an undertaking covering the excess of the policy.[70]

The final situation where the proceedings of a case will be automatically stayed is where an appeal is taken in a medical, dental, or podiatric malpractice case more than $1 million.[71] To stay the proceedings, there are three things that must be done. First, the insurance carrier must post an undertaking in the amount of $1 million or the limit of the coverage, whichever is greater.[72] Next, the insurance carrier and the insured defendant must file a joint undertaking which states that the insured "will make no fraudulent conveyance without fair consideration. . . ."[73] Any liability that arises under the joint undertaking is "limited to fraudulent conveyances made by the appellant after execution of the undertaking and during the period of stay but does not limit his or her liability under other law."[74] Finally, the court will examine the undertaking and if it finds that there is "a reasonable probability that the judgment may be reversed or determined excessive" the stay will be granted.[75] While determining whether to grant the stay, the courts are encouraged not to consider "whether a stay might be available under either subdivision (a) or (b) of CPLR § 5519."[76]

If the judgment or order does not fall under one of the automatic stay situations, the court may still grant a stay when enforcement of the judgment or order would "have the effect of changing the status quo pending appeal."[77] CPLR § 5519(c) enables a court "from or to which an appeal is taken" to "stay all proceedings to enforce the . . . order appealed from pending an appeal."[78] Pursuant to CPLR § 2201, courts are also vested with discretion to grant a stay of proceedings

---

69. *Id.* § 5519(b)(3).

70. *Id.*

71. *Id.* § 5519(g). Note there is pending legislation on this section of CPLR § 5519 as of June 2017. The changes to this section would change "fraudulent conveyances" to "voidable transactions."

72. *Id. See also* JOHN A. GEBAUER, J.D. ET AL., 10A CARMODY-WAIT 2D § 70:266 (West 2018).

73. CPLR § 5519(g).

74. GEBAUER ET AL., *supra* note 72.

75. *Id.*

76. STECICH & GOLD, *supra* note 26.

77. GEBAUER ET AL., *supra* note 72.

78. CPLR § 5519(c). *See also* High Definition MRI, P.C. v. MAPFRE Ins. Co. of N.Y., 2016 NY Slip Op 31336(U), at *6 (N.Y. Sup. Ct. Jul. 14, 2016) (citing Schwartz v. New York City Housing Authority, 641 N.Y.S.2d 885 (App. Div. 1996)).

in actions pending before it in a proper case and upon terms as may be just.[79] It is well settled that "[a] court has broad discretion to grant a stay in order to avoid the risk of inconsistent adjudications, application of proof and potential waste of judicial resources."[80] Further, "[o]n Rule 2201 motions, courts should explore their decisions' prejudicial impact, that is, the prejudice to the movant by denying a motion balanced against the prejudice to the non-movant by granting the motion."[81] CPLR § 2201 allows the court in which an action is pending to grant a stay of proceedings in a proper case.[82]

In deciding whether to exercise their discretion to grant a stay pursuant to CPLR § 5519(c), courts typically consider a variety of factors, including "the merits of the appeal, harm that might accrue to the appellant if the stay is denied, and potential prejudice to the respondent if the stay is granted."[83] These are also commonly referred to as: (1) likelihood of success on the merits, (2) irreparable harm, and (3) balancing of equities.[84] This standard by which the court judges motions of a stay is similar to the one used for preliminary injunctions.[85]

1. Likelihood of Success on the Merits

One element that must be proved for the court to grant a motion for a stay is that the movant has a likelihood of succeeding on the merits of the claim. The movant must demonstrate "a clear right to relief which is plain from the undisputed facts."[86] "[A] prima facie showing of a reasonable probability of success is sufficient"[87] to succeed on this element. This can be done through the papers the

---

79. Asher v. Abbott Labs, 763 N.Y.S.2d 555 (App. Div. 2003); CPLR § 2201.

80. Morreale v. Morreale, 923 N.Y.S.2d 876 (App. Div. 2011) (quoting Zonghetti v. Jeromack, 541 N.Y.S.2d 235, 237 (App. Div. 1989)); OneBeacon America Ins. Co. v. Colgate-Palmolive Co., 949 N.Y.S.2d 14 (App. Div. 2012).

81. Nezry v. Haven Ave. Owner LLC, 958 N.Y.S.2d 62 (N.Y. Sup. Ct. 2010).

82. CPLR § 2201.

83. WEINSTEIN, KORN & MILLER, NEW YORK CIVIL PRACTICE: CPLR ¶ 5519.13; *see also* 1 NEW YORK APPELLATE PRACTICE, *supra* note 1 § 6.04[1]; CPLR§ 5519 (C5519:4) (McKinney 2018); DaSilva v. Musso, 559 N.E.2d 1268, 1271 n.4 (N.Y. 1990).

84. *Matter of Povoski*, 2011 NY Slip Op 33091(U), at *4. The *Povoski* court believed that the standard for judging motions for a stay should be the same as the standard for preliminary injunctions. *Id.*

85. Levkoff v. Soho Grand-West Broadway, Inc., 981 N.Y.S.2d 922 (App. Div. 2014).

86. Lezell v. Forde, 891 N.Y.S.2d 606, 612 (N.Y. Sup. Ct. 2009) (citing Matter of Related Props., Inc. v. Town Bd. of Town/Village of Harrison, 802 N.Y.S.2d 221, 224 (App. Div. 2005)).

87. Barbes Restaurant Inc., v. ASRR Suzer 218, LLC., 33 N.Y.S.3d 43, 45 (App. Div. 2016); Matter of Riccelli Enters., Inc., v. State of New York Workers' Comp. Bd., 2012 NY Slip Op 31250(U), at *60 (N.Y. Sup. Ct. Apr. 30, 2012).

movant submits to the court.[88] It may also be sufficient to prove this even when the facts are in dispute.[89]

The level of success that a movant must show is not as clear as how they can show it. This element depends on the determination of other factors as well. It is often decided in connection with some evaluation of the irreparable harm element.[90] In some cases, the less evidence of likelihood of success, the more the movant would need to show irreparable harm, and vice versa.[91]

2. Irreparable Harm

Another element to prove is that there will be some irreparable harm to the movant because of the denial of the stay. Irreparable harm is defined as "any injury for which an eventual monetary award alone cannot be adequate compensation."[92] If the harm is only speculative it will not be sufficient to establish this element.[93] For a movant to be successful on this element, they will need to show that the actions required by the judgment would harm them in a way that no amount of money could cure the damage done.[94]

3. Balancing of Equities

The final element that must be proven is that the balance of equities leans in favor of the movant. This can be thought of as who will suffer more if the motion for

---

88. *Matter of Riccelli*, 2012 NY Slip Op 31250(U) at *60.
89. Vanderbuilt Brookland, LLC v. Vanderbuilt Myrtle, Inc., 48 N.Y.S.3d 251, 254 (App. Div. 2017); Ruiz v. Meloney, 810 N.Y.S.2d 216, 218 (App. Div. 2006); Waldron v. Hoffman, 13 N.Y.S.3d 684, 685 (App. Div. 2015).
90. *Matter of Riccelli*, 2012 NY Slip Op 31250(U) at *56.
91. Cayuga Indian Nation v. Vill. of Union Springs, 317 F. Supp.2d 152, 155 (N.D.N.Y. 2005), (citing Mohammed v. Reno, 309 F.3d 95, 101 (2d Cir. 2002) (quoting Washington Metropolitan Area Transit Commission v. Holiday Tours, Inc., 559 F.2d 841, 843 (D.C. Cir. 1977))).
92. Kaloyeros v. Fort Schuyler Mgt. Corp., 49 N.Y.S.3d 867, 874 (N.Y. Sup. Ct. 2017) (citing Town of Liberty Volunteer Ambulance Corp. v. Catskill Regional Med. Ctr., 816 N.Y.S.2d 246 (App. Div. 2006)).
93. *Matter of Povoski*, 2011 NY Slip Op 330391(U).
94. *See* Denza v. Independence Plaza Assocs., 2007 NYLJ LEXIS 5056, at *16-17 (N.Y. Sup. Ct. Oct. 17, 2007) (citing Weisent v. Subaqua Corp., 847 N.Y.S.2d 899 (N.Y. Sup. Ct. 2007) (extensively discussing the effects of sale of such information). Here, the court held that the tenants of an apartment complex had sufficiently showed irreparable harm because the Housing Court would sell the eviction case data to landlords and this information would "effectively blacklist them from being able to rent a new apartment." *Id.* This is distinguishable from the situation in *Silbert*, where the court held that the plaintiffs failed to show irreparable harm from the auction sale of an apartment complex because they did not live in the apartment complex and the debt could be compensable with money. Silbert v. Emigrant Sav. Bank, 2012 NY Slip Op 32227(U), at *6-9 (N.Y. Sup. Ct. 2012).

a stay is granted. The court will look at all the facts of the case and determine whether the movant has shown that the irreparable harm it will sustain if the stay is denied will be more burdensome than the harm that the respondent will sustain if the stay is granted.[95] This standard is also referred to as the harm to the movant being "decidedly greater" than the harm to the respondent.[96]

The court will also look to external factors outside the harm to both sides when balancing the equities. Some of the factors they look at include how the determination will affect public interests;[97] whether a stay will go against public policy; and whether, in the absence of a stay, the appeal will be rendered moot.[98] If the court determines based on all this information that the movant would suffer harm more burdensome if the stay is denied, the court will grant the stay.

4. *Appellate Division Rules*

Each department of the Appellate Division has its own rules and procedures that supplement the CPLR sections. For motions for a stay, the rules are similar, with a few distinctions between the departments.

In the First Department, the movant must submit a notice of motion to the clerk. The movant must also "inform the clerk at the time of submission whether the opposing party has been notified of the application and whether such party opposes or consents to the granting of the relief sought."[99] This process is the same for interim stays or "other relief pending determination of a motion."[100]

The rules for the Second, Third, and Fourth Departments call for the movant seeking a stay to move for it by a notice of motion or an order to show cause. An order to show cause is defined as "an order directing a party to appear in court and explain why the party took (or failed to take) some action or why the court should or should not impose some sanction or grant some relief."[101] These three

---

95. Robert L. Haig & Harry S. Davis, 3 New York Practice, Commercial Litigation in New York State Courts § 18:10 (4th ed. 2018); Klein, Wagner & Morris v. Lawrence A. Klein, P.C., 588 N.Y.S.2d 424, 426 (App. Div. 1992).

96. Fischer v. Deitsch, 563 N.Y.S.2d 836, 838 (App. Div. 1990). To meet this standard, the movant must show that the failure to grant the stay or preliminary injunction would cause greater harm to the movant than it would to the respondent. Laro Maintenance Corp. v. Culkin, 681 N.Y.S.2d 79, 80 (App. Div. 1998).

97. Seitzman v. Hudson River Associates, 513 N.Y.S.2d 148, 150 (App. Div. 1987) (citing Barney v. City of New York, 83 A.D. 237, 241 (App. Div. 1903)).

98. 1 New York Appellate Practice, *supra* note 1, § 6.04 *et seq.*

99. 22 N.Y.C.R.R. § 600.2(a)(7).

100. *Id.*

101. *Show-Cause Order*, Black's Law Dictionary (10th ed. 2014).

departments also require that the movant give the opposing party reasonable notice of the date, time, and place that the motion will be heard.[102]

The Second Department rules require that the movant submit an affidavit or affirmation that describes the manner of notification with their notice of motion or order to show cause.[103] The rules also require that if the notice was not given, the movant must state whether they attempted to notify the opposing party and the reasons why they were unsuccessful.[104] If the movant did not attempt to notify the adversary, the movant must explain why they did not attempt to notify the opposing party.[105]

In the Third Department, motions made to the court must give notice to adverse parties that their personal appearance is "neither required nor permitted."[106] Orders to show cause must also give notice to the adverse parties of whether the motion will be argued or submitted and whether their appearance is permitted.[107] If the movant is seeking a temporary stay through the order to show cause, the movant must inform the clerk or justice at the time of submission that the opposing party has been notified and either consents or opposes the granting of a stay.[108]

The Fourth Department rules state that the movant must give reasonable notice of the time, date, and place to all other parties in the case and all counsels have the right to be present when the order is presented to the court.[109] There is a similar requirement in the Second Department, where the movant must submit an affidavit if opposing counsel's presence could not be obtained.[110] This affidavit must state the method that was used to give notice and explain why the movant failed to obtain opposing counsel's presence.[111]

5. Appellate Term Rules

The Appellate Term follows the rules under the CPLR and the NYCRR for guidance on handling motions for a stay. The First Department's rules explicitly state

---

102. 22 N.Y.C.R.R. § 670.5(e) (for the Second Department); § 800.2(d) (for the Third Department); and § 1000.13(b)(1) (for the Fourth Department).
103. *Id.* § 670.5(e).
104. *Id.*
105. *Id.*
106. *Id.* § 800.2(a).
107. *Id.*
108. 22 N.Y.C.R.R. § 800.2(d).
109. *Id.* § 1000.13(b)(1).
110. *Id.*
111. *Id.*

that a party may apply to the court for an order to incorporate a stay while there is a pending determination of a motion for leave to appeal or reargue.[112] The Second Department does not have a codified section in its rules for motions for a stay in civil appeals.

A notice of appeal is required in the Appellate Term for the movant to be able to seek a stay.[113] This does not, however, mean that a stay will be automatically granted for the case. This will only happen in the express situations of CPLR § 5519(a).[114] A movant seeking a stay may do so through a motion or, where allowed, an order to show cause.[115] A stay may be granted if the court finds a showing of "a potentially meritorious appeal."[116] The stay does not, however, "prevent the lower court from proceeding in any matter not affected by the judgment or order appealed."[117]

The Appellate Terms require that a motion for a stay contain the following information: "a copy of the judgment or order being appealed; the notice of appeal; any related orders or decisions; any relevant exhibits; a brief procedural history; and a statement of the merits of the appeal, as part of the affirmation or affidavit or a concise memorandum of law."[118]

A stay that is granted in the Appellate Term will remain in effect for five days from the date the movant is served with the order and notice of entry.[119] If the movant takes the appeal within the five days, then stay will be effective until five days from the date the appeal is determined.[120] If the Appellate Term denies permission to appeal, then the stay will be effective for five days from the date the movant is served with the order and notice of entry.[121]

---

112. *Id.* § 640.9(c).

113. THE COMMITTEE ON COURTS OF APPELLATE JURISDICTION OF THE NEW YORK STATE BAR ASSOCIATION, NEW YORK'S APPELLATE TERMS: A MANUAL FOR PRACTITIONERS 10 (N.Y.S.B.A. 2014).

114. *Id.* at 11. These situations are where the movant is a government entity under CPLR § 5519(a)(1) or where the judgment directs "the payment of a sum of money and that judgment has been bonded." HON. PAUL KENNY, CIVIL AND CRIMINAL APPEALS IN THE APPELLATE TERM, SECOND DEPARTMENT 4 (N.Y.S.B.A. 2013).

115. THE COMMITTEE ON COURTS OF APPELLATE JURISDICTION OF THE NEW YORK STATE BAR ASSOCIATION, *supra* note 113.

116. *Id.*

117. *Id.* (citing CPLR § 5519(f)).

118. *Id.* at 11.

119. *Id.*

120. *Id.*

121. THE COMMITTEE ON COURTS OF APPELLATE JURISDICTION OF THE NEW YORK STATE BAR ASSOCIATION, *supra* note 113 at 11 (citing CPLR § 5519(c)).

6. Interim Stays

In some situations, a motion for a stay may not be determined in enough time to prevent the harm from occurring. This could occur where "(1) an order or judgment appealed from directs a party to immediately perform some act, or (2) legal proceedings are about to commence which might cause irreparable harm or render the appeal academic[.]"[122] The movant in these situations can move for an interim stay, which will stay the proceedings while the court determines the motion for the stay pending appeal.[123] It is recommended that the motion for interim relief be filed with or immediately after the notice of appeal.[124] If the movant does not move for an interim stay, the court may find that one is necessary, as it did in *Equities Holding Corp. v. Kiam.*[125] The court may not come out the same way in every case.

A motion for an interim stay is filed in a similar way as the notice of motion for a stay pending appeal as described above. In the Second, Third, and Fourth Departments, the movant files an order to show cause.[126] In the First Department, the movant files a motion for a stay and the court will attach an order for interim stay if it is granted.[127] If a party seeks an interim stay in the Court of Appeals, they must bring it to the clerk's attention because there is no codified procedure for interim stays.[128]

7. Other Types of Temporary Relief

In some cases, even though a motion for a stay was denied, the court may still grant the movant some form of temporary relief. The court will use the same standard as with motions for a stay. If the movant will be aggrieved and the court denies a stay, the movant may invoke the court's power to stay such acts under CPLR §§ 5518 or 6301.[129]

---

122. 1–6 New York Appellate Practice, *supra* note 1, § 6.04[2].
123. *Id.*
124. *Id.*
125. 469 N.Y.S.2d 2, 2–3 (App. Div. 1983). Plaintiff moved for a stay of proceedings on an order. The motion was not heard before the order to turn over documents had expired. The court held that the stay excused the plaintiff from complying with the order until the appeal was determined. The court allowed the plaintiff time to comply with the order.
126. 1–6 New York Appellate Practice, *supra* note 1, § 6.04[2].
127. *Id.*
128. *Id.*
129. CPLR § 5518 states "the appellate division may grant, modify or limit a preliminary injunction or temporary restraining order pending an appeal or determination of a motion for permission to

8. Undertaking

The CPLR defines an undertaking as

> (1) any obligation, whether or not the principal is a party thereto, which contains a covenant by a surety to pay the required amount . . . if any required condition, as specified therein . . . is not fulfilled; and (2) any deposit, made subject to the required condition, of the required amount in legal tender of the United States or in face value of unregistered bonds of the United States or of the state."[130]

An undertaking is used to "secure both the order and the judgment or order which is affirmed."[131] The purpose of an undertaking is "to assure the continued integrity of a judgment through the appellate process, while enabling the appellant to test error without prematurely, and perhaps unnecessarily, forfeiting his property."[132]

The amount of the undertaking must be reasonable under the circumstances.[133] If an appellate court affirms a judgment, and another appeal is taken, the undertaking that was given during the first appeal will also be deemed to secure the appellate order of affirmance of the higher court.[134]

B. Notice of Appeal

After the final judgment or order of the court has come down, the party who has been aggrieved by this determination has the option to take the appeal to either the Appellate Division, the Appellate Term, or the Court of Appeals. To "take an

---

appeal in any case specified in section 6301." Section 6301 allows for the court to grant other forms of temporary relief in cases where "it appears that the defendant threatens or is about to do, or is doing or procuring or suffering to be done, an act in violation of the plaintiff's rights respecting the subject of the action, and tending to render the judgment ineffectual, or in any action where the plaintiff has demanded and would be entitled to a judgment restraining the defendant from the commission or continuance of any act, which, if committed or continued during the pendency of the action would produce injury to the plaintiff."

130. *Id.* § 2501. Article 25 of the CPLR governs undertakings.

131. *Id.* § 5519(d).

132. Kreitzer v. Chamikles, 434 N.Y.S.2d 123, 125 (N.Y. Sup. Ct. 1980). *See also* Recon Car Corp. of New York v. Chrysler Corp., 495 N.Y.S.2d 639 (N.Y. Sup. Ct. 1985), *rev'd on other grounds*, 515 N.Y.S.2d 829 (App. Div.), *appeal denied*, 518 N.E.2d 7 (N.Y. 1987).

133. Hall v. Hall, 802 N.Y.S.2d 781, 784 (App. Div. 2005) (holding that the undertaking in this case did not "impermissibly stray beyond its broad discretion in making such a determination"). *See also* Chase Manhattan Mortg. Corp. v. Murphy, 768 N.Y.S.2d 374, 374 (App. Div. 2003).

134. La Rocco v. Federal Ins. Co., 321 N.E.2d 551 (N.Y. 1874). An undertaking given to secure an old judgment will not be deemed to secure the new one.

appeal,"[135] the movant must either submit a notice of appeal or a motion for leave to appeal. A notice of appeal is the document filed with the clerk of the court of original instance by the part wishing to appeal, which tells the court and any adverse parties that there is an intent to appeal a judgment or order.[136]

As with the motion for a stay, the appeal may be taken by "an aggrieved party or a person substituted for him."[137] A party may be "aggrieved" in two ways: First, a person is aggrieved when he or she asks for relief but that relief is denied in whole or in part. Second, a person is aggrieved when someone asks for relief against him or her, which the person opposes, and the relief is granted in whole or in part.[138] A party will be considered aggrieved when their pecuniary interests are adversely affected by a judgment or order.[139] A party cannot appeal a judgment that was granted in their favor. If the party obtains a complete judgment in the proceedings below, they are not considered "aggrieved."[140] This is true even if they disagree with the particular findings or rational of the court.[141] The requirement that a party be aggrieved is a jurisdictional requirement, meaning that if it is not met, the appeal will be denied.[142]

---

135. "Taking an appeal" in this section means filing and serving a notice of appeal in the proper time limit to the court and the adverse parties, as required by the court rules.
136. *Notice of Appeal*, BLACK'S LAW DICTIONARY (10th ed. 2014).
137. CPLR § 5511 (McKinney 2018).
138. Mixon v. TBV, Inc., 904 N.Y.S.2d 132, 142 (App. Div. 2010).
139. Fitch v. Turner Constr. Co., 671 N.Y.S.2d 446, 449 (App. Div. 1998).
140. *Mixon*, 904 N.Y.S.2d at 136.
141. *Id. See also* Matter of Seney v. Bd. of Educ. of the E. Greenbush Cent. Sch. Dist., 962 N.Y.S.2d 397 (App. Div. 2013).
142. Lincoln v. Austic, 401 N.Y.S.2d 1020 (App. Div. 1978) (holding that being aggrieved is "jurisdictional in nature . . ."). *See also* Kaplan v. Rohan, 165 N.E.2d 197 (N.Y. 1959); 492 Kings Realty, LLC v. 506 Kings, LLC, 964 N.Y.S.2d 215 (App. Div. 2013); Charles v. William Hird & Co., Inc., 959 N.Y.S.2d 506 (App. Div. 2013); Jones v. Rochdale Vil., Inc., 948 N.Y.S.2d 80, 83 (App. Div. 2012) (holding the appeal dismissed because the defendants were not aggrieved by the part of the orders being appealed); Dance Magic, Inc. v. Pike Realty, Inc., 926 N.Y.S.2d 588, 589 (App. Div. 2011) (holding the appeal is dismissed because the defendant was not aggrieved by the order being appealed); Stein v. McDowell, 905 N.Y.S.2d 242, 244 (App. Div. 2010) (holding that the defendant was not aggrieved by the order being appealed); Abreo v. URS Greiner Woodward Clyde, 875 N.Y.S.2d 577, 578 (App. Div. 2009) (holding the appeal dismissed because the defendant was not aggrieved by the part of the order being appealed); Matter of Harry Y., 880 N.Y.S.2d 662, 665 (App. Div. 2009) (holding that a party who consents to an order is not aggrieved by the order); Pierre-Louis v. DeLonghi Am., Inc., 888 N.Y.S.2d 100, 101 (App. Div. 2009) (holding the appeal dismissed because the defendant was not aggrieved by the order being appealed); Richardson v. Lindenbaum & Young, 868 N.Y.S.2d 116 (App. Div. 2008) (holding the appeal dismissed because the second law firm was not aggrieved by the summary judgment order in favor of a law firm on a malpractice case); Lowery v. Lamaute, 836 N.Y.S.2d 650, 651 (App. Div. 2007) (holding the cross-appeal dismissed

If the appeal can be taken as of right, the movant must file and serve the notice of appeal in accordance with the CPLR and the rules of the court in which they are taking the appeal.[143] If the court has granted permission to take the appeal, the movant does not have to file a notice of appeal.[144]

Under the CPLR, the notice of appeal must contain the following information: "the party taking the appeal; the judgment or order of the specific party appeal from; and the court to which the appeal is taken."[145] The notice of appeal must bear the caption of the case "as it appears in the court of original jurisdiction."[146]

There is a two-step process that must be followed for a movant to successfully take an appeal. The movant must (1) file the notice of appeal with the clerk of court and (2) serve a copy of the notice to the adverse parties involved, depending on the court.[147] The CPLR states that the movant may serve the adverse parties with a notice of appeal through any means that are acceptable in CPLR § 2103.[148] The methods of filing the notice of appeal with the clerk depend on the court in which the appeal is being taken. In the counties where electronic filing is allowed, the clerk may require the notice be submitted only electronically.[149] If electronic filing is not an option, the clerk may allow for the notice of appeal to be sent through the mail.[150]

---

because the plaintiff was not aggrieved by the order which did not grant relief to any party other than the plaintiff); Matter of Broda v. Monahan, 767 N.Y.S.2d 111, 112 (App. Div. 2003) (holding the appeal dismissed because the cross-appellants were not aggrieved by the order being appealed); Lukas v. Trump, 721 N.Y.S.2d 394 (App. Div. 2001); Matter of Chiakpo v. Obi, 680 N.Y.S.2d 869 (App. Div. 1998) (holding that a party who consents to the order is not aggrieved by it); Backus v. Lyme Adirondack Timberlands II, LLC, 947 N.Y.S.2d 639, 641 (App. Div. 2012) (holding the appeal dismissed because the appellant was no longer a party to the action and was not aggrieved by the order being appealed); Gadani v. DeBrino Caulking Associates, Inc., 926 N.Y.S.2d 724, 728 (App. Div. 2011) (holding the appeal dismissed because the appellant received full relief at the trial and was not aggrieved from the order); Reyes-Dobles v. Chaudhry, 576 N.Y.S.2d 735, 736 (App. Div. 1991) (holding that the defendant forfeited the right to appeal when the defendant accepted the sanctions that were part of the court's conditional order).

143. STECICH & GOLD, *supra* note 26, § 7:1. The differences between when appeals may be taken as of right and when the movant must seek permission from the court will be explained later in this section.

144. CPLR § 5513(1).

145. *Id.* § 5515.

146. 1 NEW YORK APPELLATE PRACTICE, *supra* note 1, § 5.02[2].

147. CPLR § 5515.

148. STECICH & GOLD, *supra* note 26, § 7:3. CPLR § 2103 is the section that states the various methods of service of papers that are allowed under New York law.

149. *Id.* In other counties (*e.g.*, Westchester and Kings) the clerk will require in-person filing along with electronic filing. *Id.*

150. *Id.*

Depending on the type of appeal that is being taken, the movant has a speci-fied number of days in which they must file and serve the notice of appeal. If the appeal is being taken as of right, the movant must file and serve the notice within thirty days after receiving a "copy of the judgment or order appealed from and written notice of entry."[151] If the court has granted permission to take the appeal, the movant has thirty days from the date the movant was served with a copy of the judgment or order or, if permission was denied, the time will be from the date of service of the copy of the judgment or order that denied the permission.[152] If the notice of appeal is electronically filed and served, each court has specific rules for when the thirty days begins.[153] If the notice is filed and served by any other method, the date is determined by the relevant section in CPLR § 2103.[154]

One issue that could arise regarding the time limit is when there is a dispute as to whether the documents were served within the time limit. If a dispute arises, the respondent bears the burden of showing "strict compliance with the notice requirements of CPLR 5513."[155] The respondent must also show that copies of the judgment or order and a written notice of entry were "actually served" and the thirty-day period started at that time,[156] since courts will not assume that an appeal is untimely.[157]

The CPLR also allows for additional time to be given when the judgment or order being appealed is sent through the mail. The CPLR states that if the service was done through the mail, an extra five days is added to the thirty-day limit.[158] The service under this section will be complete when the notice is placed in "a post office or depository under the custody of the United States Post Office."[159]

If the service of the judgment or order is sent by overnight delivery, the CPLR allows for one additional business day to be added to the thirty-day time limit.[160] Service under this section will be complete "upon deposit of the notice in a properly addressed wrapper in the custody of the overnight delivery service for

---

151. CPLR § 5513(a).

152. *Id.* § 5513(b).

153. STECICH & GOLD, *supra* note 26, § 7:3.

154. *Id.*

155. 1 NEW YORK APPELLATE PRACTICE, *supra* note 1, § 5.02[1][b] (citing Eigenbrodt v. Eigenbrodt, 629 N.Y.S.2d 328, 329 (App. Div. 1995)).

156. *Id.*

157. *Id.*

158. CPLR § 5513(d).

159. *Id.* § 2103(f)(1); Hull v. Feinberg, 493 N.Y.S.2d 382, 383 (App. Div. 1985).

160. CPLR § 5513(d).

overnight delivery, but it must be so deposited prior to the latest time designated by the overnight delivery service for overnight delivery."[161]

In addition to providing for additional time based on the type of service used, the CPLR also provides for certain situations where the court will grant an extension of time limit to serve and file a notice of appeal. In most situations, CPLR § 2004 would allow the court to grant an extension of time for "good cause shown."[162] This section states, however, that this can be used unless "where otherwise expressly prescribed by law. . . ."[163] CPLR § 5514 is one of those sections that falls under that exception.[164] Under CPLR § 5514, there are four instances where the court will grant an extension for the time of service. The first is in the case where the notice of appeal or motion for permission was dismissed or denied and some other method of taking the appeal is available.[165] In this case, "the time limited for such other method of service shall be computed from the dismissal or denial unless the court to which the appeal is sought to be taken orders otherwise."[166]

The second situation is where the attorney for the movant "dies, is removed or suspended, or becomes physically or mentally incapacitated or otherwise disabled before the expiration of the time limited for taking an appeal or moving for permission to appeal without having done so. . . ."[167] In this situation, the time limit will be extended for sixty days from the date the attorney became unable to file the notice of motion.[168] It is important to note that the court will not grant an extension of time if the attorney was voluntarily discharged by the movant.[169]

The third situation is where the time to take an appeal has not expired and there is an event that permits the substitution of a party.[170] In this situation, the time will be extended until fifteen days from the date the substitution was made.[171] If the case was dismissed, the fifteen days will be from the date of dismissal.[172]

---

161. *Id.* § 2103(b)(6).
162. *Id.* § 2004.
163. *Id.*
164. David D. Siegel, New York Practice § 534 (4th ed. 2005).
165. CPLR § 5514(a).
166. *Id.*
167. *Id.* § 5514(b).
168. *Id.*
169. 1 New York Appellate Practice, *supra* note 1, § 5.02[1][b].
170. CPLR § 1022.
171. *Id.*
172. *Id.*

The fourth situation is where the movant has filed the notice of appeal before the expiration of the time limit but there was some defect in the form or omission that was made.[173] The court has broad discretion to extend the time limit for a movant to cure the notice.[174] The notice must have been filed within the time limit. If the notice was not timely filed, the court has no discretion and cannot extend the time limit to cure.[175] The CPLR does not state the length of time for the extension.

An omission may be cured if the notice was timely filed but there was some "mistake or excusable neglect" which caused a problem, such as failure to serve a copy of the notice on the proper parties.[176] Another example of mistake or excusable neglect is where the movant inadvertently writes the wrong court on the notice of appeal.[177]

The court may also allow time to cure where the movant fails to take one of the two steps for taking an appeal (filing with the clerk or serving on an adverse party).[178] As long as one of the two was done in a timely manner before the expiration, the court may extend the item for the movant to complete the other.[179]

The court may decide that the issue or controversy that was at the heart of the appeal has become moot or academic. If this is the case, the court will dismiss the appeal. A case is considered moot or academic when "a change in the circumstances of the case has occurred . . . so that an actual controversy no longer exists between the parties."[180] The court may still hear the case where "the controversy

---

173. *Id.* § 5520.
174. *Id.*
175. *Id.*
176. People *ex rel.* Wilson v. Williams, 631 N.Y.S.2d 275, 275–276 (App. Div. 1995). In this case, the petitioner failed to properly serve the attorney general as the statute required. The court allowed the petitioner to cure this because it was because of "mistake or excusable neglect." *Id.*
177. El Dorado Aluminum Products, Inc. v. Jeros, 224 N.Y.S.2d 329 (App. Div. 1962) (where the plaintiff inadvertently specified on the notice that the appeal was in the appellate division instead of the appellate term). The New York Constitution also provides that if an appeal is taken in the wrong court, the court will transfer the appeal to the proper court. N.Y. CONST. art. VI, § 5(b).
178. Peck v. Ernst Bros. Inc., 439 N.Y.S.2d 515 (App. Div. 1981) (Here, the plaintiff filed the motion with the court in a timely manner but failed to give notice to the defendant until thirty-six days after the entry of the order. The court held that this was not enough to defeat the case and granted extension to serve.); Middleton v. Calhoun, 821 N.Y.S.2d 444 (Rensselaer County Ct. 2006).
179. Gamble v. Gamble, 259 N.Y.S.2d 910 (App. Div. 1965).
180. WEINSTEIN, CPLR MANUAL § 26.07[d] (citing ARTHUR KARGER, THE POWERS OF THE NEW YORK COURT OF APPEALS 425–444 (3d ed. 1997); HENRY COHEN & ARTHUR KARGER, POWERS OF THE NEW YORK COURT OF APPEALS, 412–421 (ev. ed. 1992); WEINSTEIN, NEW YORK CIVIL PRACTICE ¶ 5522.08; Lehman Commercial Paper, Inc. v. Point Prop. Co., LLC, 45 N.Y.S.3d 662 (App. Div. 2017); Matter of Williams v. Annucci, 42 N.Y.S.3d 894 (App. Div. 2016); Matter of People *ex rel.* Green v. Saunders, 42 N.Y.S.3d 812 (App. Div. 2016); People *ex rel.* Mason v. Warden, 28 N.Y.S.3d 308 (App. Div. 2016); Matter of Raven K. (Adam C.), 13 N.Y.S.3d 469 (App. Div. 2015); Villafane v. Macombs Grocery Superette, Corp., 3 N.Y.S.3d 584 (App. Div. 2015); Matter of Baines v. Berlin,

is of a character which is likely to recur not only with respect to the parties before the court but with respect to others as well."[181]

1. Finality Requirement

Appeals are usually taken by a party when there has been a final judgment on the matter. CPLR § 5611 states that a judgement or order will be final "if the appellate division disposes of all the issues in the action . . . and a subsequent appeal may be taken only from that order and not from any judgment or order entered pursuant to it."[182] There are four statutory exceptions to the finality requirement, but unless a case falls into one of them, the courts will require a judgment or order to be final before a party can take an appeal.[183]

The finality requirement under CPLR § 5601(d) means that the order or judgment being appealed from must be final. A judgment or order will be considered final if "the Appellate Division disposes of all the issues in the action . . ."[184] Put another way, a judgment or order is final if it is one that "disposes of all the causes of action between the parties in an action or proceeding and leaves nothing for further judicial action apart from mere ministerial matters."[185]

The biggest question when determining finality is whether the order or judgment being appealed from meets the definitions stated above. The New York courts have analyzed many cases and determined what constitutes disposing of all the issues. One example of where the Court of Appeals determined the finality of the issues was where they denied leave to appeal.[186] Another situation where finality has been decided was where the court specifically did not address a motion or

---

999 N.Y.S.2d 738 (App. Div. 2015); Matter of Colon v. Annucci, 57 N.Y.S.3d 512 (App. Div. 2017); Matter of Kirkland v. Annucci, 54 N.Y.S.3d 40 (App. Div. 2017)).

181. East Meadow Community Concerts Assoc. v. Board of Education, 219 N.E.2d 172, 175 (N.Y. 1966).

182. CPLR § 5611.

183. WEINSTEIN, CPLR MANUAL § 26.02[d]. The four statutory exceptions to the finality requirement are stated in CPLR §§ 5601(c), 5602(b)(2)(iii), 5602(a)(2), and 5602(b)(i). *Id.*

184. CPLR § 5561.

185. Burke v. Crosson, 647 N.E.2d 736, 739 (N.Y. 1995). One example of an order that commonly is a final determination is a grant of summary judgment that dismisses a complaint. *See* WEINSTEIN, CPLR MANUAL § 26.02[d] (citing Rovello v. Orofino Realty Co., 357 N.E.2d 970 (N.Y. 1976); WEINSTEIN, NEW YORK CIVIL PRACTICE ¶¶ 5611.01, 5611.02). An order that dismisses one cause of action and not the other will be final for that cause of action under the theory of implied severance. Sirlin Plumbing Co. v. Maple Hill Homes, 230 N.E.2d 394 (N.Y. 1967).

186. Jiggetts v. Dowling, 788 N.Y.S.2d 460 (App. Div. 2005). Another court held that a denial of a stay of arbitration was final. Wilaka Construction Co. v. New York City Housing Authority, 216 N.E.2d 696 (N.Y. 1966).

part of the motion.[187] In these cases, the court held that the failure to specifically address the issues was the same as a denial from the court.[188] An order would not be considered final if the court remanded the case for further determinations.[189]

If an appeal is brought on a final judgment or order under CPLR § 5601, the appeal brings up for review "only the prior nonfinal order of the Appellate Division which is predicate for the appeal."[190] This means that during the review of the order or judgment, the court will look at the nonfinal orders or judgments that influenced the order or judgment being appealed.[191] The court in *Farber* stated that the prior order must have "necessarily affected" the order or judgment being appealed or have been decisive of it.[192]

---

187. Klansky v. Weiden Lake Prop. Owners Ass'n., Inc., 7 N.Y.S.3d 659 (App. Div. 2015). *See also* Matter of Rose v. Albany County Dist. Attorney's Off., 34 N.Y.S.3d 753 (App. Div. 2016).
188. *Id.* at 755.
189. Spears v. Berle, 397 N.E.2d 1304 (N.Y. 1979) (holding that the order was nonfinal because the court remanded the proceedings to the Commissioner for further determination of the costs); *Id.* at 1309.
190. Gilroy v. American Broadcasting Co., 389 N.E.2d 117 (N.Y. 1979).
191. Farber v. U.S. Trucking Corp., 256 N.E.2d 521, 528 (N.Y. 1970) (holding that the appeal from the order which affirmed an award would bring up for review "only the prior order of the Appellate Division which had reversed the earlier decision of the board."); *see also* Buffalo Electric Co. v. State, 201 N.E.2d 869, 870 (N.Y. 1964) (holding that the prior order of the Appellate Division must "itself have been one of reversal, or have been with dissent, or have involved a constitutional question.").
192. *Farber*, 256 N.E.2d at 528. A judgment or order is said to "necessarily affect" the final judgment is one that "if reversed, would necessarily require a reversal or modification of the final judgment" and "there was no further opportunity during the litigation to raise the issues decided by the non-final determination." WEINSTEIN, CPLR MANUAL § 26.05[a][2], *see also* Oakes v. Patel, 988 N.E.2d 488, 493 (N.Y. 2013) (holding that "when an order granting or denying a motion to amend relates to a proposed new pleading that contains a new cause of action or defense—the order necessarily affects the final judgment."); Siegmund Strauss, Inc. v. East 149th Realty Corp., 980 N.E.2d 483, 487 (N.Y. 2012) (holding that the order necessarily affected the final judgment because "Supreme Court's dismissal of the counterclaims and third-party claim necessarily removed that legal issue from the case (i.e., there was no further opportunity during the litigation to raise the question decided by the prior non-final order) . . . ."); Rupert v. Rupert, 764 N.E.2d 954, 955 (N.Y. 2001) (holding that the judgment did not necessarily affect the final determination because "the final judgment of the Supreme Court rests on an alternative basis for the result reached by the Appellate Division"); Karlin v. IVF America, Inc., 712 N.E.2d 662, 665 (N.Y. 1999) (holding that because the order dismissing the plaintiffs' claims and dismissing of five other claims does "necessarily affect the final judgment," so they may be brought up on review); Javarone v. Pallone, 684 N.E.2d 276, 276–277 (N.Y. 1997) (holding that an "order denying appellant's motion to vacate his stipulation of discontinuance does not 'necessarily affect' the final judgment"); Matter of Aho, 347 N.E.2d 647, 651–652 (N.Y. 1976) (holding that "reversal of an order denying the motion for change of venue in any proceeding to determine competency would strike at the foundation on which the final judgment was predicated" and would necessarily affect the judgment).

The finality requirement is not always determinative of whether an appeal will be dismissed. The Court of Appeals has held that the finality requirement is not jurisdictional because there are situations where the court will permit interlocutory appeals.[193] The First Department also held in *Dewey Ballantine LLP v. Philippine Natl. Bank* that the First Department does not require finality and "regularly reviews conditional orders."[194]

2.   Taking an Appeal as of Right to the Appellate Division

Under the CPLR, there are certain situations where the movant may take an appeal as of right based on the final determination. In these situations, the movant must simply file a notice of appeal and any other required documents with the clerk and serve a copy to the adverse parties. For appeals that are taken from the Supreme Court or county courts to the Appellate Division, there are three situations where a movant may take an appeal as of right. The first situation is where a movant seeks an appeal from "any final or interlocutory judgment except one entered subsequent to an order of the appellate division which disposes of all the issues."[195]

The second situation is where the movant seeks an appeal from "an order . . . where the motion it decided was made upon notice" and it deals with one of the listed orders in the statute.[196] This list includes an order that (1) deals with a provisional remedy; (2) deals with an application to resettle a transcript of statement on appeal; (3) deals with a new trial not for specific questions of fact from the triable issues; (4) deals with "some part of the merits;" (5) "affects a substantial right"; (6) "in effect determines the action and prevents a judgment from which an appeal might be taken"; (7) deals with a statutory provision that was determined to be unconstitutional and "the determination appears from the reasons given for the decision or is necessarily implied in the decision"; or (8) grants a motion for leave to reargue or renew.[197]

Under CPLR § 2211, a motion is defined as "an application for an order."[198] This section also defines a motion on notice as a motion made "when notice of the motion or an order to show cause is served."[199] This means that the movant

---

193. State Office of Drug Abuse Services v. State Human Rights Appeal Board, 397 N.E.2d 1314, 1317 (N.Y. 1979).
194. Dewey Ballantine LLP v. Philippine Natl. Bank, 757 N.Y.S.2d 4, 5 (App. Div. 2003).
195. CPLR § 5701(a)(1).
196. *Id.* § 5701(a)(2).
197. *Id.* §§ 5701(a)(2)(i)-(viii).
198. *Id.* § 2211.
199. *Id.*

has served the opposing party with the motion. The courts of New York have heard numerous cases on what it means for a motion to be made "on notice." An order from a request for relief without a notice of motion or, in some cases, a notice of cross motion will not be considered a motion made upon notice.[200] The consensus of the opinions is that a motion is not made on notice when the order is granted *ex parte* or *sua sponte*.[201] In the *Reyes* case, the defendant sent a letter to the court requesting a telephone conference.[202] The plaintiff argued that this was a motion made by the defendant and therefore the order issued by the court was from a motion made on notice.[203] The court rejected this argument, holding that the letter was not a motion because it did not meet the definition of CPLR § 2211 as it was only seeking a telephone conference and not an order.[204] In the cases of an *ex parte* or *sua sponte* order, the courts have held that the proper way to appeal these orders would be to move to vacate the order and, if denied, appeal that determination.[205]

New York courts have also held that an order ruling on a motion *in limine* is not appealable as of right or by permission because it is an order "made in advance of trial which merely determines the admissibility of evidence" and is therefore an "unappealable advisory ruling."[206] There is an exception to this rule that is recognized by many courts. This exception is for motions *in limine* that are mistakenly used as the "procedural equivalent of a motion for partial summary judgment" and have the effect of limiting "the scope of issues to be tried."[207]

The third situation is where the movant seeks an appeal from "an order, where the motion was made upon notice, refusing to vacate or modify a prior order, if

---

200. Fried v. Jacob Holding, Inc., 970 N.Y.S.2d 260, 267 (App. Div. 2013). *See also* Free in Christ Pentecostal Church v. Julian, 881 N.Y.S.2d 773, 774 (App. Div. 2009) (holding that plaintiff could not appeal as of right because the relief was requested in the opposition papers and not in a motion); New York State Div. of Human Rights v. Oceanside Cove II Apt. Corp., 835 N.Y.S.2d 246, 247 (App. Div. 2007) (holding that the plaintiff could not appeal as of right because there was no motion made. Instead, the plaintiff requested the relief in the opposition papers.).

201. Sholes v. Meagher, 794 N.E.2d 664, 665–666 n.2 (N.Y. 2003); Tribovich v. Tribovich, 997 N.Y.S.2d 855 (App. Div. 2014); Reyes v. Sequeira, 883 N.Y.S.2d 494 (App. Div. 2009); Davidson v. Regan Fund Mgmt., 788 N.Y.S.2d 598 (App. Div. 2005).

202. Reyes v. Sequeira, 883 N.Y.S.2d 494, 500 (App. Div. 2009).

203. *Id.*

204. *Id.*

205. Davidson v. Regan Fund Mgmt., 788 N.Y.S.2d 598 (App. Div. 2005).

206. Calabrese Bakeries, Inc. v. Rockland Bakery, Inc., 32 N.Y.S.3d 667, 669 (App. Div. 2016).

207. *Id. See also* Voss v. Netherlands Ins. Co., 24 N.Y.S.3d 809 (App. Div. 2016); Dischiavi v. Calli, 3 N.Y.S.3d 491 (App. Div. 2015); Nineteen Eighty-Nine LLC v. Icahn, 984 N.Y.S.2d 358 (App. Div. 2014); Scalp & Blade v. Advest, Inc., 765 N.Y.S.2d 92 (App. Div. 2003).

the prior order would have been appealable as of right had it decided a motion made upon notice."[208]

Appeals may also be taken as of right to the Appellate Division from other appellate courts. The movant in this situation seeks an appeal from an order of the "county court or a special term of the supreme court which determines an appeal from judgment of a lower court."[209]

3.   Taking an Appeal as of Right to the Court of Appeals

As with the Appellate Division, there are several instances where a movant may take an appeal as of right to the Court of Appeals. The first situation is where a final judgment or order has been determined and there are at least "two justices dissenting on a question of law in favor of the party taking the appeal."[210]

The second situation is where there is an order from the Appellate Division that involves the construction of the Constitution of New York or the United States or where the only question from a judgment or order is the "validity of a statutory provision of the state or the United States under the constitution of the state or of the United States."[211]

---

208. CPLR § 5701(c).

209. *Id.* § 5703(b).

210. *Id.* § 5601(a). *See also* Matter of Anonymous, 34 N.E.3d 51 (N.Y. 2015); Matter of Daniel H., 938 N.E.2d 966, 967 (N.Y. 2010) (holding that the appeals were denied because the dissents were not based on a question of law); Michaelis v. Graizano, 835 N.E.2d 650 (N.Y. 2005) (holding that the appeal was permitted because it was based on two dissenting judges determining a question of law); *In re* Peter G., 816 N.E.2d 566 (N.Y. 2004); DeMaria v. Sweeney, 678 N.E.2d 498 (N.Y. 1997) (holding that the appeals were denied because the dissents were not based on a question of law); Crowley v. O'Keefe, 543 N.E.2d 744 (N.Y. 1989) (holding that the appeal was denied because it was based on an error that the movant did not object to on administrative appeal, which is not a question of law); Merrill v. Albany Med. Ctr. Hosp., 524 N.E.2d 873 (N.Y. 1988) (holding that the appeal was denied because, although it was based on a question of law, the arguments that the dissent is based on were not raised at trial by the movant); Feldsberg v. Nitschke, 404 N.E.2d 1293, 1295 n.1 (N.Y. 1980) (the dissent was based on a question of law because it was focused on the trial court's limitation to use a deposition under CPLR 3117); Gilles Agency, Inc. v. Filor, 298 N.E.2d 115 (N.Y. 1973) (holding that the appeal was denied because it was not easily discernable whether the dissent was based on a question of law or fact. It must be clear that the dissent is based on a question of law for this section to apply); Javits v. Association of Bar, 271 N.E.2d 701 (N.Y. 1971) (holding the appeal was denied because the dissent was based on a question of law in favor of the movant.).

211. CPLR § 5601(b). *See also* Matter of Baldwin Union Free Sch Dist. v. County of Nassau, 9 N.E.3d 351 (N.Y. 2014) (appeal taken as of right for determination of question of validity of local tax law under state constitution); Levenson v. Lippman, 827 N.E.2d 259 (N.Y. 2005) (appeal taken as of right to determine whether the Chief Administrative Judge's actions to amend the rules of the court were within the powers granted by the state constitution); Hernandez v. Robles, 829 N.E.2d 670

The third situation is where the movant seeks an appeal from an order of the Appellate Division which either grants or affirms a new trial or hearing where the movant "stipulates that, upon affirmance, the judgment absolute shall be entered against him."[212]

The fourth situation is where the movant seeks an appeal from a judgment or order which is the final judgment, determination, arbitration award, or Appellate Division judgment which affirms any of these and the Appellate Division has made an order in a prior appeal that "necessarily affects the judgment, determination, or award and which satisfies the requirements of subdivision (a) or of paragraph one of subdivision (b) except that of finality."[213] If the previous order being appealed does not "necessarily affect" the nonfinal judgment, the appeal will not be permitted.[214]

(N.Y. 2005) (appeals cannot be taken as of right under § 5601(b) when there are other questions than whether a statute is valid under the constitution); Courtroom TV Network, LLC v. State, 833 N.E.2d 1197 (N.Y. 2005) (appeal taken as of right to determine the validity of a statute that bans video recording of the activity in the courtroom violating the New York and U.S. Constitutions); Cohen v. State, 720 N.E.2d 850 (N.Y. 1999) (for an appeal to be taken as of right under paragraph 2 of § 5601(b), the constitutional question must be the only question on appeal); Board of Education v. Wieder, 527 N.E.2d 767, 771 (N.Y. 1988) (citing Matter of Haydorn v. Carroll, 121 N.E. 465 (N.Y. 1918). For an appeal to be taken as of right under § 5601(b), the appellant must "demonstrate that the ground for appeal is 'directly and primarily an issue determinable only by our construction of the Constitution of the state or the United States'"); Sonomax, Inc. v. New York, 372 N.E.2d 9, 11 (N.Y. 1977) (an appellant may take an appeal as of right to determine the validity of a local law under the state constitution because the local law constitutes a "statutory provision of the state"); Merced v. Fischer, 345 N.E.2d 288 (N.Y. 1976) (an appellant may take an appeal as of right under § 5601(b) when the only question is the validity of a statute under the state or federal constitutions. If there is a procedural question and a constitutional question, the appeal will be denied.).

212. CPLR § 5601(c). An order granting a new trial is generally not appealable. Coury v. Safe Auto Sales, Inc., 297 N.E.2d 88, 89 n.1 (N.Y. 1972). This type of order will be appealable when the party seeking the appeal has stipulated to the judgment being applied against them if the court on appeal affirms the order. Morales v. City of Nassau, 724 N.E.2d 756 (N.Y. 1999).

213. CPLR § 5601(d). A nonfinal determination would "necessarily affect" the final judgment if its reversal "would necessarily require a reversal or modification of the final judgment." WEINSTEIN, CPLR MANUAL § 26.05[a][2]. *See also* Siegmund Strauss, Inc. v. East 149th Realty Corp., 980 N.E.2d 483, 486 (N.Y. 2012) (holding "where the prior nonfinal order dismissed a cause of action or counterclaim pleaded in a complaint or answer" the nonfinal order would necessarily affect the final judgment); Rupert v. Rupert, 764 N.E.2d 954, 955 (N.Y. 2001) (holding that the nonfinal order did not necessarily affect the final determination because the Supreme Court's final judgment had an alternative basis than the result of the Appellate Division); Karlin v. IVF Am., Inc., 712 N.E.2d 662, 665 (N.Y. 1999) (holding that an order that dismisses a cause of action necessarily affects the final determination).

214. Bobak v. AIG Claims Services, Inc., 985 N.E.2d 425 (N.Y. 2013); Huff v. Rodriguez, 962 N.E.2d 276 (N.Y. 2012); Peterson v. Corbin, 742 N.E.2d 121 (N.Y. 2000); Javarone v. Pallone, 684 N.E.2d 276 (N.Y. 1997); Morgan Guar. Trust Co. of New York v. Solow, 492 N.E.2d 789 (N.Y. 1986); Barker v. Tennis 59th Inc., 481 N.E.2d 570 (N.Y. 1985); Kountz v. State University of New York, 445 N.E.2d 207 (N.Y. 1982); Quinn v. Stuart Lakes Club, Inc., 435 N.E.2d 403 (N.Y. 1982);

4. Taking an Appeal with Permission to the Appellate Division

When an appeal cannot be taken as of right, the movant must get permission from the court to take an appeal. The judge who made the order is the one who also gives permission to appeal.[215] A movant may also seek permission from a justice of the department of the Appellate Division department that the appeal can be taken if the judge who made the order refuses.[216]

There are three instances where appeals from the Supreme Court or county court cannot be taken as of right. These situations include (1) an order made against a government body or officer under Article 78, (2) an order requiring or refusing to require a "more definite statement in a pleading", (3) an order or refusal to order that "scandalous or prejudicial matter be stricken from a pleading."[217]

Permission to take an appeal may also be granted where the appeal is coming from a court of original instance other than the Supreme Court or the county court. In this situation, the movant must follow the statutes governing practice in that court to get permission to appeal.[218]

A movant must seek permission to appeal an order from the Appellate Term which "determines an appeal from a judgment or order of a lower court."[219] The Appellate Term may grant permission if the Appellate Division refuses.[220] If the appeal is being taken from an order of the Appellate Term, the movant must stipulate that "upon affirmance, judgment absolute may be entered against him."[221] This means that, if the movant loses the appeal, the judgment that was appealed will be the final judgment.

5. Taking an Appeal with Permission to the Court of Appeals

The permission to take an appeal when the movant cannot take the appeal as of right can be granted either by the Appellate Division or the Court of Appeals.[222]

Tillman v. Lincoln Warehouse Corporation, 434 N.E.2d 259 (N.Y. 1982); Ferrer v. Hill, 427 N.E.2d 768 (N.Y. 1981); Rusciano & Son Corp. v. Roche, 427 N.E.2d 510 (N.Y. 1981); Zipay v. Benson, 369 N.E.2d 770 (N.Y. 1977).
215. CPLR § 5701(c).
216. *Id.*
217. *Id.* § 5701(b).
218. *Id.* § 5702.
219. *Id.* § 5703(a).
220. *Id.*
221. *Id.* § 5703.
222. *Id.* § 5602(a).

The Court of Appeals may grant permission if the Appellate Division refused to grant permission or if the movant applies for permission directly to them.[223]

The CPLR lists three situations where permission to take the appeal may be sought from either the Appellate Division or the Court of Appeals. One situation is where an order from a lower state court has been finally determined by the Appellate Division and is not appealable as of right.[224] Another situation is where an order on a prior appeal in an action by the Appellate Division would affect the final judgment, determination, or award of a court or administrative agency of arbitration and it is not appealable as of right.[225] The last situation is where the Appellate Division order does not finally determine a proceeding against a public officer, a board, commission, or other body of public officers.[226]

Along with the list of situations where permission to take an appeal may be granted from the court, the CPLR also lists when permission may be sought from the Appellate Division. Two of the situations are the same as the first two situations above. The only difference between the two sections is that permission may be sought from the Appellate Division when there is an order which grants or affirms a new trial or hearing and the movant stipulates that if the order is affirmed, "judgment absolute shall be entered against him."[227]

6.   Appellate Division Rules for Notice of Appeal

Each department of the Appellate Division has its own rules for filing a notice of appeal. The rules are similar in some regards, with differences in what is required when filing. For each of the departments, the filing fee is sixty-five dollars.[228]

In the First Department, the movant must file a notice of appeal as well as a "pre-argument statement,"[229] proof of service, and a copy of the order which

---

223. *Id.*
224. *Id.* § 5602(a)(1)(i).
225. *Id.* § 5602(a)(1)(ii).
226. *Id.* § 5602(a)(2).
227. *Id.* § 5602(b)(2)(iii).
228. *Id.* § 8022.
229. A "pre-argument" statement must state "title of the action; full names of original parties and any change in the parties; name, address and telephone number of counsel for appellant or petitioner; name, address and telephone number of counsel for respondent; court and county, or administrative body for which the appeal is taken; nature and object of the cause of action or special proceeding; result reached in the court or administrative body below; and grounds for seeking reversal, annulment or modification." 22 N.Y.C.R.R. § 600.17(b). The pre-argument statement must also include if there is a related action or proceeding pending in any court and what the status of that action is. *Id.*

contains a memorandum.[230] These documents must be filed in the court where the judgment or order was entered. The pre-argument statement must be filed in all civil actions unless the action is from family court.[231]

In the Second Department, the rules are slightly different for filing a notice of appeal. The movant must file the notice in the court where the judgment or order was entered and must provide two copies of the notice of appeal, as well as a request for Appellate Division intervention (RADI), a copy of the judgment or order appealed from, and a copy of the opinion or decision if available.[232] If there is more than one judgment or order that is being appealed, the movant must also attach "an Additional Appeal Information for (form B) describing the additional judgments or order appealed from, and . . . copies of the judgments or order and the opinions or decisions upon which they were based . . ." to the RADI.[233]

In the Third Department, a movant shall file a notice of appeal, a "pre-calendar statement," a copy of the order or judgment being appealed, and a copy of the opinion or decision if available in all cases, except for the listed civil actions.[234] The pre-calendar statement requires similar information as the pre-argument statement in the First Department.[235]

The rules of practice for the Fourth Department use the term "appeals" to refer to appeals and cross-appeals.[236] In the past, the Fourth Department required

---

230. *Id.* § 600.17(a).

231. *Id.* § 600.17(b).

232. *Id.* § 670.3(a).

233. *Id.*

234. 22 N.Y.C.R.R. § 800.24-a(c). The listed civil actions include "appeals in proceedings pursuant to Election Law and CPLR articles 70 and 78, family court proceedings for child abuse or neglect, juvenile delinquency or persons in need of supervision, appeals from decision of the Unemployment Insurance Appeal Board and Workers' Compensation Board, appeals pursuant to section 168-n(3) of the Correction Law, and appeals from orders entered in proceedings pursuant to Mental Hygiene Law articles 9, 10 and 15 . . ."; *Id.*

235. This information includes "the title of the underlying action or proceeding and the date of commencement; the full names of the original parties and any change in the parties; the name, address, telephone number and facsimile telephone number of counsel for appellant; the name, address, telephone number and facsimile telephone number of counsel for each respondent and counsel for each other party; the court, judge or justice, and county for which the appeal is taken, together with the index number and the request for judicial intervention (RJI) number; the specific nature and object of the underlying action or proceeding; a clear and concise statement of the issues to be raised on the appeal and the grounds for reversal or modification to be advanced; and whether there is another pending appeal or pending related action or proceeding, briefly describing same." *Id.* § 800.24-a(b).

236. *Id.* § 1002.2(a).

a pre-argument statement to be filed with the notice of appeal.[237] In 2007, the Fourth Department did away with this requirement.[238] Now all that is required to be filed is a notice of appeal, proof of service, and the filing fee.[239]

7. Appellate Term Rules for Notice of Appeal

The Appellate Term follows similar rules as the Appellate Division for taking an appeal. The first step is to determine whether the appeal may be taken as of right or by permission.[240] To do this, the moving party must look at the Uniform Court Act (UCA), specially § 1702.[241] Section 1702 is nearly identical to CPLR § 5701, with two distinctions.[242] Under § 1702, the situations where a moving party may take an appeal as of right are identical to the situations in the CPLR.

After the moving party has determined whether the appeal may be taken as of right or by permission, UCA § 1703 provides for the procedure governing appeals to the Appellate Term. Section 1703 states that the rules and procedures that govern the appeal are those under Article 55 of the CPLR unless this section states otherwise.[243] As discussed above, Article 55 of the CPLR governs the time to take the appeal and how the moving party can take an appeal. By stating Article 55 governs, the UCA adopts the thirty-day time limit to take an appeal after service of the judgment or order and notice of entry and the rules that govern the notice of appeal.

The UCA provides two sections for when appeals may be taken from the appellate court and when they may be taken to the Court of Appeals. Under

---

237. STECICH & GOLD, *supra* note 26, § 7:9.

238. *Id.*

239. *Id.*

240. 1 NEW YORK APPELLATE PRACTICE, *supra* note 1, § 12.02.

241. *Id.* The moving party needs to look to the UCA because the rules of the Appellate Term do not state what the moving party must do to take an appeal. *Id.*

242. *Id.* The first distinction is that § 1702 does not address appeals of Article 78 proceedings because the Appellate Term does not have jurisdiction over these cases. *Id.* The second distinction is that § 1702 states that "on appeal, 'the appellate court shall have full power to review any exercise of discretion by the court of judge below.'" *Id.* (citing § 1702(d)). This language does not appear in the CPLR but the scope of review for both statutes is basically the same. *Id.*

243. N.Y. CITY CIV. CT. ACT § 1703 (Lexis 2019); N.Y. UNIFORM DIST. CT. ACT § 1703; N.Y. UNIFORM JUST. CT. ACT § 1703. Section 1703(b) states "an appeal as of right from a judgment entered in a small claim or a commercial claim must be taken within thirty days of the following, whichever first occurs: (1) service by the court of a copy of the judgment appealed from upon the appellant. (2) service by a party of a copy of the judgment appealed from upon the appellant. (3) service by the appellant of a copy of the judgment appealed from upon a party." N.Y. CITY CIV. CT. ACT § 1703(b). This section also provides that if service of one of these three subdivisions is done by mail, then an additional five days will be added to the thirty-day period. *Id.*

§ 1706, appeals that are taken from a judgment or order of an appellate court are governed by the rules of the CPLR.[244] The New York City Civil Court Act (NYCCA), New York Uniform District Court Act, and New York Uniform Justice Court Act all have the same sections for the information discussed above, but only the NYCCA has a section that governs appeals taken to the Court of Appeals. Under §1707 of the NYCCA, an appeal may be taken from any judgment or order that "finally determines an action or special proceeding where the only question involved on the appeal is the validity of a statutory provision of the state or of the United States under the constitution of the state or of the United States."[245]

8.   Court of Appeals Rules for Notice of Appeal

Taking an appeal to the Court of Appeals is done in a similar way as taking an appeal to the Appellate Division. The movant must pay close attention to the specific rules that the Court of Appeals has articulated. The rules for the Court of Appeals are more detailed than the departments of the Appellate Division.

When taking an appeal to the Court of Appeals, the movant must file a copy of the notice of appeal, a "preliminary appeal statement," a copy of the signed order, judgment, or determination being appealed from, a signed copy of the order, judgment, or determination that is the subject of the order brought up on review, a copy of all decisions or opinions relating to the order, and proof of service or the original affidavit of service.[246] If the movant is arguing in the appeal that a statute is unconstitutional, then a copy of the notice of appeal must be sent to the attorney general and a copy must be included in the documents required to be filed.[247] Along with filing these documents with the clerk of the court of original instance, the movant must also serve a copy of the notice of appeal on the adverse parties to the appeal.[248]

A "preliminary appeal statement" is similar to the pre-argument/pre-calendar statements. A preliminary appeal statement must be filed within ten days of taking the appeal.[249] The biggest difference with the preliminary appeal statement is that the Court of Appeals has a sample form that can be used to create it.[250] This form

---

244. *Id.* § 1706; N.Y. Uniform Dist. Ct. Act § 1706; N.Y. Uniform Just. Ct. Act § 1706.
245. N.Y. City Civ. Ct. Act § 1707. When the appeal is being determined, the court will only consider the constitutional question.
246. Stecich & Gold, *supra* note 26, §7:5.
247. *Id.*
248. *Id.*
249. 22 N.Y.C.R.R. § 500.9.
250. *Id.*

can be found on the Court of Appeals' website.[251] The Court of Appeals does not require that a fee be paid when filing the preliminary appeal statement.[252]

The Court of Appeals has similar discretion as the Appellate Division to allow the movant to cure any defects or omissions if the notice of appeal was timely filed and doing so would not prejudice the other parties.[253] There is no time limit for moving to cure a defect under the CPLR. The motion can be made whenever the omission or defect is discovered.[254]

C.   Notice of Cross-Appeal

After a notice of appeal has been filed and served with the court and the nonmoving party, there may be instances where the appellee wishes to appeal part of the judgment or order. When there is more than one appeal, the second appeal is generally referred to as a "cross-appeal."[255] A cross-appeal is taken in a similar way as an appeal and the notice of cross-appeal is governed by similar rules and procedures, with some differences among the departments of the Appellate Division.[256]

The party that may file a notice of cross-appeal is the party that was served with a notice of appeal by an adverse party.[257] As discussed in section II.B, the party taking the cross-appeal must have been aggrieved in some way by the judgment or order.[258]

There are two situations where a party must file a notice of cross-appeal. The first situation is where the party seeks "relief other than an affirmance of the judgment or order below."[259] The second situation is where the party seeks "review of

---

251. Stecich & Gold, *supra* note 26, §7:5.

252. 22 N.Y.C.R.R. § 500.9.

253. *Id.*

254. *Id.*

255. 1 New York Appellate Practice, *supra* note 1, § 5.06. Black's Law Dictionary defines "cross-appeal" as "[a]n appeal by the appellee, usu. [sic] heard at the same time as the appellant's appeal." *Appeal*, Black's Law Dictionary (10 ed. 2014).

256. Robert L. Haig, 4A N.Y. Practice, Commercial Litigation in New York State Courts § 56:33 (4th ed. 2015).

257. CPLR § 5513(c).

258. Mudge, Rose, Guthrie, Alexander & Ferdon v. Penguin A.C. Corp., 633 N.Y.S.2d 493, 493 (App. Div. 1995) (holding defendant's cross-appeal "dismissed as taken by a party not aggrieved by the order (CPLR 5511), without costs"), *see also* Mena v. D'Ambrose, 377 N.E.2d 466 (N.Y. 1978); Finkelstein v. Lincoln Natl. Corp., 967 N.Y.S.2d 733 (App. Div. 2013); Village of Croton-on-Hudson v. Northeast Interchange Ry., LLC, 846 N.Y.S.2d 606 (App. Div. 2007).

259. 1 New York Appellate Practice, *supra* note 1, § 5.06.

a ruling below."[260] Although these two situations seem to cover most cases where an appellee would want to take an appeal, there is an exception where a notice of cross-appeal does not have to be filed. This is where the appellee is seeking to "reinstate a jury verdict that was reduced or increased by the trial court on a motion to set aside a verdict."[261]

As with the notice of appeal, the CPLR prescribes a time limit for when a notice of cross-appeal must be filed. The party seeking a cross-appeal has the greater of (1) ten days after service of a notice of appeal or (2) the time prescribed by either sections (a) or (b) of CPLR § 5513, if either apply.[262] If the ten days is longer than the thirty days under sections (a) or (b), the ten days will apply, and vice versa.[263] The time limit begins when the notice of appeal has been accepted.[264] If the notice of appeal or cross-appeal is filed before the judgment or order is entered, then the notice will be considered premature and the court will deny the appeal or cross-appeal.[265] The additional time allowed under sections (a) or (b) is not applicable to a notice of cross-appeal when the parties are not adverse.[266]

A notice of cross-appeal is dependent on the notice of appeal that is filed first. The notice of appeal must be timely filed before a party can file a notice of cross-appeal.[267] The two notices also follow similar rules regarding filing. Any document that is required for filing a notice of appeal (i.e., pre-argument statement, RADI, preliminary appeal statement, and so on), must also be filed with the notice of

---

260. *Id.*

261. *Id.* (citing CPLR § 5501(a)(5)). This section of the CPLR lists the different issues that are brought up on review when an appeal is taken. These issues do not need to be brought up on cross-appeal. All that needs to be done is an appeal in a case where one of these happened.

262. CPLR § 5513. Section (a) states the time to take an appeal as of right. The time limit is thirty days from the date the appellant is served with a copy of the judgment or order and notice of entry. *Id.* Section (b) states the time to move for permission to appeal. The time limit is thirty days from the service of judgment or order with notice of entry or thirty days from the service of judgment or order from denial of permission to appeal. *Id.* § 5513(b).

263. WEINSTEIN, NEW YORK CIVIL PRACTICE ¶ 5513.08.

264. *See* Kubiszyn v. Terex Div. of Terex Corp., 201 A.D.2d 974 (App. Div. 1994). In this case, the notice of appeal was not properly filed but the court extended the deadline to file by motion to extend the time until a later date. The respondent had to file ten days later but failed to do so. *Id.* at 974.

265. Culen v. Culen, 69 N.Y.S.3d 881 (App. Div. 2018); Matter of Richard S. (Lacey P.), 14 N.Y.S.3d 400 (App. Div. 2015); Plato Gen. Constr. Corp./EMCO Tech Constr. Corp., JV, LLC v. Dormitory Auth. of State of New York, 932 N.Y.S.2d 504 (App. Div. 2011); Marini v. Lombardo, 835 N.Y.S.2d 332 (App. Div. 2007).

266. KARGER, *supra* note 182, § 12:1 n.14 (citing Raquet v. Zane, 732 N.E.2d 946 (N.Y. 2000)).

267. STECICH & GOLD, *supra* note 26, § 6:4.

cross-appeal.[268] A notice of cross-appeal also has the same effect of staying proceedings as the filing of a notice of appeal.[269]

It is important to note that, like a notice of appeal, if a notice of cross-appeal
does not address a specific issue or part of the judgment or order being appealed,
the court will not consider this issue or part before the court.[270] This will not,
however, prevent a court from exercising its ability to grant relief even if no appeal
or cross-appeal has been filed.[271] Under CPLR § 3212(b), the court has the power
to grant summary judgment without "the necessity of a cross-motion" if "it shall
appear that any party other than the moving party is entitled to a summary judgment."[272] The Appellate Division has taken this section to mean that it has the
"power and responsibility" to grant summary judgment in favor of the nonap-
pealing party even if there was no cross-appeal "once it determined that no issue
of material fact existed as to plaintiff's . . . cause of action and that defendants
were entitled to judgment as a matter of law. . . ."[273]

The Appellate Term does not have specific rules for cross-appeals in the court
rules or the UCA. The Appellate Division has specific rules for notices of cross-
appeal like it does for a stay and notices of appeal. In the First Department, the
first party to file a notice of appeal is referred to as the "appellant."[274] The party to
file a second appeal is referred to as the "cross-appellant."[275] The First Department

---

268. Id. at § 7:1.
269. GEBAUER ET AL., *supra* note 72, § 70:267 (citing Craige v. Consolidated Edison Co. of New
York, Inc., 511 N.Y.S.2d 359 (App. Div. 1987). In *Craige*, the court held that the order was stayed
under CPLR § 5519(a)(1) because the city had filed a notice of cross-appeal. *Id.*
270. Whitfield v. JWP/forest Elec. Corp., 637 N.Y.S.2d 4 (App. Div. 1996); Carlin v. Carlin,
7 N.Y.S.3d 230 (App. Div. 2015); Douglas Elliman, LLC. v. Bergere, 949 N.Y.S.2d 766 (App. Div.
2012); Levitt v. Levitt, 948 N.Y.S.2d 108 (App. Div. 2012); Hemmings v. St. Marks Hous. Assoc.,
Phase II L.P., 707 N.Y.S.2d 667 (App. Div. 2000); O'Donnell v. O'Donnell, 836 N.Y.S.2d 703 (App.
Div. 2007); Clark v. 345 East 52nd St. Owners, 666 N.Y.S.2d 207 (App. Div. 1997); Lynn v. McDonnell Douglas Corp., 520 N.Y.S.2d 804, 806 (App. Div. 1987); Blue v. Wilkins, 419 N.Y.S.2d 759,
760 (App. Div. 1979); Carr v. Carr, 738 N.Y.S.2d 415, 417 n.1 (App. Div. 2002); Matter of Stewart
v. Chautauqua County Bd. of Elections, 894 N.Y.S.2d 249 (App. Div. 2010).
271. *See* Ironwood, L.L.C. v. JGB Props., LLC, 14 N.Y.S.3d 248, 249 (App. Div. 2015). The Fourth
Department in this case used its discretionary power to treat the plaintiff's cross-appeal in the second appeal as a cross-appeal in the first appeal. *Id.*
272. CPLR § 3212(b).
273. Merritt Hill Vineyards v. Windy Hgts. Vineyard, 460 N.E.2d 1077, 1081 (N.Y. 1984); *see also*
Spencer, White & Prentis v. Southwest Sewer Dist. in County of Suffolk, 477 N.Y.S.2d 681, 683
(App. Div. 1984) (citing Kornfeld v. NRX Technologies, 465 N.E.2d 30 (N.Y. 1984); *Merritt Hill
Vineyards*, 460 N.E.2d at 1079.).
274. 22 N.Y.C.R.R. § 600.11(d).
275. *Id.*

rules state that if there is a cross-appeal, the appellant and the cross-appellant will both be responsible for filing a joint record or appendix.[276] This joint record must also include a copy of the notice of cross-appeal.[277] The parties shall also be responsible jointly for paying the filing fee at the court.[278] The appellant will have the duty of perfecting the appeal when the time comes.[279]

The Second Department rules are the same as the First Department when it comes to the designation of the parties when there is a cross-appeal. The rules are different when determining what constitutes a cross-appeal. The rules of the Second Department differentiate between a "cross-appeal" and a "concurrent appeal."[280] For all cross and concurrent appeals in the Second Department, the parties are to use the document number that was given to the first notice of appeal.[281] The Second Department rules are similar to the First Department rules, which require that all the parties file and serve a joint record or appendix for the appeal.[282] This joint record or appendix must include copies of all the notices of appeal in the case.[283] The parties will all equally bear the cost of the appeal. One difference between the First and Second Departments is that the Second Department measures the time to file the joint record or appendix in a concurrent appeal from the latest date of the several concurrent notices of appeal.[284]

The Third Department rules are different from the other three departments. In the Third Department, the designation of the parties is not based on who appeals first. The plaintiff at the trial court is deemed the appellant.[285] It does not matter if the plaintiff is the party appealing or not.[286] The rules of the Third Department require the appellant to serve and file the record and brief on appeal.[287] The

---

276. *Id.*

277. *Id.*

278. *Id.*

279. *Id.*

280. A cross-appeal is an appeal "taken by a party whose interests are adverse to a party who previously appealed from the same order or judgment." 22 N.Y.C.R.R. § 670.2(a)(6). A concurrent appeal is an appeal "taken separately from the same order of judgment by parties whose interests are not adverse to one another." *Id.*

281. *Id.* § 670.2(e).

282. *Id.* § 670.8(c).

283. *Id.*

284. *Id.*

285. 1 New York Appellate Practice, *supra* note 1, § 5.02.

286. *Id.*

287. *Id. See also* 22 N.Y.C.R.R. § 800.9(e); Matter of Prat v. Melton, 413 N.Y.S.2d 527 (App. Div. 1979). The plaintiff in the Third Department is considered to be "the 'more aggrieved' party responsible for progressing the appeal process and keeping a watchful eye on the nine-month abandonment period." 1 New York Appellate Practice, *supra* note 1, § 5.02 (citing 22 N.Y.C.R.R. § 800.12).

appellant is also responsible for the full cost of the appeal.[288] The parties to the appeal may stipulate as to who will perfect the appeal.[289]

In the Fourth Department, the party that is appealing the judgment or order is referred to as the "appellant or appellant-respondent."[290] The party that is opposing the appeal is referred to as the "respondent or respondent-appellant."[291] The rules of the Fourth Department state that when the word "appeal" appears, it refers to both appeals and cross-appeals, unless otherwise specified.[292] Appeals and cross-appeals in the Fourth Department follow the same rules and procedures. One distinction that the Fourth Department makes is defining a "consolidated appeal." According to the statute, a "consolidated appeal" occurs where "there are multiple appellants to an order or judgment."[293] In this situation, "there must be a stipulation designating the party who will bear primary responsibility for filing the record and shall be duly filed with the court."[294]

D. Motion for Leave to Appeal

When a judgment or order cannot be appealed as of right, the movant will need to seek permission from the court to take an appeal. Under CPLR § 5519(d) "an appeal may be taken to the Court of Appeals by permission of the Appellate Division granted before application or the court of appeals *or* by permission of the Court of Appeals upon refusal by the Appellate Division *or* upon direct application."[295] As with the notice of appeal, when making a motion for leave to appeal, the movant should raise every issue they intend to raise on appeal.[296] When a party seeking leave limits the issues they want to raise on appeal, the movant is bound to those issues and cannot raise any others. Because of this limitation, the motion

---

288. Derr v. Fleming, 970 N.Y.S.2d 100 (App. Div. 2013).
289. 1 New York Appellate Practice, *supra* note 1, § 5.02. If the plaintiff believes there is a "more aggrieved" party, the plaintiff may make a motion to the court to designate a different appellant to prepare the record and bear the cost of the appeal. *Id.* (citing 22 N.Y.C.R.R. § 800.9(e)).
290. 1 New York Appellate Practice, *supra* note 1, § 5.06.
291. *Id.*
292. 22 N.Y.C.R.R. § 1000.2(a).
293. *Id.* § 1000.4(b)(1).
294. *Id.*
295. CPLR § 5602 (emphasis added).
296. Quain v. Buzzetta Const. Corp., 507 N.E. 2d 294, 295 (N.Y. 1987) ("Ordinarily when the court grants a motion for leave to appeal all issues of which the court may take cognizance may be addressed by the parties. Where, however, the party seeking leave specifically limits the issues to be raised, it is bound thereby and may not thereafter raise other questions.")

for leave to appeal should single out the issues that can support a case for leave, convincing the court to grant the motion.

A party can make motions for leave to appeal both to the Appellate Divisions and the Court of Appeals. Because the Court of Appeals can act without waiting for the Appellate Division, if the Court of Appeals denies the motion, the Appellate Division cannot subsequently accept the motion.[297] It is important to note that, as with the other sections, the rules for motions for leave to take an appeal may be different for each court.

1. Appellate Division Rules

The rules of the Appellate Division for seeking permission to appeal are codified in the NYCRR. Each department has its own rules for how the motions should be made and the procedures for seeking permission. For the First Department, the rules are specified in 22 NYCRR §§ 600.3 and 600.14. A motion for leave to appeal is made in the First Department after the Appellate Term denied the motion.[298] When a motion is made from a court other than the Appellate Term, the rules state that the movant must make the motion within the thirty-day time as specified in CPLR § 5513.[299] In this time limit, the movant must file the motion and the papers in support. These papers must include a copy of the judgment or order and an opinion if available, a copy of the record below; a concise statement of the grounds of the alleged error; and a copy of the order of the lower court that denied leave if available.[300] The First Department also requires that the movant submit a pre-argument statement with the motion. This is the same pre-argument statement that is required for the notice of appeal.

The rules for the Second Department can be found in 22 NYCRR §§ 670.2, 670.3, 670.5, 670.6, and 670.13.[301] The rules for the Second Department divide what is required for when the motion is being made to the Appellate Division, the Appellate Term, or the Court of Appeals. If the motion is being made to the Appellate Division, the rules state that the motion must be addressed to the court and

---

297. Lumsby v. Donovan, 892 N.E.2d 857 (N.Y. 2008) ("Where motions for leave to appeal to the Court of Appeals are made in the Court of Appeals and the Appellate Division simultaneously, the Court of Appeals has the power to entertain the motion without waiting for the Appellate Division to issue its determination of the motion.")

298. 22 N.Y.C.R.R. § 600.3(a).

299. *Id.*

300. *Id.*

301. STECICH & GOLD, *supra* note 26, § 7:16.

have a copy of the judgment or order appealed from attached to it.[302] If the motion is being made to the Appellate Term, the motion must include the same papers as are required for the First Department.[303] In either department, the movant may be required to stipulate to judgment absolute upon affirmation.[304]

If the movant is seeking permission to appeal to the Court of Appeals from the Second Department, the rules state that the movant must "set forth the questions of law to be reviewed by the court and, where appropriate, proposed questions of law decisive to the correctness of this court's determination."[305] Regardless of where the motion is made, the Second Department requires that the movant submit the RADI, similar to the one that is required for the notice of appeal.[306]

For the Third Department, the rules that govern a motion for leave to appeal can be found under 22 NYCRR §§ 800.2, 800.3, and 800.24-a.[307] The biggest difference between the Third Department and the other three departments is that the rules do not state specifically what must be submitted in the moving papers.[308] The Third Department does require that "the notice of motion must give notice to adverse parties that the motion will be submitted on the papers and that their personal appearance in opposition to the motion is neither required nor permitted."[309]

The Fourth Department rules can be found under 22 NYCRR § 1000.13(a).[310] The CPLR section here governs the thirty-day time limit to file the motion. The rules of the Fourth Department are similar to the rules for the other three departments, with some differences. The rules require that the movant submit with the papers in support a notice of motion, supporting affidavits, proof of service on all the parties, a copy of the judgment or order being appealed, the court's order denying leave if any, and a copy of any prior order from the Appellate Division.[311] The Fourth Department is also the only department that has expressly stated "incomplete filings are not acceptable and that a failure to comply with the rules for the submission of a motion will result in the rejection of the motion papers."[312]

---

302. 22 N.Y.C.R.R. § 670.6(a).
303. *Id.*
304. *Id.*; 22 N.Y.C.R.R. § 600.3(a).
305. *Id.*
306. 22 N.Y.C.R.R. § 670.13(b).
307. Stecich & Gold, *supra* note 26, § 7:17.
308. *Id.*
309. *Id.* (citing 22 N.Y.C.R.R. § 800.2(a)).
310. Stecich & Gold, *supra* note 26, § 7:18.
311. 22 N.Y.C.R.R. § 1000.13(a)(5).
312. Stecich & Gold, *supra* note 26, § 7:18 (citing 22 N.Y.C.R.R. § 1000.13(a)(5)(iv)).

2. Appellate Term Rules

As with a motion for a stay and notice of appeal, the Appellate Term also has different rules for motions for leave to appeal. The First and Second Department rules have similarities and differences. The main similarity is that both rules state a movant may seek permission to appeal from one of the following: (1) from a judge who made the order, (2) from a justice of the Appellate Term if permission was refused by a judge of the lower court, or (3) from appealing directly to the Appellate Term.[313]

The rules for the First Department can be found under NYCCCA § 1702(c) and 22 NYCRR §§ 640.8 and 640.10.[314] The same thirty-day time limit as stated above applies to the motions made in the First Department.[315] The biggest difference between the departments of the Appellate Term is what the movant is required to file with the motion. In the First Department, the supporting papers must include a return date, the relief requested, the parties to the motion, a copy of the opinion and the record, a concise statement of the alleged error and the grounds, and a copy of the order from the lower court that denied leave to appeal.[316]

The rules for the Second Department are divided by the different districts. For the Second and Eleventh Judicial Districts, the rules can be found under 22 NYCRR §§ 731.10 and 731.7.[317] For the Ninth and Tenth Judicial Districts, the rules can be found under 22 NYCRR §§ 732.10 and 732.7.[318] The movant must submit the following with the motion as part of the supporting papers: "a copy of the opinion, if any . . . a concise statement of the grounds of alleged error . . . whether a similar application was made in the court below, and if one was, a copy of the order denying leave."[319]

3. Court of Appeals Rules

Most appeals that are brought to the Court of Appeals are taken with permission from either the Appellate Division or the Court of Appeals itself.[320] If the motion was first made in the Appellate Division and it was denied, then the movant

---

313. N.Y. City Civ. Ct. Act § 1702(c).

314. Stecich & Gold, *supra* note 26, § 7:19.

315. *Id.*

316. *Id.* (citing CPLR § 2214(a); 22 N.Y.C.C.R. 640.10(b)).

317. Stecich & Gold, *supra* note 26, § 7:20.

318. *Id.*

319. *Id.* (citing 22 N.Y.C.R.R. §§ 731.10, 732.10).

320. Stecich & Gold, *supra* note 26, § 7:13.

may move in the Court of Appeals.[321] The movant cannot have two simultaneous motions for leave to appeal in both the Appellate Division and the Court of Appeals though.[322] The movant also cannot make a motion in the Court of Appeals while the same motion is pending in the Appellate Division.[323] As stated in section II.B, if the Court of Appeals grants a motion for leave to appeal, then the movant does not need to file a notice of appeal.

The rules that govern motions for leave to appeal in the Court of Appeals depend on where the motion was made. If the motion was made to the Court of Appeals, then the rule that governs is 22 NYCRR § 500.22.[324] If the motion was made to the Appellate Division, then the rules of that department apply.[325]

The supporting papers for a motion must include notice of the motion, a statement of procedural history, a showing that the Court of Appeals has jurisdiction, a concise statement of the questions that are presented for review and an explanation why these questions merit review, a disclosure statement if the movant is a corporation, and a copy of the judgment or order and memorandum.[326] The notice of motion must include the relief sought by the movant, the return date for the motion, and the contact information of the attorneys for the parties.[327]

The rules for the Court of Appeals state that the movant must submit an original and six copies of the motion with the court, as well as proof of service and the filing fee.[328]

III. STANDARD OF APPELLATE REVIEW

Knowledge of the particular standard of review to be applied by the appellate court is crucial, as it addresses the applicable burdens of proof and plays a vital role in shaping and framing the manner in which attorneys draft their appellate briefs. Regarding appeals generally, the standard of review reflects the level of deference that the appellate court will afford the lower court's determination. In New York, the standard of review essentially falls within one of two categories: (a) de novo review; and (b) deferential review (or discretionary review).

---

321. *Id.*
322. *Id.*
323. *Id.*
324. *Id.*
325. STECICH & GOLD, *supra* note 26, § 7:13.
326. *Id.*
327. *Id.* (citing 22 N.Y.C.R.R. § 600.2(a)(3)).
328. *Id.* (citing 22 N.Y.C.R.R. §§ 500.22(a), 500.3(b)). The filing fee for this motion would be forty-five dollars. CPLR § 8022.

Appellate courts generally apply de novo review in cases involving the appellate review of questions of law, including, for example, cases involving matters of statutory interpretation. Where de novo review is applied, the appellate court typically gives little deference to the lower court's determination. In contrast to de novo review of questions of law, appellate courts reviewing questions of fact typically afford greater deference to the lower court's determination, and generally apply a number of different deferential or discretionary standards that address whether the lower court abused its discretion.

A. De Novo Review

As a general matter, under circumstances where the appellate court applies the de novo standard of review, the appellate court must conduct an independent review of the appellant's claim of error, and must make its own determination as to the merits of the appeal without regard for the lower court's determination.[329] Accordingly, with de novo review, the appellate court's determinations are based on a review of the underlying action from which the appeal arose, rather than a simple review of the lower court's determination. Examples of circumstances where the de novo standard of appellate review applies include appeals involving: (1) questions of law, (2) questions of statutory interpretation, (3) summary judgment, (4) judgment as a matter of law, (5) failure to state a cause of action, and (6) jury instruction issues.[330]

In New York, appeals involving questions of law to which the de novo standard of review applies include, inter alia, the interpretation of contract language[331] and determinations of actual malice in connection with defamation claims involving public figures.[332] Appellate courts likewise apply the de novo standard of appellate review when addressing appeals that involve the interpretation of statutes, including, for example, appeals involving the interpretation

---

329. Thomas R. Newman & Steven J. Ahmuty, Jr., *Issue Selection and the Applicable Standard of Review* (N.Y.L.J. July 1, 2015) ("The de novo standard empowers and requires an appellate court to make an independent 'first impression' judgment about an appellant's claim of error without giving any deference to adverse findings or conclusions of the lower court.").

330. *Id.*; *see also* Trump Vil. Section 3, Inc. v. City of New York, 974 N.Y.S.2d 469, 473 (App. Div. 2013), *aff'd*, 24 N.E.3d 1086 (N.Y. 2014); Jones v. Bill, 890 N.E.2d 884, 885-86 (N.Y. 2008).

331. Dreisinger v. Teglasi, 13 N.Y.S.3d 432, 435 (App. Div. 2015); Duane Reade, Inc. v. Cardtronics, LP, 863 N.Y.S.2d 14, 16 (App. Div. 2008); Gulf Ins. Co. v. Transatlantic Reins Co., 788 N.Y.S.2d 44 (App. Div. 2004).

332. Eastwood v. Hoefer, 24 N.Y.S.3d 391 (App. Div. 2016).

of tax laws.[333] In that regard, in recognition of the fact that appellate courts are equally as adept at interpreting statutes as are administrative agencies, the Court of Appeals has observed that "[i]interpretations of the agency charged with administering a statute are not entitled to such deference when, as here, the issue is one of pure statutory construction."[334] Likewise, in the criminal context, appellate courts apply the de novo standard of appellate review in reviewing claims of ineffective assistance of counsel.[335]

B.   Discretionary Review (Deferential Review)

Discretionary review entails various formulations of the "abuse of discretion" standard, including (1) whether the decision rests on an error of fact or law, (2) whether the decision cannot fit within the range of permissible decisions, and (3) whether the decision fails to consider all relevant factors or fails to adequately balance them.[336]

Appellate courts apply the abuse of discretion standard in connection with appeals addressing, inter alia, the following: (1) determinations as to the reasonableness of attorneys' fees,[337] (2) denial of a motion to change venue,[338]

---

333. *Trump Vil.*, 974 N.Y.S.2d at 473.

334. Debevoise & Plimpton v. New York State Dep't. of Taxation & Fin., 609 N.E.2d 514, 517 (N.Y. 1993).

335. People v. Settembre, 544 N.Y.S.2d 486 (App. Div.), *app. denied*, 547 N.E.2d 959 (N.Y. 1989).

336. Thomas R. Newman and Steven J. Ahmuty Jr., *Appellate Division Review of Discretionary Rulings* (N.Y.L.J. Nov. 4, 2009) ("In reviewing a court's exercise of discretion, an appellate court examines the record to determine whether the decision (1) rests on an error of law or erroneous finding of fact, (2) cannot be located within the range of permissible decisions, or (3) fails to consider all the relevant factors or unreasonably balances them."); *see* Steinbuch v. Stern, 770 N.Y.S.2d 106, 107 (App. Div. 2003) ("It is well settled that the determination of a witness' qualification to testify as an expert rests in the sound discretion of the trial court, and will not be disturbed in the absence of a serious mistake, an error of law or an improvident exercise of discretion.") (citations and internal quotations omitted); SKR Design Group, Inc. v. Avidon, 822 N.Y.S.2d 3, 5 (App. Div. 2006) (finding that trial court abused its discretion in denying motion to adjourn trial date for failing to "indulge in a balanced consideration of all relevant factors, including the merit of the action, prejudice or lack thereof to the plaintiff, and intent or lack of intent to deliberately default or abandon the action").

337. Casper v. Cushman & Wakefield, 931 N.Y.S.2d 55, 56 (App. Div. 2011), *app. denied*, 970 N.E.2d 431 (N.Y. 2012); Pelc v. Berg, 893 N.Y.S.2d 404, 405 (App. Div. 2009) (stating that the "trial court is in the best position to determine those factors integral to fixing [attorney's] fees" and its determination should not be overturned unless the trial court abused its discretion).

338. Saks v. Guignard, 433 N.Y.S.2d 622, 623 (App. Div. 1980).

(3) evidentiary rulings,[339] (4) sentencing,[340] and (5) the imposition of sanctions awarded by the trial court for discovery abuses.[341]

C. Other Standards of Appellate Review

In addition to the foregoing standards of appellate review, there are specific instances that do not fit within the above-described standards of review.

For example, with regard to appellate review of trial court decisions addressing discovery disputes, an appellate court, although rarely and reluctantly invoked, may "substitute its own discretion for that of the trial court . . . even in the absence of an abuse of discretion."[342]

Additionally, with regard to appellate review of administrative agency determinations, the standard of appellate review depends on whether the administrative agency conducted an evidentiary hearing prior to rendering its determination. Accordingly, appellate review "of a determination rendered by an administrative body following a hearing is limited to whether it is supported by substantial evidence."[343] However, where "an administrative agency takes action without an evidentiary hearing, the standard of review is not whether there was substantial evidence in support of the determination, but rather, whether the determination has a rational basis, and was not 'arbitrary and capricious.'"[344]

IV. PERFECTING THE APPEAL

A. Record on Appeal Based on the Standard of Review

Under CPLR § 5501(b), the Court of Appeals has narrow appellate jurisdiction that is limited to reviewing "questions of law only," with one enumerated

339. Mazella v. Beals, 57 N.E.3d 1083, 1093 (N.Y. 2016); People v. Carroll, 740 N.E.2d 1084, 1089 (N.Y. 2000) ("Trial courts are accorded wide discretion in making evidentiary rulings and, absent an abuse of discretion, those rulings should not be disturbed on appeal.")
340. People v. Hayes, 653 N.Y.S.2d 738 (App. Div.), *app. denied*, 682 N.E.2d 989 (N.Y. 1997); People v. West, 382 N.Y.S.2d 849, 850 (App. Div. 1976) (holding that "[t]he imposition of the sentence rests with the discretion of the trial court and this court should not reduce the sentence unless there is a clear abuse of discretion").
341. Tantaro v. All My Children, Inc., 19 N.Y.S 3d 159 (App. Div. 2015); Figueroa v. City of New York, 11 N.Y.S.3d 600, 601 (App. Div. 2015).
342. H.P.S. Mgmt. Co., Inc. v. St. Paul Surplus Lines Ins. Co., 7 N.Y.S.3d 462, 463 (App. Div. 2015); MSCI Inc. v. Jacob, 992 N.Y.S.2d 224, 228 (App. Div. 2014); Estate of Yaron Ungar v. Palestinian Auth., 841 N.Y.S.2d 61, 63 (App. Div. 2007).
343. Lozada v. Hook, 54 N.Y.S.2d 688, 689 (App. Div. 2017).
344. Ball v. New York State Dept. of Envtl. Conservation, 826 N.Y.S.2d 698, 699 (App. Div. 2006).

exception.[345] Regarding that exception, the Court of Appeals "shall also review questions of fact where the appellate division, on reversing or modifying a final or interlocutory judgment, has expressly or impliedly found new facts and a final judgment pursuant thereto is entered."[346]

In contrast, under CPLR §§ 5501(c) and 5501(d), the Appellate Divisions, as well as the Appellate Terms, have broad appellate jurisdiction that encompasses appellate review of "questions of law and questions of fact."[347]

The record on appeal generally consists of "everything upon which the lower court based its determination . . . [and] [a]ll appeals are heard on an original record, the contents of which varies depending upon whether the appeal is from a judgment, an interlocutory judgment or any order."[348] In compiling the record on appeal, the practitioner needs to be mindful of the finite universe of documents that made up the record before the lower court, as the appellate court, with few exceptions discussed next, will likely disregard materials that were not part of the lower court's record.

As a general matter, an appellate court will not consider factual material that is included in an appellate brief where such factual material was not included as part of the record in the lower court proceedings (and, thus, not part of the record on appeal).[349] Accordingly, an appellate court will disregard the submission of an

---

345. CPLR § 5501(b); People v. Nieves, 811 N.E.2d 13 (N.Y. 2004) (noting that "[the Court of Appeals'] jurisdiction is limited to review of issues of law"); People v. Turriago, 681 N.E.2d 350 (N.Y. 1997) (noting that "[u]nlike the trial courts and the Appellate Division, [the Court of Appeals'] jurisdiction is limited to issues of law").

346. CPLR § 5501(b); see N.Y. CONST. Art. VI, § 3(a); see also Glenn v. Hoteltron Systems, Inc., 547 N.E.2d 71, 73 (N.Y. 1989) (citing CPLR § 5501(b) and acknowledging the Court of Appeals' power to "review questions of fact" where the "Appellate Division 'expressly or impliedly found new facts'"); see also Stiles v. Batavia Atomic Horseshoes, Inc., 613 N.E.2d 572, 572–573 (N.Y. 1993) (noting that "[a] trial court's finding of fact, if affirmed by the Appellate Division, is beyond the powers of [the Court of Appeals] . . . provided the finding is supported by evidence on the record.").

347. CPLR §§ 5501(c), (d).

348. ROBERT L. HAIG & JONATHAN K. COOPERMAN, 4A N.Y. PRACTICE, COMMERCIAL LITIGATION IN NEW YORK STATE COURTS § 56:38 (4th ed. 2018) ("The CPLR provides the appellant with three alternative methods of presenting the record on appeal: (1) the full record method (CPLR 5528(a)(5)), (2) the appendix method (CPLR 5528 and 5529), and (3) the agreed statement method (CPLR 5527).")

349. Gagen v. Kipany Prods., 735 N.Y.S.2d 225, 226 (App. Div. 2001) ("Preliminarily, we agree with plaintiff's observation that defendant's brief contains many factual statements and arguments based on documents outside the record. Consequently, because 'we cannot consider factual allegations in [defendant's] brief that are not included in the record on appeal', our review will be limited to facts contained in the record and any arguments based thereon.") (citations and internal quotations omitted); Heinemeyer v. State Power Authority, 645 N.Y.S.2d 660, 663 (App. Div. 1996) ("Appellate review is limited to the record before the court of first instance. Thus, portions of the original record on appeal and of claimants' brief and appendix will not be considered on this appeal."); Ughetta

affidavit on appeal that alleges new facts that were not before the lower court.[350] Indeed, the inclusion of material in the record on appeal that was not part of the record before the lower court has been held to be conduct warranting the imposition of sanctions.[351]

Although appellate review is generally limited to factual matters that are presented as part of the record on appeal, and new facts typically cannot be injected for the first time at the appellate level, there are certain exceptions to this general rule. First of all, an appellate court may consider factual matters that may be judicially noticed notwithstanding the failure to make such facts part of the record on appeal.[352] Specifically, an appellate court may consider certain factual matters that were omitted from the record on appeal to the extent that these factual matters constitute public documents, the existence and accuracy of which is undisputed.[353]

---

v. Barile, 619 N.Y.S.2d 805, 807 (App. Div. 1994) ("We note that the argument as to whether this appeal has been rendered moot by virtue of a subsequent settlement agreement entered into by defendant and the APA in an administrative proceeding is not properly before this court as it is based on matters outside the record on appeal and we decline to consider it."); D.B.S. Realty Inc. v. State Dept. of Environmental Conservation, 615 N.Y.S.2d 484, 487 (App. Div. 1994) ("We cannot consider factual allegations in petitioner's brief that are not included in the record on appeal."); Puff v. Jorling, 592 N.Y.S.2d 107, 110 (App. Div. 1992) ("Petitioner also argues that the penalty is not in accordance with respondent's civil penalty policy issued in 1990. This policy is not included in the record on appeal and will not be considered.").

350. Mulligan v. Lackey, 307 N.Y.S.2d 371, 373 (App. Div. 1970) ("Finally, it was improper for Elia to attach to its brief an affidavit alleging new facts which were not before Special Term and to argue before the court for the first time a new theory for dismissal of the petition based upon the facts in this affidavit. It is well established that review by this court is limited to the record made before Special Term and the court is bound by the certified record on appeal. Matters contained in the brief, not properly presented by the record, are not to be considered by an appellate court.").

351. DeRosa v. Chase Manhattan Mortg. Corp., 793 N.Y.S.2d 1, 2 (App. Div. 2005) (imposing sanctions under 22 N.Y.C.R.R. § 130-1.1 where appellant supplemented appellate record with documents that were not part of the record before the trial court).

352. Mendoza v. Plaza Homes, LLC, 865 N.Y.S.2d 342, 343 (App. Div. 2008) ("However, matter dehors the record is not to be considered on appeal. [A]ppellate review is limited to the record made at the nisi prius court and, absent matters which may be judicially noticed, new facts may not be injected at the appellate level.") (citations and internal quotations omitted); Khan v. State Univ. of New York Health Sci. Ctr. at Brooklyn, 706 N.Y.S.2d 192, 193 (App. Div. 2000) ("Appellate review is limited to the record made at the Supreme Court and, absent matters that may be judicially noticed, new facts may not be injected at the appellate level."); Chimarios v. Duhl, 543 N.Y.S.2d 681, 682 (App. Div. 1989) (declining appellant's motion for leave to file supplemental record on appeal "comprised wholly of information not available to the nisi prius court for its consideration," as "[t]his court is limited to a review of facts and information contained in the record and that which may be judicially noticed").

353. Amalgamated Warbasse Houses, Inc. v. Tweedy, 822 N.Y.S.2d 763, 765 (App. Div. 2006) ("We note that although the resolution is dehors the record, it may be considered on appeal as it is a

Furthermore, an appellate court may consider incontrovertible documents for purposes of sustaining a judgment notwithstanding that such documents may have been omitted from the record on appeal.[354]

B. Brief Based upon Burden of Proof

After the record on appeal is compiled, an appellant must "prepare, file and serve an appellant's brief . . . [where] the respondent(s) will [then] have an opportunity to file a respondent's brief which addresses the arguments raised in the appellant's brief."[355] In the situation of a cross-appeal, "the respondent(s) may raise arguments concerning the judgment or order appealed from that are not raised in appellant's brief."[356]

---

matter of public record, and its existence and accuracy are not disputed."); Chateau Rive Corp. v. Enclave Development Associates, 802 N.Y.S.2d 366, 367 (App. Div. 2005) ("[W]e exercise our discretion in this matter and enlarge the joint record by taking judicial notice of the recorded deeds, maps, and site plans referable to those parcels, which, as public documents, evince indicia of authenticity and reliability.") (citation omitted); Park Realty Corp. v. Hydrania, Inc., 793 N.Y.S.2d 611, 612 (App. Div. 2005) ("Although dehors the record, reliable documents—such as Chancery Court's order, the existence and accuracy of which are not disputed—may be considered for the purpose of modifying or reversing an order under appellate review.")

354. O'Neill v. Bd. of Zoning Appeals of Town of Harrison, 639 N.Y.S.2d 961, 962 (App. Div. 1996) ("Although it is generally true that the record on appeal is limited to the documents submitted before the Supreme Court, it is well settled that an incontrovertible official document, even though it is dehors the record, may be considered on appeal for the purposes of sustaining a judgment. . . . The material to which the appellant objects consists of deeds, building permits, and tax records, all of which can be said to be incontrovertible official documents.") (citations and internal quotations omitted); Bravo v. Terstiege, 601 N.Y.S.2d 129, 131 (App. Div. 1993) ("While ordinarily material dehors the record will not be considered on appeal, there is an exception for a reliable document, whose existence and accuracy is undisputed. For the purposes of sustaining a judgment, incontrovertible documentary evidence dehors the record may be received by an appellate court. Here, the survey map is based on the descriptions in the contracts of sale of both parcels, which were before the Supreme Court and are part of the record on appeal, and the defendants do not contend that the map is inaccurate. Accordingly, we will consider the map on this appeal.") (citations omitted); Brandes Meat Corp. v. Cromer, 537 N.Y.S.2d 177, 178 (App. Div. 1989) ("We recognize, of course, the general rule that documents which were not submitted to the court of original instance may not be considered on appeal. This rule, however, is subject to certain exceptions. It has long been the law that an incontrovertible official document, even though it [is] dehors the record, may be considered on appeal for the purposes of sustaining a judgment. The Court of Appeals has also recognized a narrow exception, which allows the consideration, on appeal, of reliable documents, the existence and accuracy of which are not disputed, even for the purposes of modifying or reversing the order under review. Also, this court may, in general, take judicial notice of matters of public record.") (citations omitted).

355. HAIG & COOPERMAN, *supra* note 348, § 56:42.

356. *Id.*

When considering the contents of the appellate brief, there are several important issues concerning whether factual issues or legal issues that were not raised in
the lower court may be raised for the first time at the appellate level.

1. Raising A Factual Issue on Appeal for The First Time Is Generally Not Permitted

Just as an appellate court will not consider factual material omitted from the
record on appeal but for certain enumerated exceptions, an appellate court will
likewise decline to consider and grant appellate review of factual arguments and
issues that are being raised for the first time on appeal, as the opposing party had
no opportunity in the lower court to address such newly injected factual issues.[357]

2. Raising A Purely Legal Theory on Appeal for The First Time May Be Permitted Under Certain Circumstances

In contrast to the foregoing cases, however, "where a party does not allege new
facts on appeal but argues a legal theory that is apparent on the face of the record

---

357. Titova v. D'Nodal, 985 N.Y.S.2d 229, 230 (App. Div. 2014) ("Plaintiff's argument that
defendant is not exempt from Administrative Code § 7-210(b) because defendant used the premises for commercial purposes is improperly raised for the first time on appeal. The issue, which
is not purely legal and apparent on the face of the record, requires resolution of facts that were
not brought to defendant's attention on the motion."); Sassen v. Lazar, 962 N.Y.S.2d 126, 127
(App. Div. 2013) ("Plaintiff's argument that we may review the issue as it is a legal one, clear from
the face of the record, is unavailing. The facts necessary to support plaintiff's position, namely
that a cardiac thrombus existed in plaintiff's artificial heart valve, are not part of the record, and
defendants and their medical experts had no opportunity to respond to plaintiff's claim."); Botfeld
v. Wong, 961 N.Y.S.2d 77, 78 (App. Div. 2013) ("Defendant's argument that she had no duty to
maintain the gas valve or cap is improperly raised for the first time on appeal since the issue is
not a purely legal issue apparent on the face of the record but requires for resolution facts not
brought to plaintiff's attention on the motion."); Corgan v. DiMarco Group, 895 N.Y.S.2d 270,
271 (App. Div. 2010) ("It is well settled that an appellate court should not, and will not, consider
different theories or new questions, if proof might have been offered to refute or overcome them
had those theories or questions been presented in the court of first instance. Here, plaintiff might
have presented evidence to refute or overcome both contentions, and we thus do not consider
those contentions on appeal.") (citations and internal quotations omitted); Lindgren v. New York
City Hous. Auth., 704 N.Y.S.2d 30, 34 (App. Div. 2000) (finding that issue had not been preserved
for appellate review as "[t]his is not a case where the facts are undisputed and only a purely legal
point is being raised for the first time on appeal"); Oram v. Capone, 615 N.Y.S.2d 799, 800 (App.
Div. 1994) ("an issue may not be raised for the first time on appeal, however, where it could have
been obviated or cured by factual showings or legal countersteps in the trial court.") (citation and
internal quotations omitted).

and could not have been avoided by the opposing party if raised at the proper juncture, the issue is reviewable."[358]

Appellate courts have opted to review such purely legal issues injected for the first time on appeal under circumstances where the purely legal issues are "determinative" of the issues on appeal.[359]

As these purely legal arguments appear on the face of the record and could not have been avoided had they been brought to the opposing party's attention in the lower court, appellate courts permit appellate review of such newly injected purely legal issues, as doing so would not prejudice the opposing party.[360]

---

358. Carlyle CIM Agent, LLC v. Trey Resources I, LLC, 50 N.Y.S.3d 326, 329 (App. Div. 2017); *see also* Harrington v. Smith, 28 N.Y.S.3d 590, 591 (App. Div. 2016) ("Although respondents failed to raise this issue in opposition to the petition, we reach it, because it presents a legal issue that appears on the face of the record and could not have been avoided if raised at the proper juncture."); Nuevo El Barrio Rehabilitacion De Vivienda y Economia, Inc. v. Moreight Realty Corp., 928 N.Y.S.2d 510, 513 (App. Div. 2011) ("Although Moreight failed to make these arguments below, a purely legal argument may be considered for the first time on appeal."); DeRosa v. Chase Manhattan Mortg. Corp., 782 N.Y.S.2d 5, 7 (App. Div. 2004) ("However, this Court has authority to reach the merits of an argument first made on appeal, but only when the argument is clearly supported by facts already in the record."); Oram v. Capone, 615 N.Y.S.2d 799, 800 (App. Div. 1994) ("A question of law appearing on the face of the record may be raised for the first time on appeal if it could not have been avoided by the opposing party if brought to that party's attention in a timely manner."); Daubman v. Nassau Cty. Civil Serv. Com'n, 601 N.Y.S.2d 14, 15 (App. Div. 1993) ("While as a general rule an appellate court will not consider an issue which was not raised in the court of first instance, such an issue is reviewable where the question presented is one of law which appeared upon the face of the record and which could not have been avoided by the respondents if brought to their attention at the proper juncture.") (citations and internal quotations omitted).

359. W & W Steel, LLC v. Port Auth. of New York & New Jersey, 37 N.Y.S.3d 80, 84 (App. Div. 2016) ("However, where a party does not allege new facts, but merely raises a legal argument that appeared upon the face of the record, we are free to consider the argument 'so long as the issue is determinative and the record on appeal is sufficient to permit our review'") (citations and internal quotations omitted); 13th & 14th Street Realty LLC v. Bd. of Managers of A Bldg. Condo., 17 N.Y.S.3d 867 (App. Div. 2015) ("We may consider plaintiff's argument, which was raised during oral argument on the motion but was excluded from the parties' briefs to the motion court, because it is determinative and because the record on appeal is sufficient to permit appellate review."); Application of Allstate Ins. Co., 549 N.Y.S.2d 713, 714-15 (App. Div. 1990) ("We agree with respondents, Allstate and Mr. Perez that usually we will not consider an issue raised for the first time on appeal. However, Appellate Courts make an exception to that general rule, when there is a sufficient record on appeal, and, the issue is determinative.") (citations omitted).

360. Chateau D'If Corp. v. City of New York, 641 N.Y.S.2d 252 (App. Div. 1996) ("Where, as here, a party does not allege new facts but, rather, raises a legal argument which appeared upon the face of the record and which could not have been avoided . . . if brought to the opposing party's attention at the proper juncture, the matter is reviewable. In such circumstances, raising such an issue for the first time on appeal does not prejudice the opposing party's legal position in any respect. Since the record on appeal is sufficient for its resolution and the issue is determinative, it should be reviewed.") (citations and internal quotations omitted).

Examples of such purely legal issues that may be injected for the first time on appeal include matters of contract interpretation, such as the interpretation of an insurance policy.[361]

C. Oral Argument Based upon Burden of Proof

Oral argument is the last phase of an appeal before the appeal is decided. In New York, "[m]ost appeals to the Appellate Division may be orally argued before the panel who determines the appeal."[362] For instance, "[i]n the Second, Third, and Fourth Departments, oral argument is requested on the brief cover."[363] "In the First Department, the parties preserve their right to orally argue the appeal by notifying the clerk in writing on or before the court's scheduled date therefore in that particular term."[364]

Further, each department has its own rules regarding the time limit for oral argument.[365] In the First Department, while "any party [is permitted] to make a written request for additional time before the day of argument 'for good cause,'"[366] generally, counsel for each side is permitted a maximum of 15 minutes.[367] Thus, "[a]fter taking an appeal, perfecting it, and arguing the case before an Appellate Division panel, there is very little for counsel to do but wait for the court's disposition."[368]

---

361. Dreisinger v. Teglasi, 13 N.Y.S.3d 432, 435 (App. Div. 2015) ("Initially, although defendants' arguments on appeal differ from those made in support of their motion, they may be considered by this Court because they present a pure legal issue of contract interpretation, which appears on the face of the record and could not have been avoided if raised below."); Broad St., LLC v. Gulf Ins. Co., 832 N.Y.S.2d 1, 4 (App. Div. 2006) ("In any event, this Court has the authority to reach the merits of defendant's argument, even if it were made for the first time on appeal, because such argument is clearly supported by facts already in the record. Further, as this Court has previously stated, the interpretation of an insurance policy is a question of law, which can be raised for the first time on appeal.") (citations and internal quotations omitted).

362. HAIG & COOPERMAN, *supra* note 348, § 56:48.

363. *Id.*; 22 N.Y.C.R.R. §§ 670.10-c(g), 670.20(f).

364. HAIG & COOPERMAN, *supra* note 348, § 56:48; 22 N.Y.C.R.R. § 600.11(f)(1).

365. HAIG & COOPERMAN, *supra* note 348, § 56:48.

366. 22 N.Y.C.R.R. § 600.11(f)(2) ("[However,] the Fourth Department requires the parties to indicate on the cover of the brief 'the amount of time requested.'").

367. *Id.*; *Id.* § 670.20(a) (Generally, the Second and Third Department allow fifteen minutes for argument; however, under certain circumstances, thirty minutes was permitted.); *Id.* § 1000.11(b) ("[on the other hand, in the Fourth Department,] [t]he amount of time allowed shall be within the discretion of the court.").

368. HAIG & COOPERMAN, *supra* note 348, § 56:48 ("one exception is counsel's duty to inform the court of the settlement of the appeal or any issue therein or when an appeal or proceeding or any issue therein has been rendered moot.").

Table of Cases

M

R

Index